DIV: *C P U*

Department for Culture, Media and Sport
2-4 Cockspur Street
London, SW1Y 5DH   - 8 APR 1998

ART TREASURES AND WAR

A study on the restitution of looted cultural property,
pursuant to Public International Law

by

Wojciech W. Kowalski

Edited by Tim Schadla-Hall

D1556031

First published in Great Britain in 1998 by the Institute of Art and Law, Bank Chambers, 121 London Road, Leicester, LE2 0QT, UK.
Tel: +44 (0)116 255 5146; fax: +44 (0)116 255 1782; e-mail: ial@pipemedia.co.uk

© Wojciech W. Kowalski and Institute of Art and Law

The author is currently Professor of Law at the University of Silesia, Katowice, Poland.

Cover illustration: third century A.D. glass goblet owned by the Czartoryski family and looted during the Second World War from the Goluchów Palace. Documented in W. Froehner, Collections du Chateau de Goluchów, Verres Chrétiens, Paris 1899, pp. 10-11, no. 155, pl. XXI, XXII.
Pen and ink illustration by James Redmond-Cooper.

Typeset by Emily Beswick, Institute of Art and Law

ISBN: 0 9531696 1 8

The Institute of Art and Law
The Institute of Art and Law is an independent institution which has as its main object the increase of public knowledge concerning the contribution of law to the development of cultural tradition. It offers educational, advisory and adjudicatory services across the fields of art, history and law.

All rights reserved. No part of this book may be reproduced or transmitted in any form or by any means, electronic or mechanical, including photocopying, recording or any information storage or retrieval system without prior permission from the publisher, except in accordance with the provisions of the Copyright, Designs and Patents Act 1988 or under the terms of a licence issued by the Copyright Licensing Agency Ltd.

DEDICATION

TO MY MOTHER

TABLE OF CONTENTS

Preface

The looting of works of art on an unprecedented scale in Europe during World War II has become a subject of growing interest in recent years. To some extent, this results from something more than the mere passing of time and consequently, the more appropriate distance from those events. Since the beginning of the 1980s, there have been several famous court cases in the United States concerning the return of items of cultural property which were exported from Germany during the War. We all remember well the several years' struggle over Dürer's portraits of Hans and Felicitas Tucher, as well as the remarkable history of the collection of 56 rare Hebrew books and manuscripts sold at Sotheby's, New York, and the incredible find of the Quedlinburg treasure.

The collapse of the USSR, the unification of Germany, and the changes in Central and Eastern Europe suddenly made it possible to 'thaw' the unsolved legacy of World War II. The path towards the search for, and return of works of art and books taken away from different countries by the Nazis and the Red Army has opened. The issues surrounding, for example, the collection of drawings by F. Koenigs from Rotterdam, the Priam treasure from Berlin, and the Amber Chamber from St. Petersburg have once again hit the headlines of many newspapers.

Interesting new publications have also appeared concerning the war histories of many looted works of art and the efforts of British and American Monuments, Fine Arts and Archives Officers to find and recover them. For the first time, citizens of the former Soviet Union have begun to play a role.

The vast majority of publications, however, concentrate on the descriptive, historical, and often sensational aspects of the events. We still lack more profound and systematic works on the mechanisms of both looting and the eventual reversal of its effects. Furthermore, there is a distinct dearth of publications concerning the legal basis for return — the Allied Restitution Law. This book is intended to fill this gap.

The objective of the first chapter is to define the meaning of the term restitution in international law in contrast with other terms in the same area. In chapter II, opinions of various lawyers and academics are considered, and the development of rules of international law as regards the return of cultural goods is discussed, alongside a study of the development of the practice of restitution. In the light of this general discussion, specific issues receive more detailed treatment, in particular the regulations of the Allied Restitution Law, which came into force in various forms and situations after World War II. The book concludes with a summary of the historical evolution of the legal model of restitution, which, in the post-war period, has found its place in the Protocol signed together with the Convention for the Protection of Cultural Property in the Event of Armed Conflict on May 14, 1954 in the Hague. Some other more recent developments, such as, for example, the widely criticised draft Russian law concerning cultural property removed to the former USSR at the end of the war, are also discussed.

The reader should note that this book was written on the basis of archival materials available in Polish libraries and archives, as well as books found in British, French, American and German libraries. Beside general works on international law, especially the Law of War, and detailed works (of which there are still relatively few), the book takes into account numerous official publications of various military occupation authorities. The main sources, however, were the legal acts regulating the restitution procedures, including the documents of the Allied Control Council for Germany and the military authorities in individual zones of occupation in Germany and Austria. The documentation of the Soviet occupation authorities has not been used, since access to the original source materials in the Soviet archives is still being denied.

There was, however, a large number of documents regulating in a very detailed manner the procedures for the search and return of cultural goods, the functioning of the Allied restitutional missions, etc., for each individual zone. Hence the need for a selection of sources which will still allow for the reconstruction of the basic model of restitution common to all occupation zones.

As far as the sources on the works which led to establishing the restitution law are concerned, the author had the opportunity of using the UNESCO Archive in Paris. It contains the documentation of the Conference of Allied Ministers of Education which held its meetings in London in the years 1942-1945, as well as a number of documents containing the principles of the post-war restitution of works of art and libraries.

In conclusion, I would like to state that I have been amazed at the generosity of everyone with whom I have come into contact in the course of my research. My first thanks must go to librarians, archivists, and museum personnel, always ready to help; as well as to scholars and other persons in many scientific and cultural institutions across Europe, on the basis of whose knowledge and collections this work was written. I am indebted to Bogdan Barylko, Hanna Mausch, and Krystyna Carter, who helped me greatly with the translation of this book into English, and most particularly to William F. Archerd and Patrick O'Keefe for their final expert's comments on the text before publication. Tim Schadla-Hall and Emily Beswick performed sterling work on the editing of the text. Last but not least, I would like to thank the University of Edinburgh, Institute for Advanced Studies in Humanities, and in particular its director Professor Peter Jones for their kind hospitality during my visit there in autumn 1997, which enabled me to complete the English version of this work.

FOREWORD
Tim Schadla-Hall

Hardly a month passes without new examples of demands for restitution of cultural property.[1] In most cases, the items whose return is sought have been appropriated during times of war, or as a result of conflict.[2] The need to understand the complexity of restitution issues has never been greater. Professor Kowalski's analysis of the applicability of international law to events leading up to, during and after the Second World War is both timely and critical to an understanding of the complex factors, social, economic, cultural, political as well as legal, which surround issues of restitution. The complex nature of the restitution process is underlined by the fact that many issues remain unresolved more than half a century after the cessation of hostilities, and, as Kowalski observes,[3] new chapters continue to unfold even today.

In retrospect, it may well be that the restitution activity relating to the Second World War has been more coherently handled than the restitution problems engendered by more recent wars. Two clear points emerge, however: first, that restitution is a lengthy process, even within the framework of international law, and secondly, that the range of potential factors which can affect restitution both before, during and after conflict, as Kowalski demonstrates in chapter III, is considerable.

The Second World War and the period preceding it, with the appearance of the National Socialist Party in Germany, appears to represent the most coherent attempt by one group of people to loot material on a systematic basis and on a breathtaking (and fortunately, as yet unsurpassed) scale.[4] Whatever the eventual results of this scheme were, the intention of some organs of the Nazi party was clearly to collect all cultural artefacts and works of art not only from German territory, but also from the occupied territories. There was no recognised legal basis for this process; interestingly, however, there was a clear cultural policy behind the process of collection: officially, in some quarters at least, the various looting procedures also involved the segregation of 'germanic' from non-germanic and degenerate material.[5] Even before the War, the Nazi party had sought to destroy or even sell degenerate art (often for personal profit, although ostensibly to raise funds for the purpose of acquiring more 'germanic' cultural material).[6] This loosely enunciated policy of looting with a clear set of

---

1   February 1998 saw a series of demands for the return to the UK of Winnie the Pooh and friends from New York.
2   *The Times* 25 February 1998, reported the return of a fourth century obelisk by Italy to Ethiopia; the removal had taken place in 1937. Remarkably, the Ethiopians had apparently offered to replace the obelisk with a "work of modern art sculpted from the same kind of stone."
3   At pp. 80-90.
4   See L.H. Nicholas, *The Rape of Europa; the Fate of Europe's Treasures in the Third Reich and the Second World War*, Macmillan, London 1994.
5   See J. Petropoulos, 'German Laws and Directives Bearing on the Appropriation of Cultural Property in the Third Reich' in *The Spoils of War* ed. E. Simpson, pp. 106-111, Harry N. Abrams, New York 1997.
6   By 1937, following the Hans der Kunst exhibition, German museums were purged of all works officially clased as 'degenerate' or 'Judo-Bolshevist', and from 1938 not only German expressionist painting, but also foreign works, including impressionists and the likes of Van Gogh, Gauguin and Picasso were classified as degenerate. From then on, "many works were destroyed, although a significant number were auctioned at Lucerne in June 1939": see *the Expressionist Revolution in German Art 1871-1933* by B. Herbert and A. Hinshelwood, Leicester, 1978.

(misguided) cultural objectives represents a new departure from looting in time of war, even if it was not adhered to.

The Nazi looting during World War Two was, as Kowalski points out, relatively well-documented and clearly in contravention of the Hague Convention of 1907. It also ran counter to preceding historical trends and agreements.[7] Despite the numerous international and national committees developed to discuss the process of restitution when hostilities ceased,[8] the process of restitution never worked particularly effectively in practice. From the outset of peace, the Allied Nations adopted different approaches, often without any basis in international, or even national, law. The Soviet Union, through the Soviet Trophy Organisation, pursued a form of 'restitution in kind',[9] or even cultural reparations, whilst the bulk of the remaining Allied Nations followed the Resolution passed at the Paris Conference of 1945[10] to which, as Kowalski notes, the Polish were not a party. The Allies, and particularly the United States, were more fastidious in their approach, leaving the cultural treasures of the defeated Western Germany (as opposed to East Germany) intact, at least to some degree,[11] although Kowalski points to a number of interesting anomalies. Of course, during the debate about the basis for restitution among the Allied Nations (in which the Soviet Union does not appear to have figured to any great degree) none of the parties seems to have anticipated the development of the Iron Curtain, and the considerable scale of border realignment which succeeded the Second World War. The process of political and border realignment triggered a whole series of new problems for the restitution process, of which one of the more bizarre was that of the Polish-Canadian dispute.[12] More importantly, and possibly more intractably, at least from the viewpoint of international law, these same realignments have brought into play groups, rather than recognised States, with particular concerns about restitution.

The Western Allied Nations (i.e. with the exception of the USSR) produced the mechanism of the MFA&A officers – and what amounted to specialist units to recover stolen/looted artworks and cultural items within their occupied zone, and their activities were on a remarkable scale, particularly when compared with subsequent recovery mechanisms. These units possessed a clear legal basis, and although recent accounts vary about their effectiveness,[13] it is clear that they remain the most effective instrument yet developed to aid the process of restitution. It is not therefore surprising that suggestions have been made to revive MFA&A units to be assigned to UN Peacekeeping Forces on a permanent basis.[14]

Professor Kowalski has deliberately chosen to restrict his book to the development of international law in the field of restitution following the Second World War and its aftermath,

---

7   Pp. 27-33.

8   For example, the International Committee for the Cultural Reconstruction of Europe, p. 37.

9   See p. 17.

10   See p. 42.

11   Walter I. Farmer's essay 'Custody and Controversy at the Wiesbaden Collecting Point' in *The Spoils of War* at 131-134 deals with one example of a lack of consistency which involved the shipment to the USA of a number of high value works in 1945, although these were, subsequently, returned.

12   See below p. 64, and also S.E. Nahlik, 'The Case of Displaced Art Treasures, History and Appreciation of a Polish-Canadian Strife', *German Yearbook of International Law* 1980, vol 23, p. 255.

13   See, for example, B. Taper, 'Investigating Art Looting for the MFA&A in *The Spoils of War* pp. 133-138.

14   C.E. McConney, 'Draft Proposals for the Creation of a Permanent Monuments, Fine Arts and Archives Unit within the UN Peacekeeping Forces' (summary) in P.J. Boylan, *Review of the Convention for the Protection of Cultural Property in the Event of Armed Conflict (The Hague Convention of 1954)*, UNESCO 1994, CLT-93/WS/12.

and yet in so doing, by implication he has raised a series of questions which go far beyond the purely legal basis of restitution law.

The debate surrounding restitution of cultural material, resulting not only from war, but also from commercial and other activities, has increased in volume and intensity since the end of the Second World War. The development of the United Nations, and particularly UNESCO, has undoubtedly created a forum for such debate, although it would be wrong to suggest, as some have done, that UNESCO is responsible for the current level of discussion and controversy. In 1956 the UNESCO Convention and Protocol for the Protection of Cultural Property in the Event of Armed Conflict (The Hague Convention and Protocol of 1954) came into force. This Convention, which has now been ratified by 88 States, was based on the Hague conventions of 1899 and 1907, and also the Washington Pact of 1935, and effectively superseded them. It stands as a key document in the development of the protection of cultural property, but seems to have been more honoured in the breach than the observance.[15] For example, although both the Lebanon and Israel were signatories, damage to *Krak des Chevaliers* in South Lebanon has taken place in recent years, although whether the 'distinctive emblems' were displayed on the monument with the "appropriate authorisation duly dated and signed by the competent authority of High Contracting Party" is unclear. UNESCO has also been a key mover in the production of the UNESCO Convention on the Means of Prohibiting and Preventing the Illicit Import, Export and Transfer of Ownership of Cultural Property in 1970, and the UNIDROIT Convention on Stolen and Illegally Exported Cultural Objects in 1995. Both Conventions can be applied to cultural material acquired during times of war.

The UNESCO Convention "deals with the problem of illicit traffic by the means of administrative procedures and State action",[16] and has had a considerable impact particularly on museum related organisations. In the UK, for example, the Museums Association enthusiastically endorsed this Convention. However, the UK Government not only steadfastly refused to sign, but even withdrew from UNESCO, rejoining only after a change in Government in 1997. There still seems little active desire on the part of the current Government to sign, although currently numerous organisations are pressing the UK Government to do so. One of the major influences behind the previous Government's unwillingness to sign the Convention was determined opposition from the auction houses, primarily in London, and the desire to maintain the UK's dominant position in the world art market, a factor which contributes significantly to the UK balance of payments.

The UNIDROIT Convention has recently been extensively discussed by L.V. Prott. This Convention "provides direct access to the courts of one State by the owner of a stolen cultural object, or by a State from which it has been illicitly exported."[17] At the time of writing, there appears to be some likelihood that the UK Government is actively considering ratification, although it is this author's view that there is a degree of complementarity of the two conventions which would suggest that both should be ratified.

Notwithstanding the progress, evinced by Kowalski, towards a coherent international legal approach, looting continues apace in wars which have erupted since the cessation of hostilities in 1945. "Has there been such an effort to rescue humankind's heritage? Is there a possibility that this [i.e. attempts to restitute cultural property] can be encouraged henceforth in conflicts

---

15   Boylan, *op. cit.* note 14.
16   L.V. Prott, *Commentary on the UNIDROIT Convention*, Institute of Art and Law, Leicester, 1997.
17   *Ibid.*

elsewhere?"[18] The answer appears to be "no". The demands for restitution[19] have grown worldwide since the end of the Second World War. Over the last 40 years, a number of cultural artefacts appearing on the international art and antiquities market (as well as many which do not) have been the subject of claims for their restitution. Many of these artefacts appear on the market as either a direct or indirect result of armed conflict, including civil war, and, in many instances, not as a matter of State intervention, but as a result of individual activity. [20] The prevalence of individual looting during and at the end of the Second World War to which Kowalski refers, is another area of considerable difficulty, although it is to be hoped that, as they become more widely adopted, both the UNESCO and UNIDROIT Conventions will be employed to deal with the consequences of such activities.

The growth in demands for restitution has not resulted in any streamlining or acceleration of restitution processes. Indeed, there seems to be a marked reluctance to take strong affirmative action not only on the part of those directly involved in looting, but even among those States which have clearly declared themselves committed to processes of restitution and opposed to looting. This may be because concern over human loss and suffering is quite rightly a matter of greater concern than the looting and restitution of cultural property, but as Lyndel Prott recently wrote: "we at UNESCO are constantly confronted by the pleas of people who are physically suffering to help them save their cultural heritage, for their suffering is greatly increased by the destruction of what is dear to them. Their cultural heritage represents their history, their community and their identity. Preservation is sought, not for the sake of the objects but for the sake of the people for whom they have a meaningful life."[21] Professor Kowalski has dealt with the development of the international legal basis leading up to the Second World War in order to contextualise developments at the end of and since that conflict, and it is clearly no part of his remit to look at those areas outside conflict, or indeed analyse the apparent reluctance to implement international law to deal with such problems. However, he does give examples of the long-lived nature of restitution cases: for example, the case of the return of the Heidelberg manuscript[22] in 1815, *not* to the Vatican Library from whence it had been looted by Napoleon, but back to Heidelberg from whence it had been looted nearly two hundred years earlier during the Thirty Years War. The debate surrounding the return of the Elgin Marbles, although not arising out of warfare also serves to demonstrate the longevity of restitution demands, and incidentally, raises an issue not dealt with by Kowalski because it falls outside the remit of this volume, about whether most removal of cultural property takes place from the 'weak' by the 'strong' whether or not war is involved. Protests over the removal of the more properly termed Parthenon Marbles started nearly 200 years ago, and continue up to the present day; indeed, the publication of Christopher Hitchens' volume this year – some fifteen years after it was first published, and the continuing publication of various newspaper articles, merely serve to underline the fact that calls for restitution do indeed take place over very long periods.[23] I referred earlier to the apparent reluctance of nations to act over

---

18   C.H. Smyth, 'The Establishment of the Munich Collecting Point', in *The Spoils of War,* ed. E. Simpson, New York 1998 at p. 130.
19   It is important to distinguish restitution from reparation and restitution in kind; the definition of these terms is dealt with by Kowalski at pp. 4-17.
20   Note, for example, the case of the Quedlinburg Church Treasures; the most recent and complete assessment of all the issues surrounding the treasures, their history and 'acquisition' by Lieutenant Joe T. Meador in 1945 is contained in *The Spoils of War,* ed. E. Simpson, New York 1997 at pp. 148-158, with papers by C. Lowenthal; W.H. Honan; W. Korte; and T.R. Kline.
21   L.V. Prott, 'Principles for the Resolution of Disputes Concerning Cultural Heritage Displaced During the Second World War' in *The Spoils of War, op. cit.* note 3 at pp. 224-230.
22   P. 28.
23   C. Hitchens, *The Elgin Marbles: Should They be Returned to Greece?,* London 1998.

matters of restitution and it is worth noting that the Secretary of State for Culture Media and Sport recently stated that the Marbles were "… an integral part of the British Museum…" a remarkable statement under any circumstances! The reluctance to part with what is clearly removed (even if not in time of war) surely has roots which are deeper than the merely legal, and an understanding of what creates such views and feelings may well help to understand why the inexorable march towards more effective restitution law has not been matched by increasingly speedy restitution processes.

There is no doubt that at the end of the Second World War the USSR, unlike most other Allied Nations (in all but name), adopted an approach of *de facto* restitution in kind, or reparations (although the Polish might well have made a case for a similar approach had they been represented at the 1945 Paris Conference).[24] It might be argued that the Soviet attitude was based on the level of damage done to the Soviet cultural heritage, whilst by contrast, the stated approach of the other Allies was to try and ensure integrity of German cultural property as well as restitution; this may have been because the level of damage to their cultural heritage was far lower, by comparison. However, although it falls outside the subject of Kowalski's book, it may be worth considering the existence of much more significant, if less definable influences, which may lie behind looting, and help to explain attitudes towards it. Consideration of these issues might also offer some explanation as to why there is an apparent reluctance to restitute cultural property even with an emerging framework of international law. Whilst such influences do not have any direct relevance to the legal actions concerned with restitution, and would not enter into any legal arguments concerned with restitution, they do exist, and cannot be avoided within the overall debate.

As Kowalski observes in chapter II, looting in time of conflict has a long, well-documented history. Greenfield in her recent overview used the case of Sargon II in 714 BC to make the same point;[25] looting to effectively make a 'profit' out of conflict is frequently recorded, but the reasons for looting may well be more complex, and based on a form of cultural domination through the possession, or plunder of the vanquished's most important cultural identity through the acquisition of objects. Strong refers to the removal of the statues of the gods from conquered Veii as being "taken as part of the process known as *evocatio* and not as *objets d'art* taken by right of conquest." "The gods of the conquered city were to serve new masters."[26] The case is increasingly made that the visible removal of the Menorah and other religious and cultural items to Rome after the sacking of Herod's Temple represents a further example of cultural domination through the acquisition of cultural icons demonstrating power,[27] although one wonders who in Rome understood this powerful symbolic gesture; was it only the upper classes who saw and appreciated an additional meaning in the relief on the Arch of Titus?

The Heidelberg manuscripts referred to above were originally part of the Palatine Library which, founded in the fifteenth century, was enlarged by material looted from monasteries. During the Thirty Years War following the battle of the White Mountain and "when that great victory for the church had been followed by the capture of the usurper's own capital", the Palatine Library was removed to Rome: "what more natural than that the Pope should signalise his triumph by cannibalising his most dangerous enemy: by absorbing his intellectual

---

24   See p. 42.

25   J. Greenfield, 'The Spoils of War' in *The Spoils of War, op. cit.* note 3.

26   D.E. Strong, 'Roman Museums' in *Archaeological Theory and Practice*, ed. D.E. Strong, pp. 247-264, Seminar Press, London 1973.

27   R. Brilliant, 'Jewish Art and Culture in Ancient Rome' in *Gardens and Ghettos: the Art of Jewish Life in Italy* ed. V.B. Mann, Oxford, 1989.

sustenance, his *mana*; by swallowing up the *Palatina* into the *Vaticana*?"[28] This description of the purposes behind the looting again echoes the need for cultural, or even spiritual domination which is so hard to define; in fact, Trevor-Roper hints that plunder in the seventeenth century is a form of competitive consumption between princes, but it is clearly far more than that.[29] The first glimmerings of mass identification with cultural property apparently emerge with unrest among the Mantuans about the sale of the Duke's pictures in 1627, although how widespread this was is difficult to discern.[30] Perhaps the most remarkable and bizarre restitution of recent years is the return of the Stone of Scone to Scotland from Westminster Abbey in 1997 from whence it was removed in 1294 by Edward I. The stone was looted because of its deep symbolic and cultural significance because it did represent a domination of a weaker nation, and remarkably enough it was still seen as a symbol 700 years later.

These examples merely serve to underline the potentially long-lived and ill-defined but apparently ever-present, underlying influences which reinforce looting not only by nations in times of conflict, but also in times of peace when 'cultural' domination by strong nations is still practised, but only in a more subtle form. Kowalski singles out the rise of the Nation State as a major factor in repatriation claims,[31] but it is clear that the process and the underlying motivation is far more long-lived than the last two hundred years. Cultural identity, indeed the relationship between politics and ethnicity, and the definition of ethnicity lie outside the scope of Kowalski's analysis, and the burgeoning literature on these areas already demonstrates the difficulty of arriving at any conclusions or rules.[32]

The development of international law relies on the existence of States which still change their boundaries and laws, and takes no account, apparently, of far deeper influences which help to explain possibly, why restitution processes, even backed by international law, take so long to resolve. The non-legal reader, and the lawyers who read this volume will need to bear in mind that the problem of restitution is not purely a legal one; if it was then the solutions to the problem would be much simpler.

---

28   H. Trevor-Roper, *'The Plunder of the Arts in the Seventeenth Century': the Second Walter Neworth Lecture* Thames and Hudson, London 1970.
29   *Ibid.*
30   *Ibid.*
31   See p. 23.
32   See, for example, *Archaeological Approaches to Cultural Identity*, ed. S.J. Shennan, Routledge, London 1994, and particularly the Introduction; *The Politics of the Past* eds. P. Gathercole and D. Lowenthal, Unwin Hyman Inc., London 1990 and particularly the Foreword; P.L. Kohl and C. Fawcett eds. *Nationalism, Politics and the Practice of Archaeology*, Cambridge University Press, 1995.

CHAPTER I

THE CONCEPT OF RESTITUTION
IN INTERNATIONAL LAW

Introduction

Restitution, with its Latin roots, has a rich 'biography' in the history of law; both the explanation and definition of the term are complex. The term has been used to indicate different legal notions in different historical periods, as Brownlie comments succinctly: "the terminology of the subject is in disorder".[1] The task of examining the essence of such notions as "reparation", "restitution", "compensation", "indemnity", was undertaken by Kocot[2] who questioned whether these terms, which frequently appear in international treaties, court verdicts and international legal literature, were fixed to such an extent that it was possible to determine a set of rules qualifying the scope of accepted or imposed obligations exclusively on the basis of the term used. The answer, Kocot concluded in his extensive study, was:

> definitely negative. The result of the evolution of individual notions and related terms (in various languages) is that they often become equivalents or synonyms. It is not unlikely that a term that is broader than another one in an agreement, court verdict, or expert opinion, has a narrower meaning when used in another document. Mutually exclusive relations are exceptional and can be found only within one document.[3]

Working on the same subject, Martin commented: "The organic connection between reparations, restitution, restoration, retention, and compensation has to some extent been obscured by the drafting technique of both the 1919 and the 1947 Treaties".[4] Martin came to this conclusion by comparing the peace treaties of 1947. In the Peace Treaty with Italy, the problem of reparations and restitution was regulated in Article 6, entitled *Claims Resulting from the War*, while "restoration, retention, and debts" were covered separately in Article 7 *Property, Rights, and Interests*. The remaining four Peace Treaties dealt with these issues jointly, under a common title: *Economic Clauses*.[5]

---

1. I. Brownlie, *Principles of Public International Law*, Oxford 1979, p. 457. He further concludes that this fact "reflects differences of opinion on matters of substance".
2. K. Kocot, *Problem pojec: reparacje wojenne, restytucja, odszkodowania itp., w aspekcie umowy poczdamskiej, traktatow pokojowych, umow zawartych przez NRF, wyrokow sadowych i doktryny prawa miedzynarodowego* [The Question of the Notions: War Reparations, Restitution, Compensation, etc., in Light of the Potsdam Agreement, Peace Treaties, Agreements Signed by FRG, Court Verdicts, and the International Law Doctrine] Warsaw 1974.
3. *Ibid*, p. 64.
4. A. Martin, 'Private Property, Rights, and Interests in the Paris Peace Treaties' *British Yearbook of International Law* 24 p. 274.
5. Peace Treaty with Italy, Paris, 10 February 1947; Peace Treaty with Hungary, Paris, 10 February 1947 in: *Treaties of Peace with Italy, Romania, Bulgaria, Hungary and Finland. Texts for signature in Paris on 10 February, 1947*, London HMSO, Cmnd. 7022, p. 117; Peace Treaty with Romania, Paris, 10 February 1947. *Ibid*, p.79; Peace Treaty with Finland, Paris, 10 February 1947; *Ibid*, p.138; Peace Treaty with Bulgaria, Paris, 10 February, 1947 *Ibid*, p. 99.

The problems of terminology were also discussed by Klafkowski, who suggested solving them using a comparative method.[6] The bibliography on the subject does not give clear answers either: beside the basic notions that appear in documents, such as "restitution", "reparation", "restoration", "compensation", "indemnification", their compound forms are present as well; "*restitution par*/by equivalent", "réparation par/by equivalent", "restitution in kind", "restitution *in natura/naturalis*". More variations such as "genuine restitution", "restitution *in specie*", "making good", "recompense", are also used. Special attention is required while reading scholarly works, as many of the terms do not possess universally accepted meanings and are frequently used interchangeably, as in Personnaz's work.[7]

Occasionally, when discussing a given problem, authors use terms which have already been agreed to denote other concepts. For example, in their analysis of Article 75 of the Peace Treaty with Italy ("Restitution by Italy"),[8] McNair and Watts use the word "restoration" in a different sense from the almost universally accepted one, which defines legal means covered by a common term of "properties, rights, and interests," as used in the English versions of the Versailles Treaty (Article 297)[9] or in the Treaty with Italy (Article 78). This practice can easily lead to misunderstandings, and makes it more difficult to define the essence of the term used. In order to avoid this, some authors refrain from the use of certain words, and introduce new phrases and expressions, which they believe are more precise. Vasarhelyi, for example, writes about "general restitution" when he means returning to the previous state, but "restitution in the sense of the term" or "restitution in the technical sense of the term" when he means restitution claims following breach of the law of war, independent from the general responsibility for war.[10] The term "restitution" is avoided by Oppenheim and Lauterpacht in their fundamental work, and was not included in some legal dictionaries.[11]

Restitutio in Integrum

The term *restitutio in integrum* derives from Roman Law. The legal institutions described this way included, for example, means of protection that did not involve legal proceedings but led to the annulment of litigation effects and court verdicts, or alternatively meant litigation to restore to the State before the fraud was committed (*restitutio in integrum propter dolum*),[12] or before the legal action taken under duress (*restitutio in integrum propter metum* and *actio quod metus causa*).[13] Therefore, generally, this term meant a restoration of the state of affairs

---

6. A. Klafkowski, *Podstawowe problemy prawne likwidacji skutkow wojny 1939-1945 a dwa panstwa niemieckie* [Basic Legal Problems of the Liquidation of the Effects of the 1939-1945 War and the Two German States] Poznan 1966, p. 367.

7. J. Personnaz, *La Réparation du Préjudice en Droit International Public*, Paris 1939, p. 74 ff.

8. A. McNair and A. Watts, *Legal Effects of War*, Cambridge 1966, p. 412.

9. Peace Treaty between the Allied and Associated Powers and Germany, signed in Versailles on 28 June 1920, 112 British and Foreign State Papers 1; (henceforth: the Treaty of Versailles). See also I. Vasarhelyi, *Restitution in International Law*, Budapest 1964, p. 11.

10. *Ibid*, pp. 10, 38 ff. Sometimes, however, this method does not help if it is applied inconsistently. See *ibid*. pp. 41 and 100.

11. L. Oppenheim, *International Law*, ed. by H. Lauterpacht, London 1940. See also *Dictionnaire de la Terminologie du Droit International*, Union Académique Internationale, Paris 1960.

12. In such a case *actio doli* could be used. R. Sohm, *Institutionen des Romischen Recht*, Leipzig 1908, p. 238 (English translation: *The Institutes. A Textbook of the History and the System of Roman Private Law*, Oxford 1907); see also, W.W. Buckland, A. D. McNair, *Roman Law and Common Law*, Cambridge 1936, p. 300, ff.

13. This situation gave the plaintiff *actio quod metus causa*. R. Sohm, *op. cit.* p. 237, see also J. A. C. Thomas, *The Institutes of Justinian. Text, Translation and Commentary*. Amsterdam-Oxford 1975, p. 280.

preceding the events that later were adjudicated illegal, or shortly, "by restoring the party injured to his original position (*in integrum*)".[14] This definition of *restitutio in integrum* has been maintained to this day. In Public International Law, this term appears in connection with the question of the responsibility of the State.

Under international law, every State has various duties resulting from the fact of belonging to the international community, as well as from individually accepted obligations. These duties delimit the range of legally protected interests of other States. There is no doubt that the failure to fulfil any of these duties lays responsibility on those States who infringe the rights of the other State. As Brownlie says:

> In international relations as in other social relations, the invasion of the legal interests of one subject of the law by another legal person creates responsibility in various forms determined by the particular legal system.[15]

Consequently, the responsibility of the State is one of the most fundamental principles of international law. In some ways, it is essential for its existence. However, the question of responsibility has not been fully defined and has been shaped by practice. An attempt to systematise it has been made by doctrinal legal writings and by the United Nations' International Law Commission.[16] Many issues still remain open and are widely discussed without questioning the very principle and its main purpose, most frequently defined as "*le rétablissement de l'Etat de fait qui existerait si l'acte illicite n'avait pas été commis.*"[17] It is clear that we are dealing with this concept in its traditional meaning. Therefore, many authors state directly that what they mean is "*rétablissement de la situation antérieure, la* restitutio in integrum".[18]

We encounter formulations with identical content in practice, as opposed to theory. The decision of the Permanent Court of International Justice in the Chorzow Factory Case, the most frequently quoted verdict in cases of liability, includes the following directive: "*...rétablir l'Etat qui aurait vraisemblablement existé si ledit acte n'avait pas été commis.*"[19] The *restitutio in integrum* principle was also adopted to define Germany's responsibility for World War I. The drafts of the Peace Treaty discussed before signing suggested that it would be, *inter alia:* "making good the losses which an injured party has sustained by wrongful acts and their natural consequences, so as to place him in as good a position as that which he occupied before the wrong was done".[20]

The United States' Delegation to the conference used a more suggestive term: "physical restoration," proposing "Belgium and the occupied areas of France, Romania, Serbia and Montenegro to be physically restored to a condition as near as possible to that which would

---

14. J. Jolowicz, B. Nicholas, *Historical Introduction to the Study of Roman Law*, Cambridge 1972, p. 229; see also *in integrum restitution* in general, R. Sohm, *op. cit.* p. 341 ff.
15. See above, note 1 p. 431.
16. I. Brownlie, *System of the Law of Nations. State Responsibility*, Part I, Oxford 1983; D. W. Greig, *International Law,* London 1970, p. 396 ff.; J. G, Starke, *Introduction to International Law,* London 1988, p. 293 ff.
17. P. Anzilotti, *Cours de Droit International*, Vol. 1, Paris 1929, p. 526.
18. P.P. Guggenheim, 'Les Principes de Droit International Public' *Recueil des Cours* 1952, Vol. 88, Part 2, p. 133 ff. See also J. Personnaz, above note 7 p. 74 ff; Rousseau, *Droit International Public,* Paris 1976, p. 130; C. Eagleton, *The Responsibility of States in International Law,* Washington 1928, p. 26 ff.
19. *Publications de la Cour Permanente de Justice Internationale,* Série A. No. 17. Leiden 1928, p. 47.
20. The British Delegation's draft. P. Burnett, *Reparation at the Paris Peace Conference from the Standpoint of the American Delegation,* Vol. 2, New York 1940, p. 299.

have existed had war not occurred."[21] In the final version of the Treaty, it was articulated in a more concise form: "Germany and its allies, being the perpetrators, are responsible for all damages and losses resulting from the war sustained by the Allied and associated governments as well as their citizens ..." (Article 231 of the Treaty of Versailles).

In summary, the term *restitutio in integrum* can be said to specify the purpose of the international responsibility of the State. It defines the range of obligations of the party which has infringed the interests of another party. According to Lachs:

> *Cette obligation ne découle pas toutefois seulement des normes du droit écrit et exclusivement du droit de la guerre. C'est en effet une règle générale de droit que toute violation du droit impose en premier lieu au responsable l'obligation de rétablir le statu quo ante.*[22]

Of course, with the consequences referred to so widely, what really matters is its exclusively theoretical purpose. Usually, the full re-establishment of the previous state is difficult or practically impossible. Legal academics and judges are well aware of this and thus, provision is made that the obligation should be fulfilled *"autant que possible"*, or that *"la restitutio in integrum, ce qui, dans une certaine mesure, est toujours une fiction"*.[23] In discussing the manner in which the State's responsibility can be fulfilled in practice, we enter an area where the notion of "restitution" functions in a different way from that which has been discussed so far.

Restitution — Forms of Implementation

The Permanent Court of International Justice has stated: *"C'est un principe de droit international que la violation d'un engagement entraîne l'obligation de réparer dans une forme adéquate."* In another of the Court's verdicts, these "adequate" forms were specified as follows:

> *Restitution en nature ou, si elle n'est pas possible, paiement d'une somme correspondant à la valeur qu'aurait la restitution en nature, allocation, s'il y a lieu de dommage-intérêts pour les pertes subies et qui ne seraient pas couvertes par la restitution en nature ou le paiement qui en prendra la place.*[24]

The basic consequence of responsibility is the obligation of restitution in *"natura"* or the repayment of the value of the work subject to restitution, and only then, the payment of the reimbursement for losses which could not be covered by restitution. Here, the concept of "restitution in nature" reflects this method, meaning the action whose result is a 'physical' restoration of the previous state of affairs. The actual situation will determine the procedure; therefore actions may be of various types.[25] Their character may be rendered by such words

---

21.   *Ibid,* p. 303.
22.   M. Lachs, 'Le Problème de la Propriété dans la Liquidation des Suites de la Seconde Guerre Mondiale', *Annuaire Francais de Droit Internationale,* Paris 1961, p. 48.
23.   In the *Chorzow Factory* decision. See above note 19 Serie A. No. 17, p. 47, as well as P. Guggenheim, above note 19 p. 134. See also J. Personnaz, above note 7 p. 88 ff. The Treaty of Versailles also assumes that it may be impossible to pay the reparations that should be lawfully exacted.
24.   See above note 19 Série A. No. 9, p. 21 and No. 17, p. 47.
25.   See on this subject, I. Brownlie, above note 1, Part VIII, para 11: *The Types of Damnum and the Forms and Function of Reparation,* p. 457 ff; *ibid.* above note 16, 199 ff. C. Eagleton, *The Responsibility of States in International Law,* New York 1928, p. 182 ff.

as "return", "restoration", "extradiction", "reconstruction", "recreation", "repeal". Sometimes, these actions cannot be taken, thus the Court has conditioned the application of restitution in nature to the possibility of its realisation. If the above considerations are applied to the problems of elimination of the effects of war in nature, we notice that a more complex system of legal means serves to achieve the general theoretical aim of *restitutio in integrum*. The legal means allow for this aim to be achieved in varying degrees, because not only do factual circumstances determine their efficacy, but also the different methods which can be used. First of all they include claims to return looted objects or restoration of properties, rights and interests in the enemy's territory, as well as restitution by division and restitution in kind. Such claims make possible the achievement of a complete or nearly complete restoration of the pre-existing conditions. A complete restoration results from the application of a direct method, i.e. returning the looted objects or restoring seized properties, rights and interests. A restoration which is less than complete is accomplished by an indirect method, which involves equivalent items — either identical items, such as gold for looted gold, or comparable items, such as a painting by the same painter or school for a lost painting.

These methods and the fact that the realisation of the aim is possible, enable us to call those legal means restitutional claims. For Lachs, this was a sufficient reason to place these in a single legal category under the common title of "restitution";[26] all that is needed is a closer specification as to which of the "restitutional claims" is in question, e.g. restitution in kind. An attempt to incorporate all forms of restitution into a single definition has also been made. However, the different forms of restitutional claims make this task difficult, and even the most general of the suggested definitions does not usually cover all the possible cases. Lachs stated that restitution *"comprend les droits et les objets et elle a pour motif l'acte illicite, c'est-à-dire une violation du droit au sens le plus large et la prise illicite d'un bien au sens le plus étroit."*[27] Similarly, Vasarhelyi stressed the illegality of actions that lead to the obligation of restitution. According to him: "Restitution in the sense of the term as used in international law...is aimed at the reparation of the effects of a proceeding that was unlawful under international law."[28] Beyond the domain of these definitions, however, remain the cases of restitution of properties, rights and interests which have been legally seized as the enemy's property. For Kaufmann, the delinquent character of the cause for restitution is less important, while the essence of claims lies in the restoration of legal status: *"Restitution ist die Wiederherstellung des Rechtslage, die durch ausserordentliche, der normalen Abwicklung des Rechtsverkehrs nicht entsprechende Umstande gestort worden war."*[29] However, this would lead to the most frequent cases of restitution being overlooked; those which meant making the actual status agree with the legal status: for example, the return of looted property to its rightful owner. In the light of this matter, the term "restitution" may be explained only if the method of accomplishing its aim is examined. It is a comprehensive concept describing a few kinds of claims which aim at restoring the previous state of affairs in a direct way, i.e. by the real restoration of the same actual or legal state of affairs (possibly with some tolerance).

It is important to distinguish claims for *restitutio in integrum* in an indirect way, from the concept of restitution presented above. This indirectness means a transfer of general 'lump' equivalents defined in a peace treaty (or another document), such as money or certain amounts

---

26.   M. Lachs, above note 22 p. 47 ff.
27.   *Ibid*, pp. 47 and 48.
28.   I. Vasarhelyi, above note 10 p. 10.
29.   E. Kaufmann, 'Die volkerrechtlichen Grundlagen und Grenzen der Restititutionen', in *Archiv des offentlichen Rechts*, Bd. 75, Tubingen 1949, p. 13.

of consumer goods, raw materials, or means of production. These are claims for indemnities, sometimes referred to briefly as "reparations." They achieve their aim only partially. Examination of the individual elements of these systems will provide an indication of their origins and will highlight the differences between them. This initial examination will deal with the problems connected with restitution in general. More detailed questions concerning the reclamation of works of art will be discussed in chapter III.[30]

The restitution of looted property

The obligation to make restitution of looted property appears historically in connection with the original unrestricted 'prize law'. Basically, obligations of this type do not appear to have existed in antiquity; according to Roman law, the enemy's property was considered ownerless — *res nullius* — from the moment of declaration of war. When the conqueror came into possession of this property, it became the conqueror's property according to prize law (*ius praedae*). If the former owner managed to regain his property, it was not automatically treated as the restitution of his lost right.[31] Prize law was explicitly restricted by the medieval doctrine of a "just war".[32] The principle was that only the belligerent party which had a justified right to wage war had the right of unlimited looting of its enemies. In the words of Stanislas of Scarbimiria, a medieval Polish lawyer:

> If one wages war on the guilty because of unavoidable necessity, as in defence of motherland or to reclaim property, whatever is conquered from the enemy is his, and he is not obliged to return it ... every lay person that goes to a just war with his lord does not have to return something he acquired at war, and with his lord's consent may keep it.[33]

The late fifteenth century Professor of Law at the Jagiellonian University in Cracow, Paul Wlodkowic, explained that the whole prize coming from an unjust war should be returned because the sin cannot be remitted until the loot is returned. The war prize acquired during an unjust war cannot be legalised even after a long period of time, as the right of prescription does not apply in the case of things that have been looted or taken by force. Even those who obtained property in good faith from a winner of an unjust war cannot become the owner of it by acquisitive prescription.[34] Thus he who wages a just war is not obliged to return what he has gained. Only the party who wages an unjust war is always burdened with the obligation of restitution. Half a century later, another Polish philosopher, Andrzej Frycz Modrzewski, added that it is not proper to avoid a just war in order to regain lost property:

> A ruler who would avoid this kind of war and after having gathered an army would not try either to defeat the enemy or to take back what has been taken away, or to take revenge for injuries, would only give his enemy the opportunity to repeat the felony in future.[35]

---

30. P. 37 below.
31. C. Berezowski, *Ochrona prawno miedzynarodowa zabytkow i dziel sztuki w czasie wojny* [International Legal Protection of Historic Monuments and Works of Art during War] Warsaw 1948, p. 81; S.E. Nahlik, *Grabiez dziel sztuki. Rodowod zbrodni miedzynarodowej* [Plunder of Works of Art. Descent of an International Crime] Wroclaw-Krakow 1958, p. 72. See also by the same author, 'La Protection Internationale des biens culturels en cas de conflit armé', *Recueil des Cours* 1967, vol. 120.
32. See general historical overview of the doctrine I. Brownlie, *International Law and the Use of Force by States*, Oxford 1963, p. 2 ff.
33. L. Ehrlich, *Polski wyklad prawa wojny XV wieku* [The Polish Exposition of the Fifteenth Century's Law of War] Warsaw 1955, p. 107. English summary at p. 249.
34. L. Ehrlich, *Pawel Wlodkowic i Stanislaw ze Skarbimierza* [Paul Wlodkowic and Stanislas of Scarbimiria] Warsaw 1954, p. 172.
35. Andrzej Frycz Modrzewski, *De Republica Emendanda*, (the Polish translation by E. Jedrkiewicz), Warsaw 1953, p. 317.

At the same time, it was beyond any doubt that if during a war, a ruler took more than he had lost and had been fighting for, he was not allowed to keep the surplus and had to give it back. As Wlodkowic indicates, these principles of restitution were greatly influenced by religious norms. They can be traced not only through the views of scholars, but were shared by their contemporaries as well and instances of their practical application are also known; for instance, the obligation to return the *injusta possessa* prize, following the Avignon adjudication in the litigation against the Teutonic Knights brought to the Papal Court by the Polish king Wladislaw Lokietek in 1321, and the Peace Treaty of 1441 ordering a return to Venice of "*omnes et singulares terras, Castra, Villas et Loca,... possessiones et res*" by the Duke of Milan.[36] It should be added, however, that international practice of that time allowed for the return of prize, in most cases on the basis of reciprocity.[37]

In the course of time, the division between just and unjust wars lost its importance, although it has never disappeared completely. Restrictions and prescriptions based on religion were replaced by those following the law of nature. Theoreticians, however, said very little of restitution and the father of international law, Hugo Grotius, only summarised what had been established before him:

> If the reason for the war is unjust, all activities resulting from this war are unjust because of their intrinsic injustice, even if the war is waged in the way a formal war should be waged ... The obligation of restitution lies with the persons who perpetrated the war, either by starting it, being rulers themselves, or by giving advice to rulers. This obligation extends to all wrongdoings that usually result from war, and even to other misdeeds these people ordered to be done or did not prevent when it was possible ... A person who did not do any wrong or did it without guilt, and holds an object that has been taken by someone else in an unjust war, is obliged to give it back, because, according to the law of nature, no just reason exists for another person to be deprived of the object; he has not agreed to this or deserved such punishment, nor is there a need to fulfil any obligation.[38]

Gradually, the discussion on the right to wage war turned to the analysis of an independent right to take prize. From this the classification of legal (*praeda licita*) and illegal (*praeda illicita*) prize developed, which made it possible to distinguish these from ordinary theft. The legality of prize depended on what kind of goods were involved, who their owner was and when they fell into enemy hands.

By the turn of the seventeenth century, the entire legal ground for the right of prize was questioned. It was Locke who recognised the full right of the winner to take his enemy's life. This right, however, did not extend to his property, in accordance with the following reasoning:

---

36. M. Iwanejko, *Prawo zdobyczy wojennej w doktrynie XVI-XVIII wieku* [War Prize Law in the Doctrine of the Sixteenth to the Eighteenth Centuries] Krakow 1961, p. 11.
37. *Ibid*, p. 12.
38. H. Grotius, *De jure belli et pacis libri tres* accompanied by an abridged translation by W. Whewell. Vol. III. Cambridge 1853, pp. 192-194. "*...si belli causa injusta sit, etiamsi bellum solenni modo susceptum sit, injustos esse interna injusticia omnes actus qui inde nascuntur: ... Ad restitutionem autem tenentur, secundum ea quae generaliter a nobis alibi explicata sunt, belli auctores, sive potestatis jure, sive consilio, de his scilicet omnibus, quae bellum consequi solent: etiam de insolitis, si quid tale jusserunt aut suaserunt, aut cum impedere possent non impedientur.... Neque admittendam putem exceptionem, quam nonnuli adferunt de his, qui aliis operam navant, si modo in ipsis aliquid haereat culpae: ad restitutionem enim sine dolo culpa sufficit.... Non dissimile est, quod ex contractu sine dolo initio, cui inest inaequalitas, jure gentium nascitur facultas quaedam cogendi eum qui contraxit ad implenda pacta: nec eo tamen minus, qui plus aequo stipulatus est rem ad aequalitatem reducere ex probi ac pii hominis officio tenetur*".

... so that he that by Conquest has a right over a Man's Person to destroy him if he pleases, has thereby a right over his Estate to possess and enjoy it. For it is the brutal force the Aggressor has used, that gives his Adversary a right to take away his Life, and destroy him if he pleases, as a noxious Creature; but this damage sustained that alone gives him Title to another Man's Goods: For though I may kill a Thief that sets on me in the Highway, yet I may not (which seems less) take away his Money and let him go; this would be Robbery on my side. His force, and the state of War he put himself in, made him forfeit his Life, but gave me no Title to his Goods. The right then of Conquest extends only to the Lives of those who joined in the War, but not to their Estates, but only in order to make reparation for the damages received, and the Charges of the War, and that too with reservation of the right of the innocent Wife and Children.[39]

The rapidly developing practice of treaty-writing in the seventeenth century was penetratingly investigated by Nahlik. In the light of his studies, the crucial meaning for the understanding of these problems is the Franco-Austrian Treaty signed in Munster in 1648, which introduced the principle of general amnesty and restitution of private property. Exempt from that rule were only "the movable goods and movables, as well as harvested crops, return of which is impossible." The obligation of restitution became self-evident. From that time on, it appeared in the majority of peace treaties.[40]

Further development of the idea of restitution was greatly influenced by the views of Rousseau, who advocated a new concept of war. For Rousseau, war was a relation between States only, not between their citizens, who became enemies only as soldiers fighting in defence of their homelands; only they participated in the war. Inhabitants and their property were excluded from it. "War is not a relation between one man and another, but a relation between States, in which individuals become enemies only by accident, neither as men nor as citizens, but solely as soldiers, not as members of the fatherland, but as its defenders". Further on, the author argues that those principles "were not established by Grotius; neither were they based on the authority of poets, but they result from the very nature of things, and are founded on wisdom".[41] What follows from Rousseau's analysis is the full exclusion of private property from military operations and submission of it to absolute protection. It is not subject to any form of annexation and is always included in the obligation of restitution whenever it is necessary. These principles were fully established in the nineteenth century, and complementing the development of customary law, became standards of the international law of war codified by the end of that century.

The regulations on the Laws and Customs of War on Land, included in the 1907 (IV) Hague Convention,[42] protect the enemy's property from expropriation in separate clauses dealing with military operations and the occupation of foreign territory. In the latter case, a different kind of protection is provided for private and State property. During hostilities, it is forbidden to destroy or capture enemy property except when such destruction or expropriation is required

---

39. J. Locke, *Two Treatises of Government,* London 1698, pp. 309-310.
40. S.E. Nahlik, above note 31 p. 133. Also on the amnesty clauses see: F. Philimore, *Three Centuries of Treaties of Peace and Their Teaching,* London 1919, p. 8 ff.
41. J. J. Rousseau, Du contrat social ou principes du droit politique. Strasbourg 1796, p. 14. "*La guerre n'est (donc) point une relation d'homme à homme, mais une relation d'Etat à Etat, dans laquelle les particuliers ne sont ennemis qu'accidentellement, non point comme hommes ni même comme citoyens, mais comme soldats; non point comme membres de la patrie, mais comme ses défendeurs*". Those principles "*... ne sont pas ceux de Grotius; il ne sont pas fondés sur des autorités de poètes, mais ils dérivent de la nature de choses, et sont fondés sur la raison*".
42. *Convention Concerning the Laws and Customs of War on Land,* LIV L.N.T.S. 437, LXXII L.N.T.S. 458, CLX L.N.T.S. 456.

by military necessity (Article 23.g). Moreover, it is forbidden to pillage cities and other places, even if they are taken by storm (Article 28). However, during the exercise of the war authority on enemy territory, private property is not subject to confiscation (Article 46), while looting is formally banned (Article 47). Only a portion of State property can be seized: the army occupying a given place can requisition only cash, funds and bonds (securities) belonging to the State, as well as military depots, means of transportation, warehouses and stocks of food, and all other movable property of the State which can be used for military purposes (Article 53).

The above formulations of regulations have often been, and still are, subject to severe criticism. They have been criticised for their perceived loopholes and anachronisms, as well as their difficulties of interpretation; for example, in 1943, an American commentator on new acts of international law and the 1907 (IV) Hague Convention stated: "These rules are not entirely precise or adequate for all situations and give an unscrupulous occupant opportunity for evasion and abuse of discretion or allow interpretation according to the caprice of the commander."[43] These rules, however, acquire special meaning in the light of Article 3 of the Convention, in which they were included. Article 3 provides for the explicit responsibility of the belligerent party for infringing any of the regulations and obliges it to pay compensation (indemnification). Moreover, the section includes a very important principle, according to which the belligerent party is responsible for any action of persons who are members of its armed forces. The belligerent party is responsible for acts committed by soldiers both on and off duty.[44]

The introduction of the principle of responsibility was generally interpreted as representing considerable progress in the development of international law. Garner even stated that:

> adoption of this provision marks an important step toward making international law something more than a code of etiquette, by expressly affirming the principle of civil responsibility for injuries committed by belligerents or members of their armed forces in violating of the commands and prohibitions of the Hague Convention and by creating a legal liability upon the basis of which the injured belligerent may demand compensation.[45]

This opinion was shared by Freeman: "State impunity for such offences as pillaging has yielded to an international responsibility, construed as a duty to make compensation for the loss sustained." But he further added: "Doubtless because this form of redress could not satisfactorily respond to the scale on which forced seizures occurred in World War II, the despoiled owner was given a right to restitution of his property."[46] Does the right not follow from Article 3 then? This doubt arises because Article 3 does not include an explicit statement about the obligation of restitution, which has resulted in different interpretations of this section; Berezowski argues that compensation for infringing the regulations means there is an obligation to return the objects that have been illegally taken into possession by the enemy, and compensation is paid only when the object of restitution has been destroyed.[47] It is important to note that by establishing the obligation of compensation, the Hague Convention goes beyond simple restitution, so it includes solutions that are new in comparison to those hitherto existing. So-called 'war reparations', which had not been known before, were based on the right of the

---

43.   L. Woolley, 'The Forced Transfer of Property in Enemy Occupied Territories' *The American Journal of International Law* 1943, 37, No. 2, p. 284.

44.   A. Freeman, 'Responsibility of States for Unlawful Acts of Their Armed Forces' *Recueil des Cours* 1955, 88, Part 2, p. 324.

45.   J. Garner, *International Law and the World War 1*, Vol. 2, London 1920, p. 469.

46.   A. Freeman, above note 44 p. 409.

47.   C. Berezowski, above note 31 p. 132. See also I. Vasarhelyi, above note 9 p. 30.

victor and had a completely different character. Therefore it can be assumed that Article 3 of the Convention 'absorbed' restitution, and that seems to be the assumption of Berezowski. A different opinion, however, was presented by Nahlik, who claimed that the obligation of restitution "has nothing to do with the question of guilt or responsibility" and "none of the official enactments has dealt with that problem, thus leaving it to custom or individual peace treaties."[48]

This latter opinion had quite strong grounds, especially in the context of the practice in the nineteenth century wars and the proceedings of the Hague Convention. It may be assumed that while drafting Article 3, the writers did not refer to restitutional claims, because after 1815, the nineteenth century was exceptionally peaceful by comparison with certain earlier centuries which had been characterised by many infamous lootings. Instances of respect for enemy property which could not be used in direct warfare were much more frequent than cases of its violation and thus, apparently, the problem was not seen as a critical one, calling for a special solution. At the same time, the customary norms regarding restitution had already been well embedded in common consciousness and were sufficient to resolve all problems that were likely to appear. It is also true that restitutional issues were not taken up during the codification processes. This must have resulted in the appearance of certain differences between international and national laws when restitution was applied.[49] An additional argument in favour of Nahlik's argument also follows from use of the French term "indemnification" and the English "compensation" in Article 3. These terms usually denote compensation to the civilian population for so-called "civil damages," which was indicated by Kocot and confirmed by the debate on the section's language. The terms are applied particularly when compensation means providing one item of value in place of another item of value. Within the general category of claims resulting from war, indemnification for civil damages occurs independently of the restitution of individual objects.[50]

It seems clear that the (IV) Hague Convention did not create a new obligation of restitution. It only sanctioned the existing state of international law in that area and accepted the already existing norm of case law, or rather supplemented it with the obligation of indemnification. If we assume that the Hague Convention is a normative base for the obligation of restitution, it would only constitute a stage in the development of that obligation. The effect of two World Wars, which followed, developed it on a much larger scale. After the conclusion of World War I, the injured States considered the restitution of looted property a matter of great importance. They understood it to be a speedy repair of a part of the damage and the improvement of their economy by regaining their own property which had been removed to the enemy's territory. On the other hand, reparations required much bargaining and negotiation, so could not be settled quickly. Besides Belgium, Serbia, and Poland, the country that pressed the hardest for taking restitutional action was France, where in 1918 the press promoted a slogan "restitution, reparations, guarantees".[51] Several proposals to define restitution were put forward during the Peace Conference of Versailles. Two of them reflected particularly well the attitude towards restitution prevailing at that time. The British delegation formulated

---

48.   S.E. Nahlik, above note 31 pp. 219 and 302.
49.   The reluctance of some countries to codify the principles of restitution can be shown by the history of *The Convention for the Protection of Cultural Property in the Event of Armed Conflict* 1954, 249 U.N.T.S. 240. Eventually, resolutions regarding restitution were included in a Protocol independent of The Convention; see S.E. Nahlik, above note 31 p. 372 ff.
50.   For the proceedings of the debate see S.E. Nahlik, above note 31 p. 219 ff; K. Kocot, above note 2 p. 10, which also includes an explanation of the term "indemnification", p. 65 ff.
51.   P. Burnett, above note 20, p. 110.

it in the following way: "where objects, which have been taken from their owners against their will, continue to exist and can be identified, reparation involves that they should be re-delivered to their owners, who may also have a claim for compensation for having been deprived of them".[52]

The British formula assumed the following premises for restitution:

- the object must have been taken against the owner's will (under duress),
- the object must still exist,
- the object must be identifiable,
- the object should be delivered to its owner.

The French delegation insisted on fulfilling the following criteria:

The enemy States must make immediate restitution of all property, generally, and of whatsoever kind, belonging to the Allied Powers and their citizens of which they have possessed themselves for any purpose and which is now [to be] found on their territory.[53]

According to the French then, restitution should:

- be immediate,
- be general (i.e. include all taken goods, whatever they are and whoever their owner is), and
- include objects that are on enemy territory.

The definition of restitution finally accepted in the Treaty of Versailles was as follows:

Apart from the payments provided above [i.e. reparations], Germany, applying the procedure decided upon by the Commission of Reparations, will make restitution in cash of taken (*enlevées*), seized (*saisies*) or sequestered monies, as well as of animals, all kinds of objects and assets that have been taken away, seized or sequestered, whenever it is possible to identify them on the territory of Germany or the territory of its Allies (Article 238).

Further regulations in the Treaty provided that restitution was to be exercised "immediately" (Article 239) and "under no circumstances" could the objects covered be treated as German assets (Article 243), i.e. they were not included in the German "reparation total".

The above provisions were used as a model for the other peace treaties signed "around Paris",[54] and were included in Chapter 7 of the treaty, entitled *Reparations*. Placing restitution under that title suggested that it was a form of reparations and had not been fully developed as a legal concept.[55] This view is reinforced by the delegation of the entire task of supervising and implementing restitution to the Commission of Reparations. On the other hand, however, this suggestion is not supported by the way in which the issue of restitution was dealt with, and although the construction of the Treaty does obliterate the differences between restitution

52. *Ibid*, Vol. 2, p. 299.
53. *Ibid*, p. 671.
54. A term used by Vasarhelyi, above note 9 p. 4, means, primarily two Treaties: Treaty of Peace between the Allied and Associated Powers and Austria, signed in Saint-Germain-en-Laye on 10 September 1919, 112 British and Foreign State Papers 317 (henceforth: the Treaty of St.Germain) and Traité de la paix entre les Puissances Alliées et Associées, et la Hongrie, signé a Trianon du 4 juin 1920, Société des Nations. *Recueil des Traités* 1920, Vol. 1, No. 10 (henceforth: the Treaty of Trianon).
55. The opinion of Vasarhelyi, above note 9 p. 38.

and reparations, this did not influence the evaluation and interpretation of the document. Opinions on that issue, published almost at the same time, unequivocally differentiated between the two types of claims. According to Temperley, restitution "of recognisable articles of stolen property is, of course not regarded by the Treaty as a part of Reparations. Integral restitution of such property must be made independently of all other claims".[56] Similarly, a Polish author, Figlarewicz, indicated that the main difference between restitution and compensation in kind lies in the exclusion of the returned object from the calculation of reparations. After an analysis of the Protocol of the Commission of Reparations in which the restitutional procedure is laid down, Figlarewicz mentions the following principles of restitution:

> - a necessary condition for restitution is the identification of the object in the territory of Germany or its Allies,
> - the Germans are obliged to deliver the identified object to the place it was taken from,
> - all ensuing costs are covered by the German government, and naturally, they will not be included in the account of reparations.[57]

The most fundamental of these principles bases restitution on resolute and consistent identification without any investigation of the issue of the ownership of the returned objects. Hence, if a given object was identified as "taken away, seized, or sequestered" by enemy authorities, it had to be irrevocably and immediately returned. It is worth noting that the range of objects subject to restitution considerably increased compared to those in the resolutions of the Hague Convention. The obligation to return includes the goods that, according to Article 53 of the Convention, are covered by the notion of 'legal prize'. Another important decision was to accept the principle of making restitution independent of responsibility for war in general. The Treaty of Versailles underscored this form of responsibility in Article 231, and in its further parts it focused entirely on realisation of the appropriate reparational claims. Restitution, despite being included in the chapter devoted to these issues, is a completely different legal institution. The Treaty of Versailles did not address certain problems, such as the return of objects that were subject to restitution but were in the territory of neutral States. Some of the criteria were not developed. Those shortcomings, however, did not affect the essence of restitution, which found its full expression within the Treaty.

The next step in the development of this legal concept was restitutional law, elaborated and enforced after World War II had ended. The erstwhile construction of restitution had to be adjusted to a new situation, because never before had pillaging taken place on such a large scale. Besides certain complicated legal questions, restitution posed another practical and very difficult problem. To avoid repetition, the discussion of this subject is postponed until chapter III.[58] At this point, it is necessary to deal with the so-called law of retrieval: *ius postliminii*.

Ius postliminii

Unlike restitution, which aimed at restoration of reality to the legal status, the law of retrieval dealt purely with legal relations. If these relations underwent changes as a result of certain legal occurrences, the return to the former actual state meant, through the application of *ius postliminii*, the restoration of the appropriate legal relations.

---

56. H. Temperley, *A History of the Peace Conference of Paris*. Vol. 2: *The settlement with Germany*, London 1920, p. 68.

57. A. Figlarewicz, *O Komisji Odszkodowan. Ustroj, kompetencje i dzialalnosc na podstawie traktatow pokojowych: w Wesalu, w Saint Germain, w Trianon, w Neuilly-Seine, w Sèvres i w Lozannie* [On the Commission of Reparations. System, Competence and Activity on the Basis of the Peace Treaties: in Versailles, in Saint Germain, in Trianon, in Neuilly-Seine, in Sèvres and in Lausanne] Warsaw 1927, p. 49 ff.

58. P. 37 below.

Ius postliminii was formed in Roman law in order to define the legal status of a Roman citizen coming back from captivity. As the Roman State did not maintain legally sanctioned friendly relations with some countries, its citizens could be taken prisoner in their territories. For a Roman, this meant a civil death and the loss of all rights he had at home. But, if by any chance, that Roman managed to escape and return to his country, owing to *ius postliminii* he retrieved all his lost rights.[59]

This concept was transferred into international law. Grotius discussed it extensively in chapter IX (*De Postliminio*) of his three works on war and peace.[60] Gradually, *ius postliminii* became more like restitution, with which it was sometimes identified.[61] According to Bluntschli:

> *Les territoires, les populations et les personnes ou choses qui étaient tombés pendant la guerre au pouvoir de l'ennemi, peuvent en être affranchis sans traité de paix et les droits antérieurs être rétablis comme s'ils n'avaient pas cessé d'être en vigueur. Ce rétablissement de l'ordre de choses renversé par la guerre, porte le nom de postliminie.[62]*

Especially emphasised here was the importance of the restoration of rights through the reconstruction of old legal relations after military occupation, because, Hall explained, ... "the legitimate owner is under no obligation to recognise as a source of rights the disorder which is brought into his household by an intruder".[63]

The *ius postliminii* doctrine was used in 1918 to support and justify the right of the Polish State to its old territories. It was also applied by Polish Courts of Justice in adjudicating the restoration of certain legal relations in municipal law.[64]

The idea of the law of retrieval also had its place in the development of the war prize concept. Iwanejko argued, on the basis of his analysis of opinions presented by various writers on international law, that it was helpful in solving certain questions connected with acquiring ownership rights to captured objects. In principle, *ius postliminii* could not cover objects obtained illegally, as in that case they would be subject to restitution. However, if rights of ownership had already been transferred to the conqueror, the former owner could regain the title to the lost object by recapturing it. And while the capture of a given object gave the captor the right to it after certain requirements of the law of war were met, the use of the law of retrieval by the object's former owner gave him title to the object at the moment when it was in his territory. Continuity of ownership was assumed in such cases, as if the object had not been taken by the enemy and then won back.[65]

---

59. R. Sohm, *op. cit.* p. 201 ff. , B. Nicholas, *An Introduction to Roman Law,* Oxford 1962, p. 71.
60. H. Grotius, above note 37 p. 167 ff.
61. *Ius postliminii* as applied by the law of nations is discussed, among other authors, by E. Hall, *A Treatise on International Law,* Oxford 1909, p. 577 ff; L. Oppenheim, above note 11 p. 481 ff; S.E. Nahlik, above note 31 pp. 132, 178 ff; M. Iwanejko, above note 36 p. 116.
62. M. Bluntschli, *Le Droit International Codifié,* Paris 1870, para. 727, p. 368.
63. E. Hall, note 61 p. 578; See also L. Oppenheim, above note 35 p. 481.
64. L. Oppenheim, above note 11 p. 484. In the Polish literature of that time, a deep analysis of the *ius postliminii* issue was conducted by Hubert, who believed that the law of retrieval served to justify the restitution of the State's authority over a territory (or its portion), which had belonged to it in the past. See S. Hubert, *Zasady restytucji panstwowosci w zastosowaniu do Republiki Genewskiej w r. 1814-1815* [The Principles of Restitution of State Authority in the Case of the Republic of Geneva in 1814-1815] "Rocznik Prawa i Ekonomii" 1932; S. Hubert, *Odbudowa Panstwa Polskiego jako problemat prawa narodow* [The Reconstruction of the Polish State as an Issue of International Law] Warsaw 1934; S. Hubert, *Przywrocenie wladzy panstwowej* [The Restoration of the State Authority] Lwow 1936.
65. M. Iwanejko, above note 36 p. 121.

Ius postliminii is still traditionally discussed in literature on international law, but gradually, it is losing its former significance.

"Properties, rights and interests"

In peace treaties, it is this section which deals with the restoration of all properties, rights and interests that were confiscated from the enemy, including any right of use that had been restricted or limited in any way.

Originally, all movable and immovable property, both public and private, belonging to the enemy could be confiscated completely and irrevocably. This right was not questioned and was usually exercised by both sides. Over time, however, under the influence of the doctrines that limited the law of prize, it became a custom that properties were returned to their former owners. Each time, this process was unequivocally regulated by peace treaties. Such provisions were for example included in the Pyrenees Treaty of 1659 (Article XXII) and the 1783 Peace Treaty of Paris.[66] The practice of returning property was accompanied by limiting confiscations. The French *Décret de la Convention nationale du 14 mai 1793, relatif au séquestre des biens possédés sur le territoire français par les princes ou puissances avec lesquels la République est en guerre* was one of the last acts of this kind.[67] However, a new development appeared to include various provisions for taking "exceptional war measures against the business and property of enemies, which, though not confiscation, inflicted great loss and injury".[68] The scope of these measures was very broad. The Treaty of Versailles classified them as "exceptional war ordinances" and "means of execution." The former included all kinds of legislative, administrative, judicial, and other measures aimed at establishing supervision, compulsory administration, sequestration, etc. or seizure, use or hold up of the enemy's property "for any reason, in any form, and in any place." The further text listed possible ways to enforce this provision. According to Paragraph 3 of the Annex to Chapter 4 of the Treaty, the means of execution includes those measures that affected or will affect the ownership of the enemy's property by handing them over, totally or partially, to a person other than the enemy owner, without his consent, and especially those measures that mean selling, liquidation, or transfer of the ownership of the enemy's property, invalidation of titles and securities.

During both World Wars, such limitations were introduced in the territories of many States, and in many cases they included confiscations.[69] The Peace Treaties which concluded each of the World Wars aimed at removing these limitations and their results. Article 297a of the Versailles Treaty stated that all extraordinary war regulations and executive measures would be lifted or suspended, in the event that they had not already been removed, "while the properties, rights, and interests mentioned before will be returned to the entitled persons." At the same time, these assets were to be returned to the legal status that the properties, rights and interests of German citizens had under the pre-war law (Article 298a).

After World War II, the resolutions concerning the return of properties, rights, and interests were included in the Legal Acts of the Allied Control Council for Germany and the Peace Treaties. The Control Council regulated those matters through separate documents issued

---

66. I. Vasarhelyi, above note 9 p. 29.
67. L. Oppenheim, above note 11 Vol. 2, p. 261; M. Iwanejko, above note 36 p. 129.
68. L. Oppenheim, above note 11 Vol. 2, p. 263.
69. Restrictive laws and regulations are listed in, among others, E. Schuster, 'The Peace Treaty and its Effects on Private Property' *The British Yearbook of International Law* 1920-1921, p. 167; *The Post-war Settlement of Property Rights*, New York 1945.

over a few years, which were foreshadowed in the Proclamation No. 2 on certain additional demands from Germany of 20 September 1945. Chapter 6 of the Proclamation included a provision that the German authorities would implement all regulations issued by the Allies' representatives concerning properties, rights, and interests that were in Germany and belonged to any of the United Nations or its citizens. The German authorities were made responsible for their protection and maintenance, and for safeguarding them against dispersal. All persons in the territory of Germany who were in possession of these goods had to notify the authorities of that fact and wait for a regulation that would oblige them to return them.[70] An example of a specific regulation is Law No. 8 on rights attaching to the industrial, literary and artistic property of other nations or citizens of 20 October 1949. This law restored foreign patents and copyrights that had been "impaired by the existence of a state of war or as a result of German war legislation".[71]

The 1947 Peace Treaties include resolutions on properties, rights, and interests based on a unified common formulation.[72] Its basic tenets were as follows:

> - all existing rights and legal interests of the Allied Nations and their citizens will be restored;
> - all properties, that is all movable and immovable, material and non-material goods, including industrial, literary, and artistic property rights, will be returned in "entirely good shape";
> - properties, rights and interests will be returned without mortgage or any other charges that might have resulted from war;
> - all ownership transfers of properties, rights, and interests will be nullified, if they were a result of the use of force or duress by the Axis governments or their agents.

From all the above mentioned legal acts issued after World War I as well as after World War II, it follows that claims for the return of property, rights, and interests from the enemy territory to the status ensuing before the war, possess the character of restitutional claims. This form of restitution, however, is of a special kind, as the introduction of war restrictions did not contravene international law.[73] Hence the lifting or suspension (the Treaty of Versailles) or nullification (the 1947 Peace Treaties) of the legal measures under which the restrictions were introduced is a necessary element of the restitutional procedure. This kind of restitution is usually referred to as "restoration".

Restitution by distribution

The isolation of restitution by distribution as a separate and unique type of restitutional claim follows the analysis of a specific case of restitution that took place after World War II. It concerned the return of so-called monetary gold. It is well known that the numerous and diverse lootings committed by Nazi Germany in occupied Europe included the pillage of gold from banks and private deposits of the citizens of many countries. After the termination of

---

70. *Official Gazette of the Control Council for Germany,* 29 November 1945, No. 1, p. 8.
71. *Ibid,* 27 November 1947, No. 2, p.18.
72. See Article 78 of the Peace Treaty with Italy; Article 23 of the Peace Treaty with Bulgaria; Article 25 of the Peace Treaty with Finland; Article 24 of the Peace Treaty with Romania, and Article 26 of the Peace Treaty with Hungary. The problem is also discussed by M. Lachs, above note 22 p. 50 ff. and A. Martin, above note 4 p. 282 ff.
73. G. Hackworth, *Digest of International Law,* Vol. 6, Washington 1943, p. 199 ff; I. Vasarhelyi, above note 9 p. 29. The Treaty of Versailles accepted their legality.

military operations, a problem arose in connection with returning this gold to the wronged States. The amount of gold found in Germany and returned from neutral countries such as Switzerland and Sweden, where the Nazis had sold it, was not equal to the amount claimed by the occupied countries. Moreover, in the case of most of the recovered gold, it was not possible to determine its origin. The issue was taken up by the Reparations Conference in Paris.[74]

Since the complete recovery of the looted gold, and indeed the identification of the origin of the gold that had been discovered would evidently be impossible, the participants in the Conference decided on the following principles of restitution of the monetary gold in the Final Act of the Conference:[75]

> - the total amount of the gold found in Germany and recovered from the third party countries would be pooled in *la banque centrale du pays demandeur*;[76]
> - from this pool, coins of numismatic and historic value would be excluded and, if positively identified, returned to their owners according to the principle of direct restitution;
> - the pool would be placed at the disposal of a specially appointed international body, which would divide it among the concerned countries proportionally to the losses they sustained;
> - the wronged countries would present a detailed and verifiable account of the losses.

In 1946, a Trilateral Commission on Restitution of Monetary Gold was created in Brussels, which divided the gold according to the directives of the Conference.[77]

What overall conclusions can be drawn from this? The fundamental problem is the identification of the original place from which the object was looted; it is this identification which allows restitution by distribution to be specific. The case of gold is special and had been a controversial issue even before 1946. During the drafting of the Versailles Treaty, a suggestion was put forward that this precious metal should be excluded from restitution altogether, because "gold, notes, etc., cannot be identified, and a subject of reparation, as distinguished from restitution, it is like the 'tonne per tonne' principle applicable to destroyed shipping".[78] It should be noted, however, that the difficulties over the determination of the place of origin may also happen in the case of other kinds of looted goods, because their origins are not obvious from their structure or form. Therefore, there is no reason to exclude other categories of objects from restitution by division if their origins cannot be determined. Indeed, it seems to be the only way to execute their restitution. Another possibility would be to deal with these objects within the category of reparations, but this solution is unacceptable because reparations are not to be rendered from the property of the injured party. The burden of reparations must be borne by the country responsible for war.

As a result of restitution by distribution, the claimant country does not regain exactly what it was deprived of. It receives an equivalent, which may bear scant relation to the loss sustained.

---

74. The Reparations Conference took place in Paris on 9 November-21 December, 1945; eighteen countries participated. See J. Howard, *The Paris Agreement on Reparations from Germany*, United States Government Printing Office 1946.
75. Final Act of the Paris Conference on Reparations, 21 December 1945, London, HMSO, Cmnd, 6721.
76. The formulation after M. Lachs, above note 22 p. 54.
77. On some of the faults of division see M. Lachs, 'Problem prawny podzialu zlota zagrabionego w czasie wojny' [Legal Problem of the Division of Gold Looted during the War], *Panstwo i Prawo* 1960, No. 6, especially p. 6 ff.
78. An opinion of one of the delegates to the peace conference. See P.Burnett, above note 20 Vol. 1, p. 792.

In the case of gold, the equivalent happens to be identical, and thus restitution by distribution may have the same result as direct restitution. This is also true for other materials, such as minerals. On the other hand, if other kinds of goods are divided, restitution is similar to reparations, though it cannot be equated with it.

Restitution in kind

When direct restitution proves impossible, it is permissible to apply so-called restitution in kind. Generally speaking, this means providing an equivalent object in place of the lost item. In the event that a given object no longer exists, direct restitution will clearly be impossible; it may indeed prove impracticable in numerous other situations. Restitution in kind is not considered an ordinary method of restoring the *status quo ante*.[79] It is viewed as an exceptional measure that cannot reduce reparational obligations. The Peace Conference after World War I did not recognise restitution in kind, apart from the special case of the Louvain library.[80] The French general motion regarding restitution in kind through the use of goods similar to those taken by the Germans, and the exclusion of this category from reparations, was totally rejected. It was argued that restitution did not provide for such a procedure and applied only to objects that had actually been taken from France illegally.[81]

The restitution law established after World War II allowed for the application of restitution in kind in certain, precisely defined, cases: Firstly, goods that no longer existed or those that could not be found could be replaced by equivalent goods, but only in the case of lost works of art of high value or objects destroyed or stolen after the regular restitutional procedure had been initiated.[82] Secondly, when the item subject to restitution existed, yet restitution in kind applied, such restitution could take place only when the claimed object was necessary to maintain a technological process in a factory. However, it had to be a factory earmarked for reparations. Instead of restitution of the given object, so-called compensation took place, or in other words, restitution in kind by delivery of a similar object.[83]

From the above examples, it can be stated that restitution in kind consists of the delivery of an equivalent object that replaces in the most complete way the object subject to restitution. In a sense, restitution in kind is similar to reparations, and some authors treat it as such.[84] Nevertheless, it differs from reparations in that the substituted goods are selected individually through a search for items most similar in their type, value, etc. Reparations are accomplished in a completely different way. They may be expressed as a certain amount of money or goods of another kind, but must always be given as a total, without reference to individual components of reparations or particular losses.

---

79. In Brownlie's opinion this "specific restitution is exeptional, and the vast majority of claims, conventions and *compromis* (agreements to submit to arbitration) provide for the adjudication of pecuniary claims only". However, "writers and, from time to time, governments and tribunals assert a right to specific restitution, but, whilst it is safe to assume that this form of redress has a place in the law, it is difficult to state the conditions of its application with any certainty". He then gives examples of writers' opinions and quotes proper cases. I. Brownlie, above note 1 Chapter XX, *Responsibility of States*, under heading: 'Restitution in Kind and Restitution in Integrum', p. 461. See also note 16 p. 210 ff.
80. See below ch. 2 pp. 33-36.
81. See above note 16 pp. 111 and 792. The practice of restitution after World War I developed so-called substitution, or a supply of an equivalent, if the search for the item subject to restitution was too demanding. Both sides had to consent. A. Figlarewicz, above note 57 p. 50.
82. I. Vasarhelyi, above note 9 p. 113.
83. Military Government Regulations. Title 19: *Restitutions*; effective date 15 April 1945. Office of Military Government for Germany (U.S.). Item 19, 100. 2.C.
84. For example C. Berezowski, above note 31 p. 134; A. Martin, above note 4 p. 276; S. Turner, in: W. Fiedler (Hrsg), *Internationaler Kulturgüterschutz und deutsche Frage*, Berlin 1991, p. 37.

CHAPTER II

THE RESTITUTION OF WORKS OF ART AND THE DEVELOPMENT OF RESTITUTION AS A RULE OF CUSTOM IN INTERNATIONAL LAW

The Development of the Doctrine and Practice

Since time immemorial wars have provided numerous examples of looting of works of art. One author wrote that "history was frequently written in booty rather than in books, and the upward surge of nation after nation can still be traced through the remains of wartime plunder".[1] Looting has always been criticised by contemporaries; voices of disapproval and contempt for looters can be found in the Bible and texts of ancient writers.[2] For many centuries, however, such condemnations were merely opinions of scholars and there was no power to enforce action against looting. The Catholic Church was the only institution which, for religious reasons, attempted to give a legal cause of action, supported by the obligation of restituting war prizes. However, this applied only to ecclesiastical objects. The Polish chronicler, Dlugosz, for example, described the pillage of the Gniezno Cathedral by Bretislaw of Bohemia in 1039. The prize included relics of saints, sculptures, vessels, and even bells. The case was brought before Pope Benedict IX, who listened to both parties. The Bohemians maintained that "our Prince Bretislaw and the Bohemian people were deeply convinced that it was justified for them to pillage by the right of war they waged against the Poles." Hearing that, the Pope:

> scolded the envoys and concluded that their excuse had no sense and was groundless. It is not proper to loot God's churches of their sanctities and articles devoted to God in any war, even if it is a just war... since wars are waged against people only, not against objects related to the Heavens and worship. Therefore, they should return all relics looted from the Gniezno Cathedral and other Polish churches, or they must be aware of the fact that the Holy See, with all severity, will excommunicate Bretislaw and the Prague bishop, Severus.[3]

From this discussion, it may be concluded that the prohibition on looting churches was already well established in medieval mentality, which, of course, does not mean that it was generally observed. In the above case, as Dlugosz related, the Bohemian envoys pledged in the name of their Prince and Bishop to return everything that had been looted, but never kept their promise.

With the waning of the Middle Ages, the religious motivation weakened, giving way to the Renaissance admiration for Reason and Beauty, according to which works of art were appreciated for their own sake. Keeping abreast with the times, the Polish lawyer, Jakub Przyluski, for the first time in the doctrine of international law, formulated a rule stating that not only were objects of worship excluded from the right of war prize, but masterpieces of

---

1. D. Rigby, 'Cultural Reparations and a New Western Tradition' *The American Scholar* 1944 13 p. 274.
2. One of the most frequently quoted writers is Polybius. See Ch. de Visscher, 'International Protection of Works of Art and Historic Monuments' *The Department of State Publication* 3590 1949 p. 823; S.E. Nahlik, ch. 1 above note 31 p. 73, also for opinion of other writers.
3. *Jana Dlugosza Roczniki, czyli kroniki slawnego Krolewsta Polskiego* [The Annals of Jan Dlugosz, or The Chronicles of the Famous Kingdom of Poland] Warsaw 1969, Book 3, pp. 10-11.

literature and art as well. He believed that during military operations, *sacra, literarum et artificum nobilium monumenta conservabit integra, cunctis ab injuriis defensa*. What is more, he proposed sparing the lives of men famous for their virtues and knowledge: *Viris item et virtutibus, et eruditione conspicuis parci jubebit*.[4] To justify his opinion, Przyluski quoted examples from antiquity: the Consul Marcellus spared Archimedes' life after the conquest and sack of Syracuse, and Demetrius, who while besieging Rhodes, refrained from destroying a building because the portrait of Ialisos painted by the famous artist Protogenes was inside.[5] Przyluski's arguments are of particular significance because long after him, other international law theoreticians limited themselves only to negative evaluation of the practice of looting works of art, still rendering it legal. Assuming the legality of widespread pillaging, Alberico Gentili stated only that "Although this is the law I would prefer people were guided by shame and honesty, and refrained from what is allowed by law".[6]

Grotius developed and expanded this point of view. He, like earlier writers, observed and acknowledged the practice, but following the teachings of the law of nature, he wrote: "even if it is permissible to devastate, it would be unreasonable to do wrong to someone, not doing good to oneself at the same time, unless it is motivated by the expectation of some other advantage." Therefore, "that kind of devastation which makes the enemy immediately ask for peace, should be tolerated".[7] Among his other arguments in favour of restraining from "devastation" Grotius presents conclusions that follow the examination of objects' usefulness for military purposes. He wrote:

> It happens that some things are of such nature that they are of no effect in making or carrying on war; and these, as is reasonable, should be spared during the war. To this case belongs the pleading of the Rhodians to Demetrius the City-taker, in favour of the painting of Ialysius, which Gellius gives. They tell him that if he destroys that part of the city, he will be supposed to make war upon Protogenes the great painter. Polybius says that it is a mark of savage mind to make war on things which neither weaken the loser nor strenghten him who destroys them; as temples, porticos, statues, and the like. Cicero says that Marcellus "spared the buildings of Syracuse, public and private, as if his army had come to defend, not to destroy them". And again, that "Our ancestors left to them what is a gratification to the conquered and a trifle to us.... And as this is true in all ornamental works, for the reason which we have mentioned, there is, besides, an especial reason in things dedicated to sacred uses. [8]

---

4. J. Przyluski (Priluscius), *Leges seu Statuta ac privilegia Regni Poloniae omnia ...* Cracoviae 1553, Liber VI, cap. I: 'De expeditione ad bellum', f. 875.
5. *Ibid:"Sic captis Syracusis M. Marcellus Imperator, machination(n)ib(us), Archimedes Philosophi, multum ac diu victoria sua(m) inhibita(m) senserat, eximia tame(n) hominis prudentia delegatus, ut capiti illius parceret, edixit: pene tantu(m) gloriae in Archimede seruato, quantu(m) in oppressis Syracusis hostis reponens."*
6. *"Ceterum ut hoc jus est, quantum quidem ipse puto, tamen malim sequi pudorem, et honestatem, et a iure licito abstinere."* A. Gentili, *De iure belli libri tres*, 1598 Liber III, cap. 6: 'Victos ornamentis spoliare', p. 509.
7. H. Grotius, ch. 1 above note 38 p. 230-231."*Ceterum, nisi causa utilitatis suadeat, stultum sit, nullo suo bono nocere alteri. Ideo, qui sapiunt, utilitatibus moveri solent.... Et illa quidem polulatio ferenda est, quae brevi ad pacem petendam hostem subigit."*
8. The original passage runs as follows: *Ibid*: p. 239-240 *"...ut res quaedam ejus sint naturae, quae ad bellum faciendum aut ducendum nihil momenti habeant: quibus rebus parci etiam, manente bello ratio vult. Huc pertinent Rhodiorum oriatio ad Demetrium urbicapum pro pictura Ialysi, sic a Gallio Latine expressa: Quae malum ratio est, ut tu imaginem istam velis incendio oedium facto disperdere? nam, si nos omnes superaveris, et oppidum hoc totum ceperis, imagine quoque illa integra et incolumi per victoriam potieris: sin vero nos vincere obsidendo nequieris, petimus consideres, ne turpe tibi sit, quia non potueris Rhodios vincere, bellum cum Protogene mortuo gesisse. Polybius rabiosi esse animi ait, ea perdere, quae nec hosti perdita vires adimant, nec perdendi emolumentum adferant, qualia sunt templa, porticus, statuae, et similia. Marcellus, laudante Cicerone, aedificis omnibus Syracusarum, publicis et privatis, sacris et profanis, sic pepercit, quasi ad ea defendenda cum exercitu non expugnanda venisset. Idem postea: majores nostri relinquebant iis, quae jucunda victis, nobis levia videbantur.... Hoc vero sicut in aliis ornamentis valet ob eam, quam jam diximus, causam: ita specialis ratio accedit in iis, quae sacris usibus dicata sunt."*

This was followed by a reference to religious motives, which have already been discussed.[9] Obviously, Grotius considered works of art to be objects useless in war, since he gives the examples already mentioned by Przyluski in a similar context. There is however, a clear and significant difference between these two authors: Przyluski advocated the protection of works of art during war for completely different reasons; for him, it was willingness to preserve the values that were worth respecting, while Grotius seems to have been guided by a negative motive: not to destroy things that are useless in warfare. Also interesting are the other advantages cited by Grotius to encourage moderation in military operations. He wrote for example that "moderation in devastation, which finds its expression in sparing objects that do not prolong war, deprives the enemy of his crucial weapon — despair." Moreover:

> moderation in devastation at war creates the illusion of being certain of victory, while mere gentleness is enough to reduce enemy's pugnacity and makes him more conciliatory. According to Livy, Hannibal did not demolish anything in the territory of Tarentum; 'it was obvious', says Livy, 'that it was not because of the soldiers and their chief's moderation, but was aimed at winning the heart of Tarentians'.[10]

The issues raised by academics and theoreticians gradually began to appear in the practice of international relations. Initially, the instances of restitution in peace treaties refer only to religious objects; a good example of restitutional clauses of this kind can be the provisions included in the Peace Treaty concluded between Poland and Moldavia in 1510 in Kamieniec. In the Treaty, the Moldavian hospodar Bohdan promised the Polish king Sigismund I that he would give back gold, silver and other goods looted from the church in Rohatyn and from other Polish sanctuaries:

> *Imprimis de rebus Ecclesiae Rohatinensis, quaecunque invenientur in veritate, sive sint de auro, sive de argento, sive sint vestes sacrae, et alia ornamenta, Magnificus Bohdanus Woiewode, omne debet restituere sine fraude et dolo. Idem fiat de rebus aliarum Ecclesiarum, ut quaecunque invenientur, utrinque restituantur. Similiter et de companis, quotquot reperientur ab utraque parte, ut restituantur.*[11]

The inclusion of such clauses was not exceptional, but neither was it common practice. Other well known cases include, for example, the return of Raphael's tapestries by Constable Montmorency to Pope Julius III in 1553. The tapestry was stolen from Rome during the famous *Sacco di Roma*.[12]

In the seventeenth century, treaty clauses dealing with restitution became more common, although cultural goods were not directly mentioned. The first such case was the 1660 Treaty of Oliva, in which it was decided that, besides archives, the Royal Library would be returned to Poland. Article IX of the Treaty read: "*Restituentur quoque a parte Svecorum, omnia archiva, acta publica, Castrensia, Iuridica, Ecclesiastica, necnon Biliotheca Regia, quae ex Regno*

---

9.   P. 18 above.

10.   H. Grotius, ch.1 above note 38 p. 245 "*...moderatio ista in servandis rebus, quae bellum non morantur, magnum hosti telum eripit, desperationem. ... Adde quod speciem hoc praefert, manente bello, magnae de victoria fiduciae: et quod clementia apta per se frangendis et conciliandis animis. Annibal apud Livium in Tarentino agro nihil violat: apparebat, ait, non id modestia militum aut ducis, nisi ad conciliandos Tarentinorum animos fieri*".

11.   '*Conditiones Pacis inter Sigismundum I Regem Poloniae et Bohdanum Palatinum Moldaviae ... Datum in Kamieniec 23 Januar 1510*', in M. Dogiel, *Codex Diplomaticus Regni Poloniae et Magni Ducatus Lithuanie* Vol.1 Vilnea 1758, p. 607.

12.   S.E. Nahlik, ch. 1 above note 31 p. 133.

Poloniae et magno Ducatu Lithuanie avecta...". [13] There were also the first instances of establishing joint bodies to supervise the correctness of the restitutional process and to adjudicate in contentious cases; this type of solution was provided for in the so-called Treaty of the Pyrenees, signed by France and Spain in 1659.

> As it might well happen that the particular Persons interested on both sides, in the restitution of the Goods, into the Propriety and enjoyment whereof they ought to re-enter by virtue of the present Treaty, should find under divers Pretences, Difficultys and Resistance in their Re-establishment by such as are now in possession of the said Goods, or that any other Obstructions should arise in the full execution of the Premises; it hath been concluded and agreed, that the said Lords and Kings shall appoint each of them one of their ministers to repair to the Court of the other, and other places if need be, to the end that hearing jointly, at the place where the said Ministers shall meet, such Persons as shall apply themselves to them about those Affairs, and taking Cognizance of the Contents of the Articles of the Treaty, and of what the said Partys shall offer unto them, they might declare together unanimously, briefly and summarily, without any other formality of Justice, what ought to be executed, issuing thereupon the necessary Act and Instrument of their Declaration; which Act shall be perform'd without admitting or leaving any room to any Contradiction or Reply. [Article CXII] [14]

The wars of the following century did not provide examples of famous lootings of works of art, and this is why the eighteenth century author Martens could state that:

> *depuis longtemps on avait reconnu comme loi de la guerre sur le continent, non-seulement de conserver aux sujets ennemis la propriété de leurs biens-fonds, mais aussi d'épargner tant les biens privés du monarque que les biens-meubles des sujets, et particulièrement les monuments de l'art et de l'industrie ...*" [15]

One of the key writers on international law of that time, Emer de Vattel, accounted for this state of affairs in the following way:

> The usefulness of literature and the fine arts, and necessity of encouraging them are quite generally recognised today. The immortal Peter I believed that he could not fully civilise Russia and make the country prosperous without their help. In England knowledge and ability lead to honours and wealth... France also deserves special praise in this matter; it owes to the munificence of its Kings several institutions no less useful than renowned. [16]

---

13.   '*Tractatus pacis inter regem poloniae Joannem Casimirum eiusque foederatus Leopoldum Romanorum imperatorem, electorem Brandenburicum Fridericum Wilhelmum ab una et Carolum XI Sueciae regem a parte altera...*' Oliva, 3 May 1660, in *Volumina Legum*, Vol. 4 Petersburg 1859. See also 'Acta Pacis Oliviensis inedita' Vratislaviae 1763.
14.   'Major Peace Treaties of Modern History 1648-1967' with an introductory essay by Arnold Toynbee, Vol. 1 F. Israel, ed., New York 1967, p. 108.
15.   G.F. Martens, *Précis du droit des Gens moderne de l'Europe*, Vol. 1 Paris 1864, p. 252.
16.   E. de Vattel, *The Law of Nations or the Principles of the Natural Law Applied to the Conduct and to the Affairs of Nations and of Sovereigns* translation of the 1758 edition by Ch. G. Fenwick, Washington 1916, special edition 1993, Book I, Ch. XI, para. 113 'The Arts and Sciences', p. 48. The original text reads as follows: "*On reconnoit assez généralement aujourd'hui l'utilité des Lettres & des Beaux-Arts, & la nécessité de les encourager. L'immortel Pierre I ne crut point pouvoir sans leur secours civiliser entièrement la Russie, & la rendre florissante. En Angleterre la science & les talens conduisent aux honneurs & aux richesses, ... La France mérite aussi à cet egard des louanges particulières: Elle doit à la magnificence de ces Rois plusieurs Etablissemen non moins utiles que glorieu.*" E. De Vattel, Les Droits de Gens. ou Principes de la Loi Naturelle, Appliqués à la conduite & aux affaires des Nations & des Souverains, Tome I, A Londres 1758, p. 104.

> For whatever cause a country be devastated, those buildings should be spared which are an honour to the human race and which do not add to the strength of the enemy, such as temples, tombs, public buildings, and all edifices of remarkable beauty. What is gained by destroying them? It is the act of a declared enemy of the human race thus wantonly to deprive men of these monuments of art and models of architecture.

Finally he concluded:

> What we have said is sufficient to give a general idea of the moderation with which, in the most just war, a belligerent should use the right to pillage and devastate the enemy's country.... All acts of hostility which injure the enemy without necessity, or which do not tend to procure victory and bring about the end of the war, were unjustifiable, and as such condemned by the natural law.[17]

From this examination, it is possible to identify different arguments for the respect of works of art during war, and their restitution in cases where they are pillaged. Apart from the protection ensuing from the generally accepted treatment of movable goods, their special status was also recognised on different grounds in different historical periods. Initially, there was a religious basis; then, the 'liberal' admiration for beauty of art created by famous artists. Next, the purely logical and practical conclusion was added that works of art do not strengthen any of the belligerents and do not help in achieving the lawful purpose of war; on the contrary, by sparing them, one can even win the goodwill of the enemy. Writing about this period, Hall also added that "works of art and the contents of collections were spared, as royal palaces were spared, on the ground of the personal courtesy supposed to be due from one prince to another".[18]

Extremely turbulent and important events at the beginning of the nineteenth century added an entirely new dimension and scale, and shed a different light on the function of restitution of works of art in international law, in terms of the development of doctrine. Nahlik described it accurately as "the great chapter in restitution of works of art — Paris 1815." This event was the return of the collection of art gathered on the orders of Napoleon in the capital of France, to the places of its origin. Napoleon's plans for making Paris a great centre of art, comprising the most famous works from all over Europe had meant that the period of his reign was one of continuous looting. The pillaging often assumed a hidden form, maintaining the appearances of legality, as for example, in the form of benevolence or compensation, usually coerced at Armistices and Peace Treaties.[19] Napoleon's defeat brought an inevitable reckoning of the accounts. After a prolonged period of bargaining, intense diplomatic activity, and political

---

17.   *Op. cit.* Book III, Ch. IX, para. 168: 'What Property Should be Spared', p. 293, and para 172: 'General Rule in Limitation of the Injury which may be done to the Enemy', p. 294. Original text reads as follows: "*Pour quelque sujet que l'on ravage un pays, on doit épargner les Edifices qui sont honneur à l'humanité, & qui ne contribuent point à rendre l'Ennemi plus puissant; les Temples, les Tombeaux, les Bâtiments publics, tous les Ouvrages respectables par leur beauté. Que gagne-t-on à les détruire? C'est se déclarer l'ennemi du Genre-humain, que de le priver de gaieté de Coeur, de ces Monuments des Arts, de ces Modèles du Goût;... En voila assez pour donner une idée de la modération avec laquelle on doit user, dans la guerre la plus juste, du droit de piller & ravager le pays ennemi.... Tout le mal que l'on fait a l'Ennemi sans nécessité, toute hostilité qui ne tend point à amener la Victoire & la fin de la guerre, est une licence, que la Loi Naturelle condamne*", E. De Vattel, above note 16 Tome II, p. 139 and 142.
18.   E. Hall, ch. 1 above note 61 p. 505.
19.   For example, the Albanii and Braschi collections as well as Pope Pius VI's collection were handed over as 'compensation' for the murder of General Duphot in Rome. See Ch. de Visscher, above note 2 p. 825. Extensive descriptions of such practices can be found in S.E. Nahlik, ch. 1 above note 31 p. 25 ff.

complications,[20] the collection was removed from the Louvre, almost forcefully.[21] According to contemporary reports, the return of the works of art to their places of origin had all the attributes of a triumph. Crowds of people with flowers greeted them at the Brandenburg Gate in Berlin, while in Dusseldorf, the bells pealed, the streets were illuminated and gun salutes were fired on the banks of the Rhine.[22]

An explanation of the uncompromising attitude of the Allies towards the issue of restitution, and the unusual social response restitution engendered, can be found in socio-political processes occurring at the end of the eighteenth century; the period was characterised by deep changes in the mentality of Europeans which resulted in the rise of national consciousness. The genesis of a modern Nation-State, as Niec wrote "is characterised by the development of a link between the newly isolated national group and cultural goods that belong to it".[23] These 'cultural goods' are necessary for each nation, and contribute to the definition of its identity, creating the so-called cultural heritage — a testimony of historical tradition that gives the Nation-State its 'historical legitimation'.[24]

The diplomatic documents from the time of the events in Paris stressed the demand for the "return of statues, pictures, and other works of art," because "the States in question, one after another, had been systematically pillaged by the former Revolutionary Government of France, in spite of all principles of justice and customs of modern war".[25] Thus, alongside the traditional and purely logical arguments, a new motivation emerged. At first, it appeared in letters and petitions from people who protested against looting the works of art and called for their return. Thirty nine artists living in Rome emphasised the necessity of leaving "works of every school" under the sky that witnessed their birth, "and in the environment for which they were created by their authors".[26] From the British note,[27] de Visscher assumed that "the restitution ordered by the Allied Powers was based on the very general principle of the integrity of the artistic heritage of conquered nations".[28]

This argument for restitution meant giving the process a new function and new tasks. The need for its implementation was no longer dictated by the nature of a given object, as it had been in the case of *res sacrae*, or by the fact that the prize was recognised as *praeda illicita* because of the circumstances of its seizure. From now on, restitution was to be founded on the new principle of protection of the integrity of national cultural heritage. This principle was to be developed in the twentieth century, but it had its roots in the nineteenth. It is worth noting

---

20.   Because the Allies, who were re-establishing the ancient regime in France, supported the Bourbons and did not want to weaken their position by too blatant restitutional operation. For the details see S.E. Nahlik, ch. 1 above note 31 p. 150.
21.   The Prussian works of art were taken from the Louvre by a unit of 200 soldiers under the command of Eberhard von Grote, and it almost ended in a clash with an intervening detachment of the French National Guard. For details see W. Treue, *Art Plunder. The Fate of Works of Art in War, Revolution and Peace,* London 1960, p. 192.
22.   *Ibid,* p. 190.
23.   H. Niec, *Ojczyzna dziela sztuki. Miedzynarodowa ochrona integralnosci narodowej spuscizny kulturalnej* [Fatherland of Works of Art. International Protection of the Integrity of the National Cultural Heritage], Warsaw-Krakow 1980, p. 106. See also this work for an extensive analysis of this subject.
24.   After S. Zaryn, *Dlaczego chronimy zabytki* [Why We Protect Historical Monuments], Warsaw 1966, p. 19.
25.   The note of Lord Castlereagh, the British foreign minister, handed to the diplomatic representatives of the Allied Powers on 11 September 1815. In G.F. Martens, *Nouveau recueil de traités,* Vol. 2, Goettingue 1818, p. 632 *et seq.*
26.   Ch. de Visscher, above note 2 p. 826; also there, more opinions on this subject.
27.   The note of Lord Castlereagh, above note 25 p. 105.
28.   Ch. de Visscher, above note 2 p. 826. See also B. Hollander, *The International Law of Art for Lawyers, Collectors and Artists,* London 1959, p. 21.

that some nineteenth century pronouncements went even further in their argument for the protection of cultural goods during war, paving the way for the idea of a World Heritage, a contemporary concept for us. How else could the decision of the Halifax Vice Admiralty Court be interpreted? In 1813, the Court ordered that a collection of paintings and engravings captured by a British ship during its transportation from Italy to the United States, had to be returned to the Academy of Fine Arts in Philadephia, on the basis:

> that the arts and sciences are admitted amongst all civilised nations to form an exception to the severe rights of war, and to be entitled to favour and protection. They are considered not as the peculium of this or that nation, but as the property of mankind at large, and as belonging to the common interest of the whole species; and that the large restitution of such property to the claimants would be in conformity with the law of nations, as practised by all civilised countries.[29]

Two years later, in a similar spirit, Sir John Mackintosh MP spoke during a debate in the House of Commons in London, of the bombardment of Washington by the British:

> It was an attack, not against the strength or the resources of a State, but against the national honour and public affections of a people. After 25 years of the fiercest warfare, in which every great capital of the European continent had been spared, he had almost said, respected by enemies, it was reserved for England to violate all that decent courtesy towards the seats of national dignity, which, in the midst of enmity, manifest the respect of nations for each other, by an expedition deliberately and principally directed against palaces of government, halls of legislation, tribunals of justice, repositories of the muniments of property, and of the records of history — objects among civilised nations exempted from the ravages of war, and secured, as far as possible, even from accidental operation, because they contribute nothing to the means of hostility, but are consecrated to purposes of peace, and minister to the common and perpetual interest of all human society.[30]

Most important for this discussion is the fact that as a result of the complete and consistent restitution that concluded the Napoleonic lootings, the full protection of works of art and a ban on their capture during war was established. This was vividly formulated by Rigby:

> Probably no one would have been more amazed than Napoleon himself to learn how his ravenous fingers were closing the looting gate in Europe — closing it so well, in fact, that it could be sealed by the peace-makers of World War I, and kept sealed until Adolf Hitler blew off the hinges.[31]

Those principles were then confirmed by the doctrine of international law. In 1819, Klüber wrote the following on the issue of war prizes: "Nowadays, works of literature and fine arts, as well as objects used in religious ceremonies are respected and usually spared and left undisturbed".[32] An American author Wheaton was even more firm when he stated:

> By the ancient law of nations, even what was called *res sacrae* were not exempted from capture and confiscation. Cicero has conveyed this idea in his expressive metaphorical

---

29.   The verdict of the Vice Admiralty Court in Halifax of 21 April 1813 [Judge Sir A. Croke], in J.B. Moore, *A Digest of International Law*, Vol. 7, Washington 1906, para. 1197, p. 460.

30.   The speech of Sir John Mackintosh before the House of Commons on 11 April 1815, in J.B. Moore, above note 29 para. 1123, p. 200.

31.   D. Rigby, above note 1 p. 276.

32.   J.L. Klüber, *Droit des gens modernes de l'Europe,* Paris 1874, para. 253.

language, in the Fourth Oration against Verres, where he says that: 'Victory made all the sacred things of the Syracusans profane.' But by the modern usage of nations, which has acquired the force of law, temples of religion, public edifices devoted to civil purposes only, monuments of art, and repositories of science, are exempted from the general operations of war.[33]

The essence of the formulated rules of customary law finally found its place in legal enactments too. Instructions for the US Army drafted on the order of President Lincoln included directives that called for respect for cultural goods. These goods, defined as "classical works of art, libraries, scientific collections," had to be, according to Article 35, "secured against all avoidable injury, even when they are contained in fortified places whilst besieged or bombarded." If, however, they could be removed without exposing them to the danger of damage:

> the ruler of the conquering State or nation may order them to be seized and removed for the benefit of the said [enemy] nation. The ultimate ownership is to be settled by the ensuing treaty of peace. In no case shall they be sold or given away, if captured by the armies of the United States, nor shall they ever be privately appropriated, or wantonly destroyed or injured.[34]

These military instructions became a starting point for work on the codification of international law. The principles included in its provisions cited here were first found in Bluntschli's private code. His formulation was as follows:

> *La destruction intentionelle ou la dégradation des monuments et oeuvres d'art, des instruments et collections scientifiques, par les troupes d'occupation du territoire ennemi, ne sont plus permises en temps de guerre et sont considérées aujourd'hui comme des actes de barbarie (para. 649).*

> *Le droit international actuel n'interdit pas encore au vainqueur d'emposter et d'installer ailleurs les objets d'art qui peuvent être transportés sans dommages. Mais l'opinion publique reprouve aujourd'hui la mise en vente ou la donation de ces objets par le vainqueur pendant la guerre. On regarde déjà actuellement comme contraire aux idées civilisées, l'enlèvement des collections ou instruments scientifiques et bibliothèques, destinées à satisfaire les besoins intellectuels d'une contrée (para. 650).[35]*

Bluntschli's prohibition on looting was supplemented by the separate provision regarding restitution:

> *La restitution des autres objets [except for archives and other documents connected to the territory and which make "un accessoire du territoire" — para 722] pris sur l'ennemi, et spécialement des collections scientifiques ou artistiques et des oeuvres d'art enlevées avant la conclusion de la paix, doit être expressément stipulée (para 723).[36]*

---

33.   H. Wheaton, *Elements of International Law*, London 1864, p. 596.
34.   *Instructions for the Government of Armies of the United States in the Field, General Orders.* No. 100, 24 April 1863, Articles 35 and 36, in J.B. Moore, above note 29 para. 1123, p. 204. After the author of the draft, Francis Lieber, the instruction is referred to in the literature as the Lieber Code. See, among others, L. du Boff, *The Deskbook of Art Law*, Washington 1977, pp. 134 and 135; S. Williams, *The International and National Protection of Movable Cultural Property. A Comparative Study*, New York 1978, pp. 15 and 16.
35.   M. Bluntschli, *Le droit international codifié*, Paris 1870, p. 331.
36.   *Ibid*, p. 366.

Through the important but unratified Brussels Declaration of 1874, the formulations also influenced the solutions used in the official codifications of the international war law of 1898 and 1907.[37] The Hague Regulation of 1907 regarding the laws and customs of war on land ordered that during hostilities all necessary steps must be taken to spare, as far as possible, buildings dedicated to religion, art, science, and historical monuments (Article 27). During a military occupation:

> The property of municipalities, that of institutions dedicated to religion, charity and education, the arts and sciences, even when the State's property, shall be treated as private property. All seizure, destruction of, or wilful damage to, institutions of this character, historic monuments, works of art or science, is forbidden, and should be made the subject of legal proceedings. (Article 56).[38]

The ban on looting was mirrored in the absolute obligation of restitution, which, since the nineteenth century, had a new motivation — that of respect for the integrity of national cultural heritage. From that time on, it developed, slowly but constantly, enriched by new legal means that reinforced the possibility of its application.

The Protection of the Integrity of the National Cultural Heritage

Although there is no universally accepted scholarly definition of the concept of national cultural heritage, it has a rich bibliography. At the basis of its structure lies the general acceptance of a territorial link for a 'cultural good'. The criterion of territoriality is determined by various premises. Particular aspects of the problem were first investigated by de Visscher[39] and Nahlik, who added problems of peacetime into the field of analysis of the law of war. These included, *inter alia*, the question of restrictive legislation regarding the export of works of art, conflicts resulting from property law and the regulation of archaeological excavations.[40] In this case, it is more important that the principle of the integrity of national cultural heritage allows for claims of a restitutional nature. According to Seferiades, as early as 1815, we could talk about the establishment of a custom that *"tous objets d'art ou historiques appartenant au domaine public d'un pays et directement ou indirectement extorqués par un autre doivent être restitués au premier"*.[41] De Visscher added that "the very general principle of the integrity of the artistic heritage of conquered nations ... tends to condemn as having an unlawful purpose, any cession, even conventional, of an art object, which is imposed under moral duress".[42] Legal norms referring to the times of peace were examined by Niec. She arrived at a conclusion that national law includes the right to keep artistic goods within the State's borders. This right is complemented by a right to demand the return of an object that has been taken away without

---

37.   It must be noted that the provisions on the protection of cultural goods included in the Brussels Declaration were later adopted, practically unchanged, by the Hague Conventions.

38.   The Regulations Concerning the Laws and Customs of War on Land, 1907.

39.   Ch. de Visscher, 'La protection internationale des objets d'art et des monuments historiques', *Revue de Droit International et de Legislation Comparée* 1935, No. 1 and 2; Ch. de Visscher, 'La protection des patrimones artistiques et historiques nationaux', *Mouseion* 1938, Vol. 43-44; Ch. de Visscher, 'Les monuments historiques et les oeuvres d'art en temps de guerre et dans les traites de paix', in *Manuel technique et juridique*, Paris 1939; Ch. de Visscher, above note 2.

40.   See S.E. Nahlik, ch. 1 above note 31 p. 187 in which the "territorial and national" character of many of the peace treaty resolutions are pointed out.

41.   S. Seferiades, 'La question du repatriement des "Marbres d'Elgin" considérée plus spécialement au point de vue du droit des gens', *La Revue de Droit International* 1932, Vol. 3, p. 20.

42.   Ch. de Visscher, above note 2 p. 826.

the State authorities' consent.[43] The task of fully examining the nature of the principle of integrity was undertaken by Engstler[44] and Williams.[45] Engstler tried to establish certain points in order to systematise the whole problem. Recapitulating the work of his predecessors, he stated that in international relations, the principle of integrity (*Integrität des nationalen Kunst und historischen Erbes*) is based, among other things, on the principles of the inviolability (*Unantastbarkeit*) and inalienability (*Unantziehbarkeit*) of individual elements of national cultural heritage, as well as on the principle of reconstitution (*Rekonstitution*) of this heritage in the case of territorial cession or dissolution of a multi-ethnic State.[46] To provide a balance of opinions it should be noted, however, that not all authors share the above mentioned views. They are questioned strongly in particular by Merryman in several of his works.[47] Assuming, however, that all these emerging principles are binding, what forms does restitution take and how does it function?

The Restitution of Works of Art Looted in Time of War

The starting point for this analysis of the restitution of works of art looted during war is an evaluation of the events in Paris in 1815 (when the Allies did not use a uniform principle of return) which makes it possible to formulate some generalisations, as well as a number of more varied conclusions.

First of all, it is possible to speak of the application of the principle that was later defined as the principle of identification. According to this principle, only the objects that are identified

---

43.   H. Niec, 'Sovereign Rights to Cultural Property' *Polish Yearbook of International Law* 1971, Vol. 4, p. 239, ff.; 'Legislative Models of Protection of Cultural property', *Hastings Law Journal* 1976, Vol. 27, p. 1089 ff. See also other conclusions of this author regarding the customary norms of respect for cultural goods as public property and the general principle of international law regarding an independent right to cultural goods, above note 23, p. 149 ff.

44.   L.L. Engstler, *Die territoriale Bindung von Kulturgütern im Rahmen des Volkerrechts*, Köln-Berlin-Bonn-Munchen 1964.

45.   S. Williams, above note 34. The author pointed, *inter alia*, to consequences of practical application of the concept of the common heritage of mankind, which implies not only "an obligation by states to protect one another's national cultural heritages, as a part of the cultural heritage of mankind, but it could also justify the establishment of a concrete international heritage, a new sort of property, owned by the international community as such, administered by an international agency (e.g. UNESCO) and made available to all persons for them to enjoy." *Ibid*, pp. 201 and 202.

46.   L. Engstler, above note 44, p. 279. The principle of integrity is also accomplished, according to Engstler, by the principles of inalienability (Unveräusserlichkeit) and non-transferability (Unübertragebarkeit) of works of art and archaeological objects representative of the cultural heritage of a given country. These principles are enforced through the passing of appropriate restrictive legislation. The criterion for incorporating cultural goods in a cultural heritage is included in another principle that the author called the principle of retention of cultural goods within the country of their origin (Bewahrung der Kulturgüter auf ihrem Herkunft-und Schöpfungsgebiet). Besides these principles, Engstler underlined, in his opinion, the rising importance of the protection of the integrity of works of art treated as individual units, as well as of the integrity of whole collections. This he did in the principle that concluded his systematisation: "Integrität gesschlossener Einheiten," which allows for re-integration of dispersed works of art and the protection of the integrity of collections of world importance (Grundsatz der Integrität organischer und historisch gewachsener Kollektionskörper). *Ibid*, p. 279 ff.

47.   See, for example, J. H. Merryman, 'International Art Law: from Cultural Nationalism to a Common Cultural Heritage' *New York Journal of International Law and Politics* 1983, 15, p. 757 ff.; 'Trading in Art: Cultural Nationalism v. Internationalism' *Stanford Lawyer* 1984, 18, p. 24 ff. ; 'Two Ways of Thinking about Cultural Property' *American Journal of International Law* 1986, Vol. 80, p. 831 ff. ; 'The Retention of Cultural Property' *University of California Davis Law Review* 1988, 21, p. 477 ff.; 'The Protection of the Cultural heritage?' *American Journal of Comparative Law* 1990, 38, Supplement.

as looted can be subject to restitution. In 1815, the Allies took from Paris only those works of art they had been previously deprived of. Some other works of art they took accidently from the former royal collection were returned to the Louvre in 1816.[48]

Secondly, there had been times in the past when looting had been ignored. Some of the restituted works of art had been stolen by General Bonaparte under an order from the Directoire in 1792, that is, more than twenty years earlier. A special case where time limits on restitutional claims were overlooked was the return of the Heidelberg manuscripts that had been looted from that German city nearly 200 years before.[49]

Next, it is clear that the principle of territoriality was applied, according to which objects were returned to the territory from which they had been looted, notwithstanding changes or other circumstances. Thus, the paintings taken from the Habsburg Flanders were returned to the Dutch King, the new ruler of the country.

Finally, the principle of a special territorial link of works of art developed — the principle which had been recognised and applied up to that time exclusively for archives.[50] This was the basis for the return of the Heidelberg manuscripts not to the Vatican, from where Napoleon's emissaries took them, but to Heidelberg, from where they were looted during the Thirty Years War in 1622. In this case, the manuscripts were obviously recognised as belonging to the cultural heritage of the place of their origin.

The application of this principle was also confirmed in several treaties concluded in the nineteenth century, such as the Austro-Prusso-Danish Treaty of 1864, in which the signatories pledged to co-operate for reconstruction of the scattered "ancient collection" connected with Schleswig's history, and the Hessian-Prussian Treaty of 1866, according to which the Cologne Chapter reclaimed the collection it had lost in 1794. These treaties settled old problems through the application of, as Nahlik called them, the rules that gave "priority to territorial and national claims".[51]

An example of restitution of works of art on a larger scale is provided by the Peace Treaties that concluded World War I.[52] The Treaties of Versailles, Saint Germain, and Trianon include general provisions on restitution, which cover all objects identified in the enemy territory as having been looted during the war (Articles 238, 184, and 168, respectively). The Treaties of Saint Germain and Trianon also include special provisions, of similar intent, which broaden the scope of general restitution. Under them, Austria and Hungary had to:

> return to each of the Allied and Associated Powers all legal records, documents, historic and artistic objects, as well as all scientific and bibliographic materials taken over from the territories which they invaded and which is the property of State or local governments, cities, charity and church institutions, or to other public and private institutions. (Article 191 of the Treaty of Saint Germain).

Besides the general Article 238, the Treaty of Versailles includes a special resolution regarding restitution for France, with the time limit shifted to include the Franco-Prussian War. Article 245 states that:

---

48.   D. Rigby, above note 1 p. 277.
49.   For this and other examples see S.E. Nahlik, ch. 1above note 31 p. 150.
50.   *Ibid*, p. 134 ff.
51.   *Ibid*, p. 187.
52.   See in particular Temperley, ch. 1 above note 56.

the German government will be obliged to return to the French government the trophies, archives, historic relics, works of art that were taken away by the German authorities during the 1870-1871 war, as well as during the recent war, according to an inventory that will be sent by the French government, and especially the French military banners taken during the 1870-1871 war, and all the political documents, taken by the German authorities from the Castle of Cercay near Brunoy (Seine-et-Oise) on 10 October 1870, which at that time belonged to Mr Rouher, a former Minister of State.

This article permits the following conclusions regarding the principle of restitution applied here: first, the public law character of restitution was stressed in such clauses as "the German government will be obliged to return to the French government", without differentiating between State, public, or private property; secondly, the principles of identification and territoriality also applied; and thirdly, in the case of the Treaty of Versailles, it is possible to refer to a particular application of the latter in connection with the principle of preserving national cultural heritage. This seems to be the only plausible interpretation of the provisions in Article 246, according to which, "Germany will be obliged to return to His Royal Highness, the King of the Hejaz, the original copy of the Koran, which belonged to Caliph Osman and was taken from Medina by the Turkish authorities in order to present it to the former Emperor Wilhelm II," because the King of the Hejaz assumed control over Medina only in 1916.

The Restitution (Repatriation) of Works of Art in Connection with Territorial Changes

Peace treaties often regulate the border changes resulting from wars. Such changes bring about additional problems connected with the status of works of art belonging to the cultural heritage of the areas that are ceded.[53] On a larger scale, this problem first appeared in 1866, when certain Italian territories, including the area of the former Republic of Venice, were incorporated within united Italy. Up to that time, these areas had been under rule of the Habsburgs, who had displaced several 'cultural goods' within the Austro-Hungarian Empire. The Italians went to extreme lengths to get some of them back to their places of origin, especially those objects that were in Vienna. The case was settled in the Austro-Italian Treaty in such a way that land and legal archives, "as well as political and historic documents of the former Republic of Venice" and "works of art and science connected with the ceded territory" were to be handed over to the Italians, while the "property titles and the documents of administration and civil courts related to the Austrian territory that may happen to be among the archives of the ceded territory will be handed over, in their totality, to the commissioners of His Imperial and Royal Highness" (Article XVIII).[54] Thus, the principle of complete reciprocity was applied, based on the criterion of a territorial link, and, at the same time, the aim of preserving the integrity

---

53.   The author suggests that the term 'repatriation' is used in the context of this restitution, as is based on entirely different legal grounds (which are in fact *sui generis*) from all types of restitution discussed above. In the following subchapter however, both terms will be used, because in the treaties discussed, restitution of looted works of art and repatriation of heritage resulting purely from territorial changes were regulated together and a full separation of them would be difficult without further lengthy explanation.

54.   The Peace Treaty between Austria-Hungary and Italy signed in Vienna on 3 October 1866 (henceforth: the Vienna Treaty); Ch. de Martens, F. de Cussy, *Recueil manuel et pratique de traités, conventions et autres actes diplomatiques...* 2è série, par F. H. Geffcen, Vol. 1, Leipzig 1885, p. 387. The original language of Article 18 of the Vienna Treaty is as follows: " *Les archives des territoires cédés contenant les titres de propriété, les documents administratifs et de justice civile, ainsi que les documents politiques et historiques de l'ancien République de Venise, seront remis dans leur intégrité aux Commissaires qui seront désignés a cet effet auxquels seront également consignés les objets d'art et de science spécialement affectés au territoire cédé.*"

of the historical heritage of Venice was emphasised. In the Treaty itself, however, these principles were limited as the private property rights of the members of Imperial Family to certain masterpieces of Italian art were recognised. This led to further complications, as the Italians did not want to hand them over to Austria and an additional agreement had to be concluded, which, in turn, impaired the achievement of mutual restitution.[55] The Italian claims in this area were eventually fulfilled after more than 50 years, in the Treaties of Saint Germain (Article 194), and Trianon (Article 179). These Treaties included very expanded provisions on the repatriation of works of art related to territorial changes after World War I. Three types of restitution of that sort can be distinguished on the basis of those treaties.

Type I:
repatriation of cultural goods that during the war were taken away from a territory that later was ceded. The appropriate provisions of the Treaties stated that Austria and Hungary were to return works of art, documents, etc., "which were taken away after 1 June 1914 from the ceded territorries, with the exception of objects that were purchased from private owners".[56]

Type II:
the obligation to release cultural goods relating to the ceded territory that were taken from it during a specified period before the war. Thus, Austria and Hungary "will return to each of the concerned Allied and Associated Powers, all records, documents and historic relics that are in possession of their public institutions, that are directly related to the history of the ceded territories, and that were removed from them after 1 January 1868," in the case of Hungary (Article 177 of the Treaty of Trianon), and "for the last ten years" in the case of Austria (Article 193 of the Treaty of Saint Germain). As far as Italy was concerned, "this period will be marked by the date of proclamation of the kingdom (1861)" for both countries obliged to make restitution (Articles as above).

Type III:
repatriation in order to reconstruct the national cultural heritage of certain countries by the return of 'cultural goods' being in the possession of Austria, and which had been taken from the ceded territories a long time ago. For this type of restitutional claim, no time limit was set. Countries that were allowed to lay such claims included Italy, Belgium, Poland and Czechoslovakia. These States presented lists of objects which they claimed. Some of the goods included in those lists had been removed from their original places 200 or more years before the Treaty was signed. To justify the filed claims, the Repatriation Commission was to be establish a "Committee of Three Lawyers", whose decisions were pledged to be recognised by all concerned States (Article 195 of the Treaty of Saint Germain).[57]

---

55. Eventually, two separate agreements were signed. Under the first one, Italy pledged to pay four million lira in order to keep the majority of the disputed works of art, and gave only a few of them. See articles 3, 4, and 5 of *Convention pour régler les questions financières entre les deux Pays à la suite des articles 6, 7 et 22 du traité de paix du 3 octobre1866* ... Florence du 1 janvier 1871. According to the second one — Protocol additionnel — Raphael's *Madonna*, which since that time has been called "*Madonna del Granduca*" because it had belonged to Archduke Ferdinand Habsburg, remained in Florence; G. F. Martens, *Nouveau recueil général de traités et autres actes relatifs aux rade droit international,* 2è serie, Vol. 1, Goettingue 1876, p. 328 ff.

56. Article 176 of the Treaty of Trianon, and Article 192 of the Treaty of Saint Germain.

57. Italy backed out of this procedure and concluded a separate agreement with Austria concerning her claims in 1920. See, Ch. de Visscher, above note 2 p. 834. See also I. Vasarhelyi, *Restitution in International Law,* Budapest 1964, p. 45. The author believes that the goods subject to restitution based on this principle were "for a long time illegally kept at a place they did not belong to". As far as the work of the Committee of Three Lawyers is concerned, see "'O', International Arbitrations under the Treaty of Saint Germain', *The British Yearbook of International Law* 1923-1924, Vol. 4, p. 124 ff. It is worth adding that none of the claims presented to the Committee was accepted, so, for example, Poland also had to enter into additional negotiations with Austria. The respective agreement was reached in 1938.

If the above types of claims are compared, it is clear that they are based on the principle of a territorial bond of the returned goods, and their aim is obviously to preserve the integrity of the national cultural heritage of the ceded territories and, in a broader sense, of the countries that take over these areas. The effort to achieve this aim can also be discerned in treaty provisions concerning a limited protection of collections. In this case, the integrity of national cultural heritage took precedence over the principle of integrity of "complete artistic collections of a greater value".[58] Analogous provisions of the Treaties of Saint Germain (Article 196) and Trianon (Article 177) pronounced that "in regard of the objects and documents of artistic, archaeological, scientific, and historical character that belonged either to the government of Austria-Hungary, or to the Crown," — in the case where these objects are not subject to other provisions of this treaty — Austria and Hungary are obliged:

> a) to conduct negotiations with the concerned States, on their demand, in order to conclude a conciliatory agreement, under which all parts of the collections and all objects and documents described above that should belong to the intellectual heritage (*patrimoine intellectuel*) of these States could be repatriated (*repatriés*) to the countries of their origin, on the principle of reciprocity;

> b) not to disperse the said collections and not to dispose of any of the above-mentioned objects for twenty years, unless a special agreement is signed before the end of this period, to provide security and good maintenance, and to render the collections, as well as their inventories, catalogues, and administrative documents, to researchers who are citizens of the Allied and Associated Powers.

In order to give a universal meaning to the principle of integrity of national cultural heritage, it was necessary to treat all nations alike. A step toward this was the provision of reciprocity — limited as it was — included in the Treaties. According to Article 193 of the Treaty of Saint Germain and Article 178 of the Treaty of Trianon:

> the newly created States, isolated out of the former Austro-Hungarian Empire, as well as the States that will receive a portion of the territory of that Empire, are obliged to return to the government [of Hungary or Austria] the records, documents, and historical relics originated from the period not longer than twenty years of age, that are directly related to the history or administration of [Austrian or Hungarian] territory, and which happen to be in the ceded territories.

The analysis of the question of repatriation resulting from the ceding of territories is also affected by two other issues relating to the Treaty of Versailles. The first one is related to the transfer of the former German East Africa to Great Britain as its mandate territory. It was not a cession in the proper meaning of the word, nevertheless, Article 246 of the Treaty of Versailles obliged Germany to hand over to Britain the skull of Sultan Makaoua, which had been taken out of East Africa during German rule. Obviously, the principle of territoriality was applied in this case, but owing to special circumstances, the object of repatriation was to be transferred to the country that assumed protection over the object's place of origin. According to Hollander, the skull was never found in Germany.[59]

The second issue concerned Polish claims to cultural goods that had been taken by Germany from the territories handed over to Poland. At the Peace Conference, the Polish government

---

58.   As underlined especially by H. Niec, above note 23 p. 149.
59.   B. Hollander, *The International Law of Art for Lawyers, Collectors and Artists*, London 1959, p. 32.

presented an extensive *Memorandum on some questions related to reparations and finances* .[60]
Article I of this document, calling upon the "requirements of justice", assumed that:

> Germany will return to Poland all libraries, museum collections, and all artistic, scientific
> and religious collections, as well as historical relics, that have been, for many reasons,
> seized, confiscated, or taken to Germany by German public officials, civilian and military,
> or by private persons, German citizens, from any Polish territories, at any time, even if
> these objects have become a part of public or private collections that are now located in
> Germany. This obligation applies not only to the property of the former Polish
> Commonwealth, but also to the property of the Polish Crown and public, religious,
> municipal, scientific and artistic institutions, as well as to that of private owners".[61]

The above-mentioned objects were to be handed over to Polish commissioners. Disputed
cases were to be resolved by a joint Polish-German commission in Poznan. The German
authorities were supposed to make available to the Polish commissioners all relevant
institutions, museums, archives, libraries, government buildings, etc., in which there might
be objects covered by Polish restitutional claims. Germany was also to cover the costs of
packing and shipping the restituted goods to the Polish border.[62] As the Peace Conference did
not accept these demands for procedural reasons, they were not included in the Treaty of
Versailles. Consequently the Polish side began direct talks with Germany, which resulted in a
Polish-German *Financial Agreement* in 1920.[63] This included a general restitutional clause,
essentially not different from the clauses on repatriation of cultural goods cited above.

The scope of repatriation of cultural property was much wider in the 1921 Peace Treaty between
Poland, Russia and the Ukraine.[64] The extensive clauses of this Treaty included two types of
restitution according to the classification used to analyse the Treaties of Saint Germain and Trianon.

The first type concerned the objects "evacuated" to Russia or the Ukraine, voluntarily or
under duress, from the area of the Republic of Poland since the beginning of World War I.
This "re-evacuation" was to cover, among other items, libraries, art collections and archives
with their inventories, works of art, historical relics, and "all kinds of collections and objects
of historical, national, scientific, artistic, or cultural character (in any sense), bells and all
sorts of objects pertaining to the religious cult of any confession", that belonged to "the State
or its institutions, self-government bodies, social institutions, or to any legal or natural persons"
(Article XI. 9 and 10).

The second type was the repatriation of cultural goods, in a broad sense of the word, that had
been taken from the territory of Poland to Russia or the Ukraine after 1 January 1772. Even all
war trophies were subject to this repatriation, (excluding those from the Polish-Russian-
Ukrainian war of 1938-1921), as well as all objects "of cultural character" listed above. Return
of these objects was to be conducted no matter "under what circumstances, or by what orders
of the then authorities they were taken away, and whether they belonged to a legal or natural
person, originally or after their removal" (Article XI.1).

---

60.   The full text in P. Burnett, ch. 1 above note 20 Vol. 1, pp. 885-889.
61.   *Ibid*, pp. 886-887.
62.   See *ibid*, Article II of the *Memorandum*, pp. 887 and 888.
63.   S. E. Nahlik, ch. 1 above note 31 p. 244.
64.   Peace Treaty between Poland, Russia and the Ukraine, signed at Riga 18 March 1921. Martens, *Nouveau
      Recueil Général de Traités*, 3è sér., Vol.13, Goettingue1924, p. 152 (henceforth: Treaty of Riga).

From these quotations — as has been stressed in various works[65] — it is clear that the repatriation provided for by the Treaty of Riga was unprecedented because of its scope and absolute character. The basic criterion for the range of objects subject to both types of restitution was territoriality. All cultural goods taken away from the territory of Poland were to be given back. This represents a substantial extension of this form of restitution, compared to the Treaties of Saint Germain and Trianon, (above) which allowed for repatriation of goods related to the ceded territory only. It should be noted that the Treaty of Riga did not distinguish between public and private property, and called for reciprocity. The limitations to restitution provided in the Treaty had two bases. The principle of integrity of national cultural heritage was applied also to the objects of Belorussian and Ukrainian culture. These were to be returned to Poland, if they had been taken from the areas east of the border established in the Treaty, and earlier, if they had been brought to Poland "not by the way of voluntary transaction or inheriting" (Article XI.2). The other limitations followed the principle that "systematically, scientifically described and complete collections that belong to a collection of universal cultural importance, should not be destroyed" (Article XI.7). In such cases, however, an exception was made for the repatriation of an object that while belonging to collection of that kind was closely related to Polish history and culture.

The implementation of all restitutional provisions of the Treaty of Riga was delegated to the Special Joint Commission in Moscow. The documentation of the Commission's work, which in practice proved to be very difficult, was published in nine volumes soon afterwards.[66]

The Problem of Restitution in Kind and Cultural Reparations

The analysis of restitution of cultural goods so far needs to be supplemented by a short discussion of restitution in kind and reparations as applied to cultural objects; these are the most contentious issues both in theory and practice. To date, international law has not developed complete and universally accepted norms in this area, but questions concerning this type of restitution have been raised in cases of especially drastic thefts and destructions of works of art. Nahlik's research has shown that in the nineteenth century, there was no practice of paying compensation for the losses of works of art.[67] The problem appeared most acutely after World War I, owing to the wide devastation of monuments by the Germans in Belgium and France. The public was horrified to learn of the results of shelling of some of the Belgian cities and the intentional burning of the Louvain Library.

A logical reaction to this damage was to demand appropriate compensation. Memoranda and proposals on this issue were put forward by scientific and artistic circles; numerous press

---

65.   See for example Ch. de Visscher, above note 2 p. 836; Nahlik, ch. 1 above note 31 p. 250 ff. L. V. Prott, P. J. O'Keefe, *Law and the Cultural Heritage*, Vol. 3, *Movement* London-Edinburgh 1989, p. 829. See also the comprehensive analysis of this treaty: J. Kumaniecki, *Pokoj polsko-radziecki 1921* Geneza, Rokowania, Traktat, Komisje Mieszane [The Polish-Soviet Peace of 1921. The Origins. The Negotiations. The Treaty. The Mixed Commissions] Warsaw 1985.

66.   Les Travaux des Délégations Polonaises aux Commissions Mixtes de Réévacuation et Spéciale en Moscou. Varsovie 1922. Dokumenty dotyczace akcji Delegacji Polskich w Komisjach Mieszanych Reewakuacyjnej i Specjalnej w Moskwie [Documents of the actions of the Polish Delegations to the Re-evacuation and Special Mixed Commissions in Moscow] Vols 1- 9, Warsaw 1922-1924. It is also worth mentioning the secret report of P. Wojkow, who was then head of the Russian delegation to the Mixed Commissions. This important report, describing Russian policy to minimalize the results of repatriation, was discovered in Moscow archives and published by J. Kumaniecki, *Tajny raport Wojkowa* [Wojkow' s Secret Report] Warsaw 1991.

67.   S.E. Nahlik, ch. 1 above note 31 p. 179.

articles appeared.[68] The most appropriate approach seemed to be the compensation in nature from Germany. A statement by Khnopff serves as an example for this form of demand. He referred to what the Prime Minister of Bavaria had said in his speech at the opening of L'Exposition Bruxelles of 1910. At this exhibition, many paintings from the Munich Pinakotheca were shown, and the Bavarian Prime Minister, when asked what would have happened if the paintings had been damaged or destroyed, said:

> *Les oeuvres des grands maîtres, ecrivait-il, ne peuvent se payer avec de l'argent; elles peuvent seulement se remplacer par des oeuvres équivalentes. La perte d'un même mérite à choisir dans vos musées de Bruxelles.*[69]

Thus, in Khnopff's opinion, the Germans themselves proposed the principle of compensation in nature for damages in the world of art caused by their vandalism. Consequently, he suggested that Belgium should get a number of works of art from German collections, including two paintings that belong to the Van Eyck brothers' polyptych *The Mystic Lamb,* from Berlin, *The Last Supper* by D. Bouts, of which two panels were in Munich and Berlin, *The Last Judgement* by H. Memling, from the Church of Our Lady in Danzig, and many others.[70] By compensation, Khnopff understood the amount estimated for the totality of damages, while others thought about equivalents, set up individually according to the principle: "*une autre oeuvre d'art au choix de la victime; tableau pour tableau, statue pour statue, manuscrit pour manuscrit*".[71] Arguments for excluding the possibility of compensation in kind altogether were also abundant.[72]

The Peace Conference was not free from this dispute either. At first, reparations in kind, also called "reparation by equivalent" or "payment in kind", were suggested, to be distinguished from the payments in cash that were being settled. They were to include transfer of ships, machines, cattle, and works of art. In the case of the latter, the French draft of the Treaty provided: "*Dans le but de rétablir dans toute la mesure du possible le patrimoine d'art des régions dévastées, la France sera autorisée à faire choisir en Allemagne des objets d'art détruits*".[73] The value of a work of art was to be estimated by the Allied Commission of Experts, with the participation of German experts as well. This value would be added to the total amount of reparations. The French draft was accepted by the committee of experts, although not without some doubts. The British delegate said: "I accept this Article if the French want it. I think it questionable whether it is wise politically, but this is France's affair. The bartering about of objects of art caused very bitter feeling in 1814." The US delegate added: "I sympathise with the replacement of works of art. It is impossible to create them anew".[74] Eventually, the suggestion of reparation in works of art was definitely rejected. Because Belgium repeatedly insisted on it, and because compensation for that country was given priority, special provisions were included in the treaty "at the last moment", as is twice

---

68. See among others J. Garner, *International Law and the World War*, Vol. 2, London 1920, p. 456; F. Khnopff, 'Les compensations pour dommages artistiques', *Bulletin de la Classe des Beaux-Arts* 1919, No. 1-3, p. 59; G. Hulin de Loo, 'Des compensations à réclamer pour les dommages artistiques', *Bulletin de la Classe des Beaux-Arts* 1919, No. 4-5, p. 75.

69. F. Khnopff, *ibid*, s. 61.

70. *Ibid*, p. 62.

71. H. de Loo, above note 67 pp. 77 and 78.

72. *Ibid*, p. 75 ff.

73. P. Burnett, ch. 1 above note 20 Vol. 1, p. 865. The Polish Memorandum, also called for cultural reparations, "at least partially." See *ibid*, p. 886.

74. *Ibid*, p. 877.

stressed by Burnett.[75] According to the Treaty, Germany was obliged to submit to the Louvain University "manuscripts, *incunabula*, printed books, maps, and other objects of the collection corresponding in number and value to the similar objects destroyed in the fire set by the Germans to the library in Louvain." Moreover, "in order to make possible the reconstruction of two great masterpieces," Belgium was to be handed:

> 1. The panels of *The Mystic Lamb* polyptych by the Van Eyck brothers, formerly located in Saint Bavon's Church in Ghent, now in the Berlin Museum.

> 2. The panels of *The Last Supper* polyptych by Dierk Bouts, formerly located in St. Peter's Church in Louvain, two of which are in the Berlin Museum, two others in the Old Pinakotheca in Munich. (Article 247 of the Treaty of Versailles).

How could these provisions be interpreted? Burnett, a commentator and editor of the documents of the Peace Conference, already had doubts whether the obligations following Article 247 should be classified as restitution or reparations. Since the Treaty did not include the value of these works of art in the amount of the German reparations, the author decided that the Belgian claims "perhaps fell actually under the principle of restitution rather than under that of reparation". [76]

Legal commentators have not paid too much attention to the issue of restitution in kind. Some authors treat it as a form of reparation in kind,[77] while others in such cases prefer to use the term 'restitution in kind'.[78] A more detailed analysis of the substance of Article 247 reveals that the obligations it contained were of a very different nature. The obligation to deliver manuscripts, *incunabula*, printed books, etc., to the library in Louvain to replace similar objects burned in the fire should be recognised as an instance of restitution in kind, which means a delivery of an equivalent object, set up individually, in place of a concrete work that was destroyed. This is exactly the case here. The library materials given to Belgium were to "correspond in number and value to the similar objects destroyed." The principle adopted here was "book for book, manuscript for manuscript," etc. In the case of printed matter, the replacement may be complete in the literal meaning of this word.

Restitution in kind also occurs when the object that is subject to it cannot be transferred, although it has not been destroyed and its whereabouts are known. Such cases were provided for in the Treaty of Riga, by the adoption of the principle of protection of complete collections of universal importance. "If the elimination of any object subject ... to return to Poland, would impair the completeness of such a collection, this object should remain where it is, with the approval of both sides in the Mixed Commission ... and an equivalent object, of the same scientific or artistic value" should be handed over (Article XI.7). The Treaty of Riga also provides for the application of restitution in kind in other cases.[79]

---

75. *Ibid*, pp. 122 and 129. See also W. Schivelbusch, *Die Bibliothek von Löwen. Eine Episode aus der Zeit der Weltkriege*, München-Wien 1988.

76. *Ibid*, p. 122.

77. For example C. Berezowski, *Ochrona prawnomiedzynarodowa zabytkow i dziel sztuki w czasie wojny* [International Legal Protection of Historic Monuments and Works of Art during War] Warsaw 1948, p. 134; S.E. Nahlik, ch. 1 above note 31 p. 240.

78. A. Martin, 'Private Property, Rights and Interests in the Paris Peace Treaties', *The British Yearbook of International Law* 1947, Vol. 24, p. 277; I. Vasarhelyi, ch. 1 above note 9 p. 96; In his commentary on Article 247, Ch. de Visscher uses the term "restitution", above note 2 p. 829. I. Brownlie, ch. 1 above note 1 p. 461 ff, and see ch. 1 note 16 p. 210 ff.

79. See Article XI 9.

However, except for the case of the Louvain Library, the other obligations of Germany ensuing from Article 247 of the Treaty of Versailles do not match the requirements of restitution in kind as presented above. The delivery of the wings of *The Mystic Lamb* and *The Last Supper* polyptychs, which for a long time had been held legally in German art collections, was not related to any particular loss. It has to be considered as some kind of symbolic reparation for all Belgium's artistic losses. The justification included in Article 247, saying that they had to be brought to Belgium in order to reconstruct "two masterpieces of art", was an additional and extra-legal argument that later seemed to be unduly highlighted.[80] This sentence, together with the whole Article 247, was included into the Treaty of Versailles "at the last moment" after a prolonged debate. The argument was most probably intended to soften the strictly compensatory character of the obligation, in the face of the conference's definitive and consistent rejection of reparations 'paid' in cultural goods.

---

80.   It is one of the reasons for Ch. de Visscher to put the principle of integrity of outstanding works and collections before the principle of integrity of national cultural heritage (see above note 2 p. 836). See also T. Bodkin, 'The Reconstitution of Dismembered Masterpieces by International Action', in XIV *Internationaler Kungstgeschichtlicher Kongress* 1936, Kongressakten. Bd. 2. Bern 1938, p. 205 ff.; The limitation of the cultural reparations after World War I was approved by D. Rigby, who wrote that "the writers of the World War treaties exercised conscious and enlightened volition to prevent the retaliative looting of cultural objects. It was not an easy victory. Feeling ran high in those days just as it does today [in 1944], and strong determination had to be called up to resist the tide" (above note 1 p. 279).

CHAPTER III

WORKS OF ART AND RESTITUTION LAW: WORLD WAR II, ITS AFTERMATH AND SUBSEQUENT DEVELOPMENTS

Recognition of the Problems

The restitution of works of art looted during World War II constituted an extremely complex and difficult task. Apart from the necessity of solving purely technical problems in relation to the search for looted works of art, the identification and recovery of such a huge number of high value objects required a legal basis with an international scope. Obviously, the need for restitution itself was beyond question at that time. The Treaty of Versailles and other peace treaties concluded after World War I had finally confirmed the validity of appropriate regulations in international law. In the 1930s, in particular after the experience of the Spanish Civil War, an attempt was made to protect art objects in time of war by means of a special convention. However, this attempt, undertaken by the International Museums Office, did not go beyond the stage of preparation and consultation projects.[1] As a result, after the outbreak of World War II, the Museums Office published, but only as a 'reminder', regulations concerning the protection of cultural property and the need to prohibit looting. These regulations were taken from the annex to the fourth Hague Convention concerning the Laws and Customs of War on Land.[2] When the Allies realised the scale and organisation of Nazi looting, it became obvious that restitution on an unprecedented scale would be necessary: the work of the Polish Government in Exile helped to make clear the size of the problem.[3] The problems of restitution were initially handled by unofficial organisations, one of the first of which was the International Committee for the Cultural Reconstruction of Europe formed in 1941 through the Central Institute of Art and Design in London. Members of over ten countries joined the action and in 1943 the Committee, functioning as an advisory body of the Foreign Office, published an analysis entitled *Looting and Destruction of Works of Art by Axis Powers*.[4] This document provided a clear illustration of the potential problems and difficulties which might be faced by the ravaged countries after the war. It is worth listing its main points, especially in so far as legal issues are concerned. In the introduction to the analysis, the authors pointed out that when the War ended the situation with regard to looted art objects would be very complex and that the methods of dealing with them would depend on:

1.　'La protection des monuments et oeuvres d'art en temps de guerre. Manuel technique et juridique', Paris, p. 180; Ch. de Visscher, ch. 2 above note 2 p. 859.
2.　*Mouseion* Supplement, Septembre-Octobre 1939: p. 5 ff. The same issue also included the correspondence between the President of the United States, the German Chancellor and the governments of Poland, France and Great Britain regarding the observance of the international law of war: see p. 8 ff.
3.　On this subject see W. Kowalski, 'Udzial Karola Estreichera w alianckich przygotowaniach do restytucji dziel sztuki zagrabionych w czasie II wojny swiatowej' [Contribution of Charles Estreicher to Allied Preparations for the Restitution of Works of Art Looted During World War II] (1986) *Muzealnictwo*, 30, 24; also the same author: *Liquidation of the Effects of World War II in the Area of Culture*, Warsaw 1994. See also Annexes 1 and 2.
4.　The Archives of New Records in Warsaw, records of the Ministry for Congress Affairs of the Republic of Poland (henceforth: ANR, records of MCA RP) sign. 152, p. 9 ff.

1. The history of each work of art preceding the act of its looting. Looting was understood in this document to be any illegal acquisition under different forms of duress, not only by theft. A given object could:

    a) belong to the State, or a municipality, or a private owner,

    b) be acquired by purchase or by exchange from a foreign State, or private owner,

    c) be ceded by a foreign State as a condition of a treaty of peace,

    d) be looted during the war and not returned.

2. Circumstances concerning the art object after looting. The object:

    a) may still be in the possession of the enemy State,

    b) may be handed over to a neutral State,

    c) may be sold to a neutral State,

    d) may be handed over or sold to a citizen of the enemy State; that person could have either bought the object in good faith or have been aware of the facts,

    e) may be handed over or sold to a citizen of the neutral State directly or through the authorities of the neutral State; again, the buyer could either be innocent, or aware of the relevant facts.

    f) may not exist any more.

After presenting different types of scenario, the authors of the analysis suggested that the government should answer the following questions:

i) As far as 2a is concerned:

    - Should the work of art be returned irrespective of the circumstances described in 1?

    - Could the enemy State keep the work of art only in certain cases and if so, in what cases?

ii) As far as 2b and 2c are concerned:

    - Should the neutral State be obliged to return the art object, and should certain conditions be imposed on it?

iii) As far as 2d and 2e are concerned:

    - Should the art object be 'pursued' irrespective of circumstances?

In the document's summary, the authors pointed out that the Committee suggested that the government adopt the principle of returning each work of art to its owner. However, if this solution was not possible or was inappropriate, the decision could be made as to whether the country responsible for looting should:

    - pay compensation, or

    - hand over some other work of art as an equivalent.

Similar preliminary work on the scope of the law of restitution also took place in the United States; the delegate of the Polish Government in Exile, Charles Estreicher, played a key role in developing solutions.[5] On the eve of 1943, he gave several lectures in the United States on the activity of the Nazis in occupied territories. A memorandum entitled *The Destruction and Plunder by the Germans of Works of Art and the Necessary Cultural Revindication Resulting from it* was given by Estreicher to a group of specialists interested in the subject. Estreicher suggested that certain indispensable steps should be taken. The following, he proposed, were the most important tasks to be accomplished immediately after the end of the war:

---

5.   See comments by L. Woolley in *A Record of the Work done by the Military Authorities for the Protection of the Treasures of Art and History in War Areas*, London 1947, p. 5.

- placing all German museums and art collections under compulsory management until the origin of all objects was known, and it was clear whether the museum's personnel had participated in the looting,
- transferring a certain number of outstanding works of art from German collections to the liberated nations to guarantee that Germany would fulfil the restitution obligation and pay off the damages,
- introducing a total prohibition on the buying and selling of any art objects on the territory of Germany in order to eliminate the possibility of trade in looted works of art.[6]

Moreover, Estreicher suggested establishing the principle of reparations in kind and taking initial steps in order to organise the entire action, such as training experts who would handle the whole process. During the Polish delegate's visit to the United States, the American Council of Learned Societies appointed a special commission which was intended to handle the restitution matters. A few months later, President Roosevelt approved the appointment of the American Commission for Protection and Salvage of Artistic and Historic Monuments in Europe.[7] In 1944, within the framework of an inter-governmental body, the Conference of Allied Ministers of Education, the Committee for the Protection and Restitution of Cultural Material was appointed. The additional aim of this committee was to prepare an organisational scheme and suggest some legal regulations concerning, *inter alia*, the restitution of works of art after the liberation of Europe.[8]

The process of restitution proved difficult; according to the memoirs of Sir Leonard Woolley, the archaeological adviser to the War Office, the preparation of adequate directives for the Commanding Staff:

> meant much discussion with officers of other branches of the War Office and of the Foreign Office and with USA representatives, attendance at Committees, and constant writing and re-editing of briefs... The claims of the arts were not always easy to reconcile with other interests; there was always the fear that the regulations made for the arts might be a dangerous precedent when extended to other subjects and, on the other hand, there might be a tendency to relegate art objects to a position in which they would be subordinate to rules of general application. It was essential to maintain that they were *sui generis* and required special legislation. The interdepartmental correspondence on

---

6. For more details, see Kowalski, above note 3.
7. It was known as the Roberts Commission after the U.S. Supreme Court judge who was appointed its chairman. One of its main tasks consisted of recommending experienced members of American museums' staff to the Army's posts of 'Officers for Monuments, Fine Arts and Archives,' popularly called 'MFA&A Officers'. See *Report of The American Commission for the Protection and Salvage of artistic and historic Monuments in War Areas*, Washington 1946. See J.B. Eggen, 'La Commission américaine pour la protection et le sauvetage de monuments d'art et d'histoire dans les zones de guerre', *Mouseion* 1946, Vol. 55-56, p. 61. Parallel Commissions were later appointed in France, Great Britain and other countries. See M. Florisoone, 'La commission française de récuperation artistique', *Mouseion* 1946, Vol. 55-56, p. 67 ff; L.Woolley, *A Record of the Work Done by the Military Authorities for the Protection of the Treasures of Art and History in War Areas,* London 1947, p. 5 ff.
8. The Vaucher Committee, named after its chairman, elaborated the following documents: *Scheme for restitution of objets d'art, books and archives; Recommendation as to the methods of arranging and pooling information; Memorandum upon the measures to be taken immediately upon the occupation of Germany;* The Archives of UNESCO in Paris, records of Conference of Allied Ministers of Education. Documents in order: Doc. AME/A/30 and Doc. AME/a/48, document in volume 9, pages not numbered, and Doc. AME/A/74. For a detailed analysis of these documents see W. Kowalski, *Liquidation...*(note 3 above) p. 97.

these and similar subjects, in all of which not only Governmental but Allied agreement had to be obtained, assumed very large proportions and accounted for a great deal of time.[9]

Basic Sources of Law

A survey of the basic international documents produced at the end of World War II, leads to the conclusion that the issue of restitution was completely separate from the matter of reparations. During the Yalta Conference, the issue of damage caused to the Allied Nations by Germany was thoroughly discussed. It was resolved that the duty to repair these damages in nature, on the broadest possible scale, should be imposed on Germany. Following this resolution, the Potsdam Agreement specified a form of compensating damages utilising German assets. In both the resolutions and during the conferences themselves, the subject of restitution claims was left untouched; consequently, the documents mentioned above could not provide a basis for restitution. They could be considered, however, as a legal basis for possible reparation claims in the sphere of cultural damages. One can agree with Nahlik that[10] the matter of restitution in itself was not in issue during World War II as the principles of customary international law had been well established. Therefore, it was simply 'announced' in the *Declaration of the Allied Nations against acts of dispossession committed in territories under enemy occupation or control* published in London, Moscow, and Washington on 5 January 1943; this document requires further analysis.

The Declaration of the Allied Nations Against Acts of Dispossession Committed in Territories Under Enemy Occupation or Control

The text of the Inter-Allied Declaration is relatively short.[11] In the Declaration, the governments of seventeen countries and the French National Committee warned those it might concern, especially persons in neutral countries, that "they intended to do their utmost to defeat the methods of dispossession practised by the governments with which they were at war against countries and peoples who have been so wantonly assaulted and despoiled." For this purpose they reserved "all their rights to declare invalid any transfers of, or dealing with, property, rights and interests situated in the territories which have come under the occupation or control, direct or indirect," of the enemy, "or which belonged, or have belonged, to persons, including juridical persons, resident in such territories". This warning concerned every form of transfer of property irrespective of "whether such transfers or dealings have taken the form of open looting or plunder, or of transactions apparently legal in form, even when they purport to be voluntarily effected". The conclusion included a declaration of solidarity among the governments. The reception of the Declaration was of great legal and political importance, and as a result, it was decided that it should be given wide publicity. The governments of other Allied Nations members were also invited to subscribe to its principles. Additionally, the text of the Declaration was officially communicated to the neutral countries; as an international agreement it had a specific legal form, although it was not concluded by an international conference but by way of three simultaneous publications. This is a rare example of an open group agreement; it was initially concluded by three countries, and subsequently joined by fourteen other countries and the French National Committee.

---

9.   The duties of the archaeological adviser to the War Office included all matters connected with the protection of monuments, and the restitution of works of art on the territories occupied by the British Army. See L. Woolley, above note 5 p. 8 ff.
10.   S.E. Nahlik, ch. 1 above note 31 p. 288.
11.   S.A. Williams, *The International and National Protection of Movable Cultural Property. A Comparative Study,* New York 1978, p. 22. See Annex 3.

The aims and legal character of the Declaration were clear from the very beginning, and could not be changed, although its form might suggest a certain reserve on the part of the main signatories in binding themselves to any definitive obligation.[12] The contents of the document were commonly accepted as an unequivocal agreement to undertake restitution on a wide scale.[13] To facilitate its implementation, the Declaration reserved the right to invalidate all changes concerning property rights introduced in the occupied territories. The accomplishment of this task rested with the legal authorities of particular countries from the moment they returned to their territories. The Declaration stressed the solidarity of all the signatory governments as far as this crucial issue was concerned. This meant that the interested governments would help one another in inspecting and possibly invalidating the transfer of property rights and interests, if these went beyond the borders of a given country and the co-operation of two or more countries was required.[14] Publishing the Declaration with such contents and provisions indicated a disavowal of the principle of protecting a person who had acquired looted works of art in good faith. This also applied to the neutral countries as it was crucial to introduce a general principle that no one could profit from unlawful acts. Therefore the neutral countries were also obliged to undertake restitution. As a result, the Declaration acquired a 'revolutionary' character, in the context of the existing norms of international law. Prior to the Declaration, as can be seen in the Treaty of Versailles for example, this duty had not gone beyond the borders of defeated countries.[15] The Declaration was later included in many legal documents, for example, in Peace Treaties. It provided a general interpretation clause according to which all aspects of the restitution of property looted by Nazi Germany from the Allied countries should be investigated:[16] It is not surprising that the Declaration was severely criticised by German authors.[17]

Final Act of the Bretton Woods Conference
The United Nations Monetary and Financial Conference was held in Bretton Woods on 1-22 July 1944. The Final Act, which included a separate chapter concerning the protection of

---

12.   Certain doubts concerning the legal character of this Declaration arose in the circles connected with the Ministry for Congress Affairs of the Polish Government in Exile. They concerned the statement of the British Government published together with the Declaration as: *Note on the Meaning, Scope and Application of the Inter Allied Declaration*, ANR, records of MCA RP, sign. 190, (pages not numbered). In the later period, the British Government, it seems, maintained its specific interpretation of the Declaration, which was shown in the utterance of the Foreign Office representative on the eighteenth meeting of the Anglo-Polish Committee on Non-Political Matters, 13 May 1949. It was stressed there that: "it should be pointed out that this Declaration did not itself constitute a formal and binding treaty"; Department of Archives and Historic Documentation of the Ministry of Foreign Affairs [from now on: DAHD MFA], sign. paper 10, verse 34, vol. 291, p. 18.
13.   For Example: I. Vasarhelyi, ch. 1 above note 9 p. 78 ff; C.G. Fitzmaurice, 'The Juridical Clauses of the Peace Treaties', *Recueil des Cours* 1948, Vol. 81, part 2, p. 327.
14.   Some governments issued legislation concerning this matter even earlier, for example: Decree of the President of the Polish Republic of 30 November 1939 on the invalidity of Legal Acts of the Authorities in Occupation, *Republic of Poland, Journal of Laws* 1939, No. 102 [Angers], item 1006. As far as other countries are concerned, see: *The Postwar Settlements of Property Rights,* New York, 1945, p. 4 ff. A special committee of experts was appointed to enact a common policy concerning these matters.
15.   I. Vasarhelyi, ch. 1 above note 9 p. 78 ff; S. Williams, above note 9 p. 22; A. Martin, ch. 1 above note 4, Vol. 29, p. 276.
16.   See, for example: 'The Allied Control Commission for Germany. The Definition and Interpretation of the Notion of Restitution', *Zbior dokumentow* 1946, No. 9, p. 277. See Annex 5. Peace Treaty with Italy signed in Paris on 10 February 1947. 49 U.N.T.S. 3 [henceforth: Peace Treaty with Italy], Article 77.1.
17.   For example: E. Langen and E. Sauer, *Die Restitution im internationalen Recht,* Dusseldorf 1949, p. 11 ff. Langen and Sauer point out many inconsistencies within the Declaration and stress that it lacks the character of an international legal enactment. According to them, it resulted from the fact that during the war, the Declaration was accepted by only one fighting party, which meant that other countries, including for example, the neutral ones, were disregarded. It is usually the case, as Langen and Sauer remark, that in such situations "egoistic purposes" prevail and "there is no room for objectivity."

enemy assets as well as the control and restitution of looted property, was signed by the representatives of 44 countries.[18] Referring to the Declaration of 5 January 1943, the participants of the Conference wholly supported the actions undertaken by the Allied Nations in order to recover and return these assets to their legal owners: the Declaration called upon the neutral countries to undertake immediate measures to prevent any disposition or transfer of property belonging to the countries occupied by the enemy and their citizens. It also ordered that special attention should be paid to the possible disposition and transfer of looted works of art; these needed to be protected and handed over to the appropriate authorities after the liberation of occupied territories. The statements dealing with the holding of assets belonging, or probably belonging to the enemy commanders and their collaborators in the territories of the neutral countries were also of crucial importance. The Final Act of the Bretton Woods Conference covered the issue of restitution even more clearly than the Declaration of 5 January 1943. It also constituted a complete basis for common actions aimed at the restitution of looted objects remaining in the territories of the neutral countries.

The Resolution on the Subject of Restitution passed at the Paris Conference on Reparations

From 9 November to 21 December 1945, the representatives of eighteen Allied countries debated in Paris the final settlement of the question of German war reparations and the division of the so-called monetary gold, seized in Germany. The Conference passed a Final Act, of which the basic document was a draft of the agreement on reparations. The Final Act was annexed to the document which included, *inter alia*, the Resolution on the Subject of Restitution.[19] Although the Resolution was passed by delegates representing only some of the countries taking part in the Conference (such as: Albania, Belgium, Czechoslovakia, Denmark, France, Greece, Netherlands, India, Luxembourg, and Yugoslavia; Poland did not take part in the Conference), it remains an important document because it states precisely the basic principles for the anticipated restitution; these principles can be found in later legal acts of the Allied Control Council for Germany. The first point of the Resolution recalled the Declaration of 5 January 1943, according to which all cases for the recovery of goods looted by the Nazis in the Allied countries should be investigated. In a further part of the Resolution it was decided that 'in general' the Resolution should concern only the objects that could be identified as already existing at the time when a given country was under occupation and taken away without payment, or even with payment, or manufactured during the time of the occupation and obtained by an act of force. However, if the looted property could not be identified, its replacement should form a part of the general reparation claim of the country concerned. An exception to this principle was established by introducing restitution in kind for cultural property which would not be returned. Moreover, the Resolution required the granting of all necessary privileges to a 'mission of experts', sent by the Allied Nations in order to search for, identify and transfer the looted objects to their countries of origin. The German holders of looted property should be compelled to declare possession of such objects to the controlling authorities; violation of this obligation should be punished.

---

18.   United Nations Monetary and Financial Conference, Bretton Woods, New Hampshire, 1 July to 22 July 1944. 'Final Act and related documents. VI: Enemy assets and looted property' 1946, p. 4.
19.   'Final Act and Annex of the Paris Conference on Reparations, Annex 1: Resolution on subject of restitution'; J. Howard, *The Paris Agreement on Reparation from Germany,* U.S. Government Printing Office, 1946, p. 19. For the full text see Annex 1.

Overview of Subsequent Documents

Matters concerning restitution and measures allowing for restitution, after the 1944 Resolution at Bretton Woods can be found in a wide range of documents, including the legislation of the authorities in occupation, bilateral and multilateral agreements, as well as Surrender and Armistice Acts (which concern the issues of restitution from the territory of one or several specified countries). These documents will be discussed under the following headings:

1. Restitution from Germany and Austria.
This was to be accomplished on the basis of legislation passed by the Allied Control Council for Germany or military governments in particular occupation zones, and later also on the basis of the Bonn Convention of 1952. In the territory of occupied Austria, the Allied Commission for Austria introduced a restitution law modelled on the law in force in Germany. Statements concerning restitution can also be found in the State Treaty with Austria of 1955.

2. Restitution from other Axis countries.
Initially this was to be carried out on the basis of the Act of Surrender in the case of Italy, and on Armistices, as far as other countries are concerned. Later, full clauses concerning restitution were introduced in peace treaties concluded in 1947.

3. Restitution from the neutral countries.
The principles of the restitution procedure used in these countries were established in the agreements concluded in 1945 between the USA, Great Britain and France on one side, and Switzerland and Sweden on the other. In 1946, in order to intensify and simplify the search for looted works of art in the territory of neutral countries, the three Allied countries cited above concluded a special agreement specifying the principles of conduct and co-operation.

4. Restitution from the territories of the Allied Nations.
In order to regulate the search for and return of looted property, found on the territory of South American countries, Resolution No.19 was passed at the Inter-American Conference on War and Peace Problems, which took place between 21 February and 8 March 1945, in Chapultepec. In Europe, bilateral agreements were concluded; for example, on the mutual return of assets concluded between Poland and Czechoslovakia in 1946 and with France in 1947 in the form of a protocol regulating mutual obligations for restitution.

5. Restitution in kind.
The announcement and basic regulation of restitution in kind for works of art which could not be returned, may be found in the directive of the Allied Control Council for Germany from 1946, concerning the definition of the term "restitution". A year later, the Council agreed another document on this subject, but further actions were not continued. However, the obligation to undertake restitution in kind was included in peace treaties concluded in 1947 with Italy, Hungary and Bulgaria.

6. Restitution on behalf of Germany, Austria and the former Axis Powers.
This, first of all, concerned regulating the return to Germany of that cultural property which was taken by the Allies, and the return of assets belonging to the Axis Powers which were taken away by the Germans near the end of the war. These restitutions were made on the basis of transfer protocols and bilateral agreements. As far as the German libraries in Italy are concerned, a special agreement was concluded between five countries in 1953. The Austrian assets and the property of the former Axis powers become the subject of restitution on the basis of the Austrian Treaty, the peace treaties of 1947, as well as the Allied restitution regulations in force on German territory.

Restitution from Germany and Austria

Shaping of the restitution law

As a result of the preparatory actions outlined above, the Allied Armies marching into Germany were provided with basic restitution instructions and could immediately proceed to prepare for acts of restitution. In Autumn 1944, soon after crossing the German border near Aachen, the Commander-in-Chief of the Allied Expeditionary Forces published regulations introducing a total blockade, and control over all assets in the occupied territories.[20] The range of these regulations was very wide and included a ban on all possible transactions and activities concerning cultural property. The present owners, possessors, or holders were obliged to preserve and protect such property until a time when further regulations would be passed. This concerned all persons holding cultural property — both private owners and managers of museums and national, local or church galleries. These regulations were aimed at imposing ultimate control over all art collections remaining on German territory, thus ensuring the return of looted works of art and the payment of compensation. These regulations also aimed to prevent possible legal complications which could arise from consequent changes of owner or simply holder. The Military Government of the U.S. Zone was the first to undertake strictly restitutional activities. The basic assumptions which lay behind these actions had been presented earlier in the form of recommendations by the U.S. delegation at the meeting of the Reparation Commission in Moscow.[21] In a general form they were included in Directive No. 1067 of April 1945 to the Commander-in-Chief of the United States Forces in Germany.[22] This Directive included the seizing or blocking of "works of art or cultural material of value or importance, regardless of the ownership thereof" (point 48.e.3). If such objects were "the subject of transfer under duress or wrongful act of confiscation, disposition or spoliation, whether pursuant to legislation or by procedure purporting to follow forms of law or otherwise", it was necessary to "institute measures for prompt restitution" (point 48.e.2 and 3). The basic aim of restitution was, according to point 4 of the Directive, "to provide relief for the benefit of countries devastated by Nazi aggression".

These requirements were enforced by Regulations passed by the Military Government, from 7 July 1945. They formed the legal basis for the temporary restitutional programme defined as the "unilateral stop-gap program for the return of stolen property in the U.S. Zone."[23] It allowed for the prompt return of the best known works of art and established the first rules of the restitution procedure, which were later further elaborated. *Inter alia*, it was suggested that the interested governments could submit lists of the objects they were searching for and carry out foreign missions.

Establishing the general legal framework for restitution covering the entire German territory was the task of the Allied Control Council for Germany. The work of this body was initiated by passing Proclamation No. 1, which, apart from announcing the appointment of the Council, did not change the legal provisions and executive regulations introduced by the military

---

20. It was the first version of Law No. 52, in force since 18 September 1944 on the Supreme Commander's Area of Control, *Monthly Report of the Military Government. United States Zone* 1946, No. 9, p. 13 (henceforth: *Monthly Report*). Law No. 52 has been amended many times since then; see note 191. For the full text see Annex 7.
21. *Monthly Report* 1946, No. 9, p. 15.
22. *Directive to Commander-in-Chief of United States Forces of Occupation Regarding the Military Government of Germany*, JCS 1067, April 1945; L. Pastusiak, *Polityka Stanow Zjednoczonych w Niemczech 1945-1949* [The United States Policy in Germany 1945-1949] Wroclaw-Warsaw-Krakow 1967, p. 589 ff.
23. *Monthly Report* 1946, No. 9, p. 13 and 15.

authorities in the Zones remaining under their occupation.[24] It is important to bear in mind that, at this point, the Council was not an administrative body with control over Germany;[25] in some zones the local governments retained control, even though, in theory, the Allied Control Council consisted of the sum total of all of these governments. The Council's task was limited to providing 'possibly uniform' administration in the occupation zones and to taking crucial decisions concerning Germany as a whole.[26] In its second Proclamation,[27] the Council imposed over all German authorities a general obligation to undertake on behalf of the Allies "such measures of restitution ... as Allied representatives may prescribe". Enforcing this obligation was the task of Zone authorities. In particular, German authorities were to release or enable the release of all property, rights etc., as well as perform all activities, provide supplies, manpower, staff and specialists etc., to be used in Germany or outside its borders, according to the requirements of the representatives of Allied Countries. Moreover, they were to observe all regulations concerning property, rights, etc., "located in Germany, belonging to any one of the United Nations or its nationals or having so belonged at, or at any time since, the outbreak of war between Germany and the Nations or since the occupation of any part of its territories by Germany." Both the German authorities and all German individuals were responsible for preserving and protecting items of cultural property, and for their transfer at the time and place appointed subsequently. It was also necessary to provide any information and facilities required during the investigations conducted by Allied authorities.[28]

In practice, the Allied Control Council turned out to be a rather formal body. Its main statements and agreements were forged by meetings of the Co-ordination Committee[29] which was also engaged in the problems of restitution. The Committee was involved in the formation of more detailed terms, and issued certain summary statements; on 6 November 1945 it turned to the interested countries, asking them to present lists of items removed from their territories[30] and nearly a month later, on 12 December 1945, it agreed on a uniform procedure of returning cultural property.[31] This was contained in a temporary document, which stipulated the restitution of only those works of art which were easily identified, and included the requirement to gather full documentation concerning the works of art undergoing restitution, for both those which were currently being sought and those already returned, as well as statements dealing with the process of identifying works of art and simplifying claims.

The period of shaping restitution law ended when the Allied Control Council agreed upon the definition of the term 'restitution', on 21 January 1946.[32] The resulting document was a

---

24.   'Control Council Proclamation No. 1: Establishement of Control Council', in B. Oppen-Ruhm (ed.), *Documents of Germany Under Occupation 1945-1954,* London 1955, p. 58. See also M. Balfour and J. Mair, *Four Power Control in Germany and Austria 1945-1946* London 1956, p. 92.

25.   M. Virally, *L'administration internationale de l'Allemagne,* Paris 1948, p. 64.

26.   'Statement by the Governments of the United Kingdom, the United States, the USSR, and the Provisional Government of the French Republic on Control Machinery in Germany', 5 June 1945, in B. Oppen-Ruhm (ed.), above note 24 p. 36.

27.   'Control Council Proclamation No. 2: Certain additional requirements imposed on Germany' in B. Oppen-Ruhm (ed.), above note 24 p. 68.

28.   *Ibid,* point 19 a, b, c.

29.   Above note 24 p. 93 ff.

30.   ANR, records of the Polish Military Mission in Germany, sign. 190/IV/57, p. 6; ANR, records of the Ministry of Culture and Art, Bureau of Revindication and Reparations (henceforth: ANR, records of MCA BRR), sign 378/53, p. 108.

31.   *Monthly Report* 1946, No. 6, p. 10.

32.   "Series of Documents" 1946, No. 9, p. 277 ff. According to other sources accepted on 20 January; See *Monthly Report* 1946, No. 7, p. 8. The document quoted later as: 'definition'. For the full text see Annex 5.

confirmation of the Declaration of 5 January 1943 and in its introduction clearly refers to this act, requiring that all matters concerning restitution should be judged "in all cases, in the light of the Declaration of 5 January 1943". The 1946 Definition was only a very general directive announcing the planned action of restitution; the definition itself was the first step towards the crystallisation of the project, the next and final stage being the restitution law introduced in particular occupation zones. The definition included a brief summary of the general principle requiring the return of all property removed from territories of the Allied Nations. As a Council document, it aimed to unify the principles applying to all German territories. It obliged Zone authorities to impose regulations based on these principles; this, in some cases, would involve changing some of the principles already in force.[33]

Despite the fact that Austria's legal situation after World War II was different from that of Germany,[34] the system of occupation established on its territory was similar to the one introduced in occupied Germany. As in Germany, all questions concerning restitution in Austria were in the hands of the Allied military authorities in each Zone. Co-ordination of all restitution activity was the task of the Allied Commission for Austria. The return of property looted by the Third Reich and remaining in Austria was initiated in the late autumn of 1946, after the definition of restitution of 21 January 1946 was accepted. Earlier, the activities of the Zone authorities were limited to accepting the country's lists of looted properties from other countries. The Allied restitution law established in Austria in mid-1946 was based on similar principles to those in Germany;[35] the discussion, analysis and conclusions concerning restitution law presented below, will consequently be held also to apply to Austria.

The definition of restitution

The definition of restitution specifies the principles for the formulation of detailed restitution norms for all occupation zones in Germany. As far as the restitution of cultural materials is concerned, the following principles should be emphasized:

1. The Public International Law Principle.[36]
This directly follows from the statement: "The Control Council will deal with all questions of restitution with the Government of the Country from which the objects were looted" (Point 5).[37] This principle established the strictly public-law character of restitutional claims.

2. The principle of 'identification'.
This follows the English text of the definition, according to which "Restitution will be limited, in the first instance, to identifiable goods ..." (Point 2). Here, 'identification' means comparing

---

33. Corrections were introduced for instance in the U.S. Zone, where until that time restitution regulations were more liberal and it was not required to present evidence of force used during the removal of property which had existed before the territory was occupied by Germany; *Monthly Report* 1946, No. 7, p. 8.

34. Austria was treated as the first "victim of the national-socialist invasion" which is why the annexation of 15 March 1938 was considered to be "imposed on Austria by German invasion, invalid and non-existent"; *The Moscow Declaration* of 1 November 1943, "Series of Documents" 1945, No. 3-4, p. 88 and 89. For the analysis of Austria's legal situation see also: R. Clute, *The International Legal Status of Austria 1938-1955*, The Hague 1962, p. 130 ff.

35. According to Vasarhelyi, restitution laws valid in Austria were "identical with those established by the Allied authorities in Germany"; ch. 1 above note 9 p. 18. On this subject, see also ANR, records of the Bureau of War Revindications and Reparations Office (henceforth: ANR, records of BWRR), sign. 224, p. 341 ff.

36. Defined by I.Vasarhelyi, ch. 1 above note 9 p. 87.

37. Quotations and division of text into points according to the text found in ANR, records of MCA BRR, sign. 387/53, part 1, p. 32 See also the text published in *Monthly Report* 1946, No. 7, p. 8.

the identity of the object found in Germany with the object taken away from the country occupied by Germany. Such an object must have existed during the Occupation or be produced in this period. It should be restituted in both cases: "Identifiable goods produced during the period of occupation ..." (Point 2) also fall within this provision.

3. The principle of 'force and duress.'

"This includes only the instances where items have been taken by the enemy by force ..." (Point 2), and states that these items should undergo restitution. However, in a more detailed discussion of restitution principles, the notion of force is extended to cover other forms of duress. The principle was therefore broadened accordingly.

4. The principle of territoriality.

According to this principle, restitution concerns all the goods taken away from the territory of the occupied country, no matter whose property or in whose possession they remained during the occupation. The definition includes only the short statement that the restitution will be limited only to goods taken "from the territory of the country" (Point 2).

5. The principle of formalised procedure.

The starting point for establishing this principle is the definition which regulates German participation in the expense and the realisation of the restitution process. It states that:

> Relevant transportation expenses within the present German borders and any repairs necessary for proper transportation including the necessary manpower, material and organisation, are to be borne by Germany and are included in restitutions. Expenses outside Germany are borne by the recipient country (Point 4).

Further statements, often very detailed, which regulated the organisation of the restitution process, are included in the regulations issued in the occupation zones by military authorities. Taken together, these regulations can be regarded as creating what might be termed a 'formalised restitution procedure'.

6. The principle of restitution in kind.

This is the only principle, included in the definition, which strictly concerns the restitution of cultural materials. It was formulated in the following way: "As to goods of unique character, restitution of which is impossible, a special instruction will fix the categories of goods which will be subject to replacement, the nature of these replacements and the conditions under which such goods could be replaced by equivalent objects" (point 3).

These are the basic principles which constitute the framework of restitution law. For practical purposes, they were formulated in detail in a number of regulations. Deeper analysis of these regulations makes it possible to reconstruct a complete model of the law regulating the restitution of cultural material after World War II. Since the great majority of objects of art looted by Germany were found in the U.S. and British Occupation Zones, the analysis will include the regulations imposed on the territories of these Zones. It is important to note that although the legal systems introduced in these Zones were independent, there were no crucial differences between them; the solutions adopted, as well as the formulation of certain regulations, were often identical, and therefore, will not be analysed separately.

Finally, it should be noted that the principle mentioned last, that of *restitution in kind*, is discussed in greater depth below.[38]

---

38.   P. 70 *et seq.*

The public international law principle

This principle is based both on the 1943 Declaration and the definition of restitution. It indicates that restitution claims work within the framework of public international law; it may be seen as defining the relationship between the State from which the work of art was taken and the State where it is presently located. The only legal basis for restitution is found in international law regulations, which establish its premises, organisational procedures etc. The restitution requirement is triggered by an act violating the norms of international law. There has been considerable discussion and disagreement about this principle, led by a number of German authors[39] who have suggested that the public-law character of restitution claims results merely from the fact that the parties to the legal proceedings happen to be States. The claim itself, they suggest, has a private-law character and should be judged according to the criteria of civil law. This opinion is based primarily on the negative slant of the civil law in respect of restitution claims; dispossession resulting from looting does not result in the complete loss of title to property. Thus the owner retains his title and can act according to the principle: *ubi rem meam invenio ibi vindico*. According to Langen and Sauer, international law does not alter this legal situation; it only transfers the right to take action to recover the property to the interested States:

> *Bei allem aber bleibt Restitution gleichbedeutend mit Rechtsverfolgung durch den Eigentumer, solange diesem nicht etwa sein Eigentum, das die Declaration von 1943 kraftigen und bestatigen will, vom eigenen Staate >>restitutionshalber<< weggenommen wird. Eine andere Rechtsperson, etwa der Staat, kann nur vertretungsweise oder subsidiar die Aktivlegitimation haben. Nur in dieser Rolle konnen sich daher die alliierten Staaten befinden, wenn sie ihrerseits als Verfolger von Restitutionsanspruchen auftreten.*[40]

This opinion is debatable; the assertion of Vasarhelyi — who allows that civil restitution claims are permissible in addition to international law claims in the case of wartime looting, — is to be preferred. However:

> the legal basis of a claim to restitution under Public International Law is in every case an injury under Public International Law.... Consequently, ... in the majority of cases civil law claims stand behind the actions of the States. This, however, only establishes the claim of public international law and does not transform it into a claim of civil law.[41]

Therefore, he concluded that there was no room for competition between these two legal systems. Any trend towards 'transferring' restitution into the domain of civil law would complicate the process of restitution and, in many cases, would make the return of looted property impossible because of the potential subsequent legal complications. It was accepted that the problem concerning restitution should be solved only by means of the rules of public international law, and only those distinctly separate cases were to be judged according to national law. Establishing the Public International Law Principle meant that the legal proceedings ended at the moment when the object was handed over to the claimant State. The subsequent location of the recovered objects and their return to lawful owners was governed by the internal regulations of that State.

---

39 .   For example G. von Schmoller, H. Maier, and A. Tobler, *Handbuch des Besatzungsrechts,* Tübingen 1957; E. Langen and E. Sauer, above note 17.

40.   *Ibid,* p. 14. see also E. Kaufmann, 'Die volkerrechtlichen Grundlagen und Grenzen der Restitutionen' in *Archiv des offentlichen Rechts,* Bd.75, Tübingen 1949, p. 23 ff.

41.   I. Vasarhelyi, ch. 1 above note 9 p. 89.

The definition of restitutional procedures between States was fully confirmed in detailed regulations. The definition of restitution itself, and the aims specified in the regulations of the U.S. Military Government for Germany, make clear that looted works of art, after being identified, would be "restituted to the governments of the countries" from which they were taken (MGR 18-106 and 110).[42] The release itself would be made "to the authorised representative of the claimant nation" (MGR 18-445.3). The appointment of military organisations to undertake the action of restitution appears later. Basic activities connected with restitution were the duty of Monuments, Fine Arts and Archives Officers (known as "MFA&A Officers") who were specialists in art and monuments, most frequently former museum officials drafted into the army during the occupation of Germany. They worked within the framework of the military administration, which was the authority in subjugated *Länder* (MFA&A Officers at the Offices of Military Governments of the *Länder*, MGR 18-107.2). Their work was supervised by the MFA&A Section of the Restitution Branch, Economics Division, Office of U.S. Military Government for Germany (MGR-18-107.1).[43] This Section was to take the final decision concerning the restitution of each work of art. It should be noted that, in time, the Occupying Authorities carrying out the restitution increasingly made use of German staff; by the end of 1946 in the British Zone, so-called German Restitution Offices were set up. According to instructions,[44] these offices had taken over "a considerable degree of responsibility for restitution from the German Administration and the greater part of the executive work in this connection" (Point 1). The Offices, which were created, paid and controlled by the German Administration, were engaged in the following activities: accepting restitution claims, searching for the claimed object, record filing, preparing the recovered object for shipment, etc. After the establishment of the German Restitution Offices, the British Administration was left with issues such as estimating the value of a given object, granting permits for its receipt by restitution missions, and arbitrating disputes. The governments of the countries concerned were represented in occupied Germany by Military Missions, which functioned at the Allied Control Council for Germany in Berlin. Every occupation zone had a specialised restitution mission, which co-operated with appropriate branches of the Allied Military Administration and, as far as the restitution of works of art was concerned, with the MFA&A Officers. The procedures and structures of these missions, as well as the number and authority of their members, were governed by appropriate regulations[45] which limited the staff to four officers, an administrator, a driver and an interpreter. The staff could perform their work only when accompanied by an officer of the occupation army. The basic tasks of the restitution missions were: "to visit the location of the property subject to restitution for purposes of identification, examination, supervision of packaging and shipping and signing of necessary receipts and other documents" (MGR 19-102.3); the mission staff had no right to search for these objects. They elaborated and submitted restitution claims and were the only

---

42. Office of Military Government for Germany, U.S. Military Government Regulations, Title 18: 'Monuments, fine arts and archives' (henceforth: MGR 18). Berlin, according to the legal situation on 12 February 1947. For the full text see Annex 10. See also parallel notes: *Civil Affairs Handbook*, which were in binding for the British Army; L.Woolley, above note 5 p. 41 ff.

43. See K. Lindsay 'Official Art Seizure under the Military Cloak' (1998) *Art, Antiquity and Law* (forthcoming). As far as the British Army is concerned, see: L. Woolley, above note 7.

44. *Control Commission for Germany, B.E. Zonal Executive Offices, Zonal Executive Instruction No. 49*, dated 24 October 1946: Institution of German restitution offices. ANR, records of BWRR, sign. 244, p. 57. It should be added that these offices were, in fact, excluded from the process of restitution of works of art, but they were often helpful.

45. Office of Military Government for Germany, U.S. Military Government Regulations, Title 19: *Restitution*, Berlin 1946 (henceforth: MGR 19) *Regulation of the Structure and Composition of the Mission* MGR 19-102. In the British Zone, *"T" Force Instruction No. 4: Allied Nations Reparations and Restitutions Teams*, ANR, records of BWRR, sign. 227, p. 12.

organisations accredited for the final and formal receipt of the recovered property. This role was included in regulation MGR 19-501, according to which "only the accredited agent of the country receiving the property (the restitution missions) are authorised to take over and to acknowledge receipt of property prescribed in the so-called permit to release". The British regulations allowed for two kinds of restitution teams; some of them had a more mobile character as their basic task was to identify objects that had already been found ("Restitution Identification Team"), while the others attended to preparing the objects already formally restituted for shipping ("Restitution Packing Team").

The principle of identification

This principle can be defined in general terms as the duty to ascertain that the object subject to restitution was identical to the property taken away from the territory occupied by the Germans. The identification had to be absolutely positive, as this was an indispensable condition for the receipt of a work of art. This condition derives from the definition of restitution and is repeated in detailed regulations as a definite formula that restitution concerns "identifiable" or, as it is often formulated "clearly identified looted cultural materials" (*inter alia* MGR 18-106, 110, 445.3). The identification of the excessively large number of objects brought to Germany from many European countries required action on a very large scale. One of the first steps was to introduce Law No. 52 concerning the blocking and control of property.[46] This law constituted a basis for blocking and strictly controlling several different categories of property (mainly public property and looted objects (Article 1)) by the Military Administration. Simultaneously, a ban on all kinds of transactions was introduced; this clearly covered a greater range of objects than Article of Law No. 52, including all works of art looted on the German territory. The ban was formulated so as to leave no room for doubt. Article 2 stated that:

> no person shall import, acquire or receive, deal in, sell, lease, transfer, export, hypothecate or otherwise dispose of, destroy or surrender possession, custody or control of any property ... (d) which is a work of art or cultural material of value or importance, regardless of the ownership or control thereof;

Foreign exchange also fell within this ban.[47]

The total 'freeze' on cultural materials was imposed so that it would be possible for members of the Military Administration to conduct a systematic survey of all works of art, as well as to find and identify all looted objects (MGR 18-400). Until these surveys were completed, owners, administrators and other persons protecting or controlling art collections were obliged to preserve and supervise the objects remaining at their disposal, as well as gather any relevant documents. When summoned by the Military Administration, they were to present all information and reports immediately or, if necessary, to hand over all accessible collections (Law No. 52, Article 3). Breach of these regulations could be met with severe punishment (Law No. 52, Article 8). Cultural material which was "clearly German-owned" could be released and turned over to the German administration only after:

- the survey of the entire collection had been completed and objects identified as looted had been excluded, and
- all records or archives had been searched in order to establish whether the documents collected there were products of "Nazi looting activities"(MGR 18-301).

---

46. Military Government for Germany. U.S. Zone. Law No. 52: 'Blocking and control of property' *Military Government Gazette* [Germany. U.S.Zone. Issue A] 1 June 1946, p. 24. See also note 166. For the full text see Annex 7.
47. Military Government for Germany. U.S. Zone. Law No. 53: 'Foreign exchange control', *Military Government Gazette* [Germany. U.S. Zone. Issue A], 1 June 1946, p. 36. All agreements concluded against this law were, on the strength of Art. 5 "null and void", whereas persons concluding them were to be punished (Art. 8).

Museums and galleries could be opened to the public under the same conditions (MGR 18-401.4). The trading activities of art and antiques dealers were placed under special control; in order to escape the ban on all transactions, they were required to possess a special licence as well as maintain all documents and reports concerning the trade of works of art with a selling value exceeding ten thousand marks (MGR 18-401.7 and 8, and 440 in connection with Article 2 of Law No. 52).

The control, search and identification activities were carried out by MFA&A Officers, who, in the case of more difficult investigations, could turn for help to military criminal investigation units (MGR 18-108). If they managed positively to identify a given work of art, the restitution process could commence. However, immediate identification was possible only for a limited number of well-known works of art. The identification of the majority of works, dispersed all over Germany, required thorough research which was carried out after the works of art had been transported to Central Collecting Points and Depots (MGR 18-440). Such Points were organised by the Military Administration in bigger cities and developed to house all works of art looted by Nazis, which had been hidden in special secret depots or included in museum collections. At the Central Collecting Points, specialised staff were engaged in the sorting of, and detailed research into these works; it was only here that representatives of foreign restitution missions were permitted to identify them. Detailed inventories and photographic records were made of all items; this requirement could be waived only if the objects remained sealed in crates which were marked in such a way that the place of restitution was identifiable (MGR 18-443.1).

A very significant source of information concerning looted property and the place from where it was taken, was declarations made by Germans; the obligation to make such declarations was introduced under Articles 1 and 3 of Law No. 52[48] which concerned property with a value exceeding 10 marks in the case of one object, and 50 marks in cases where one person possessed several objects. All persons who were or had been in possession of property, were administering or had administered it, controlled or had controlled such property or had any knowledge of cultural materials of this sort, were obliged to notify the appropriate German authorities of these facts. The copies of such declarations were to be sent to the Military Government; failure to perform this duty was punishable.[49]

The restitution missions of the countries concerned were also helpful in identifying works of art which might be subject to restitution. Their representatives were very frequently invited to examine the contents of storehouses and museums and they also had access to declarations made by the Germans. Moreover, much information on looted works of art could be found in the countries from which they were taken, which explains why the restitution regulations required the name of the last known place where the object was stored in Germany to be stated in any restitution claim (MGR 19-203).

---

48. In the U.S. Zone, this obligation resulted from MGR 19-504; in the British Zone it was introduced on the basis of General Order No. 6: *Declaration of looted property in British Zone*, 24 April 1946; ANR, records of BWRR, sign. 244, pp. 27, 29 and 30. For the full text see Annex 8.

49. This description concerns the obligations resulting from General Order No. 6. American regulations were more extensive, and the persons obliged to make such a declaration were those who:
      a. possess, hold or shelter,
      b. have possessed, held or sheltered,
      c. have or believe they have knowledge of present location of,
      d. have moved, assisted in moving, ordered the move or transmitted instructions to move any property removed from an area occupied by German forces (MGR 19-504).

The principle of 'force and duress'

Proof that the removal of property from occupied territories by Nazis had been carried out by force was a necessary prerequisite for application for restitution. Therefore, establishing the criterion of force become one of the main issues of restitution law. The often complex and concealed forms of Nazi theft necessitated a broad interpretation of this notion; consequently, as early as the Declaration of 5 January 1943, apart from "open looting and plunder," the authors mention "transactions apparently legal in form, even when they purport to be voluntarily effected." The definition of restitution uses only the term 'force' and leaves further interpretation of this notion to the laws of each individual zone. An example of the fullest interpretation of 'force' is contained in MGR 19-100.2.a, where it was held to cover duress, which may occur with or without violence, and also extended to looting, theft, larceny and other forms of dispossession whether they were carried out by order of the German authorities, or by officials of the German civil or military administration, without such orders from the German authorities, or by individuals. It also included acquisitions carried out as a result of duress, such as requisitions or other orders or regulations of the military or occupation authorities.[50] A few months after this definition was announced, the U.S. Military Government for Germany issued a memorandum which added further criteria to this complex area of interpretation.[51] The common title "Criteria of Force", included a number of situations which, if supported by appropriate evidence, satisfied the notion of force contained in the definition. These were:

1. Force in the physical sense.

2. The threat of physical force, although the presence of the occupation army was not sufficient to constitute such a threat.

3. Requisition.

4. Public sale after confiscation (sale by a sequestrator).

5. Involuntary acceptance of payment:
- if payment was reasonable, the burden of proof as to its involuntary nature lay on the party claiming restitution;
- if, however, payment was unreasonable, the burden of proof was on those opposed to restitution to show that the payment was accepted voluntarily.

6. The removal of objects during the German withdrawal from the occupied territory, except the removal of personal property of the collaborators who were leaving the country together with the German Army; (they were not considered enemies).

A crucial element of this memorandum was the acceptance of a general "presumption of force", if the property removed had already existed before the occupation began. This presumption could be rebutted by proof that a given object had not been acquired by force.[52]

---

50. MGR 19-100 (2a).
51. Office of Military Government of Germany, U.S. Property Division Reparation and Restitution Branch, *Memorandum on Restitution as Affected by Reparations, Force and the German Minimum Economy*, 15 October 1946. ANR, records of BWRR, sign. 5, p. 8 ff.
52. On the subject of presumed use of force, see I. Vasarhelyi, ch. 1 above note 9 p. 105, which refers to another memorandum.

These criteria also applied when circumstances of the seizure of cultural objects was under investigation.[53] In practice, however, there appeared to be many interpretative difficulties as a result of which the Military Government issued another memorandum introducing an additional criterion, this time excluding acting by force;[54] this was the concept of a so-called 'Normal Commercial Transaction.' The introduction to this memorandum clearly states that it was quite impossible to establish the rules of a 'normal commercial transaction' in a complete and explicit way. Consequently, it was recommended that every case be judged individually in the light of the 1943 Declaration taking into account some additional considerations which included:

1. The burden of proof of a 'normal commercial transaction' lies with the German possessor of property.

2. Acceptance of payment is not sufficient to establish that a 'normal commercial transaction' was concluded.

3. The only transaction in question is that which resulted in the deposit of a given cultural object in Germany. All subsequent transactions are of no importance.

4. All receipts for payment and the registration of any claims concerning a given object, which were signed in a territory occupied at that time "will be disregarded since restitution claims are Government claims and not those of individuals."

5. The application of the 'Normal Commercial Transaction' criterion in individual cases depends on an assessment of the wider commercial relationship existing between the German seller and the German buyer before and during the occupation.

6. If it is ascertained that property has been removed by a special organisation engaged in plunder by the order of civil or military authorities, the criterion of 'Normal Commercial Transaction' is not taken into consideration.

As far as cultural objects were concerned, the 'Normal Commercial Transaction' criterion was applied with certain modifications which were announced to the representatives of the restitution missions at a special meeting, devoted to presenting and discussing the Memorandum. The chief of the MFA&A Section informed all participants that:

Ascertaining excessive and abnormal increase in the number of transactions made by an antique dealer with a person living in the occupied country may be rightly considered evidence of acting by force and duress. Moreover, any evidence that a dealer living in Germany worked for the Nazi party or had its support, or for any other military or similar German organisation annuls the appearance of a 'normal commercial transaction.'[55]

---

53. Certain vagueness concerning the definition of the force criterion in the restitution of cultural objects may appear in reference to the definition of 'looted cultural material,' included in MGR-18-104. According to this regulation, this notion covered: "all cultural objects and materials which have been acquired since 1 January 1933 by the Nazis within Germany or those acquired in territories occupied by the Germans or their allies, either:
a. Directly by duress or wrongful acts of confiscation, dispossession or spoliation, whether pursuant to legislation, or by procedure purporting to follow forms of law, or otherwise; or
b. Indirectly by purchase or other transactions regardless of whatever consideration may have been employed. This formulation results from some generalisations made in order to apply this definition to internal restitution."

54. Office of Military Government for Germany, U.S. Property Division. Reparation and Restitution Branch, *Memorandum on procedure of restitution*, 23 June 1948. ANR, records of BWRR, sign. 5, p. 123. See also I. Vasarhelyi, ch. 1 above note 9 p. 108.

55. ANR, records of BWRR, sign. 5, p. 125.

Therefore, the belief that a transaction fulfilled all the requirements of a 'Normal Commercial Transaction' acted as a bar to restitution. However, acting by 'force', in the broad sense of the word, was sufficient justification for accepting an undeniable right to restitution. The explicit formulation of MGR 19-100.2.a. left no room for doubt: according to this regulation, if "an article has been removed by force at any time during the occupation of a country, and is identifiable, the right to its recovery is an absolute one." In practice, this basically meant removing the protection afforded to a buyer in good faith, a matter which provoked severe criticism from some German authors who maintained that annulling a traditional principle of civil law was unacceptable, even under the terms of international law.[56] This criticism seems harsh because the duty to return the object to be restituted did not result in the recovery of payment or any other form of compensation; this counter-view led Schmoller, Maier and Tobler, in defending their position, to put forward a concept of 'proper' and 'improper' restitution. They defined 'proper' restitution as restitution which could be performed on the basis of both international and civil law. 'Improper' restitution was, according to them, restitution which was in accordance with international law but could not be based on civil law regulations. In practice, this proposal would result in the protection of a buyer in good faith and the payment of compensation by the country in the case of improper restitution.[57] Distinguishing between these two types of restitution would have further consequences, and would make it impossible to recover many objects which could be restituted only on the basis of regulations introduced by international law; examples of such situations are presented by Wengler.[58]

German authors also criticised the acceptance of a general presumption of acting 'by force', to all cases where the objects removed by Germans had existed in the occupied territory since the occupation commenced. According to these authors, the introduction of this principle, which they dubbed "*Kollektivzwang*", was unacceptable because the legal judgment of acting 'by force' or under duress could be based only on the norms of civil law.[59] It should be noted that this general presumption was introduced only following the regulations issued in 1948, by which time, the Allied authorities obviously wanted to complete the process of restitution and to expedite the examination of claims which had not yet been dealt with. By that time, many claims had already been rejected because, *inter alia*, no evidence of acting 'by force' or duress had been presented, and the 1948 regulations had not yet become valid; reconsideration of rejected claims was not possible under the legal procedures then in force.

The principle of territoriality
The principle of territoriality is included in all major acts of restitution law. The 1943 Declaration considered items of property which are or were "situated in the territories which have come under the occupation or control, direct or indirect, of the governments with which they are at war..." Similar statements were included in the definition of restitution and in the MGR 19-101.b. The regulations concerning the restitution of works of art include the statement that those works which were "in existence and located in an occupied territory ..." should be subject to restitution (MGR 18-106 and 110); according to these regulations restitution should apply to all cultural materials removed from a given territory. Therefore, an object had to be carefully identified. A clear connection with a given territory was the sole criterion for

---

56. G. von Schmoller, B. Maier, and A. Tobler, above note 39 p. 16.
57. *Ibid*, p. 20 ff. See also I. Vasarhelyi, ch. 1 above note 9 p. 59, which quotes MGR 16-241, unequivocally forbidding the payment of compensation related to restitution.
58. W. Wengler, 'Conflicts of Laws. Problems Relating to Restitution of Property in Germany', (1962) 11 *International and Comparative Law Quarterly* 1133.
59. These views were definitely rejected by I. Vasarhelyi, above ch. 1 note 9 p.106 ff.

restitution, and this removed the need for the investigation of other circumstances (such as the current ownership of the objects in question or their ownership under the occupation). Vasarhelyi proposed that the territoriality principle should be applied irrespective of the citizenship of the owner:

> It is beyond doubt that the legal principle of restitution protects the interests of the political economy rather than those of the owner: restitution is not aimed at setting up the right of ownership of an individual person but at repairing the serious injury caused to the whole economic life of the countries concerned.[60]

The arbitrary character of this principle is supported by many regulations; for example, according to the Memorandum quoted above,[61] where circumstances excluding a 'normal commercial transaction' are discovered, the will of the seller is not taken into consideration, even if he shows no interest in recovering the object. The territoriality principle is supported by a country's exclusive right to raise claims relating to objects removed from its territory. This right is certainly not granted to an owner. In fact, one of the statements in a restitution claim is: "the last known resident of a claimant country, who was the owner or custodian of a claimed item ..." (MGR 19-203 a.5.). However, the supply of this information is not a necessary prerequisite for the submission of a claim and it is needed only to identify the place from where the object came. This information is merely auxiliary. Similarly, the receipt of restituted property, for instance a work of art, is possible only by an authorised representative of a given country (MGR 18-445.3). The case of the ownership of property by an emigrant provides an exception to the principle of territoriality; in this situation, restitution would not take place.[62]

In conclusion, it should be noted that restitution law does not provide a comprehensive solution to the question of recovering objects in the case of territorial changes made after World War II.

The formalised procedure

The restitution of property looted by the Germans in occupied territories proceeded in a very formal and defined way; its legal basis was the regulations passed by the military governments in particular zones, and works of art were restituted according to the general rules of this procedure. Certain issues, however, were governed by separate regulations; restitution was effected by specialised institutions and their results were recorded in different reports and statistical tables.[63] This division of duties necessitated a clear definition of the objective of restitution. According to MGR 18 the purpose of restitution was the recovery of property falling within the broad category of 'cultural materials,' which comprised "cultural objects and archives, books and miscellaneous documents", except current commercial archives (MGR 18-103). The authors further defined 'cultural objects' as:

> all movable goods of importance or value either religious, artistic, documentary, scholarly or historic, the disappearance of which constitutes a loss to the cultural heritage of the country concerned. This definition includes recognised works of art, as well as such objects as rare musical instruments, books and manuscripts, scientific documents of a historic or cultural nature, and all objects usually found in museums, collections, libraries and historic archives.[64]

---

60. *Ibid*, p. 87.
61. See note 52.
62. *Ibid*. See I. Vasarhelyi, ch. 1 above note 9 p. 92.
63. 'Cultural claims' and 'non-cultural claims' were distinguished, *Monthly Report* 1948 and 1949.
64. MGR 18-101.

Irrespective of the source of information about the property being sought, the restitution procedure was instigated by a claim submitted by restitution missions to the Occupation Authorities in Germany (with numerous copies to be given to several departments of each Authority specified in the regulations). Each claim, submitted on a standard form, was required to include the following data:
- description of the object which was the subject matter of the claim;
- as much available information as possible allowing the identification of the object, such as characteristic features and peculiarities, signatures and numbers;
- the last known place where the object had been stored in the claimant country and the approximate date of its removal;
- the last known place where the object was stored in Germany;
- personal data of an inhabitant of the claimant country who was the last owner or custodian of the object before it was taken by the enemy on the territory of this country;
- information regarding whether the item had already existed at the moment when the occupation of the claimant country started.

In addition, it was necessary to provide the most detailed information concerning the circumstances in which the item had been taken and removed from the country occupied by Germany (as required by MGR 19-203). Provided the item claimed was identified, this information was critical to the determination of the claim, which is why it had to be supported by sufficiently detailed evidence.[65] A bare assertion by a mission that the force or duress criterion had been fulfilled was not accepted as evidence of acting 'by force' or duress, (although such an attestation could be accepted if it included detailed facts of the circumstances of force or duress, and the German party did not provide evidence to the contrary). A signed attestation by a person from the country occupied by Germany was accorded some evidential value, if it detailed the circumstances in which the object was taken. Original documents of requisition, military orders, forms, inventories, sale agreements , German receipts etc. constituted conclusive evidence, provided that they were authentic and demonstrated one or several 'Force Criteria'. Similar evidentiary principles applied to a German, or any other party, who argued against restitution. General evidence of acquiring the item by means of purchase, exchange, donation or similar mechanism was not accepted, irrespective of the fact of the object being acquired from an original owner or from a dealer. The only evidence that alone could defeat a restitution claim was original documents unquestionably revealing one or several 'Criteria of lack of force'.

A claim, prepared according to these requirements, was initially submitted with five, and from 1947, seven copies to the Reparations, Deliveries and Restitutions Division of the Control Commission for Germany.[66] After an initial examination of the claim, and confirmation that it fulfilled all the requirements, the Reparations, Deliveries and Restitutions Division distributed all the copies according to a prescribed list. If a claim was based on information received from Allied military authorities, an application for a travel permit would be made in order that an expert who would be able to identify the claimed work or works of art, and examine the condition of the item or items, could carry out these procedures in the presence of an MFA&A Officer. Next, a common protocol was prepared on the basis of which, the Reparations,

---

65.   *Memorandum* as in note 54, para. 4: *Evidence on the question of force.*
66.   Control Commission for Germany; B. E. Reparations, Deliveries and Restitutions Division. *Internal procedure for the restitution of property. Works of art, historical relics, archives, etc.*, 9 February 1946. ANR, BWRR records, sign. 224, pp. 14 and 15. The instruction concerning asserting restitution claims of 28 February 1946. ANR, records of BWRR, sign. 2, p. 41.

Deliveries and Restitutions Division, after consultation with the Legal Section of the Military Government, could issue a so-called 'release to restitution' of items to be removed. Subsequently, those items would be packed and their transport prepared; the restituted objects were then handed over to the representative of the appropriate restitution mission. Receipt of the object had to be documented by a special 'Receipt for Cultural Objects', signed in eight copies, the form of which had been worked out by the President of the Reparations, Deliveries and Restitutions Division of the Allied Control Commission. A common receipt form was used for the whole of occupied Germany; it included a promise by the country receiving the work of art to return it if the wrong object had been released by mistake.[67] When a claim was prepared on the basis of information acquired from some source other than an Allied occupation administration, after checking it, the MFA&A Officers conducted a search for the item. If it produced no results, or there were difficulties in identifying the item, the Reparations, Deliveries and Restitutions Division requested the appropriate restitution mission send extra data or the aid of an expert. If the recovery of the claimed object turned out to be impossible, the procedure was discontinued.

On the basis of the general regulations, all the expenses relating to restitution made on German territory were covered by the German administration (MGR 19-400), and special regulations obliged it to pay compensation if, after asserting the claim and after identification, the item was damaged, stolen or "disposed of in some other way".[68]

Finally, it is necessary to consider the question of time limitations in relation to the formalised procedure of restitution; neither the 1943 Declaration, nor the definition of restitution, nor the subsequent detailed regulations, specified the period of time for restitution. The procedure became unavailable upon the withdrawal of the Allied military administration in Germany at the turn of 1948-1949 and at that time, the so-called dates of 'final' restitution were settled. However, these were postponed many times as a result of protests. A parallel situation occurred in the territories of Austria. The legal character of the dates of "closing restitution" is explained by Gen. J. Balmer in the following way:

> This action is without prejudice to such rights as may be given to claimants under a future treaty with Austria, and represents merely a termination of the responsibility of the United States with respect to claims for looted property in the American Zone of Austria.[69]

These fixed dates did not include the restitution of cultural materials, a fact which was confirmed by Ardelia Hall, supervising restitution on behalf of the Department of State. In an official publication of the Department from 1951, she wrote: "For the first time in history, restitution may be expected to continue for as long as works of art known to have been plundered during a war continue to be rediscovered."[70] However, the tasks of restitution which flowed from this were taken over from the Allied military administration by the appropriate German and Austrian institutions. Moreover, the regulations concerning the procedure in force until this point were changed.

---

67. In such a case, the work of art should be returned either "to the government of the Allied State if the property was removed from the territory of the State," or "to the Headquarters of the Zone from which it was shipped, if it had not been removed from the Territory of an Allied State". Moreover, the receipt included an important clause, according to which "the occupying power and all its agents and representatives shall be saved harmless from any claim for loss, damage or deterioration suffered by any item from the time of its removal from the jurisdiction or custody of the country receiving restitution until its return thereto." MGR-18-550.2 and 3.
68. I. Vasarhelyi, ch. 1 above note 9 p. 113.
69. ANR, records of BWRR, sign. 214, p. 3.
70. A. Hall, 'The Recovery of Cultural Objects Dispersed During World War II', *Department of State Bulletin* 1951, Vol. 25, No. 635, p. 339.

Internal Restitution

The legal regulations discussed so far have concerned so-called 'external restitution'; these provided the formal basis for the recovery of cultural materials removed by the Nazis from occupied territories. However, the creation of a legal basis to regulate so-called 'internal restitution' was also possible. The Allied Control Council decided that, because of the frequent confiscation of individual private persons' property within German territory since 1933, internal restitution should be introduced to cover this period. Initially it intended to produce one set of regulations for the entire territory of occupied Germany, but endless discussions over its precise form, as well as political 'dissonances' between the Allies, destroyed this intent. Finally, after two years of painstaking modifications, three acts of similar content came into force in 1947. They regulated the course of internal restitution on the territories of the Western occupied zones. After two years a parallel regulation was issued for Berlin.[71]

These regulations aimed at effecting:

> to the largest extent possible, the speedy restitution of identifiable property (tangible and intangible property and aggregates of tangible and intangible property) to persons who were wrongfully deprived of such property within the period from 30 January 1933 to 8 May 1945 for reasons of race, religion, nationality, ideology or political opposition to National Socialism.[72]

A crucial element of this law was the explicit statement that property confiscated in these circumstances was to be returned to its previous owner or his legal heir, even if it became necessary to disregard the rights of other persons who were not acquainted with these circumstances. The concept of 'confiscation' was defined very broadly. It included, on the basis of presumption, all transactions made in this period if they resulted in the dispossession of persons persecuted because of their race, religion, nationality, ideology or political opposition to National Socialism, or persons belonging to communities excluded from German cultural or economic life in connection with such persecution. A right to make a restitution claim was granted to persons whose property had been confiscated or to their legal heirs. The regulations did not state explicitly whether this right applied in respect of property confiscated only on German territory or also on the territories occupied by Nazis. The restitution of property which was not the object of individual complaint, could be performed only by so-called

---

71. These were the following laws: Military Government for Germany, U.S. Area of Control, Law No. 59: 'Restitution of Identifiable Property', *Military Government Gazette* [Germany. U.S. Zone. Issue G] No. 10, November 1947; (See Annex 10) Control Commission for Germany. B.E. Law No. 59: 'Restitution of Identifiable Property to Victims of Nazi Oppression', *Military Government Gazette* [British Zone of Control], No. 28; Allemagne. Gouvernement Militaire de la Zone Française d'occupation, 'Ordonnance No. 120 du 10 Novembre 1947 relative à la restitution des biens ayant fait l'objet de spoliation', *Journal Officiel du Commandement en Chef Français en Allemagne* No. 179, 17 juin 1949; 'Order of Allied Kommendantura Berlin', BK/O/49/180, 26 July 1949: 'Restitution of Identifiable Property to Victims of Nazi Oppression', DAHD MFA, z. 10, w. 32, Vol. 284, p. 46 ff. Many similarities between these legislative acts are pointed out in E.J. Cohn, 'A Novel Chapter in the Relations Between Common Law and Civil Law', (1955) 4 *International and Comparative Law Quarterly* 493. The research of Bentwich and Wengler shows that on the territory of the Russian Occupation Zone a similar law was not introduced. N. Bentwich, 'International Aspects of Restitution and Compensation for Victims of the Nazis', (1955/56) 32 *British Yearbook of International Law* 204; W. Wengler, above note 58 p. 1133.

72. A general formula included as Article 1 in all laws cited above.

Successor Organisations, representing missing or dead persons (Successor Organisation as Heir to Persecuted Persons). Such organisations could be appointed by military governments of a given occupation zone in Germany; this function could not be assigned to any other countries or their institutions. The restitution procedure was carried out by German organisations such as the Restitution Agency and the Restitution Chamber of the District Court. Every claimant had a right to appeal against their decisions to the Supreme Appellate Court.

Regulations concerning internal restitution obliged the Germans to submit items which came under restitution laws. This obligation existed irrespective of the obligation to make declarations relating to property looted in occupied territories.

The restitution law, characterised by aims similar to those described above, was also valid on the territory of Austria.[73]

The 1952 Bonn Convention

Although the military occupational administration in Germany was liquidated and wider powers were granted to the German authorities, the issue of restitution remained under Allied management. This was clearly confirmed in the Occupation Statutes of 1949, "in order to ensure accomplishment of the basic purposes of the occupation."[74] This situation changed when the Convention on the Settlement of Matters Arising out of the War and the Occupation was signed in Bonn on 26 May 1952.[75] This document introduced different principles for the external restitution of cultural materials and related objects, which were specified in detail. In the case of the other unspecified property, it changed the position and allowed individual complaints by owners of looted property against the then present holders, permitting them to seek judicial redress. However, in so far as cultural material, in the broad sense of the word, was concerned, the regulations remained in force, although they underwent certain modifications. Restitution claims could be made by States only according to the territorial principle. Control and implementation of the restitution procedure was handed over to the Federal Republic, which was obliged to appoint and support an 'administrative agency' engaged in searching, investigating and returning objects separately specified as 'jewellery, silverware and antique furniture' and as 'cultural property.' The choice of these categories was not fortuitous and it had certain procedural effects: the first category included objects valued at less than FF 200,000 on 1 January 1951. Additionally, in relation to furniture, it was established that the term 'antique' concerned items over one hundred years old. The restitution of objects defined in this way was impossible if one established that they were acquired through a regular commercial transaction, even if occupation currency was used. In addition, significant procedural limits were introduced, under which recovery should be claimed on the basis of claims submitted to Allied restitution authorities even before the Convention entered into force.

---

73.   General information introducing this issue can be found in I. Seidl-Hohenveldern, 'Austria. Restitution Legislation', *American Journal of Comparative Law* 1953, Vol. 2, p. 383.

74.   *The Memorandum of the Three Western Occupation Powers on the Programme for Germany,* Washington, April 8 1949. "Series of Documents" 1949, No. 5, p. 359 ff.

75.   *Convention on the Settlement of Matters Arising out of the War and the Occupation,* Bonn, 25 May 1952. Treaty Series 1959, No. 13. London HMSO, Cmnd. 656, p. 3 ff. For a concise discussion of the principles of restitution in the Convention see N. Bentwich, above note 71 p. 209 ff; B. Hollander, ch. 2 above note 59 p. 39.

The second category, 'cultural property', included objects defined as "movable goods of religious, artistic, documentary, scholarly or historic value, or of equivalent importance, including objects customarily found in museums, public or private collections, libraries or historic archives." (Chapter Five, Article 1.4). According to a special provision, 'cultural property' would also be subject to restitution when it constituted a 'gift' received by direct or indirect duress or by the use of an individual's official position. Property acquired by means of purchase was also included, unless it had been brought to a given country in order to be sold. A condition *sine qua non* of restitution in these cases was that the item existed on the territory of a country from which it was removed before the outbreak of war with this country.

The deadline for registering claims for the recovery of 'cultural property' was 8 May 1956. If the search conducted by the restitution agency was fruitless, or was unlikely to be completed before 8 May 1957, the agency could suspend the procedure. It could be resumed if the object sought was identified. Appeals against any decision of the agency could be made to the Arbitration Commission on Property, Rights and Interests in Germany, which was appointed for ten years and constituted an international organisation with the participation of representatives of occupying powers, Germany and neutral members. The Convention confirmed the right to compensation in case of damage, theft or loss of any identified object which was not restituted, if the restitution claim had been asserted by the Allied restitution bodies before this Convention became valid. The Bonn Convention upheld all existing occupation laws regulating internal restitution.

The State Treaty with Austria

While the task of conducting internal restitution on the territory of liberated Austria was handed over at once to local courts and authorities,[76] the question of restituting property originating from the countries occupied by Germany was left in the hands of Allied authorities. A change in this respect was brought about in 1955 by the conclusion of the State Treaty on Reconstructing an Independent and Democratic Austria.[77] According to Article 25 of this Treaty, Austria committed itself to return to the Allied Nations and their nationals all properties that belonged to them and were presently in Austria, in their present condition. In this context, the term 'properties' meant all property, either movable or immovable, material or immaterial, including industrial, literary and artistic property, as well as all property rights and interests concerning this property (Article 25.8.d). The tasks connected with conducting restitutional procedures were entirely taken over by the Austrian authorities. All transfers of property, brought about by force by the Axis countries and their institutions, were annulled. In cases where the property was not returned within six months from the date when the Treaty came into force, a restitution claim could be made to the Austrian authorities within the next six months, unless the party concerned was unable to assert a claim in that time. All expenses incurred in enforcing restitution claims were to be covered by the Austrian Government.

---

76.   I. Seidl-Hohenveldern, above note 73 p. 388.
77.   'The State Treaty on Reconstructing an Independent and Democratic Austria', Vienna, 15 May 1955, *Journal of Laws of the People's Republic of Poland* 1957, No. 19, item 94, Appendix.

Restitution from the Territories of the Former Axis Powers

The legal basis for the restitution of property from the territories of the former Axis powers developed in two stages. Initially, only general restitutional clauses were formulated, which related to the countries whose claims were most likely to be taken into account. The earliest document including this kind of resolution — the Act of Surrender of Italy of 29 September 1943[78] — stated that all property in the Italian territory which belonged to the Allied Nations or occupied countries, or their citizens, would be seized and safeguarded until further orders (Article 28.c). The Italian Government pledged to observe these orders, especially in cases which dealt with restitution (Article 33.a). Later, the Armistice agreements with, in succession, Romania,[79] Finland,[80] Bulgaria,[81] and Hungary[82] included similar clauses, which obliged the governments of those countries to return *"en parfait état"* all property that had been taken from the Allied Nations' territories during the war. The Armistice Agreements with Romania and Finland included the USSR, while that with Bulgaria included the USSR, Greece, and Yugoslavia; and that with Hungary included the USSR, Czechoslovakia, and Yugoslavia as the countries for which restitution would have the greatest impact. All four agreements list, *inter alia, "objets ayant un caractère historique"* as well as *"pièces de musée."*

In the second stage, the principles of restitution from the territories of former Axis powers were fully regulated in peace treaties. With the exception of the Treaty with Finland,[83] which merely repeated the clause from the Armistice Agreement, the treaties[84] included very detailed provisions concerning restitution, and were all constructed along similar lines.[85] A closer examination of these provisions makes it clear that they used the basic principles regarding the return of plundered goods incorporated in the 1943 Inter-Allied Declaration, which were fully represented in the law applied to the territory of Germany. The Treaties used the 1943 Declaration directly as a general interpretation clause in instances of returning property. In the case of Italy, for example, this followed from the statement: "Italy accepts the principles of the Allied Nations Declaration of 5 January 1943..." (Article 75.1). The principles of public international law were adopted for restitutional claims. They were to be "presented to the ... Government by the Government," and all legal and practical situations were evaluated according to international law. Only identified property was subject to restitution, and the obligation to prove the origin of a given object lay with the claimant country. The criterion of 'the use of force and duress' was also applicable, thus giving restitution the character of an

---

78. The title 'The Capitulation Act of Italy' was changed by the protocol signed in Brindisi on 9 November to 'Dispositions additionalles a la Convention d'Armistice', *Recueil de Textes a l'usage des Conferences de la Paix,* Paris 1946, p. 193 ff.
79. *Ibid,* Article 12 of the Armistice Agreement with Romania, p. 321.
80. *Ibid,* Article 14 of the Armistice Agreement with Finland, p. 155.
81. *Ibid,* Article 11 of the Armistice Agreement with Bulgaria, p. 145.
82. *Ibid,* Article 6 of the Armistice Agreement with Hungary, p. 173.
83. Treaty of Peace with Finland, Paris, 10 February 1947. In Treaties of Peace with Italy, Romania, Bulgaria, Hungary and Finland. Texts for Signature in Paris on 10 February 1947. London HMSO, Cmnd. 7022 (henceforth: Treaty of Peace with Finland), Article 24, p. 138.
84. *Ibid,* Treaty of Peace with Bulgaria, Paris, 10 February 1947 (henceforth: Treaty of Peace with Bulgaria), Article 22, p. 99; Treaty of Peace with Romania, Paris, 10 February 1947 (henceforth: Treaty of Peace with Romania), Article 23, p. 79; Treaty of Peace with Hungary, Paris, 10 February, 1947 (henceforth: Treaty of Peace with Hungary), Article 24, p. 117; Treaty of Peace with Italy, Article 75.
85. The appropriate Articles maintain the same internal division into points of the same content. Certain modifications were made but these did not relate to the principle of restitution, but were rather additional provisions resulting from the specific situation of each country. For example, in the case of Italy, the treaty included an additional point on the restitution of monetary gold (Article 75.8).

absolute law. Property "which was removed by force or duress by any of the Axis Powers from the territory of any of the Allied Nations irrespective of any subsequent transactions by which the present holder of any such property has secured possession" (Article 75.2) was subject to restitution. Negating the good faith of the purchaser of the object subject to restitution was not accompanied by the obligation to return the payment. Martin noted[86] that none of the treaties mentioned this problem, which, in his opinion, might lead to many cases of unjustified growth of fortunes, contradictory to the principles of private law.

Restitutional claims were based on the principle of territoriality, which was also noted in literature as important.[87] The deadline for filing claims was six months from the day the Treaties came into force. According to universally accepted principles, all costs of the restitutional process, labour, materials, and shipment were charged to the country obliged to carry out restitution, but this included only the costs borne within its borders.

Restitution from Neutral Countries

The original obligation of restitution — a norm of international law — did not cover looted objects that were found in territories of neutral countries. The peace treaties signed after World War I regulated only the restitution of goods from the defeated nations. For example, Article 238 of the Treaty of Versailles provided that all types of objects were subject to return if their identity could be confirmed in the territory of Germany or her Allies. During World War II, a proportion of looted goods was deposited or sold to countries that did not participate in the war. Initially, the planned restitution was limited to Switzerland, but over time the Allied Nations realised the immense scale of the transfers and decided not to restrict it to this country alone, but to extend it to the territories of relevant neutral countries as well. Since this decision was unusual, it had to be announced and information about it had to be disseminated world-wide to ensure that it should reach the governments and individuals concerned. This explains the publicity given to the 1943 Inter-Allied Declaration, in which a warning against all acts of 'dispossession' was directed "especially [to] persons in the neutral countries." The aims of the pre-emptive warning were specified in the Final Act of the conference in Bretton Woods,[88] and their implementation was secured by agreements concluded between the United States, France, and Great Britain, with Switzerland and Sweden. Negotiations with the Swiss Government took place in Berne between 8 February and 8 March 1945, before the war in Europe had ended. On 8 April 1945, the so-called Currie Protocol was signed, in which Switzerland was obliged to pass national legislation that would enable the restitution of goods looted by Nazis from the occupied territories.[89] Switzerland passed the law on 10 December 1945 and for the following two years provided a special procedure to deal with claims for the return of goods taken from territories through which the war had passed. The right to claim was vested in anyone who:

---

86. A. Martin, ch. 1 above note 4 p. 278.
87. *Ibid*, p. 282.
88. For information on the Declaration of 5 January 1943 and the Final Act of the Bretton Woods Conference, see pp. 40-42 of this work.
89. For details see I. Vasarhelyi, ch. 1 above note 9 p. 117 ff.; A. Martin, ch. 1 above note 4 p. 280 ff.; L. Engstler, *Die territoriale Bindung von Kulturgütern im Rahmen des Volkerrechts*, Koln-Berlin-Bonn-Munchen 1964, p. 174 ff. E. Thilo, 'La revendication de biens se trouvant en Suisse, dérobés en pays occupés pendant la guerre', *Journal des Tribunaux*, 1946 p. 25; 'La restitution des rapines de guerre', *Journal des Tribunaux*, 1948 p. 418 and 1952 p. 386.

a été, d'une manière contraire au droit des gens, spolié ou dépossedé de choses mobilières
ou de papiers-valeurs par la violence, la confiscation ou par des mesures de requisition
ou autres actes similaires, de la part des organes militaires ou civils ou des forces
armées d'une puissance occupante ... (Article 1.1).

The dispossession must have taken place between 1 September 1939 and 8 May 1945 within the occupied territories according to the definition in Article 42 of the Hague Convention. The claim could be directed at the purchaser, whether or not he purchased the object in good faith. Under this law, the protection ensuing from good faith, guaranteed by Article 934 of the Swiss Civil Code, was suspended for a period of two years. Every subsequent purchaser in good faith could bring a case against the seller to return payment, until the person who purchased the object in bad faith was traced. If this person remained unknown or lived outside Swiss jurisdiction, the obligation to return the payment passed on to the Swiss Treasury.

The Government of Sweden assumed even greater responsibility than the Swiss: in the Looted Objects Law of 29 June 1945,[90] whenever restitution was to take place, the Swedish citizen who was unclear of the origin of the object purchased could sue the State Treasury for the amount he paid for it. The Swiss and Swedish legislation was so far reaching in terms of State responsibility that some authors considered that it represented the establishment of a new principle of international law by the Allied Nations. Martin wrote that "indeed, it is difficult to find a legal (as distinct from a political) explanation for the Swiss precedent without resort to a new principle of international law — a more comprehensive inter-state idea of law and justice."[91] The principle was justified by Weiss,[92] and discussed in a wider context by Vasarhelyi, who, referring to Oppenheim and Lauterpacht's opinion,[93] formulated a proposition that "receiving and concealing" stolen goods was "a grave violation of the international legal order" and "has to be internationally prosecuted in order that nobody may make a profit from it ...."[94] The adoption of this principle placed an obligation on neutral States to introduce appropriate legal means for the restitution of these goods.

In the case of restitution of works of art, the effectiveness of these legal means was internationally encouraged by the Agreement on the Control of Looted Works of Art[95] which was concluded on 8 July 1946 by the United States, France, and Britain in order to undertake joint efforts to intensify the search for, and restitution of cultural goods. It was agreed that the governments of these States would request the governments of the liberated countries to provide the governments of neutral States with inventories of looted objects that had not been found in territories of Germany and Austria. These inventories were to be updated as the losses were established. At the same time, the countries which were signatories to the agreement decided

---

90. *Svensk Forfattnings Sammling* 1945, No. 589/90 of 31 July 1954. Quoted after Restitution. European legislation to redress the consequences of Nazi rule. London [not dated] p. xiii-2.
91. A. Martin, ch. 1 above note 4 p. 280.
92. G. Weiss, 'Beuteguter aus besetzen Landern und die privatrechtliche Stellung des schweizerischen Erwerbers', *Schweizerische Juristenzeitung* 15 September 1946.
93. "There is little room for doubt that acts of deprivation of property in disregard of international law are incapable of creating or transferring title. Neutral States which, by failing to take the requisite and practicable steps for preventing their subjects from acquiring the property in question, connive indirectly in the unlawful measures of the occupant and incur a responsibility whose novelty probably does not preclude it from being enforced by appropriate international remedies" : I. Vasarhelyi, ch. 1 above note 9 pp. 115-116.
94. *Ibid*, p. 116.
95. Agreement concluded 8 July 1946, between the United States, the United Kingdom, and France in respect of the control of looted articles. *Department of State Bulletin* 1951, Vol. 25, No. 635, p. 340.

to request the governments of neutral States to make searches for these objects in their territories and to order their customs authorities to prevent their export. Lists of objects that were looted had to be distributed among art dealers, museums, and interested individuals. Private persons and institutions were obliged to report to the authorities if they discovered any item included in the lists. Moreover, the governments of neutral States were obliged to warn and inform their public about the agreement and to request reports on suspicious cases.

Restitution from the Territories of the Allied Nations

Resolution No. 19 of the Chapultepec Conference

Increasing information indicating that the Germans were shipping looted items to South America resulted in South American countries joining in restitutional operations. Most South American States were already signatories of the Final Act of the Allied Nations Conference in Bretton Woods, including Resolution 6 of the Conference dealing with "the enemy countries' assets and property from looting." Resolution 19 of the Inter-American Conference on Problems of War and Peace in February and March 1945, also covered and reiterated these issues.[96] The participant countries adopted and confirmed the principles included in the 1943 Inter-Allied Declaration and other Allied Nations declarations, and pledged to undertake action to fulfil directives that followed these documents.

Firstly, they called for ways of identifying and preventing the export of all property "unjustly obtained or taken in like manner by the enemy", as well as the return of the property to its rightful owner; the signatory countries also agreed to prepare, and engage in various forms of appropriate action (point 2.b).

Secondly, they sought to establish means of preventing the use of South American countries as safe hiding-places for such property as well as the property of persons whose activities were detrimental "to the security of the Western Hemisphere and of the post-war world" (point 2.c).

Agreements on restitution concluded by Poland

There were many factors resulting from post-war difficulties in reconstruction which forced some countries to conclude special agreements despite the universally accepted principle of restitution. As a result of bilateral, explicit confirmation of the general rules, and additional regulation of the more detailed questions, such agreements provided the formal basis for mutual restitutional action. After the end of World War II, Poland signed two agreements of this kind: the first one with the government of Czechoslovakia in 1946 and the second with the government of France in 1947.

Any discussion of Polish restitution from the Allied Nations should include one particular case, although it falls outside the topic of this book. This is the so-called Polish-Canadian dispute over the return of a collection of cultural treasures which had been evacuated from Poland for the duration of the war, and had arrived in Canada in 1940. The dispute was a political rather than a legal one, and the arguments presented by the Canadian side failed to withstand critical analysis from the outset. The dispute has been adequately documented by Nahlik, and from a Canadian standpoint by Williams, with a final evaluation by Nahlik.[97] It therefore requires no further mention here.

---

96.   'Resolution 19: Final Act of the Inter-American Conference on Problems of War and Peace', 21 February-8 March, 1945, in *The Post-War Settlement of Property Rights,* New York 1945, Appendix D, p. 76 ff.

97.   S.E. Nahlik, 'The Case of Displaced Art Treasures — History and Appreciation of a Polish-Canadian Strife', *German Yearbook of International Law* 1980, Vol. 23, p. 255; S. Williams, above note 11 p. 66.

The agreement between Poland and Czechoslovakia on the mutual return of property was concluded in Prague on 12 February 1946.[98] The two countries affirmed their full acceptance of the public law character of restitutional claims. They agreed that each country would delegate two representatives "for mutual settlement, justification of restitution claims" (Article 5). Two Commissions were set up, one in Warsaw and the other in Prague. In the event of a difference of opinion between delegates, the final decision was to be taken by a mixed Commission consisting of four persons, two from each side (Article 6). Each country was obliged to inform the other about property on their territory which could be reclaimed, and to provide information on the circumstances of its displacement in order to make a proper identification (Article 3). On the assumption that in most cases there would be no original documents of requisition issued by the occupation authorities, it was decided that the verified testimony of witnesses, reliable statements of firms and relevant research institutes, as well as other documents allowing for the identification of the object in question, would be accepted (Article 4). Instead of the usual criterion of 'force or duress', this agreement included the criterion of property being removed "without payment or compensation" (Article 1). The principle of territoriality was emphasised in the document: restitution covered all property that was in the territory of one of the signatories before the war, that is, in the case of Poland, before 1 September 1939, and in the case of Czechoslovakia, before 17 September 1938, and in the territory of the other side at the moment of signing the agreement. All types of property were subject to restitution, "whether or not it was the property of the State, a legal entity, or natural person" (Article 1), and "wherever its owner is at the moment" (Article 2). The agreement listed as examples of objects subject to restitution, works of art, libraries, archives, all kinds of historic relics and valuable objects made of precious metals and gems (Article 1). There was no deadline for restitutional claims. It was decided that the agreement would be binding until both sides agreed on another regulation or until this one was fulfilled, such fulfilment being "confirmed by both sides in a joint protocol at the appropriate time" (Article 9).

In contrast to the speedily concluded Polish-Czechoslovak agreement, the regulation of Polish-French restitution took far longer. The exchange of notes began at the end of 1945[99] but the obstacle to a final settlement was the consistent French policy of basing the implementation of restitution on specifically formulated reciprocity. A problem concerning the language of the draft agreement arose during the negotiations. The French proposed to:

> specify a basic agreement between the two countries for the restitution of the totality of French goods taken by the Germans to Poland in its present borders, in exchange for the totality of Polish goods taken by the Germans to France and the French occupation zones in Germany and Austria.[100]

---

98.   'Agreement Regarding the Mutual Return of Property between Poland and Czechoslovakia', *Journal of Laws of the Republic of Poland* 1948, No. 4, item 25.
99.   Between 2 November 1945 and 17 January 1947, Poland and France exchanged fifteen notes on the subject; ANR, records of BWRR, sign. 265, pp. 4-5. The author does not share the opinion of H. Szczerbinski regarding the 'special favour' the French showed towards Poland in this matter, expressed in H. Szczerbinski, *Restytucja mienia polskiego z zachodnich stref okupacyjnych Niemiec* [Restitution of Polish Property from the Western Occupation Zones of Germany] Warsaw 1983, p. 142 ff. It should be mentioned that the Polish Restitution Mission was allowed into the French occupation zone only in the autumn of 1947, while the negotiations on the restitutional agreement took nearly a year. Of course, there are other aspects connected with this issue.
100.   The French note of 29 October 1946 in an answer to the draft of an agreement on restitution presented by the Polish side; ANR, records of BWRR, sign. 224, p. 67.

Polish experts believed that the French also intended to include in restitution those objects which France had sold to Germany and which were subsequently shipped to Poland.[101] Eventually, the agreement was signed on 28 April 1947.[102] It included a reminder of the basic principles of restitution law valid in German territory, and, at the very beginning, it referred to the appropriate documents of the Allied Council of Control. It was then agreed that Polish restitution missions would be sent to the French occupation zones in Germany and Austria, and the outline of their work was specified. As far as restitution from Poland to France — and vice versa — was concerned, it was agreed that in both countries "restitutional work would be done by diplomatic or consular representatives, which may appoint special officials for this purpose" (Point 2).

Restitution Connected with Territorial Changes (Repatriation)

The end of World War II was marked by considerable changes in the national status of many territories in Europe. These changes had a bearing on the problem of preserving national cultural heritage in affected areas, which required a solution.

Peace Treaties of 1947
The Peace Treaty with Italy.
The Peace Treaty with Italy included clauses ceding territory to three countries; certain alterations to the border with France (Article 2), a transfer of some areas to Yugoslavia (Article 3) and a dozen or so Dodecanese Islands to Greece (Article 14). As a result of these changes a general clause on repatriation of cultural goods was formulated which was included in Appendix XIV of the Treaty, dealing with the economic and financial provisions for the ceded areas. Following this clause the Italian government pledged to hand over to the successor States:

> all objects of artistic, historic or archaeological value which belong to the cultural heritage
> of the ceded territory, and which were taken without payment during the Italian rule over
> the territory, and are now in the hands of the Italian government or Italian public institutions.

The general principle of return expressed here, based exclusively on the relationship of a given object to the national cultural heritage of the ceded area, was later broadened with respect to Yugoslavia. Article 12 of the Treaty, devoted exclusively to this issue, dealt with two types of cases, although in both of them restitution had a clear 'territorial' foundation.[103] The first part of Article 12 included provisions relating to matters which may be described as overdue — matters which had not been settled in earlier treaties.[104] It was decided that Italy would return to Yugoslavia all objects of artistic, historic, scientific, religious, etc., value, which, as a result of Italian occupation, were displaced between 14 November 1918 and 2

101.　Statements expressed at the conference on 14 January 1947 regarding the confirmation of the Polish position; ANR, records of BWRR, sign. 265, p. 2.
102.　The agreement was signed in the form of a protocol entitled: *The Polish-French Protocol Regarding the Restitution of Property Looted by the Germans*. In the files that have survived, the author of this work has found a few texts of this protocol that slightly differed from one another; ANR, records of BWRR, sign. 224, p. 71 and sign. 265, pp. 16-17. DAHD MFA, z. 10, w. 35, vol. 301 A, p. 60. These texts differ from the text quoted in Szczerbinski, above note 99 p. 170.
103.　See, Brownlie, ch. 1 above note 1 p. 462.
104.　Article 7 is similar in character, and on its basis, Italy was to give back to France "all historical and administrative archives from before 1860 that are related to the territory ceded to France under the Treaty of 24 March 1860, and the Convention of 23 August 1860".

March 1924, from the territory that (by the terms of the treaties signed in Rapallo on 12 November 1920 and in Rome on 27 January 1924) was ceded to Yugoslavia. At the same time, all objects within these categories, originating in the same territory and displaced after World War I by the Italian Armistice Mission in Vienna were also to be returned.

The second part of Article 12 dealt with more current issues; it obliged Italy to hand over to Yugoslavia all objects in the above-mentioned categories if they had been public property and were displaced "after 4 November 1918 from the territory ceded to Yugoslavia by the terms of this treaty, as well as all objects related to the territory ceded to Italy by Austria and Hungary following the Peace Treaties concluded respectively in St. Germain on 10 September 1919 and in Trianon on 4 June 1920, and the Convention between Austria and Italy signed in Vienna on 4 May 1920."

The Treaty, it should be noted, also strengthened the process of repatriation to Yugoslavia, through Italy's obligation to execute restitution in kind if necessary. In the event that Italy was unable to restitute certain objects, it would return objects "of the same kind and similar value to the ones taken, if such objects are available in Italy" (Article 12.3).

The Peace Treaty with Hungary
As a result of the territorial changes decreed in the peace treaties, Hungary was obliged to restitute three separately described sets of cultural items which originated from the areas ceded to Czechoslovakia and Yugoslavia and belonged to their national cultural heritage. These items included, *inter alia*, historical archives that were created in these two countries, libraries and relics that belonged to institutions existing in these areas or to historical personalities of the nations of Czechoslovakia and Yugoslavia, as well as original works of art, literature and science by representatives of these nations. All these cultural goods were to be returned if they had come into the possession of Hungary or Hungarian public institutions. Repatriation did not extend to original works by Hungarians or objects that had been sold, given, or endowed to Hungarians (Article 11).

Regulations resulting from the territorial changes in Eastern Europe
The border changes in Eastern Europe following World War II created situations which also require discussion and analysis in terms of the restitution of cultural goods. The borders between Poland and Germany, and between Poland and the Soviet Union were shifted, and as a result, a large number of German collections found themselves in the new Polish western and northern areas, whilst in the former eastern Polish lands given up to neighbouring Soviet republics, many items of Polish cultural heritage were left behind. This situation was entirely different from the territorial changes after the First World War; the scale and the issues were much more complex, and historically exceptional, not least because of the large-scale resettlement, for political reasons, of people whose ancestors had populated the ceded territories for centuries.

In fact, the legal situation of the goods located in the north and west of Poland was clarified quite speedily. By the decrees of 8 May 1945 on abandoned and deserted property, and of 8 March 1946 on abandoned and former German property,[105] the State treasury took over "all property of the former German Reich and Free City of Danzig, German and Danzig's natural

---

105. Decree of 8 May 1945 on Abandoned and Deserted Property, *Journal of Laws of the Republic of Poland 1945*, No. 9, item 45; Decree of 8 March 1946 on Abandoned and Former German Property, *Journal of Laws of the Republic of Poland 1946*, No. 13, item 87.

and legal persons, as well as persons who fled to the enemy". These decrees did not mention cultural goods specifically, but since their main objective was to regulate, as soon as possible after the war, the legal status of all the property in the ceded territories, they clearly extended to cultural goods. According to Nahlik, this nationalisation of German art collections was additionally justified by the "horrendous" devastation of Polish culture under Nazi occupation.[106]

Among the newly nationalised cultural items were many objects closely connected with German culture; conversely, many Polish objects could be found in East Germany. The governments of these two countries consequently attempted an exchange of at least some of these objects. The issue was pursued at diplomatic level in 1953, and talks continued for two years with no definite conclusion. The Polish side handed over 117 important paintings by various German artists to East Germany, but Polish hopes of receiving the original architectural drawings of Warsaw's buildings were dashed; "the authorities of the German Democratic Republic, in return for the works of German painters that had been handed to them, presented an electron microscope to Poland in 1954".[107] Later, there were further cases of restitution, by both Poland and the German Democratic Republic.

The history of the settlement of the cultural heritage located on the territories taken over by the USSR was quite different. Initially, the mutual repatriation of cultural goods was considered; it aimed to secure the integrity of the national cultural heritage of the Poles, Ukrainians, Belorussians and Lithuanians, despite significant border changes in the areas where they lived. The Polish-Soviet agreement on the delimitation of the new borders, however, included only strictly territorial and border provisions.[108] Other issues requiring consideration, such as the relocation of people and their property, were the subject of 'repatriation agreements' concluded in 1944, 1945 and 1946. The question of cultural goods was regulated — although only partially — in the agreements of 1944 concluded with the three Soviet Republics that had a common border with Poland. Article 3 of the Agreement between the Polish Committee of National Liberation and the government of the Belorussian Soviet Socialistic Republic of 9 September, 1944 provides an example of an appropriate clause.[109] Under this Article, evacuated people were allowed to take to their country of destination, among other things, "works of art and antiques, if they made up a collection or were individual items", provided they belonged to the family and, together with other luggage, did not weigh over the 2 tonnes permitted per family (Article 3.2 and 4). The Additional Protocol to this agreement provided that priests who were to be evacuated along with their parishes to Poland could take with them church paraphernalia and objects of worship (Point 4).[110] From these statements, it is clear that the

---

106.   S. E. Nahlik, ch. 1 above note 31 p. 296. Cultural goods were not specifically mentioned in these acts but were covered by them as "all former German property". However, these cultural goods included many objects closely connected with German culture, and since many Polish objects could be also found in the territory of East Germany, the governments of these two countries tried to exchanged them.

107.   DAHD MFA, sign.10. 48. 461, p. 113. See also the introduction to the catalogue of the exhibition of the returned paintings: *Deutsche Malerei. Freundschaftsgeschenk. Des Polnischen Volkes an das Deutsche Volk. Ausstellung,* Berlin 1954.

108.   Agreement of 27 July 1944 on the Polish-Soviet border, in *Dokumenty i materialy do historii stosunkow polsko-radzieckich* [Documents and Materials for the Study of History of Polish-Soviet Relations] Vol. 8, Warsaw 1974, p. 158.

109.   'Agreement Between the Polish Committee of National Liberation and the Government of the Belorussian Soviet Socialistic Republic Regarding the Evacuation of the Polish Population from the Territory of the BSSR and of the Belorussian Population from the Territory of Poland', Lublin, 9 September 1944 in *Dokumenty* (above note 106) p.221. See also similar agreements signed with Lithuania and the Ukraine, p. 227 ff.

110.   Additional Protocol, above note 108 p. 643.

repatriation of cultural goods was allowed in a very limited form; it included only private property of the repatriated people and certain ecclesiastical items. The number of objects permitted for repatriation was also limited by the weight restriction.

The agreements which were subsequently signed did not provide a legal basis for the relocation of cultural items. For example, according to Point 6 of the Protocol to the Agreement signed with Soviet Union on 6 July, 1945:

> persons who are leaving for Poland have a right to take with them property belonging to them whose weight does not exceed two tonnes per family from a rural area and one tonne per family from an urban area, other than objects that are not permitted to be exported from the USSR.[111]

Although the 1956 repatriation agreement did not impose weight restrictions, this had no effect on works of art owing to a general ban on their export from the USSR, which was not lifted for repatriated people.[112]

The Polish public expressed their opinion in memoranda and letters directed to the authorities: the following text is an extract from one of the numerous documents that clearly illustrate the contemporary widespread concern and discussion about this issue:

> Return of Polish cultural property that has been left in the territories of the former eastern provinces is crucial for resolving the problem of borders between Poland and the Soviet Republics. This solution, achieved by way of agreement, which should guarantee its effectiveness and durability, can only be genuine if it refers not only to the land and people living on it, but also to a common good that is public cultural property.

> When the Polish population from the former eastern provinces gains the opportunity and the right to unite with its nation by moving to central Poland and to regained ancient Polish lands, everything that documents its centuries of long spiritual unity with the rest of the nation and represents a common heritage of the whole nation — that is the Polish cultural property — should also return to our common motherland.

> This demand, which is justified regardless of the time and place, has acquired a special meaning in the light of the distinctive role Lwow [Lviv] and Wilno [Vilnius] played in the development of Polish public consciousness and national culture in the nineteenth century, because of their participation in the accumulation of an all-Polish cultural heritage.[113]

---

111.   'Protocol to the Agreement Between the Provisional Government of National Unity of the Polish Republic and the Government of the Union of Soviet Socialist Republics on the Right to Change Soviet Citizenship and to Evacuation for Persons of Polish and Jewish Nationality Living in the USSR, and the Right to Change Polish Citizenship for Persons of Russian, Ukrainian, Belorussian, Ruthenian, and Lithuanian Nationality Living in the Territory of Poland, and their Evacuation to the USSR', Moscow, July 6 1945 in *Dokumenty* (above note 108) p. 503.

112.   "Persons leaving the Union of Soviet Socialist Republics on the basis of this Agreement are allowed to take with them their personal belongings duty-free, provided their export from the Soviet Union is not prohibited" (Article 8.a.1). 'The Agreement between the Government of the Polish People's Republic and the Government of the Union of Soviet Socialist Republics Regarding the Terms and Procedure of the Further Repatriation from the USSR to Poland of Persons of Polish Nationality' in *Dokumenty* (above note 106) Vol. 11, Warsaw 1987, p. 122.

113.   ANR, records of MCA BRR, sign. 387/71, p. 17.

This broad justification was followed by more detailed arguments which referred to the national character of many cultural institutions that were now located beyond Poland's eastern borders. From the very beginning of their existence, it was assumed that they were more than local institutions, and people from all parts of Poland contributed to their establishment. An official attempt to regulate the repatriation of the totality of Polish cultural heritage, especially that part that was in the public domain, was made in 1945. The preparatory work was carried out by the Bureau of Revindication and Reparations of the Ministry of Culture and Arts, which collected the essential documentation and developed the whole policy, as well as more detailed proposals and claims. The Bureau also prepared drafts of international agreements, one of these being a draft of the agreement with the Ukrainian Soviet Socialist Republic, providing a clear illustration of the principle on which reciprocal repatriation should be based. Article 1 of the draft provided as follows:

> Ensuring the definitive regulation of the State border and mutual exchange of population between the two States, and understanding that creations of national spirit, that is, cultural values, belong to a given nation nothwithstanding their place of origin, and taking into account the large losses in the cultural heritage of Poland and the Ukrainian SSR inflicted by the German aggressor, and also willing to stress the fraternal relationship between the two nations, both parties to this agreement allow for repatriation from their territories of those cultural goods that, owing to their national character, are part of the cultural property of the other party.[114]

According to this definition, cultural goods, as described in the draft, included:
- libraries, collections of manuscripts, autographs, prints, and documents, both public and private;
- monuments and museum collections;
- masterpieces of art of a 'national' character, owing either to their authors or to their collectors;
- ethnographic, prehistoric, and natural science relics;
- foundations established to protect national cultural heritage.[115]

Ultimately, however, the agreements regulating the total relocation of national cultural heritage were not signed; talks with the Ukrainian delegation in 1946 resulted in Poland receiving only a small portion of certain collections, such as the Ossolineum Foundation, and a few individual works of art, for example, the Raclawice Battle Panorama and three monuments commemorating national heroes.[116]

Restitution In Kind

Restitution in kind of works of art was introduced to a limited extent in the Treaty of Versailles, and was the subject of considerable discussion during World War II. It was not accepted by

114. A Draft Agreement Between the Provisional Government of the National Unity of the Polish Republic and the Government of the Ukrainian Soviet Socialist Republic on the Repatriation of Polish Cultural Goods from the Territory of the Ukrainian SSR and of the Ukrainian Goods from the Territory of Poland. ARN records of MCA BRR, sign. 387/71, p. 34.
115. Article 2 of the Draft Agreement. The definitions of cultural goods to be repatriated were different in draft agreements with Lithuanian SSR and the USSR; see ARN, records of MCA BRR, sign. 387/16, p. 169, and sign. 387/71, p. 19 and 21.
116. See *Dokumenty* (above note 108) Vol. 10 and 11.

museum circles in Britain, where its application after World War I was much criticised.[117] In the United States, however, the notion of restitution in kind was more enthusiastically received, although even here, moderation was advised in the administration of collections belonging to the enemy countries:

> where possible forfeitures might be collected from objects native to the country to be compensated and the bulk of Germany's own intellectual patrimony left intact: in a hundred years the fate of a thousand factories will be forgotten but not the seizure of a single treasured relic.[118]

The huge scale of Nazi pillaging resulted in a greater acceptance of restitution in kind as a necessary element capable of supplementing regular restitution in those cases where the return of certain cultural items was impossible. A *Memorandum on the Restitution or Indemnification of Property Seized, Damaged, or Destroyed during World War II*, written and published in the United States by experts from the Council of Foreign Relations provides an example of this thinking; [119] in countering the effects of war on property the most important principle in the opinion of these experts was "justice under international law." Consequently, it was recognised that in cases where the return of property "of exceptional historical, artistic, or cultural value" was not possible, the Axis nations must substitute equivalent property of their own.[120] Opinions published in the popular press went even further: the records of the Ministry of the Congress Works of the Polish Government in Exile contain a press clipping from *The Daily Telegraph*, which reads:

> I suggest that at the end of the war an International Restitution Committee should take possession of all such [German] collections with the view to distributing their contents between the various ravaged countries. The confiscation should be sweeping, so that empty museums and galleries would be a permanent reminder to the Germans that war does not pay and a contemptuous rejection of their impudent claim to be the guardians of European culture.[121]

The first international act that touched on the issue of restitution in kind was the Resolution on the Subject of Restitution, adopted at the Reparations Conference in Paris. The representatives of Albania, Belgium, Czechoslovakia, Denmark, France, Greece, India, Luxembourg, Netherlands, and Yugoslavia decided that objects of artistic, scientific,

---

117. For comments see B. Leitgeber, *A Report on Tendencies Regarding Revindication and Compensations Dominant in Allied Circles*, London, 25 January 1943. Leitgeber interviewed, among others, Sir E. MacLagan, Director of the Victoria and Albert Museum, who was considered to be a very influential person in Britain, and who participated in "the liquidation of the Austrian Empire after World War I with regard to museums and libraries". MacLagan was said to have commented on the return of the Ghent altar panels to Belgium under the Treaty of Versailles: "Wouldn't it have been better to leave the altar in Berlin, where it was well maintained and displayed to the public, than to place it back in the dark of a church in a small Belgian town, where it wasn't even prevented from being stolen?" ARN, records of MCA RP, sign. 208, p. 1. A sceptical opinion about restitution in kind was also expressed in a letter to the author from Col. C. Norris, a former British Army MFA&A officer.
118. D. Rigby, 'Cultural Reparations and a New Western Tradition', *The American Scholar* 1944, Vol. 13, p. 284.
119. 'A Memorandum on the Restitution or Indemnification of Property Seized, Damaged, or Destroyed during World War II', drafted by the Study Group of the Council of Foreign Relations in *The Postwar Settlement of Property Rights*, New York 1945, p. 1. It may be interesting to add that at that time, Allen Dulles was the Council's vice-president.
120. *Ibid*, p. 2.
121. A letter to the editor from A.E. Russel, published in *The Daily Telegraph* 16 March 1943; ANR, records of MCA RP, sign. 97, p. 118.

educational, and religious character, including books, manuscripts, and documents that had been pillaged by the enemy "shall as far as possible, be replaced by equivalent objects if they are not restored."[122]

Subsequently, the nature and process of restitution in kind varied widely, depending on the territory on which it was to be effected. It was included in most peace treaties, but it was never definitively regulated in the territory of occupied Germany. It is therefore worth examining the peace treaties in the context of the issue of restitution in kind.

The 1947 Peace Treaties

Clauses concerning restitution in kind were incorporated in the peace treaties concluded with Italy, Bulgaria, and Hungary. In each of these treaties, the clauses were phrased identically, encapsulating the formula that: if in an individual case, Italy/Bulgaria/Hungary could not restitute objects of artistic, historic or archaeological value, that belonged to the cultural heritage of one of the Allied Nations, from whose territory the given objects had been taken by the armed forces, authorities, or Italian/Bulgarian/Hungarian citizens, by force or duress, Italy/Bulgaria/Hungary would be obliged to give to the concerned Allied Nation state objects of the same kind and more or less the same value as the objects taken, if Italy/Bulgaria/Hungary could provide such objects.[123]

There are two important constraints in this formula for restitution; first of all, the equivalent object was to be provided not for every irrevocably lost cultural item, but only for those which constituted a part of the cultural heritage of the victim nation. Secondly, the obligation of restitution in kind was to be fulfilled only if it was possible to provide an equivalent object; this equivalence was not precisely defined.

Restitution in kind under the restitution law in force for the territory of Germany

Initially, it seemed natural to include restitution in kind in the first stage of a quadripartite restitutional law. There was an explicit provision for this in the definition of restitution accepted on 21 January 1946 by the Allied Control Council. According to that document, restitution was to cover a wide range of goods "of a unique character", if their return was impossible. It described "the categories of goods which will be subject to replacement, the nature of these replacements, and the conditions under which such goods could be replaced by equivalent objects."[124] Publication of the instruction was delayed and the most devastated nations became concerned; the Polish delegation referred to their worries in a memorandum, presented at the conference of deputy ministers of foreign affairs in London in January 1947, which included, *inter alia*, the following demand:

> independently of the total sum of compensations for war devastation, Germany should also cover the Polish losses in the field of culture and science. These losses should be compensated by the allocation of objects of equivalent value, which may contribute to

---

122. 'Final Act and Annex of the Paris Conference on Reparation. Annex 1: Resolution on the subject of restitution'; J. Howard, *The Paris Agreement on Reparation from Germany*, U.S. Government Printing Office 1946, p. 19. See Annex 4.
123. Article 75.9 of the Peace Treaty with Italy, Article 22.3 of the Peace Treaty with Bulgaria, and Article 24.3 of the Peace Treaty with Hungary. The Peace Treaty with Italy also includes the special clause on restitution in kind with regard to Yugoslavia (Article 12.3).
124. "Series of Documents" 1946, No. 9, p. 277. See Annex 5.

the reconstruction of these losses. According to the Allied Nations 1943 Declaration and the Potsdam Agreement, all property that was present in the territory of Poland (and areas incorporated into it under the Potsdam Resolutions) and taken to Germany during the war should be returned to Poland. If such restitution turns out to be impossible, Poland should be provided with objects of the same sort and value.[125]

Meanwhile, the principle of restitution in kind found its way into the peace treaties discussed earlier. According to Nahlik, since restitution in kind was applicable to the Third Reich's allies, it should also apply to Germany itself, and the obligations of the allies should be the "lower limit of the German burden."[126]

Eventually, the long-awaited Instruction regulating the procedural details of restitution in kind was accepted by the Council's forum on 25 February 1947.[127] The Instruction provided for the possibility of claiming the equivalent for the following cultural goods "the location of which cannot be traced":

- artistic works by great masters including paintings, sketchings and sculptures;
- the most outstanding works of masters of applied arts and outstanding anonymous examples of national art;
- historical relics of all sorts;
- manuscripts, books (such as rare *incunabula*), books of a historic character or of great value, or books that are unique, even if modern;
- objects important for the history of science.

The text of the document was sent to the restitution missions on 25 April 1947, and a detailed instruction for official use in Poland was ready by September of that year. It was drafted by the Ministry of Shipping and Foreign Trade,[128] and included a directive concerning the preparation of Polish claims to the effect that if all the losses of artistic paintings and sculptures suffered during war and occupation of the Polish territory by the German armed forces could not be compensated by the return of the specific individual works, then they should be covered by the return of the same number of objects:

- by the same artists,
- by artists of the same country and school,
- by artists of the same period as the works destroyed or lost.

As far as library collections were concerned, the Polish losses should be covered in the form of the return of:

- relevant specific works, classified according to library catalogues,

---

125. These were Demands 15 and 16 of the Memorandum of the Polish Government regarding the Peace Treaty with Germany, presented at the meeting of deputy ministers of foreign affairs in London, January 1947; DAHD MFA, z. 10, w. 23, t. 207, p. 56. Also see "Series of Documents" 1947, No. 1-3, p. 45 ff. On the ambiguity of the text see S.E. Nahlik, ch. 1 above note 31 p. 295.
126. S.E. Nahlik, ch. 1 above note 31 p. 295.
127. Document: CORC/M/46/34. Annex "A"; ARN, records of BWRR, sign. 276, p. 87 and sign. 244, p. 71. For the full text see Annex 6.
128. 'Forms of Indemnities for War Losses other than Compensation: Restitution In Kind', (Document drafted by T. Gliwic, Head of a Department in the Ministry of Shipping and Foreign Trade, 25 September 1947; ANR, records of MCA BRR, sign. 387/60, pp. 3-10 and 35.

- where these works were not available, by the return of newer works on the same subject, in the same language, or in another language, as chosen by the Polish side,
- Polish language works reprinted by Germany were to replace the destroyed Polish publications, at the expense of Germany and with the use of its technical facilities.

The Polish authorities placed a detailed claim for restitution in kind with the U.S. Forces of Occupation on 15 September 1948. This included a suggestion for delivering to Poland 117 works of art, mainly from the Munich collections, a large number of which were works connected in some way with Poland.[129] The claim, however, was never met, and no restitution in kind from the German collections has been ever made. The note was returned to Poland within a week with the following explanation: "Although quadripartite agreement was made for restitution in kind, no action was taken by this office to implement such a plan."[130]

It seems likely that the main reason for this refusal was the change in the United States' policy towards Germany, which manifested itself, *inter alia*, in a new directive from the Joint Chiefs of Staff for the Commander-in-Chief of the U.S. Armed Forces in Germany; the new directive of 11 July 1947 included the following statement:

> You will not consent to any extensive program for replacement of looted or displaced property which has been destroyed or cannot be located whenever such replacement can be accomplished only at the expense of ... the cultural heritage of the German people.[131]

This new position was partly based on the opinion of the Roberts Commission, which wrote in its resolution that "cultural objects belonging to any country or individual should not be considered or involved in reparations settlements growing out of World War II."[132] The official justification for this policy referred directly to the concept of protecting the integrity of national cultural heritage. The Department of State declared that "the policy of the United States is one of respect for artistic and historic property of all nations."

In addition to the Department of State's opinion, restitution in kind was also barred by the international obligations of the United States following the Hague regulations and the Roerich Treaty.[133] Although these were the official reasons it is clear that the real reason for not implementing the programme of restitution in kind was to a large extent due to more practical difficulties. These were explained in a report by R. Howard of the U.S. Occupation Administration, who was responsible for these matters:

129. ANR, records of MCA BRR, sign. 387/60, pp. 3-10 and 35.
130. *Ibid*, p. 35.
131. Text of directive to Commander-in-Chief of US Forces of Occupation, regarding the Military Government of Germany. JCS 1779, 11 July 1947. *The Department of State Bulletin* 1947, Vol. 17, No. 421, July 27, p. 190.
132. 'Resolution of the American Commission for the Protection and Salvage of Artistic and Historic Monuments in War Areas, 20 June 1946'. *College Art Journal* 1951, Vol. 11, No. 1, p. 34. For details of actions taken by the Roberts Commission see W. Kowalski, above note 3 p. 31.
133. 'US seeks to replace cultural property displaced during World War II', *The Department of State Bulletin* 1951, Vol. 25, No. 635, August 27, p. 345. The treaty for the protection of art and science institutions and historic monuments, signed in Washington on 15 April 1935, *The Department of State Bulletin* 1935, No. 67, 30 April, p. 55. This treaty is known as the Roerich treaty in the literature. The above-mentioned declaration of the Department of State referred to Article II of the Treaty is quoted it in its totality: "The neutrality of, and protection and respect due to, the monuments and institutions mentioned in the preceding article shall be recognised in the entire expanse of territories subject to the sovereignty of each of the signatory and acceding States, without discrimination as to the State allegiance of the said monuments and institutions. The respective Governments agree to adopt the measures of internal legislation necessary to insure said protection and respects."

This principle [replacement or restitution-in-kind] was agreed upon in the European Advisory Commission in 1944 and was vaguely reiterated in the Allied Control Authority definition of restitution. Upon the theory, however, that two wrongs do not make a right, this Headquarters has consistently refused to take steps to implement this general agreement. Also it is believed that it would be impossible to do so without the pooling of information and of available valuable German works of art throughout the four zones. Here again the Soviet removals from their zone gravely affect even a consideration of the problem. It is believed the entire matter should be forgotten.[134]

The question of restitution in kind was also to be raised at a conference summoned specially for this purpose in Paris on 23 to 25 October 1948.[135] Owing to a late notification from the Polish embassy in Paris, representatives of the Ministry of Culture arrived in France after the conference had ended. At the conference, delegates from Austria, Belgium, Denmark, France, Greece, Hungary, Italy, Luxembourg, the Netherlands, Norway, and Yugoslavia drafted a note to the governments of the United States and Great Britain, in which they raised both the question of the deadlines for restitution and the gradual liquidation of the organisational structures that dealt with the examination of claims. The problem of restitution in kind was ignored altogether. As a result, Poland declined France's invitation to join the signatories of the note, stating that:

In the opinion of the Government of Poland, the note drafted at the conference on 25 October 1948 by the representatives of the States concerned without participation of a delegate of the Polish Government, does not comply with the interests of the countries injured by Germany, especially Poland, as it completely disregards the very important question of restitution in kind. The execution of resolutions of the Allied Control Council concerning restitution in kind in the area of cultural goods is regarded by the government of Poland as an extremely important problem requiring a swift solution, and cannot be neglected in the note drafted by the participants of the conference.

The Government of Poland feels compelled also to express its surprise at the fact that the conference included in the draft note the statement that *'sur le plan juridique, on ne peut pas opposer une date de forclusion à ces demandes de restitution.'* In the opinion of the Government of Poland, this statement is contradictory to the contents of the Declaration of 5 January 1943, and to the resolutions of the Allied Control Council which do not provide for any limitations in cases concerning the restitution of property looted by Germany.

The Government of Poland stresses its readiness to participate in any action of the nations which, according to the international regulations, will lead to the enforcement of effective means for the restitution of property stolen by Germany. The Government of Poland would appreciate an explanation as to whether the conference will deal with the question of restitution in kind, and a confirmation that the conference's purpose is the complet fulfilment of obligations of the American and British authorities in Germany towards the countries that suffered the looting of their cultural goods.[136]

---

134. M.J. Kurtz, *Nazi Contraband. American Policy on the Return of European Cultural Treasures, 1945-1955,* New York-London 1985, p. 150.
135. The documentation secured by the Department of Archives and Historical Documentation of the Ministry of Foreign Affairs does not provide a clear account of the proceedings and results of the conference see DAHD MFA, z. 10, w. 33, t. 289. The French Foreign Ministry has not answered the author's letter regarding the conference.
136. Answer to the note from the French Ministry of Foreign Affairs of 25 October 1948, regarding the restitution of cultural goods. Document of 8 March 1949. DAHD MFA, z. 10, w. 33, t. 289, p. 327.

This note had no effect; the conference did not continue, and thus the question of restitution in kind at the forum of the Allied countries was closed.

Restitution to Germany and Austria and the Former Axis Countries

The policy of respect for the national cultural heritage of all nations declared by the United States Government also justified the obligation for restitution of cultural items belonging to the enemy countries which, in various circumstances, were taken from their territories during the war. Certain large and well known museum collections were taken by the Allied armies which entered Germany; in most cases the main reason given was the need to protect these collections against destruction and dispersal. In this way, a collection of over 200 major paintings from the Kaiser Friedrich Museum in Berlin, found in South Germany, was shipped to the United States under custody of the National Gallery in Washington, while the Dresden Gallery collection, including the treasures of the Grunes Gewolbe, was taken to the Soviet Union. These actions, although justified to some extent, aroused doubts and even some protests in American museum and scientific circles. Despite the publication of an official explanation by the White House on 27 September 1945, which declared that the paintings had been shipped to the United States "with the sole intention of keeping such treasures safe and in trust for the people of Germany or the other rightful owners",[137] various associations and groups published letters and resolutions opposing the retention of German collections.[138] A separate issue which emerged was the private export of works of art from Germany carried out on a considerable scale by U.S. soldiers on demobilisation or whilst on leave. As a result of this process, a great many museum pieces from German collections, as well as objects that had come from Nazi looting, were shipped across the Atlantic Ocean.[139]

---

137. 'Removal of German art objects to the United States', *The Department of State Bulletin* 1945, Vol. 13, No. 327, 30 September, p. 499. See K. Lindsay, *op. cit.* note 43.

138. A selection of these texts was published by T. Howe, *Salt Mines and Castles. The Discovery and Restitution of Looted European Art*, Indianapolis-New York 1946, p. 301 ff. Perhaps the most significant was the letter which the MFA&A officers assigned to the Central Collecting Point in Wiesbaden sent to their authorities on 7 November 1945. In this letter, called later 'Wiesbaden Manifesto', the officers considered it proper to inform their superiors about their attitude towards the removal of German art collections to the United States. The letter referred to similar German actions in the occupied territories, supposedly undertaken in order to protect the works of art, which in fact were nothing else but ordinary looting. It ended with the following statement: "We wish to state that from our knowledge, no historical grievance will rankle so long, or be the cause of so much justified bitterness, as the removal, for any reason, of a part of the heritage of any nation, even if that heritage be interpreted as a prize of war. And though this removal may be done with every intention of altruism, we are none the less convinced that it is our duty, individually and collectively, to protest against it, and that though our obligations are to the nation to which we owe allegiance, there are yet further obligations to common justice, decency, and the establishment of the power of right, not might, among civilised nations." *Ibid*, p. 275. See also recent comments on the *Wiesbaden Manifesto* and on its author, Walter Farmer, *The Economist*, 23 August 1997, p. 75.

139. B. Ratchford and W. Ross describe these practices in their report from Berlin. They wrote, *inter alia*, about a certain woman, a U.S. corporal, who had bought a large antique grandfather clock and then was "bitterly disappointed when the postal authorities told her it was too large for shipment by parcel post": B. Ratchford and W. Ross, *Berlin Reparation Assignment*, Richmond 1947, p. 17. Among the works of art shipped to the United States in this way were many objects that had been looted, a matter about which the Polish Ministry of Culture and Art was being informed; see ANR, records of MCA BRR, sign. 387/54, p. 55, sign. 387/190, p. 82, sign. 387/184, p. 429 ff.

Moves to carry out the restitution of these objects began in 1947 with the publication of an official memorandum entitled: *Return of Looted Objects of Art to Countries of Origin.*[140] It stated that bringing to the United States works of art that had been looted was contrary to the general policy of the United States and infringed the Hague Convention of 1907, and in the case of objects whose value exceeded five thousand dollars, also infringed the Federal Law. The Memorandum called for a number of steps to be taken in order to find and return cultural goods to their countries of origin. If disclosed objects came from Germany, Austria, Japan, or Korea, they would be handed over to the U.S. Military Authorities in those countries. These measures produced some results, and in the case of more important works, the restitution attracted much publicity.[141] In addition, museum objects from collections that came from the Soviet Zone, and later, from the German Democratic Republic, were returned to West Germany. To fulfil, at least formally, the principle of return to the place of origin, the 1966 agreement with the Federal Republic of Germany concerning the return of three paintings from the Weimar collections included the following statements:

1. The Federal Republic of Germany shall hold the paintings in trust for eventual transfer to the Weimar Museum on the same basis as such paintings were held by the Museum prior to 18 April 1922. The Federal Republic shall determine when conditions are appropriate for the transfer of the three paintings to the Weimar Museum. ...

2. Until the transfer is made, the Federal Republic shall hold, care for and safeguard the three paintings in the same way as it would art treasures of its own.[142]

It was only after the official recognition of the German Democratic Republic by the United States government that the New York courts could adjudicate the case of another two paintings from the same collection in favour of their rightful owner — *Kunstsammlungen zu Weimar* in East Germany.[143]

The restitution of the works of art taken to the United States for their protection took place in 1949,[144] and four years later, an agreement was signed to return to Germany library collections as well as historic immovables in Rome, such as the libraries of German scientific institutes in Italy, the collection of *Bibliotheca Herziana*, and *Palazzo Zuccari*. On the basis of the agreement signed on 20 April 1953 by France, the United States, Great Britain, Italy, and the Federal Republic of Germany,[145] these works of art were returned to their owners on the condition

---

140. 'Return of Looted Objects of Art to Countries of Origin. Memorandum by the State Department', *The Department of State Bulletin* 1947, Vol. 16, No. 399, 23 February, p. 358 ff.

141. See for example: 'Exhibition in Germany of the Returned Collection of Berlin Paintings', *The Department of State Bulletin* 1949, Vol. 21, No. 543, 28 November, p. 809 ff; 'Rare Mainz Psalter of 1457, Looted, Returned to US Zone in Germany', *The Department of State Bulletin*, 1950, Vol. 22, No. 560, March 27, p. 487; 'Mainz Exhibiting Treasured Psalter', *The Department of State Bulletin*, 1950, Vol. 23, No. 582, August 28, p. 349.

142. Transfer of Certain Paintings for the Weimar. Agreement effected by exchange of notes, signed at Washington 9 and 16 December 1966; entered into force 16 December 1966, in *United States Treaties and Other International Agreements,* Vol. 17, Washington 1968, Part 2, p. 2279. On the basis of this agreement, the Federal Republic of Germany was handed three paintings: *Self Portrait* by Rembrandt, *Portrait of A Man* by Terborch, and *Portrait of A Young Woman* by Tischbein.

143. These were two paintings by Dürer, which were the subject of a lawsuit before the New York court between 1966 and 1981. *Kunstsammlungen zu Weimar v. Elicofon* 678.F.2d 1150 (2nd Cir.) (1982). It should be noted that such cases of restitution still occur today.

144. 'Recovery of Lost European Treasures', *Department of State, The Record,* May-June 1951, Vol. 7, No. 3, p. 39 ff.

145. Agreement between the Governments of the French Republic, United Kingdom, United States of America, the Italian Republic and the Federal Republic of Germany, relating to certain libraries and properties in Italy signed at Rome, 30 April 1953 in *United States Treaties and Other International Agreements*, Vol. 4, Washington 1955, part 2, p. 377-378.

that the libraries would remain in Italy and become international scientific centres to which representatives of all nations would have access. The Italian Government promised to provide the privileges and rights that the libraries had enjoyed before the war.

A number of museum collections taken from Germany in 1945 were also returned by the Soviet Union. This followed a number of protocols of transfer concluded between 1953 and 1958; the restitution of the most precious collections took place in 1955 when the Dresden Gallery was returned and in 1958 when the collection from Grunes Gewolbe was returned to Dresden.[146]

The process of restitution to Austria and the Axis countries at the end of the war first of all required the recognition and denouncement of the seizure of property carried out by Nazis at the end of the war. The rights of these countries and their citizens were recognised in the State Treaty with Austria and in peace treaties concluded in 1947.[147] The moment that the treaties came into force, the property of the Axis countries and their citizens which was in Germany ceased to be treated as enemy property, and all restrictions and constraints regarding it were suspended. At the same time it was decided that restitution would be effected according to Allied Restitutional Law, if, in relation to the property in question, its seizure and transfer to Germany qualified it to be returned according to the provisions of that law.[148] Detailed decisions on this matter were published by the U.S. military authorities in Memorandum No. 6 of 28 May 1947.[149] This document provided for the restitution of any property from the territories of the former enemy states (also called Non-Allied Nations, to indicate the inclusion of States other than those with which peace treaties were signed) which could be identified as seized by force or without appropriate compensation between:

- 25 July 1943 and 15 May 1945 from Albania,
- 12 March 1938 and 15 May 1945 from Austria,
- 2 September 1944 and 15 May 1945 from Bulgaria,
- 2 September 1944 and 15 May 1945 from Finland,
- 15 October 1944 and 15 May 1945 from Hungary,
- 25 July 1943 and 15 May 1945 from Italy,
- 23 August 1944 and 15 May 1945 from Romania.

It should be noted that the regulations of Memorandum No. 6, which covered the Austrian property, dated back to the period before the signing of the State Treaty.

The provisions discussed in the Memorandum included special regulation of the legal situation of cultural property. It was decided that 'valuable art objects' belonging to refugees who took them while fleeing from their countries for religious or racial reasons would not be subject to

---

146.   'Abschlussprotocoll uber die Ubergabe der Gemalde der Dresdner Galerie durch die Sowjetunion und deren Ubernahme durch die DDR', 27.11.1955, in,. Bd. 4. Berlin 1954-1959, p. 51; 'Protokoll uber die Ubergabe der Kulturguter des "Grunen Gewolbes", die sich zeitweilig zur Aufbewahrung in der UdSSR befanden, an die DDR', 28.11.1958, in *Dokumente* (above note 106) Bd. 6, p. 469. See also R. and M. Seydewitz, *Die Dresdner Kunstschatze. Zur Geschichte des "Grunen Gewolbes" und der anderen Dresdner Kunstsammlungen,* Dresden 1960, especially p. 121 ff.
147.   These were treaties with Bulgaria, Finland, Hungary, Italy, and Romania.
148.   See Article 26 of the peace treaty with Bulgaria, Article 28 of the peace treaty with Finland, Article 30 of the peace treaty with Hungary, Article 77 of the peace treaty with Italy, and Article 28 of the peace treaty with Romania.
149.   Memorandum No. 6. Subject: Restitution to Ex-Enemy (Non-United) Nations, 28 May 1947. The discussion of this document is based on the text published in I. Vasarhelyi, ch. 1 above note 9 p. 128.

restitution if the refugees decided not to return home.[150] In Point 10 of the Memorandum, it was resolved that cultural items, in the broad meaning of the term, would be returned to the relevant governments not only if they had been taken from the listed countries within the dates provided above, but also if they had been "acquired in any way, whether through commercial transactions or otherwise", subject to identification.[151] This regulation, which was already in force in 1947, deserves emphasis as it facilitated the restitution of works of art to the enemy countries to a far greater extent than to the Allied Nations. The introduction of the general principle of the return of objects "acquired in any way, whether through commercial transactions or otherwise", meant removing the criterion of 'force or duress', which was a necessary condition in the case of restitution to, for example, Poland. The criterion of 'normal commercial transaction' was not used until 1948 in the case of Poland, and it was formulated in a more complex and exacting manner than Point 10 of the Memorandum.[152]

In concluding the discussion of restitution to the former Axis countries, the complications resulting from 'official' or private transfers of certain works of art from Germany to the United States should be noted; these included some objects from the former Axis countries. One of the most famous cases was the case of Hungarian regalia, taken over by the U.S. armed forces from Hungarian refugees in Germany in 1945 and kept by the U.S. Government until they were returned to the Hungarian government on 6 January 1978.[153]

---

150. Point 3 of the Memorandum.
151. Point 10 of the Memorandum. The complete text of this regulation is as follows: "Works of art and cultural works of either religious, artistic, documentary, scholastic, or historic value, including recognised works of art, as well as such objects as rare musical instruments, books and manuscripts, scientific documents of a historic or cultural nature, and all objects usually found in museums, collections, libraries, and historic archives shall be restored to the government of the country from which such property was taken or acquired in any way, whether through commercial transactions or otherwise, provided the requirement of paragraph 2a and c above are met." The regulations mentioned at the end of this text regard the requirement of identification (para. 2a) and the dates of removal (para. 2c).
152. See remarks on the application of the 'normal commercial transaction' criterion in the process of examining Poland's restitutional claims under title *The Principle or 'Force and Duress'* in ch. 3 of this work.
153. On this case read T.C. Howe, above note 136 p. 288; J.J. Rorimer and G. Rabin, *Survival. The Salvage and Protection of Art in War,* New York 1950, p. 154. The Department of State claimed that St. Stephen's Crown was stored in the United States "as property of a special status". 'U.S. seeks to replace Cultural Property Displaced during World War II', The Department of State Bulletin 1959, Vol. 25, No. 635; p. 345. E. Kovacs, Z. Loveg, *The Hungarian Crown and Other Regalia,* Budapest 1980, p. 16.

CHAPTER IV

CONCLUSIONS AND FURTHER DEVELOPMENTS

The concepts of '*restitutio in integrum*' and 'restitution' have featured in legal thinking since the development of Roman Law. Although the terms have been used in many different contexts, they have, to this day, maintained their original meaning — the restoration of the previous state of affairs. Within current international law, the phrase *restitutio in integrum* defines the objective of the State's responsibility; each violation of an interest of another subject creates the obligation to restore the situation to the *status quo ante*. For the elimination of the material effects of war, the aim thus defined can be achieved through restitution and reparations.

The most common areas of restitution are:

- the return of property looted during military operations or during the occupation of a territory;
- the restoration of property, rights, and interests seized as enemy property;
- the handing over to the wronged state a certain number of equivalent objects that compensate for losses defined individually (restitution in kind);
- restitution (repatriation) of cultural heritage in connection with territorial changes, such as the ceding of territory or dissolution of multi-national States.
  Another area of restitution is the specific case of the distribution of reclaimed goods among the wronged States, especially when the explicit place of origin of an individual object cannot be identified (restitution by distribution).

A common feature of all of the above forms of restitution is the tendency to a complete or almost complete restoration of the *status quo ante*. This is possible either directly, that is by the return of the looted objects and the restoration of the property, rights, and interests seized, or indirectly, by the handing over of an object identical with the one lost (e.g. gold for gold), or similar (e.g. one painting by the same master or from the same school of painting for another one). Restitution must be distinguished from reparations; to achieve the aim of *restitutio in integrum*, the indirect method is employed, compensating for the loss only in an approximate manner. It is usually accomplished by handing over goods or money of equivalent value.

The works of Jakub Przyluski, Hugo Grotius, Georg Friedrich Martens, John Locke, Emer de Vattel and other philosophers and writers make clear that although looting and pillaging during war was condemned centuries ago, legal restrictions on such activities have been only slowly and reluctantly implemented. The first mention of the obligation to refrain from looting works of art comes from the Middle Ages, where it mainly covered ecclesiastical objects, and had religious backing. In the Renaissance, regard for beauty led to calls for sparing the works of great artists. Subsequently, purely logical reasons appeared; destruction and looting was recognised as nonsense, because it had little or no effect on the belligerents. Through time, a ban on looting works of art became customary in international law, and eventually, found its way into regulations of the codified law of war. The obligation of the restitution of a looted work of art correlates with the ban on pillaging. As early as the nineteenth century, it was based on the principle of identification, which provided for the return of exactly the same and only the same objects which had been removed, as well as on the principle of territoriality, according to which an item is returned to the place from which it was taken. In many cases, when claims were examined, the period of time that had passed since the loss of the object was not taken into account.

From the beginning of the nineteenth century, claims relating to cultural heritage emerged, indicating the development of the principle of the special territorial bonds attaching to works of art, which had previously applied only to archives. This principle is connected with the protection of the integrity of national cultural heritage, and has increasingly influenced both bilateral and multilateral international agreements.

All the principles relating to the restitution of works of art were fully recognised and developed in the peace treaties signed after World War I.

The requirements for restitution became especially difficult in the face of the range and scale of works of art plundered during World War II. The restitution law enforced after the War's conclusion included new elements and a number of very detailed regulations. Restitution as performed in the territories of Germany and Austria was limited initially to the return of the works of art that had been removed by Nazis from the occupied areas. The Allied authorities introduced a restitution law that was based on the following principles:

- Restitution had a public-legal character, and was performed exclusively by specialised services of the Allied occupational armies and foreign restitutional missions representing the wronged States.

- Only those objects that were proved to have been looted were subject to return. The identification process was facilitated by the fact that there was a total ban on the art trade in the territory of occupied Germany, and Germans were obliged to declare all objects which were likely to be subject to return.

- A necessary condition for restitution was the need to establish that a given object had been taken 'by force' or 'under duress', in the broad meaning of these terms. To clarify this issue, in 1948, a new criterion was introduced providing that a given object was exempt from restitution only if it was proved to have been purchased by means of a 'normal commercial transaction'.

- All items that had been removed from a given territory were subject to restitution, regardless of who owned or held such items at the moment of seizure.

The Allied Restitution Law represents a very important step in the development of the restitution of looted cultural goods as a norm in international law. Never before had the rules and procedures been so elaborate and detailed, and so widely used in practice. For the first time in history, restitution covered neutral States, where special regulations removed the protection of a good-faith purchaser in order to provide a more efficient implementation of the claims of wronged persons.

At first, the restitution law that was adopted in Germany provided for restitution in kind in the case of cultural goods that could not be returned. However, this was never applied in practice on the basis that the principle of the protection of the integrity of the cultural heritage also had to be implemented in the case of Germany and its former allies; that was at least the official line used for the final refusal to undertake restitution in kind and cultural reparations which had been expected by several Allied nations, at the expense of the German cultural heritage. Resolutions regarding this issue were included in the peace treaties of 1947.

The same principle should have governed the regulations resulting from the 1944 territorial changes. It must be stressed however, that there was a considerable difference between the changes that took place after World War I and those which followed World War II. After the First World War the interested nations focused on the repatriation of cultural goods which had been removed from their territories, in some cases even from a period before they were ceded. After the Second World War, on the other hand, the whole issue was much more complicated, and in fact, historically exceptional due to the resettlement of large numbers of people away from their homelands, where they had lived for centuries. The decisive rule applied in this situation was the principle of recognising a territorial link with the cultural heritage; repatriation of cultural items was limited only to certain private property and a small number of other objects of special interest and significance.

Another form of restitution discussed in this work — restitution by distribution — was not introduced in the field of cultural property although the scale of looting, and the post-war conditions in Europe might well have justified it. Delegates to the Conference of Allied Ministers of Education as well as MFA&A Officers and officers from national allied restitution missions were fully aware of the problems surrounding items whose rightful owners, and often even countries of origin, could not be identified. The first proposal aimed at resolving the problem, namely a project to create a 'Common Exchange Museum' which would hold all cultural goods of unknown origin for the benefit of all nations who suffered during this war, was submitted to the American authorities at the end of 1942. However this idea was not accepted and the question was left open for many years; it remains a source of debate today.[1]

Following World War II, the restitution principle entered a new phase of development, and in 1954, became a treaty standard. Although it did not feature in the Convention for the Protection of Cultural Property in the Event of Armed Conflict,[2] it did appear in a Protocol signed on the same day as the Convention.[3] This Protocol included the following resolutions:

1.　Each High Contracting Party undertakes to prevent the exportation, from a territory occupied by it during an armed conflict, of cultural property as defined in Article 1 of the Convention for the Protection of Cultural Property in the Event of Armed Conflict, signed at The Hague on 14 May 1954.

1.　　The project was prepared by Charles Estreicher and presented to governmental bodies as well as to several scientific organisations during his visit to USA at the close of 1942 and early 1943. He suggested the creation of a 'Common Exchange Museum' keeping all works of art and other cultural property of unknown provenance found after the war on the territories of Germany, Japan and Italy. According to his plan, approximately every ten years, this museum should travel from one European city to another. The crucial idea behind this concept was a kind of indirect and symbolic return of the cultural goods to countries that had most probably lost them. For more details see W. Kowalski, *Liquidation of the Effects of World War II in the Area of Culture,* Warsaw 1994, p. 44.

2.　　Convention for the Protection of Cultural Property in the Event of Armed Conflict. 249 U.N.T.S., 1956, p. 240. The proceedings of The Hague Conference and the text of the Convention was keenly described by one of Conference's participants: Nahlik, ch. 1 above note 31 p.339; see also 'International Law and the Protection of Cultural Property in Armed Conflicts', *Hastings Law Journal* 1976, Vol. 27, p. 1069, and more recent studies by P.J. Boylan, *Review of the Convention for the Protection of Cultural Property in the Event of Armed Conflict* [The Hague Convention of 1954] UNESCO 1993, and by J. Toman, *La protection des biens culturels en cas de conflit armé. Commentaire de la Convention de la Haye du 14 mai 1954,* Paris 1994. The necessity to update this law was stressed also by Williams, ch. 3 above note 11 p. 46.

3.　　Writing about the exclusion of the restitution issues to the Protocol, Nahlik is right in commenting that: "If one looks at the long tradition which the restitution problem boasts, (unlike all other problems pertaining to the international protection of cultural property) the least one can say that it was not given fair treatment"; 'On Some Deficiencies of the Hague Convention of 1954 on the Protection of Cultural Property in the Event of Armed Conflict', *Yearbook of the AAA* 1974, Vol. 44, p. 100.

2. Each High Contracting Party undertakes to take into its custody cultural property imported into its territory either directly or indirectly from any occupied territory. This shall either be effected automatically upon the importation of the property or, failing this, at the request of the authorities of the territory.

3. Each High Contracting Party undertakes to return, at the close of hostilities, to the competent authorities of the territory previously occupied, cultural property which is in its territory, if such property has been exported in contravention of the principle laid down in the first paragraph. Such property shall never be retained as war reparations.

4. The High Contracting Party whose obligation it was to prevent the exportation of cultural property from the territory occupied by it, shall pay indemnity to the holders in good faith of any cultural property which has to be returned in accordance with the preceding paragraph.

5. Cultural property coming from the territory of a High Contracting Party and deposited by it in the territory of another High Contracting Party for the purpose of protecting such property against the dangers of an armed conflict, shall be returned by the latter, at the end of hostilities, to the competent authorities of the territory from which it came.

These resolutions did not conclude the process of regulating restitutional issues. Since the early 1970s, restitution has received more attention in the international arena, and the wartime aspect has become only an element of a wider problem, generally defined as the return of cultural goods to the country of their origin. It was mentioned in two resolutions of the General Assembly of the United Nations,[4] following which the work on its application was ceded to UNESCO. In 1978, at the Twentieth General Conference of UNESCO, a resolution was passed creating a special inter-governmental committee to work out forms and procedures, in the most general terms, to promote the return of works of art removed during colonial periods and in wartime, as well as in peacetime through illicit export. [5] The Committee undertook work on various aspects of restitution believing that:

> The reassembly of dispersed heritage through restitution or return of objects which are of major importance for the cultural identity and history of the countries having been deprived thereof is now considered to be an ethical principle recognised and affirmed by the major international organisations. This principle will soon become an element of *jus cogens* of international relations.[6]

One of the results of the UNESCO Committee, was the creation of the Standard Form Concerning Request for Return or Restitution, which is also to be used for filing a claim for cultural goods looted during the occupation of a foreign territory.[7]

---

4. They both had the same title: 'Resolution on the Restitution of Works of Art to Countries Victim to Expropriation'. The first was passed in 1973 (doc.: A/RES/3187/XXVIII), the second in 1975 (doc.: A/RES/3391/XXX). See also on this subject: D. Schulze, *The Restitution of Works of Art. On the International Legal Dimensions of Restitution: Resolutions Passed by the General Assembly of the United Nations,* Bremen 1983.

5. Inter-governmental Committee for Promoting the Return of Cultural Property to its Countries of Origin or its Restitution in Case of Illicit Appropriation. The Committee was created on the initiative of the Director General of UNESCO during the 20th General Conference of this organisation (doc.: 20 C/86.). On the work of the Committee see: P.J. O'Keefe, and L. Prott, *Law and the Cultural Heritage,* Vol. 3, *Movement,* London 1989, p. 855 ff.

6. One of the suggestions included in the study on the problem, prepared by the International Council of Museums for UNESCO (Doc.: CC-78/CON/609/3 Annex I, p.11).

7. Guidelines for the use of the 'Standard Form Concerning Request for Return or Restitution', Doc.: CC-86/WS/3, p. 11.

In practical terms the question of restitution emerged on a wider scale in connection with political changes in Central and Eastern Europe at the end of 1980s; changes in 1989 reopened many post-war issues, and another, and possibly the last chapter of the restitution matters resulting from World War II opened. Many of the original issues have now received wide coverage in the press and other media.[8]

An excellent example of these latest developments in the post-war restitution of looted works is provided by the return from Poznan Cathedral of seven Renaissance bronze grave plates, for which a search had been conducted for many years in Germany; they were identified accidentally in 1989 in the storerooms of the State Hermitage, in what was still Leningrad, and restored to their place of origin. In the same year the Royal Castle in Warsaw recovered four paintings by Pillement which had initially been looted by Nazis and were discovered in the reserve collections of *Tsarskoe Selo* in Russia.

Gradually, entirely new Polish-Russian, Polish-German and German-Russian relationships have allowed the issue to be formally placed on negotiation tables. In the Polish-German Treaty signed in 1991, a short and rather enigmatic Article 28.3 stipulated that "The pacting Sides will strive to resolve in this spirit [of concord and reconciliation] the problems relating to the cultural goods and archives starting with individual cases".[9]

This statement clearly reflected the difficulties both sides would face during negotiations, but the provision became the basis for the bilateral negotiations in February 1992, the first practical result of which was the return later that year of the collection of ancient gold jewellery and over 1,700 silver and some gold coins, all of them removed at the end of occupation from Poznan and Warsaw archaeological museums. The talks are still continuing.[10]

The Polish-Russian Treaty signed in 1992[11] contains a more exhaustive but less definitive statement on restitution which reflected the fact that all the objects gathered during the war by the Russian military administration were still hidden at the time the Treaty was signed. It starts with the general resolution on co-operation "in order to reveal and reunify, to introduce to the cultural currency and to insure the necessary legal, material and other protection regarding the assets, historical monuments and objects found in their territories that are related to the historic and cultural heritage of the nations of the other Side" (Article 13. 3). The next passage of the same provision states directly in relation to wartime removals that "in accord with the international standards and agreements ... the Sides will regard with favour the mutual efforts to reveal and return the cultural and historic goods, including archive material which had been seized and unlawfully removed or that by some other unlawful manner had come to be found in the territory of the other Side" (Article 13.4). After the entry into force of the Treaty, both sides nominated special governmental plenipotentiaries to fulfil the obligations undertaken in its provisions.

---

8. A special international newsletter entitled *Spoils of War* is published in Germany twice a year to give full information on the restitutional events and talks taking currently place in Europe. The full name and address of the publisher is: Koordinierungsstelle der Länder fur die Rückfuhrung von Kulturgütern beim Kulturministerium des Landes Sachsen-Anhalt, Turmschanzenstr. 32 D-39114 Magdeburg.

9. Treaty between the Republic of Poland and the Federal Republic of Germany on Good Neighbourhood Policy and Friendly Co-operation, signed 17 June 1991. Polish-German Treaties of 14 November 1990 and 17 June 1991, Bonn.

10. For more details and photographs of the return objects see: W. Kowalski, above note 1 p. 96 ff.

11. Treaty between the Republic of Poland and the Russian Federation on Friendship and Good Neighbourly Co-operation, signed 22 May 1992. For more detail, see W. Kowalski, above note 1 p. 96 ff.

It is important to note that such developments are not confined to Central or Eastern European countries. For example, irrespective of the model German-French relations established many years ago, the process of the restitution of cultural property between these two States has by no means been completed and was resumed with the return of some paintings found in former East Germany during the German State visit to France in 1993. Another round of talks on this issue took place early in 1997.

As a result of the new political climate of the early 1990s, unified Germany was also able to re-commence negotiations on the restoration of their own war losses. This process on the part of both German States started just after the war and has never been terminated. After the successful return of many objects from the USA and Russia in the 1950s, a catalogue of lost paintings was published in 1965.[12] Its publication led to the formulation of the claim the next year for the restitution of two portraits by Albrecht Dürer, which were taken from a depot in Germany by an American soldier and sold in New York to E. Elicofon just after the War. The well known and widely studied case *Kunstsammlungen zu Weimar v. Elicofon*[13] successfully ended in 1982 with the return of both pictures to the castle in Weimar. Another recent case of restitution, although not so complicated and time consuming, took place in October 1990, when Carol B. Hallett, U.S. Commissioner of Customs returned important postage stamps to Juergen Ruhfus, ambassador of the Federal Republic of Germany; the set of six postage stamps and two covers, including the outstanding rarity, the famous Twopence Mauritius of 1847, went missing from a salt mine near Leipzig, where it had been stored for safekeeping during the war.[14]

Official Russian-German talks on restitution commenced after the Treaty between the two States in 1990. In Article 16 of the Treaty, both States have bound themselves to return " the works of art lost without a trace or unlawfully held, found in their territories".[15] As a result of the first negotiations a special additional agreement was concluded in Dresden two years later for the joint conduct of the search for and return of cultural goods lost during the war. It was also agreed to set up four commissions to study detailed questions, including the form of compensation that Russia expected to obtain from Germany for destroyed or lost works of art in the event that Russia returned the German collections hidden until now in the storerooms of the Moscow and St. Petersburg museums.[16] Independently of the work of these commissions, several cultural items which were found in other countries were recently returned to Germany. For example, medieval ivory relief plates were returned by France in 1994, three albums of

---

12. *Verlorene Werke der Malarei in Deutschland in der Zeit von 1939 bis 1945, zerstorte und verschollene Gemalde aus Museen und Galerien,* Hrsg. M. Bernhard. Berlin 1965.

13. *Kunstsammlungen zu Weimar v. Elicofon,* 536 F. Supp. 829 (1981), aff'd, 678 F. 2d 1150 (1982). See, for example, S. K. Burks, 'Kunstsammlungen zu Weimar v. Elicofon: Theft of Priceless Art Treasures Gives Rise to Protracted International Legal Battle', *Texas International Law Journal* 1984, Vol. 19, No. 1, and L.V. Prott, P. J. O'Keefe, above note 156, pp. 421 and 621.

14. This restitution was possible due to the co-operation of INTERPOL, Scotland Yard and the U.S. Customs Service. See *Preserving Mankind's Heritage. U.S. Efforts to Prevent Illicit Trade in Cultural Property,* Washington 1991, p. 4.

15. Treaty on the Good Neighbourhood Policy, Partnership and Co-operation between Federal Republic of Germany and the Union of Soviet Socialistic Republics, signed on 9 November 1990. Bulletin des Presse- und Informationsamts der Bundesregierung, No. 133/S, 1379, 15 November 1990.

16. The agreement was signed on 10 February 1993. See commentaries in *Berliner Zeitung, Frankfurter Allgemeine Zeitung* and *Kommersant* of the following day. Commissions have to discuss separately libraries, museums and archives issuees. See report from the works accomplished by the Commission on Libraries: K.-D. Lehmann, 'A New Proposal for Negotiations by the German-Russian Expert Group Concerning the Repatriation of the Spoils of War'. *Spoils of War (International Newsletter)* No. 3, December 1993, p. 12.

prints by the Ukraine in 1995, and around 100,000 books, a part of the Red Army spoils from Bremen, Magdeburg, Lubeck, Hamburg and Leipzig libraries, were found in Georgia and restituted in autumn 1996. In February 1997 a painting by J. F. Tischbein was handed over by Sotheby's, New York, to a representative of the *Kunstsammlungen zu Weimar*.[17]

On the Russian side all activities connected with restitution are now co-ordinated and supervised by the State Commission for the Restitution of Works of Art set up on the strength of a Government resolution of 28 December 1992. The State Commission is to "regulate the mutual claims of Russia and other countries concerning the restitution of works of art" (part 1 of the resolution), which had been " translocated in the period of the Second World War" (part 2). In its work, the Commission is under a duty to "secure the protection of the national interest of the Russian Federation [and] prevent any harm to the cultural heritage of the people of the Federation" (part 3).

However the most important recent development is the law aimed at nationalising the cultural items gathered in Russian depots at the end of World War II which was finally adopted by the State Duma in early 1997 after a long process. President Yeltsin refused to sign it and it is now being considered by the Constitutional Court. The potential impact on the whole issue of the final liquidation of the effects of the last war in the area of cultural restitution, as well as other potentially far-reaching consequences justifies a closer examination of the main provisions of this Act.[18]

The scope of the application of this Federal Law is indicated by the statement that it "regulates relations in connection with cultural items removed to the USSR as a result of World War II and located in the Russian Federation territory" ... "irrespective of the actual possessor and the circumstances which led to this possession" (Introduction and Article 3). According to Article 6 such defined cultural items "are in the ownership of the Russian Federation and constitute federal property". There are five exceptions to this principle provided in the form of the rights to claim certain objects if prescribed conditions are met. The following objects can be reclaimed:

- cultural objects which were "plundered and taken away during World War II by Germany [or] its war allies" from the territories of the former Soviet republics, namely Belorussian, Latvian, Lithuanian, Moldavian, Estonian and Ukrainian republics, and which were their "national property" (Article 7);
- cultural objects removed from, so called, "affected States", which according to Article 4 means "any State whose territory was fully or partially occupied by the forces of former enemy States", namely Germany, Bulgaria, Hungary, Italy, Romania and Finland (Article 8.1);
- cultural objects that were "the property of religious organisations or private charities and which were used exclusively for religious or charitable aims and did not serve the interests of Militarism and/or Fascism" (Article 8.2);
- cultural objects "that used to belong to individuals who were deprived of these because of their active fight against Nazism/Fascism, including their participation in national resistance movements against the occupation regimes, and/or because of their race, religion or nationality" (Article 8.3);

---

17. See respective notes in *Spoils of War (International Newsletter)* No. 3, December 1996, and No. 4, August 1997.
18. 'Federal Law on Cultural Values Removed to the USSR as a Result of World War II and Located in the Territory of the Russian Federation'; see unofficial translation of the full text and its parliamentary history dating from 1994 in *Spoils of War (International Newsletter)* No. 4, August 1997, p. 9 ff.

- cultural objects that are "family relics (family archives, photographs, letters, decorations and awards, portraits of family members and their ancestors) which have become federal property according to Article 6 of the Federal Law" (Article 12).

All claims, with the exception of those claiming the property of the former Soviet Republics, and family relics, must be submitted to the special Federal Body within the period of eighteen months after the Law enters into force. If the return of the object is decided all claimants must pay the costs of "the expenses for its identification, expert examination, storage and restoration, as well as its transfer (transportation costs etc)" (Article 18). In the case of family relics, "the family which used to be the owner" is also expected to pay the value of the relics to be returned (Article 19.2). In the case of these objects there is another exception to the general rule, in that the interested families can file their claims directly with the Federal Body, while all other claimants must be represented by their respective States.

Finally, the condition limiting 'affected States' claims should be noted. Their cultural losses will be returned only if the States in question are able to present evidence of having produced their original restitutional claims within the time limits prescribed by post-war laws provisions, in particular Peace Treaties and procedural provisions of Soviet Union zone of occupation (Article 8.1). These time limits were: until 15 March 1948 with regard to Bulgaria, Hungary, Italy and Romania; until 15 September 1948 with regard to Finland and until 1 February 1950 with regard to East Germany.

This Federal Law met with much criticism at the outset because of its lack of co-ordination with generally accepted principles of international law.[19] It will be sufficient to emphasise two points which have not yet been raised by commentators.

The first results directly from the main objective of the Law. The intention of the State Duma was to deal with the issue of 'trophy art' on a legal, as well as on a political level; during the last few years Russia has been faced by growing international concern about the problem of collections hidden in Moscow; these could not be kept in secret any longer and some of them have recently been on show for the first time since the war.[20] Now is the time to clarify their legal status and definitive location. Serving as a remedy for these problems, the Federal Law underlines the legality of the USSR action in connection with the removal of cultural goods; Article 6 states, for example, that they "were brought into the USSR by way of exercise of its right to compensatory restitution".[21] However, such a formula raises a question: what does 'compensatory restitution' mean, especially in the context of international law? Is it a restitution in kind, as suggested by the very term itself, or is it rather a way to justify reparations? Although from the practical point of view the retention of 'trophy art', in its present form, could only be explained in terms of reparations, it is quite unlikely that the authors of the draft of this law

---

19. See comments by V. Akulenko, P. d'Argent, M. Boguslavskii, J. Geher, T. R. Kline, K. Siehr and W. Kowalski, *Spoils of War (International Newsletter)* No. 4, August 1997, p. 10 ff.

20. One of these exhibitions, entitled: *Masterdrawings in the Hermitage. Rediscovered Works of Art from German Private Collections*, was opened officially in the Hermitage Museum in St. Petersburg on 4 December 1996. See *Trophy Art* exhibition in the Hermitage; *Spoils of War (International Newsletter)* No. 3, December 1996, p. 68.

21. Article 4 is even more descriptive when defining 'removed cultural values'. This notion embodies "any cultural values that have been removed by way of compensatory restitution from the territories of Germany and its former war allies — Bulgaria, Hungary, Italy, Romania and Finland — to the territory of the USSR, pursuant to orders of the Soviet Army military command, the Soviet Military Administration in Germany or instructions of the other competent bodies in the USSR and that are now located in the territory of the Russian Federation".

(Institute of State and Law of the Russian Academy of Science) would suggest this solution. Reparations in works of art are not recognised at all by international law. Therefore the only reasonable explanation is that the term 'compensatory restitution' means restitution in kind, as adopted by post-war laws. This solution is, however, difficult to accept in this situation because Russia is not in a position to satisfy the fundamental condition upon which this form of restitution can be effected. It cannot provide the necessary documentation of losses which would allow it to follow the principle of maximum similarity or likeness of the rendered objects in relation to the lost ones ('object for similar object' rule) on which restitution in kind is based.

It should be noted that this form of restitution is likely to be adopted in other cases currently under negotiation. According to Article 28.3 of the Polish-German Treaty (above)[22] the German side claims a collection of early aeroplanes relocated for security reasons from one of the Berlin museums to the east during the carpet bombing of the cities of Germany. The collection was found after the war in western Poland and is now in the museum in Krakow. Arguing for the retention of it on the basis of restitution in kind, the Polish side was able to present a list of aeroplanes corresponding in number, quality and origin which were destroyed by the Nazis in Poland and therefore argues that the collection cannot be returned.

The second aspect of concern within the Federal Law refers to the Russia's external obligations and agreements which have already been executed. Article 22 states that:

> the Russian Federation concludes treaties under international law which promote the resolution of the aims of this Federal Law, including treaties under international law ... on the settlement of questions connected with the reimbursement of the expenses of the Russian Federation and its cultural institutions for the preservation and restoration of removed cultural items which were handed over to foreign States not by way of concluding a treaty or in accordance with international treaties that have no provisions for such reimbursement, and which were concluded by the Government of the USSR or the Government of the Russian Federation with the Governments of other States before the enforcement of this Federal Law.

Does it really mean that Russia will try to re-negotiate the terms of restitution established in 1940s and 1950s? These difficult areas help to explain why President Yeltsin refused to sign the law.

There are two further areas of restitution which need to be considered. The first is the case which to a certain extent followed the principle of 'restitution by distribution'. In the 1980s it became widely known that the Austrian authorities had kept about 8,000 cultural items deposited in 1955 in Austria by the U.S. Army in order to try to locate their owners. After very limited restitutional action, the collection remained in Austria, because the origins of its individual components could not be established. In 1984, the Government of Austria decided to close the matter by selling the collection (which included valuable works of art) at auction. This proposal was greeted with considerable public opposition.[23] As a result, after an additional round of new claims, which resulted in the return of some objects to successful claimants (350 out of a total of 3,282) the remaining items in the collection were officially transferred by the Austrian Government to the Federation of Israeli Communities of Austria

---

22.   See above note 9.
23.   See, for example, A. Decker, 'A Legacy of Shame', *Art News* 1984, No. 12, p. 55 ff.

(*Bundesverband der Israelitischen Kultusgemeinden Osterreichs*). The Federation sold them at an auction organised in 1996 by Christie's in Vienna for the benefit of the victims of the Holocaust.[24] The sale has not, however, definitively closed the Mauerbach story; there are still numerous people claiming these objects before Austrian courts.[25]

The second issue concerned territorial changes; in this field a number of recent events have occurred within the framework of the political changes of the late 1980s, although certain earlier transfers of objects originating from the neighbouring countries did take place in this context.[26] These can rightly be quoted as good examples of the growing acceptance of the 'territorial link' rule as the only solution for the final settlement of cultural heritage problems resulting from the post-war border changes, even when accompanied by mass relocation of the indigenous peoples. Further examples of such acceptance came later in the indirect form of court decisions and the direct form of bilateral international agreements. In at least two cases, courts refused to recognise the claims concerning former German private property nationalised after the war and located in Poland. One of them referred to cultural objects left in Silesia and then sold abroad; when these objects were offered for subsequent sale in Sweden, the previous owners tried to stop the auction arguing that the Polish State lacked a good title as a result of nationalisation. The Civil Court in Stockholm did not accept that argument.[27]

The 'territorial link' principle was adopted directly in Article 28 of the Polish-German Treaty. This obliges both States to protect the cultural goods of other groups located in their territories, as parts of the common cultural heritage of Europe. The same concept lies behind the Polish-Ukrainian Treaty and Agreement on Cultural Co-operation, both signed 18 May 1992. Both documents allow, however, certain exceptions: Article 5.1 of the Treaty stipulates that the sides "will co-operate ... in bringing together collections of art, libraries and archives that had been scattered due to historical events".[28] The adoption of such exceptions is dictated by the history of these two neighbouring nations. It makes possible, for example, the reunification of certain collections of the Ossolineum Foundation, which are now dispersed in various places in both countries.[29]

This principle appears to have been applied in other recent negotiations, such as the talks aimed at finding solutions to the post-war problems of the new states created after the collapse of Yugoslavia. During the talks in Brussels in September 1992 the representatives of Croatia advocated the repatriation of all the archives "taken over by the Yugoslavian Federation Republic between 1 December 1918 and 31 December 1991"; they propose to keep more recent archives together as the common property of the States (former Yugoslavian

---

24.　See auction catalogue: *Mauerbach. Items Seized by the National Socialists to be Sold for the Benefit of the Victims of the Holocaust,* Christie's, Vienna, 29 and 30 October 1996. S. Waxman, 'Austria: Ending the Legacy of Shame', *Art News* Vol. 94, No. 7.

25.　For more details, see 'The Mauerbach Case', *Spoils of War (International Newsletter)* No. 3, December 1996. Part I by J. Leistra, p. 22; part II by H. Feliciano, p. 24.

26.　For example, in the early 1980s Poland transferred a religious sculpture found near Zgorzelec which came from one of the churches in Gorlitz, the town located on the other side of the nearby new Polish-German border.

27.　The claim was dismissed in 1992 (T 3-402-92), unpublished. The second case referred to land and was held in 1991 by the German Constitutional Court (1 BvR 1268/91) and later by the European Commission of Human Rights, (20931/92).

28.　For more details, see: W. Kowalski, above note 1 p. 100.

29.　M. Matwijow, 'Ossolineum. The Case of the Dispersed Library', *Spoils of War (International Newsletter)* No. 3, December 1996, p. 14.

republics).[30]   Other negotiations are under way in connection with the dissolution of USSR; these were commenced successfully in 1992 with the signature of the agreement "on the return of cultural and historical goods to the countries of their origin" by the Presidents of eleven states — members of the Commonwealth of Independent States. This agreement was rejected by the Russian State Duma and has been followed by other agreements[31] which open the door to another field of possible research — the more general problem of the succession of states in the area of cultural heritage. This, however, will open up a whole new area of study.

30.   B. Sulc, 'Restitution and Succession of Cultural Property from Croatian Museums and Galleries', *Informatica Museologica* 1992, No. 23 (1-4), p. 16.
31.   The first agreement was signed on 14 February 1992 in Minsk, Belarus. For the full text see *Rosijskaja Gazeta,* 24 February 1992.

APPENDIX
Annex 1

Journal of the Regulations for the German-occupied Poland (No. 12/1939 p. 20) Regulation concerning confiscation of the works of art in the German-occupied Poland dated 16 December 1939.

Pursuant to Section 5 of Decree 1 issued by the Fuhrer and Chancellor of the German Reich on 12 October 1939, concerning the administration of the German-occupied Poland (Reichesgeselzbl. I.S. 2077) Journal of the Regulations of the German Reich I, p. 2077) I ordain the following:

Para. 1
Public possession of the works of art in the German-occupied Poland is hereby confiscated for the sake of public benefit and use, provided the property in question does not fall under the regulation dated 15 November 1939 (Journal of the Regulations, p. 37), concerning the confiscation of the State property of the former Polish State which is now located in the German-occupied territory.

Para. 2
The term public possession of the works of art, apart from the works and artistic collections which were State property of the former Polish State, refers to:
1. private collections of the works of art, which are subject to registration and security procedures undertaken by the appointed commissioner to protect their cultural and historical value,
2. the works of art in the exclusive possession of the Church, except for the property needed for everyday liturgy.

Para. 3
1. To determine the case of the public possession of the works of art as pursuant to this regulation, any and all works of art which are the Church property should be declared, specifying their number, type and condition.
2. Every person in possession of the said works of art since 15 March 1939 or entitled to dispose of the said property is subject to registration procedures.
3. Every person is obliged to reveal the true information concerning the possession of the said works of art, at the request of the relevant authorities.

Para. 4
The appointed special commissioner for registering and securing artistic and cultural property is entitled to settle any disputable cases and decide which works of art or which collections should fall into the category of the public possession, as pursuant to para. 2 of this regulation. He is also entitled to allow for any exemptions.

Para. 5
1. The following offenders are subject to imprisonment:
(1)   those who attempt to hide, dispose of or export from the German-occupied Poland the said works of art;
(2)   those who, being obliged by this regulation to reveal information concerning the said works of art, refuse to do so, or relate the information which is false or insufficient.
2. It is within the Special Court's jurisdiction to declare about the above.

Para. 6
The special commissioner for registering and securing the artistic and cultural property shall announce the relevant orders to execute the stipulations of this regulation.

Para. 7
This regulation comes into force on this day of 16 December 1939.

Cracow, 16 December 1939.
Governor General for the German-occupied Poland

Annex 2

Journal of the Regulations for the German-occupied Poland (No 6/1940, p. 61.)
The first executive order to the Regulation dated 16 December 1939 concerning the confiscation of the works of art in the German-occupied Poland, 15 January 1940.

To execute the Regulation concerning the confiscation of the works of art in the German-occupied Poland, dated December 16 1939 (Journal of the Regulations for the German-occupied Poland, p. 209) I order the following:

Para. 1
The declaration of the works of art pursuant to para. 3 of the said regulation should be completed until February 15 1940 at the Office of the Special Commissioner for registering and securing artistic and cultural property, Cracow, Academy of Mining.

Para. 2
(1)   All artistic, cultural and historical property made before 1850 should be declared.
(2)   The following objects are subject to obligatory declaration:
      a)   works of art
      b)   paintings
      c)   craft and handiwork (antique furniture, china, glass, gold and silver articles, carpets, tapestry, embroidery and lace works, liturgical vessels, etc.)
      d)   drawings, wood engravings, copperplate engravings, etc.
      e)   rare manuscripts, music note scripts, autographs, miniatures, prints, frames, etc.
      f)   weapons, armoury, etc.
      g)   coins, medals, rings, etc.
(3) The information about the origin, master, theme presented, dimensions and materials (e.g. wood, brass, canvas) should also be enclosed to the objects specified in (2).

Para. 3
All disputable cases or exemptions from the stipulations of para. 4, shall be settled in the written notification prepared by the special commissioner, whose decision is final.

Para. 4
This order is to be enforced by professional science clerks.
Cracow, 15 January 1940.

Dr Mühlmann, on behalf of the Governor General for the German-occupied Poland.

Annex 3

Inter-Allied Declaration against Acts of Dispossession committed in Territories under Enemy Occupation or Control

London, 5 January 1943

The following statement, corresponding to similar announcements in Moscow and Washington, was issued by the Foreign Office in London on 5 January:

H. M. Government in the United Kingdom have today joined with sixteen other Governments of the United Nations, and with the French National Committee, in making a formal Declaration of their determination to combat and defeat the plundering by the enemy Powers of the territories which have been overrun or brought under enemy control.

The systematic spoliation of occupied or controlled territory has followed immediately upon each fresh aggression. This has taken every sort of form, from open looting to the most cunningly camouflaged financial penetration, and it has extended to every sort of property — from works of art to stocks of commodities, from bullion and bank notes to stocks and shares in business and financial undertakings. But the object is always the same — to seize everything of value that can be put to the aggressors' profit and then to bring the whole economy of the subjugated countries under control so that they must slave to enrich and strengthen their oppressors.

It has always been foreseen that when the title of battle began to turn against the Axis the campaign of plunder would be even further extended and accelerated, and that every effort would be made to stow away the stolen property in neutral countries and to persuade neutral citizens to act as fences or cloaks on behalf of the thieves.

There is evidence that this is now happening, under the pressure of events in Russia and North Africa, and that the ruthless and complete methods of plunder begun in Central Europe are now being extended on a vast and ever increasing scale in the occupied territories of Western Europe.

H.M. Government agree with the Allied Governments and the French National Committee that it is important to leave no doubt whatever of their resolution not to accept or tolerate the misdeeds of their enemies in the field of property, however these may be cloaked, just as they have recently emphasised their determination to exact retribution from war criminals for their outrages against persons in the occupied territories. Accordingly they have made the following joint Declaration, and issued an explanatory Memorandum on its meaning, scope and application:

The Governments of the Union of South Africa, the United States of America, Australia, Belgium, Canada, China, the Czechoslovak Republic, The United Kingdom of Great Britain and Northern Ireland, Greece, India, Luxembourg, the Netherlands, New Zealand, Norway, Poland, the Union of Soviet Socialist Republics, Yugoslavia and the French National Committee, hereby issue a formal warning to all concerned, and in particular to persons in neutral countries, that they intend to do their utmost to defeat the methods of dispossession practised by the Governments with which they are at war against the countries and peoples who have been so wantonly assaulted and despoiled.

Accordingly the Governments making this Declaration and the French National Committee reserve all their rights to declare invalid any transfers of, or dealings with, property, rights, and interests of any description whatsoever which are, or have been, situated in the territories which have come under the occupation or control, direct or indirect, of the Governments with which they are at war, or which belong, or have belonged, to persons (including juridical persons) resident in such territories. This warning applies whether such transfers or dealings have taken the form of open looting or plunder, or of transactions apparently legal in form, even with the purport to be voluntarily effected.

The Governments making this Declaration and the French National Committee solemnly record their solidarity in this matter.

The explanatory Memorandum states that the Declaration is being communicated to the Governments of the other United Nations, with an invitation to declare their adherence to its principles, and brought to the notice of neutral Governments, and that the signatories will jointly arrange maximum publicity for it through the Press and Broadcasts.

"The Declaration makes it clear", the Memorandum continues, "that it applies to transfers and dealings effected in territory under the indirect control of the enemy, such as the former unoccupied zone in France, just as much as to transactions in territory under his direct physical control. It is obviously impossible to define exactly the action which will require to be taken when victory has been won and the occupation or control of foreign territory by the enemy has been brought to an end. The wording of the Declaration, however, clearly covers all forms of looting to which the enemy has resorted.

In so far as transfer or dealings are confined to the territory of a particular country, the procedure of examination and the decision reached regarding their invalidation will fall to be undertaken by legitimate Government of the Country concerned on its return. The Declaration marks, however, the solidarity in this important matter of all participating Governments, and of the French National Committee, and this means that they are mutually pledged to assist one another as may be required, and, in conformity with the principles of equity, to examine and if necessary to implement the validation of transfers or dealings with property, rights, etc., which may extend across national frontiers and require action by two or more Governments.

The parties are agreed as far as possible to follow in this matter similar lines of policy, without derogation to their national sovereignty and having regard to the differences prevailing in the various countries. They have accordingly decided as a first step to establish a Committee of experts, who will consider the scope and sufficiency of the existing legislation of the Allied countries concerned for the purpose of invalidating transfers or dealings of the nature indicated in the Declaration in all proper cases.

The Committee has also been asked to receive and collect information on the methods adopted by the enemy Governments and their adherents to lay their hands upon property, rights, etc., in the territories which they have occupied or brought under their control. When a report is available from this committee the whole question will be reviewed by the Governments making the Declaration and the French National Committee. The other Governments of the United Nations will be informed of the results of the inquiry."

A statement issued on the same day by the French National Committee in London as "the interpreter of the will of the French people" reaffirmed that the Declaration aimed equally at acts of depossession carried out or inspired by the Germans and by the Vichy Government.

Annex 4

Final Act and Annex of the Paris Conference on Reparations

On 14 January the following governments signed the agreement: United States, France, United Kingdom, Netherlands, Belgium, Yugoslavia, and Luxembourg. The signatures represent 84.15 per cent of Category A quotas, thus bringing the agreement into effect as of 14 January.

CONFERENCE RECOMMENDATION
The Paris Conference on Reparation, which has met from 9 November 1945 to 21 December 1945, recommends that the Governments represented at the Conference should sign in Paris as soon as possible an Agreement on Reparation from Germany, on the Establishment of an Inter-Allied Reparation Agency and on the Restitution of Monetary Gold in the terms set forth below.

DRAFT AGREEMENT ON REPARATION FROM GERMANY, ON THE ESTABLISHMENT OF AN INTERALLIED REPARATION AGENCY AND ON THE RESTITUTION OF MONETARY GOLD
The Governments of Albania, the United States of America, Australia, Belgium, Canada, Denmark, France, the United Kingdom of Great Britain and Northern Ireland, Greece, India, Luxembourg, Norway, New Zealand, the Netherlands, Czechoslovakia, the Union of South Africa and Yugoslavia, in order to obtain an equitable distribution among themselves of the total assets which, in accordance with the provisions of this Agreement and the Provisions agreed upon at Potsdam on 1 August 1945 between the Governments of the United States of America, the United Kingdom of Great Britain and Northern Ireland and the Union of Soviet Socialist Republics, are or may be declared to be available as reparation from Germany (hereinafter referred to as German reparation), in order to establish an Inter-Allied Reparation Agency, and to settle an equitable procedure for the restitution of monetary gold, HAVE AGREED as follows:

Part I: German Reparation
Article 1. Shares in Reparation.
A. German reparation (exclusive of the funds to be allocated under Article 8 of Part I of this Agreement), shall be divided into the following categories:
Category A, which shall include all forms of German reparation except those included in Category B;
Category B, which shall include industrial and other capital equipment removed from Germany, and merchant ships and inland water transport.
B. Each Signatory Government shall be entitled to the percentage share of the total value of Category A and the percentage share of the total value of Category B set out for that Government in the Table of Shares set forth below:

TABLE OF SHARES

Country	Category A	Category B
Albania	0.05	0.35
United States of America	28.0	11.80
Australia	0.70	0.95
Belgium	2.70	4.50
Canada	3.50	1.50
Denmark	0.25	0.35
Egypt	0.05	0.20
France	16.00	22.80
United Kingdom	28.00	27.80
Greece	2.70	4.35
India	2.00	2.90
Luxembourg	0.15	0.40
Norway	1.30	1.90
New Zealand	0.40	0.60
Netherlands	3.90	5.60
Czechoslovakia	3.00	4.30
Union of South Africa*	0.70	0.10
Yugoslavia	6.60	9.60
TOTAL	100.00	100.00

* The government of the Union of South Africa has undertaken to waive its claims to the extent necessary to reduce its percentage share of Category B to the figure of 0.1 per cent but is entitled, in disposing of German enemy assets within its jurisdiction, to charge the net value of such assets against its percentage share of Category A and a percentage share under Category B of 0.1 per cent.

C. Subject to the provisions of paragraph D below, each Signatory Government shall be entitled to receive its share of merchant ships determined in accordance with Article 5 of Part I of this Agreement, provided that its receipts of merchant ships do not exceed in value its share in Category B as a whole. Subject to the provisions of paragraph D below, each Signatory Government shall also be entitled to its Category A percentage share in German assets in countries which remained neutral in the war against Germany.

The distribution among the Signatory Governments of forms of German reparation other than merchant ships, inland water transport and German assets in countries which remained neutral in the war against Germany shall be guided by the principles set forth in Article 4 of Part I of this Agreement.

D. If a Signatory Government receives more than its percentage share of certain types of assets in either Category A or Category B, its receipts of other types of assets in that Category shall be reduced so as to ensure that it shall not receive more than its share in that Category as a whole.

E. No Signatory Government shall receive more than its percentage share of either Category A or Category B as a whole by surrendering any part of its percentage share of the other Category, except that with respect to German enemy assets within its own jurisdiction, any Signatory Government shall be permitted to charge any excess of such assets over its Category A percentage share of total German enemy assets within the jurisdiction of the Signatory Governments either to its receipts in Category A or to its receipts in Category B or in part to each Category.

F. The Inter-Allied Reparation Agency, to be established in accordance with Part II of this Agreement, shall charge the reparation account of each Signatory Government for the German assets within that Government's jurisdiction over a period of five years. The charges at the date of the entry into force of this Agreement shall be not less than 20 per cent of the net value of such assets (as defined in Article 6 of Part I of this Agreement) as then estimated, at the beginning of the second year thereafter not less than 25 per cent of the balance as then estimated, at the beginning of the third year not less than $33^{1/3}$ per cent of the balance as then estimated, at the beginning of the fourth year not less than 50 per cent of the balance as then estimated, at the beginning of the fifth year not less than 90 per cent of the balance as then estimated, and at the end of the fifth year the entire remainder of the total amount actually realised.

G. The following exceptions to paragraphs D and E above shall apply in the case of a Signatory Government whose share in Category B is less than its share in Category A:

(i) Receipts of merchant ships by any such Government shall not reduce its percentage share in other types of assets in Category B, except to the extent that such receipts exceed the value obtained when that Government's Category A percentage is applied to the total value of merchant ships.

(ii) Any excess of German assets within the jurisdiction of such Government over its Category A percentage share of the total of German assets within the jurisdiction of Signatory Governments as a whole shall be charged first to the additional share in Category B to which that Government would be entitled if its share in Category B were determined by applying its Category A percentage to the forms of German reparation in Category B.

H. If any Signatory Government renounces its shares or part of its shares in German reparation as set out in the above Table of Shares, or if it withdraws from the Inter-Allied Reparation Agency at a time when all or part of its shares in German reparation remain unsatisfied, the shares or part thereof thus renounced or remaining shall be distributed rateably among the other Signatory Governments.

Article 2. Settlement of Claims against Germany.

A. The Signatory Governments agree among themselves that their respective shares of reparation, as determined by the present Agreement, shall be regarded by each of them as covering all its claims and those of its nationals against the former German Government and its Agencies, of a governmental or private nature, arising out of the war (which are not otherwise provided for), including costs of German occupation, credits acquired during occupation on clearing accounts and claims against the Reichskreditkassen.

B. The provisions of paragraph A above are without prejudice to:

(i) The determination at the proper time of the forms, duration or total amount of reparation to be made by Germany;

(ii) The right which each Signatory Government may have with respect to the final settlement of German reparation; and

(iii) Any political, territorial or other demands which any Signatory Government may put forward with respect to the peace settlement with Germany.

C. Notwithstanding anything in the provisions of paragraph A above, the present Agreement shall not be considered as affecting:

(i)   The obligation of the appropriate authorities in Germany to secure at a future date the discharge of claims against Germany and German nationals arising out of contracts and other obligations entered into, and rights acquired, before the existence of a state of war between Germany and the Signatory Government concerned or before the occupation of its territory by Germany, whichever was earlier;

(ii)   The claims of Social Insurance Agencies of the Signatory Governments or the claims of their nationals against the Social Insurance Agencies of the former German Government; and

(iii)   Banknotes of the Reichsbank and the Rentenbank, it being understood that their realisation shall not have the result of reducing improperly the amount of reparation and shall not be effected without the approval of the Control Council for Germany.

D. Notwithstanding the provisions of paragraph A of this Article, the Signatory Governments agree that, so far as they are concerned, the Czechoslovak Government will be entitled to draw upon the Giro Account of the National Bank of Czechoslovakia at the Reichsbank, should such action be decided upon by the Czechoslovak Government and be approved by the Control Council for Germany, in connection with the movement from Czechoslovakia to Germany of former Czechoslovak nationals.

Article 3. Waiver of Claims Regarding Property Allocated as Reparation.

Each of the Signatory Governments agrees that it will not assert, initiate actions in international tribunals in respect of, or give diplomatic support to claims on behalf of itself or those persons entitled to its protection against any other Signatory Government or its nationals in respect of property received by that Government as reparation with the approval of the Control Council for Germany.

Article 4. General Principles for the Allocation of Industrial and other Capital Equipment.

A. No Signatory Government shall request the allocation to it as reparation of any industrial or other capital equipment removed from Germany except for use in its own territory or for use by its own nationals outside its own territory.

B. In submitting requests to the Inter-Allied Reparation Agency, the Signatory Governments should endeavour to submit comprehensive programs of requests for related groups of items, rather than requests for isolated items or small groups of items. It is recognised that the work of the Secretariat of the Agency will be more effective, the more comprehensive the programs which Signatory Governments submit to it.

C. In the allocation by the Inter-Allied Reparation Agency of items declared available for reparation (other than merchant ships, inland water transport and German assets in countries which remained neutral in the war against Germany), the following general principles shall serve as guides:

(i) Any item or related group of items in which a claimant country has a substantial pre-war financial interest shall be allocated to that country if it so desires. Where two or more claimants have such substantial interests in a particular item or group of items, the criteria stated below shall guide the allocation.

(ii) If the allocation between competing claimants is not determined by paragraph (i), attention shall be given, among other relevant factors, to the following considerations:

(a)   The urgency of each claimant country's needs for the item or items to rehabilitate, reconstruct or restore to full activity the claimant country's economy;

(b)   The extent to which the item or items would replace property which was destroyed, damaged or looted in the war, or requires replacement because of excessive wear in war production, and which is important to the claimant country's economy;

(c)   The relation of the item or items to the general pattern of the claimant country's prewar economic life and to programs for its postwar economic life and to programs for its postwar economic adjustment or development.
economic life and to programs for its post-war economic adjustment or development;

(d)   The requirements of countries whose reparation shares are small but which are in need of certain specific items or categories of items.

(iii)   In making allocations a reasonable balance shall be maintained among the rates at which the reparation shares of the several claimant Governments are satisfied, subject to such temporary exceptions as are justified by the considerations under paragraph (ii) (a) above.

Article 5. General Principles for the Allocation of Merchant Ships and Inland Water Transport.

A. (i) German merchant ships available for distribution as reparation among the Signatory Governments shall be distributed among them in proportion to the respective over-all losses of merchant shipping, on a gross tonnage basis, of the Signatory Governments and their nationals through acts of war. It is recognised that transfers of merchant ships by the United Kingdom and United States Governments to other Governments are subject to such final approvals by the legislatures of the United Kingdom and United States of America as may be required.

(ii) A special committee, composed of representatives of the Signatory Governments, shall be appointed by the Assembly of the Inter-Allied Reparation Agency to make recommendations concerning the determination of such losses and the allocation of German merchant ships available for distribution.

(iii) The value of German merchant ships for reparation accounting purposes shall be the value determined by the Tri-partite Merchant Marine Commission in terms of 1938 prices in Germany plus 15 per cent, with an allowance for depreciation.

B. Recognising that some countries have special need for inland water transport, the distribution of inland water transport shall be dealt with by a special committee appointed by the Assembly of the Inter-Allied Reparation Agency in the event that inland water transport becomes available at a future time as reparation for the Signatory Governments. The valuation of inland water transport will be made on the basis adopted for the valuation of merchant ships or on an equitable basis in relation to that adopted for merchant ships.

Article 6. German External Assets.

A. Each Signatory Government shall, under such procedures as it may choose, hold or dispose of German enemy assets within its jurisdiction in manners designed to preclude their return to German ownership or control and shall charge against its reparation share such assets (net of accrued taxes, liens, expenses of administration, other *in rem* charges against specific items and legitimate contract claims against the German former owners of such assets).

B. The Signatory Governments shall give to the Inter-Allied Reparation Agency all information for which it asks as to the value of such assets and the amounts realised from time to time by their liquidation.

C. German assets in those countries which remained neutral in the war against Germany shall be removed from German ownership or control and liquidated or disposed of in accordance with the authority of France, the United Kingdom and the United States of America, pursuant to arrangements to be negotiated with the neutrals by these countries. The net proceeds of liquidation or disposition shall be made available to the Inter-Allied Reparation Agency for distribution on reparation account.

D. In applying the provisions of paragraph A above, assets which were the property of a country which is a member of the United Nations or its nationals who were not nationals of Germany at the time of the occupation or annexation of this country by Germany, or of its entry into war, shall not be charged to its reparation account. It is understood that this provision in no way prejudges any questions which may arise as regards assets which were not the property of a national of the country concerned at the time of the latter's occupation or annexation by Germany or of its entry into war.

E. The German enemy assets to be charged against reparation shares shall include assets which are in reality German enemy assets, despite the fact that the nominal owner of such assets is not a German enemy.

Each Signatory Government shall enact legislation or take other appropriate steps, if it has not already done so, to render null and void all transfers made, after the occupation of its territory or its entry into war, for the fraudulent purpose of cloaking German enemy interests, and thus saving them harmless from the effect of control measures regarding German enemy interests.

F. The Assembly of the Inter-Allied Reparation Agency shall set up a Committee of Experts in matters of enemy property custodianship in order to overcome practical difficulties of law and interpretation which may arise. The Committee should in particular guard against schemes which might result in effecting fictitious or other transactions designed to favour enemy interests, or to reduce improperly the amount of assets which might be allocated to reparation.

Article 7. Captured Supplies.

The value of supplies and other materials susceptible of civilian use captured from the German Armed Forces in areas outside Germany and delivered to Signatory Governments shall be charged against their reparation shares in so far as such supplies and materials have not been or are not in the future either paid for or delivered under arrangements precluding any charge. It is recognised that transfers of such supplies and material by the United Kingdom and United States Governments to other Governments are subject to such final approval by the legislature of the United Kingdom or the United States of America as may be required.

Article 8. Allocation of a Reparation Share to Non-repatriable Victims of German Action.

In recognition of the fact that large numbers of persons have suffered heavily at the hands of the Nazis and now stand in dire need of aid to promote their rehabilitation but will be unable to claim the assistance of any Government receiving reparation from Germany, the Governments of the United States of America, France, the United Kingdom, Czechoslovakia and Yugoslavia, in consultation with the Inter-Governmental Committee on Refugees, shall as soon as possible work out in common agreement a plan on the following general lines:

A. A share of reparation consisting of all the non-monetary gold found by the Allied Armed Forces in Germany and in addition a sum not exceeding 25 million dollars shall be allocated for the rehabilitation and resettlement of non-repatriable victims of German action.

B. The sum of 25 million dollars shall be met from a portion of the proceeds of German assets in neutral countries which are available for reparation.

C. Governments of neutral countries shall be requested to make available for this purpose (in addition to the sum of 25 million dollars) assets in such countries of victims of Nazi action who have since died and left no heirs.

D. The persons eligible for aid under the plan in question shall be restricted to true victims of Nazi persecution and to their immediate families and dependants, in the following classes:

(i) Refugees from Nazi Germany or Austria who require aid and cannot be returned to their countries within a reasonable time because of prevailing conditions;

(ii) German and Austrian nationals now resident in Germany or Austria in exceptional cases in which it is reasonable on grounds of humanity to assist such persons to emigrate and providing they emigrate to other countries within a reasonable period;

(iii) Nationals of countries formerly occupied by the Germans who cannot be repatriated or are not in a position to be repatriated within a reasonable time. In order to concentrate aid on the most needy and deserving refugees and to exclude persons whose loyalty to the United Nations is or was doubtful, aid shall be restricted to nationals or former nationals of previously occupied countries who were victims of Nazi concentration camps or of concentration camps established by regimes under Nazi influence but not including persons who have been confined only in prisoners of war camps.

E. The sums made available under paragraphs A and B above shall be administered by the Inter-Governmental Committee on Refugees or by a United Nations Agency to which appropriate functions of the Inter-Governmental Committee may in the future be transferred. The sums made available under paragraph C above shall be administered for the general purposes referred to in this Article under a program of administration to be formulated by the five Governments named above.

F. The non-monetary gold found in Germany shall be placed at the disposal of the Inter-Governmental Committee on Refugees as soon as a plan has been worked out as provided above.

G. The Inter-Governmental Committee on Refugees shall have power to carry out the purposes of the fund through appropriate public and private field organisations.

H. The fund shall be used, not for the compensation of individual victims, but to further the rehabilitation or resettlement of persons in the eligible classes.

I. Nothing in this Article shall be considered to prejudice the claims which individual refugees may have against a future German Government, except to the amount of the benefits that such refugees may have received from the sources referred to in paragraphs A and C above.

Part II: Inter-Allied Reparation Agency
Article 1. Establishment of the Agency.

The Governments signatory to the present Agreement hereby establish an Inter-Allied Reparation Agency (hereinafter referred to as the "Agency"). Each Government shall appoint a Delegate to the Agency and shall also be entitled to appoint an Alternate who, in the absence of the Delegate, shall be entitled to exercise all the functions and rights of the Delegate.

Article 2. Functions of the Agency.

A. The Agency shall allocate German reparation among the Signatory Governments in accordance with the provisions of this Agreement and of any other agreements from time to time in force among the Signatory Governments. For this purpose, the Agency shall be the medium through which the Signatory Governments receive information concerning, and express their wishes in regard to, items available as reparation.

B. The Agency shall deal with all questions relating to the restitution to a Signatory Government of property situated in one of the Western Zones of Germany which may be referred to it by the Commander of that Zone (acting on behalf of his Government), in agreement with the claimant Signatory

Government or Governments, without prejudice, however, to the settlement of such questions by the Signatory Governments concerned either by agreement or arbitration.

Article 3. Internal Organisation of the Agency.
 A. The organs of the Agency shall be the Assembly and the Secretariat.
 B. The Assembly shall consist of the Delegates and shall be presided over by the President of the Agency. The President of the Agency shall be the Delegate of the Government of France.
 C. The Secretariat shall be under the direction of a Secretary General, assisted by two Deputy Secretaries General. The Secretary General and the two Deputy Secretaries General shall be appointed by the Governments of France, the United States of America and the United Kingdom. The Secretariat shall be international in character. It shall act for the Agency and not for the individual Signatory Governments.

Article 4. Functions of the Secretariat.
The Secretariat shall have the following functions:

A.	To prepare and submit to the Assembly programs for the allocation of German reparations;
B.	To maintain detailed accounts of assets available for, and of assets distributed as, German reparation;
C.	To prepare and submit to the Assembly the budget of the Agency;
D.	To perform such other administrative functions as may be required.

Article 5. Functions of the Assembly.
 Subject to the provisions of Articles 4 and 7 of Part II of this Agreement, the Assembly shall allocate German reparation among the Signatory Governments in conformity with the provisions of this Agreement and of any other agreements from time to time in force among the Signatory Governments. It shall also approve the budget of the Agency and shall perform such other functions as are consistent with the provisions of this Agreement.

Article 6. Voting in the Assembly.
 Except as otherwise provided in this Agreement, each Delegate shall have one vote. Decisions in the Assembly shall be taken by a majority of the votes cast.

Article 7. Appeal from Decisions of the Assembly.
 A. When the Assembly has not agreed to a claim presented by a Delegate that an item should be allocated to his Government, the Assembly shall, at the request of that Delegate and within the time limit prescribed by the Assembly, refer the question to arbitration. Such reference shall suspend the effect of the decision of the Assembly on that item.
 B. The Delegates of the Governments claiming an item referred to arbitration under paragraph A above shall select an Arbitrator from among the other Delegates. If agreement cannot be reached upon the selection of an Arbitrator, the United States Delegate shall either act as Arbitrator or appoint as Arbitrator another Delegate from among the Delegates whose Governments are not claiming the item. If the United States Government is one of the claimant Governments, the President of the Agency shall appoint as Arbitrator a Delegate whose Government is not a claimant Government.

Article 8. Powers of the Arbitrator.
 When the question of the allocation of any item is referred to arbitration under Article 7 of Part II of this Agreement, the Arbitrator shall have authority to make final allocation of the item among the claimant Governments. The Arbitrator may, at his discretion, refer the item to the Secretariat for further study. He may also, at his discretion, require the Secretariat to resubmit the item to the Assembly.

Article 9. Expenses.
 A. The salaries and expenses of the Delegates and of their staffs shall be paid by their own Governments.
 B. The common expenses of the Agency shall be met from the funds of the Agency. For the first two years from the date of the establishment of the Agency, these funds shall be contributed in proportion

to the percentage shares of the Signatory Governments in Category B and thereafter in proportion to their percentage shares in Category A.

C. Each Signatory Government shall contribute its share in the budget of the Agency for each budgetary period (as determined by the Assembly) at the beginning of that period; provided that each Government shall, when this Agreement is signed on its behalf, contribute a sum equivalent to not less than its Category B percentage share of £50,000 and shall, within three months thereafter, contribute the balance of its share in the budget of the Agency for the budgetary period in which this Agreement is signed on its behalf.

D. All contributions by the Signatory Governments shall be made in Belgian francs or such other currency or currencies as the Agency may require.

Article 10. Voting on the Budget.

In considering the budget of the Agency for any budgetary period, the vote of each Delegate in the Assembly shall be proportional to the share of the budget for that period payable by his Government.

Article 11. Official Languages.

The official languages of the Agency shall be English and French.

Article 12. Offices of the Agency.

The seat of the Agency shall be in Brussels. The Agency shall maintain liaison offices in such other places as the Assembly, after obtaining the necessary consents, may decide.

Article 13. Withdrawal.

Any Signatory Government, other than a Government which is responsible for the control of a part of German territory, may withdraw from the Agency after written notice to the Secretariat.

Article 14. Amendments and Termination.

This Part II of the Agreement can be amended or the Agency terminated by a decision in the Assembly of the majority of the Delegates voting, provided that the Delegates forming the majority represent Governments whose shares constitute collectively not less than 80 per cent of the aggregate of the percentage shares in Category A.

Article 15. Legal Capacity. Immunities and Privileges.

The Agency shall enjoy in the territory of each Signatory Government such legal capacity and such privileges, immunities and facilities, as may be necessary for the exercise of its functions and the fulfilment of its purposes. The representatives of the Signatory Governments and the officials of the Agency shall enjoy such privileges and immunities as are necessary for the independent exercise of their functions in connection with the Agency.

Part III: Restitution of Monetary Gold

Single Article.

A. All the monetary gold found in Germany by the Allied Forces and that referred to in paragraph G below (including gold coins, except those of numismatic or historical value, which shall be restored directly if identifiable) shall be pooled for distribution as restitution among the countries participating in the pool in proportion to their respective losses of gold through looting or by wrongful removal to Germany.

B. Without prejudice to claims by way of reparation for unrestored gold, the portion of monetary gold thus accruing to each country participating in the pool shall be accepted by that country in full satisfaction of all claims against Germany for restitution of monetary gold.

C. A proportional share of the gold shall be allocated to each country concerned which adheres to this arrangement for the restitution of monetary gold and which can establish that a definite amount of monetary gold belonging to it was looted by Germany or, at any time after 12 March 1938, was wrongfully removed into German territory.

D. The question of the eventual participation of countries not represented at the Conference (other than Germany but including Austria and Italy) in the above-mentioned distribution shall be reserved, and the equivalent of the total shares which these countries would receive, if they were eventually admitted to participate, shall be set aside to be disposed of at a later date in such manner as may be decided by the Allied Governments concerned.

E. The various countries participating in the pool shall supply to the Governments of the United States of America, France and the United Kingdom, as the occupying Powers concerned, detailed and verifiable data regarding the gold losses suffered through looting by, or removal to, Germany.

F. The Governments of the United States of America, France and the United Kingdom shall take appropriate steps within the Zones of Germany occupied by them respectively to implement distribution in accordance with the foregoing provisions.

G. Any monetary gold which may be recovered from a third country to which it was transferred from Germany shall be distributed in accordance with this arrangement for the restitution of monetary gold.

Part IV: Entry into Force and Signature.
Article 1. Entry into Force.

This Agreement shall be open for signature on behalf of any Government represented at the Paris Conference on Reparation. As soon as it has been signed on behalf of Governments collectively entitled to not less than 80 per cent of the aggregate of shares in Category A of German reparation, it shall come into force among such Signatory Governments. The Agreement shall thereafter be in force among such Governments and those Governments on whose behalf it is subsequently signed.

Article 2. Signature.

The signature of each contracting Government shall be deemed to mean that the effect of the present Agreement extends to the colonies and overseas territories of such Government, and to territories under its protection of suzerainty or over which it at present exercises a mandate.

In witness whereof, the undersigned, duly authorised by their respective Governments, have signed in Paris the present Agreement, in the English and French languages, the two texts being equally authentic, in a single original, which shall be deposited in the Archives of the Government of The French Republic, a certified copy thereof being furnished by that Government to each Signatory Government.

———— for the Government of ————194
———— for the Government of ———— 194

UNANIMOUS RESOLUTIONS BY THE CONFERENCE

The Conference has also unanimously agreed to include the following Resolutions in the Final Act:

1. German Assets in the Neutral Countries.

The Conference unanimously resolves that the countries which remained neutral in the war against Germany should be prevailed upon by all suitable means to recognise the reasons of justice and of international security policy which motivate the Powers exercising supreme authority in Germany and the other Powers participating in this Conference in their efforts to extirpate the German holdings in the neutral countries.

2. Gold transferred to the Neutral Countries.

The Conference unanimously resolves that, in conformity with the policy expressed by the United Nations Declaration Against Axis Acts of Dispossession of 5 January 1943 and the United Nations Declaration on Gold of 22 February 1944 the countries which remained neutral in the war against Germany be prevailed upon to make available for distribution in accordance with Part III of the foregoing Agreement all looted gold transferred into their territories from Germany.

3. Equality of Treatment regarding Compensation for War Damage.

The Conference unanimously resolves that, in the administration of reconstruction or compensation benefits for war damage to property, the treatment accorded by each Signatory Government to physical persons who are nationals and to legal persons who are nationals of or are owned by nationals of any other Signatory Government, so far as they have not been compensated after the war for the same property under any other form or on any other occasion, shall be in principle not less favourable than that which the Signatory Government accords to its own nationals. In view of the fact that there are many special problems of reciprocity related to this principle, it is recognised that in certain cases the actual implementation of the principle cannot be achieved except through special agreements between Signatory Governments.

Reference to the Annex to the Final Act.

During the course of the Conference, statements were made by certain Delegates, in the terms set out in the attached Annex, concerning matters not within the competence of the Conference but having a close relation with its work. The Delegates whose Governments are represented on the Control Council for Germany undertook to bring those statements to the notice of their respective Governments.

In witness whereof, the undersigned have signed the present Final Act of the Paris Conference on Reparation.

Done in Paris on 21 December 1945, in the English and French languages, the two texts being equally authentic, in a single original, which shall be deposited in the Archives of the Government of the French Republic, certified copies thereof, being furnished by that Government to all the Governments represented at that Conference.

――――――― Delegate of the
Government of ―――――
――――――― Delegate of the
Government of ―――――

ANNEX.

1.   Resolution on the subject of Restitution.

The Albanian, Belgian, Czechoslovak, Danish, French, Greek, Indian, Luxembourg, Netherlands and Yugoslav Delegates agree to accept as the basis of a restitution policy the following principles:

(a) The question of the restitution of property removed by the Germans from the Allied countries must be examined in all cases in the light of the United Nations Declaration of 5 January 1943.

(b) In general, restitution should be confined to identifiable goods which (i) existed at the time of occupation of the country concerned, and were removed with or without payment; (ii) were produced during the occupation and obtained by an act of force.

(c) In cases where articles removed by the enemy cannot be identified, the claim for replacement should be part of the general reparation claim of the country concerned.

(d) As an exception to the above principles, objects (including books, manuscripts and documents) of an artistic, historical, scientific (excluding equipment of an industrial character), educational or religious character which have been looted by the enemy occupying Power shall, so far as possible, be replaced by equivalent objects if they are not restored.

(e) With respect to the restitution of looted goods which were produced during the occupation and which are still in the hands of German concerns or residents of Germany, the burden of proof of the original ownership of the goods shall rest on the claimants and the burden of proof that the goods were acquired by a regular contract shall rest on the holders.

(f) All necessary facilities under the auspices of the Commanders-in-Chief of the occupied Zones shall be given to the Allied States to send expert missions into Germany to search for looted property and to identify, store and remove it to its country of origin.

(g) German holders of looted property shall be compelled to declare it to the control authorities; stringent penalties shall be attached to infractions of this obligation.

2.   Resolution on Reparation from Existing Stocks and Current Production.

The Delegates of Albania, Belgium, Czechoslovakia, Denmark, Egypt, France, Greece, India, Luxembourg, the Netherlands, Norway and Yugoslavia,

In view of the decision of the Crimea Conference that Germany shall make compensation to the greatest possible extent for the losses and suffering which she has inflicted on the United Nations,

Considering that it will not be possible to satisfy the diverse needs of the Governments entitled to reparation unless the assets to be allocated are sufficiently varied in nature and the methods of allocation are sufficiently flexible,

Express the hope that no category of economic resources in excess of Germany's requirements as defined in Part III, Article 15 of the Potsdam Declaration, due account being taken of Article 19 of the same Part shall in principle be excluded from the assets, the sum total of which should serve to meet the reparation claims of the Signatory Governments.

It thus follows that certain special needs of different countries will not be met without recourse, in particular, to German existing stocks, current production and services, as well as Soviet reciprocal deliveries under Part IV of the Potsdam Declaration.

It goes without saying that the foregoing shall be without prejudice to the necessity of achieving the economic disarmament of Germany.

The above-named Delegates would therefore deem it of advantage were the Control Council to furnish the Inter-Allied Reparation Agency with lists of existing stocks, goods from current production and services, as such stocks, goods or services become available as reparation. The Agency should, at all times, be in a position to advise the Control Council of the special needs of the different Signatory Governments.

3.   Resolution regarding Property in Germany belonging to United Nations or their nationals.

The Delegates of Albania, Belgium, Czechoslovakia, France, Greece, Luxembourg, the Netherlands, Norway and Yugoslavia, taking into account the fact that the burden of reparation should fall on the German people, recommend that the following rules be observed regarding the allocation as reparation of property (other than ships) situated in Germany:

(a) To determine the proportion of German property available as reparation, account shall be taken of the sum total of property actually constituting the German economy, including assets belonging to a United Nation or to its nationals, but excluding looted property, which is to be restored.

(b) In general, property belonging legitimately to a United Nation or to its nationals, whether wholly owned or in the form of a share-holding of more than 48 per cent, shall so far as possible be excluded from the part of German property considered to be available as reparation.

(c) The Control Council shall determine the cases in which minority share-holdings of a United Nation or its nationals shall be treated as forming part of the property of a German juridical person and therefore having the same status as that juridical person.

(d) The foregoing provisions do not in any way prejudice the removal or destruction of concerns controlled by interests of a United Nation or of its nationals when this is necessary for security reasons.

(e) In cases where an asset which is the legitimate property of one of the United Nations or its nationals has been allocated as reparation, or destroyed, particularly in the cases referred to in paragraphs b, c, and d above, equitable compensation to the extent of the full value of this asset shall be granted by the Control Council to the United Nation concerned as a charge on the German economy. This compensation shall, when possible, take the form of a share-holding of equal value in German assets of a similar character which have not been allocated as reparation.

(f) In order to ensure that the property in Germany of persons declared by one of the United Nations to be collaborators or traitors shall be taken from them, the Control Council shall give effect in Germany to legislative measures and juridical decisions by courts of the United Nation concerned in regard to collaborators or traitors who are nationals of that United Nation or were nationals of that United Nation at the date of its occupation or annexation by Germany or entry into the war. The Control Council shall give to the Government of such United Nation facilities to take title to and possession of such assets and dispose of them.

4.   Resolution on captured War Material.

The Delegates of Albania, Belgium, Denmark, Luxembourg, the Netherlands, Norway, Czechoslovakia and Yugoslavia, taking account of the fact that part of the war material seized by the Allied Armies in Germany is of no use to these Armies but would, on the other hand, be of use to other Allied countries recommend:

(a) That, subject to Resolution 1 of this Annex on the subject of restitution, war material which was taken in the Western Zones of Germany and which has neither been put to any use nor destroyed as being of no value and which is not needed by the Armies of Occupation or is in excess of their requirements, shall be put at the disposal of countries which have a right to receive reparation from the Western Zones of Germany, and;

(b) That the competent authorities shall determine, the available types and quantities of this material and shall submit lists to the Inter-Allied Reparation Agency, which shall proceed in accordance with the provisions of Part II of the above Agreement.

5.   Resolution on German Assets in the Julian March and the Dodecanese.

The Delegates of Greece, the United Kingdom and Yugoslavia (being the Delegates of the countries primarily concerned), agree that:

(a) The German assets in Venezia, Giulia (Julian March) and in the Dodecanese shall be taken into custody by the military authorities in occupation of those parts of the territory which they now occupy, until the territorial questions have been decided; and

(b) As soon as a decision on the territorial questions has been reached, the liquidation of the assets shall be undertaken in conformity with the provisions of Paragraph A of Article 6 of Part I of the foregoing Agreement by the countries whose sovereignty over the disputed territories has been recognised.

6.   Resolution on Costs relating to Goods Delivered from Germany as Reparation.

The Delegates of Albania,, Australia, Belgium, Canada, Denmark, Egypt, France, Greece, India, Luxembourg, Norway, New Zealand, the Netherlands, Czechoslovakia and Yugoslavia, recommend that the costs of dismantling, packing, transporting, handling loading and all other costs of a general nature relating to goods to be delivered from Germany as reparation, until the goods in question have passed the German frontier, and expenditure incurred in Germany for the account of the Inter-Allied Reparation Agency or of the Delegates of the Agency should, in so far as they are payable in a currency which is legal tender in Germany, be paid as a charge on the German economy.

7.   Resolution on the Property of War Criminals

The Delegates of Albania, Belgium, France Luxembourg, Czechoslovakia and Yugoslavia express the view that:

(a) The legislation in force in Germany against German war criminals should provide for the confiscation of the property in Germany of those criminals, if it does not do so already;

(b) The property so confiscated, except such as is already available as reparation or restitution, should be liquidated by the Control Council and the net proceeds of the liquidation paid to the Inter-Allied Reparation Agency for division according to the principles set out in the foregoing Agreement.

8.   Resolution on Recourse to the International Court of Justice

The Delegates of Albania, Australia, Belgium, Denmark, France, Luxembourg, the Netherlands, Norway, Czechoslovakia and Yugoslavia recommend that:

Subject to the provisions of Article 3 of Part 1 of the Foregoing Agreement, the Signatory Governments agree to have recourse to the International Court of Justice for the solution of every conflict of law or of competence arising out of the provisions of the foregoing Agreement which has not been submitted by the parties concerned to amicable solution or arbitration.

Annex 5

PRESS HANDOUT No. 151
PR. BRANCH, C.C.G. (BE), BERLIN.

DEFINITION OF THE TERM "RESTITUTION"

1. The question of restitution of property removed by the Germans from Allied countries must be examined, in all cases, in light of the declaration of 5 January 1943.

2. Restitution will be limited, in the first instance, to identifiable goods which existed at the time of occupation of the country concerned and which have been taken by the enemy by force from the territory of the country. Also falling under measures of restitution are identifiable goods produced during the period of occupation and which have been obtained by force. All other property removed by the enemy is eligible for restitution to the extent consistent with reparations. However, the United Nations retain the right to receive from Germany compensation for this other property removed as reparations.

3. As goods of a unique character, restitution of which is impossible, a special instruction will fix the categories of goods which will be subject to replacement, the nature of these replacements, and the conditions under which such goods could be replaced by equivalent objects.

4. Relevant transportation expenses within the present German frontiers and any repairs necessary for proper transportation including the necessary manpower, material and organisation, are to be borne by Germany and are included in restitutions. Expenses outside Germany are borne by the recipient country.

5. The Control Council will deal on all questions of restitution with the Government of the Country from which the objects were looted.

22 January 1946

Annex 6

To: Belgian R.D.R. Mission   April 1947
      Czechoslovak R.D.R. Mission
      Danish R.D.R. Mission
      French R.D.R. Mission
      Greek R.D.R. Mission
      Yugoslav R.D.R. Mission
      Luxembourg R.D.R. Mission
      Netherlands R.D.R. Mission
      Norwegian R.D.R. Mission
      Polish R.D.R. Mission
Allied Liaison Branch, 100 E.Q. C.C.G. (BE) BAD SALZUFLEN, BAOR

Subject: Restitution: Objects of a Unique Character

1. I am directed to inform you that the Allied Control Authority has now defined the categories of objects of a unique character which may be subject to replacement, and the method by which claims may be made for replacement of such objects, the location of which cannot be traced.
2. Objects for which a claim for replacement may be made must fall within the following categories:-

   (a)   works of art of the masters of painting, engraving and sculpture;
   (b)   the most important works of distinguished masters of applied art and outstanding anonymous examples of national art;
   (c)   historical relics of any kind;
   (d)   manuscripts, books (such as rare *incunabula*), books having an intrinsic value or historical character, or constituting rare examples even of modern times;
   (e)   objects of importance to the history of science.

Where claims have been submitted for objects and it has been found impossible to trace their location in any of the force zones, if you consider whose objects fall within the categories specified in paragraph 2 above, you may submit claims for replacement on an equivalent basis to the R.D.R. Directorate, who will take each claim on its merits and ... action on the evidence presented.

Chief, RDR DIVISION

Annex 7

Law No. 52
Amended (3 April 1945)

BLOCKING AND CONTROL OF PROPERTY (British Zone)

ARTICLE I: CATEGORIES OF PROPERTY

1. All property within the occupied territory owned or controlled, directly or indirectly, in whole or in part, by any of the following is hereby declared to be subject to seizure of possession or title, direction, management, supervision or otherwise being taken into control by Military Government:

(a) The German Reich, or any of the Länder, Gaue, or Provinces, or other similar political sub-divisions, or any agency or instrumentality thereof, including all utilities, undertakings, public corporations or monopolies under the control of any of the above;

(b) Governments, nationals or residents of' nations, other than Germany, which have been at war with any of the United Nations at any time since 1 September 1939, and governments, nationals or residents of territories which have been occupied since that date by such nations or by Germany;

(c) The NSDAP, all offices, departments, agencies and organisations forming part of, attached to, or controlled by it; their officials and such of their leading members or supporters as may be specified by Military Government;

(d) All persons while held under detention or any other type of custody by Military Government;

(e) All organisations, clubs or other associations prohibited or dissolved by Military Government;

(f) Owners absent from the Supreme Commander's Area of Control and Nationals and Governments of United Nations and Neutral Nations;

(g) All other persons specified by Military Government by inclusion in lists or otherwise.

2. Property which has been the subject of duress, wrongful acts of confiscation, dispossession or spoliation from territories outside Germany, whether pursuant to legislation or by procedures purporting to follow forms of law or otherwise, is hereby declared to be equally subject to seizure of possession or title, direction, management, supervision or otherwise being taken into control by Military Government.

ARTICLE II: PROHIBITED TRANSACTIONS

3. Except as hereinafter provided, or when licensed or otherwise authorised or directed by Military Government, no person shall import, acquire or receive, deal in, sell, lease, transfer, export, hypothecate or otherwise dispose of, destroy or surrender possession, custody or control of any property:

(a) Enumerated in Article I hereof;

(b) Owned or controlled by any Kreis, municipality, or other similar political subdivision;

(c) Owned or controlled by any institution dedicated to public worship, charity, education, the arts and sciences;

(d) Which is a work of art or cultural material of value or importance, regardless of the ownership or control thereof.

ARTICLE III: RESPONSIBILITIES FOR PROPERTY

4. All custodians, curators, officials, or other persons having possession, custody or control of property enumerated in Articles I or II hereof are required:

(a) (i) To hold the same, subject to the directions of the Military Government, and pending such direction not to transfer deliver or otherwise dispose of the same;

(ii) To preserve, maintain and safeguard, and not to cause or permit any action which will impair the value or utility of such property;

(iii) To maintain accurate records and accounts with respect thereto and the income thereof.

(b)   When and as directed by Military Government:

     (i)   To file reports furnishing such data as may be required with respect to such property and all receipts and expenditures received or made in connection therewith;

     (ii)   To transfer and deliver custody, possession or control of such property and all books, records and accounts relating thereto, and

     (iii)   To account for the property and all income and products thereof.

5. No person shall do, cause or permit to be done any act of commission or omission which results in damage to or concealment of any of' the properties covered by this law.

ARTICLE IV: OPERATION OF BUSINESS ENTERPRISES AND GOVERNMENT PROPERTY

6. Unless otherwise directed and subject to such further limitation as may be imposed by Military Government:

(a)   Any business enterprise subject to control under this law may engage in all transactions ordinarily incidental to the normal conduct of its business activities within occupied Germany provided that such business enterprise shall not engage in any transaction which, directly or indirectly, substantially diminishes or imperils the assets of such enterprise or otherwise prejudicially affects its financial position and provided further that this does not authorise any transaction which is prohibited for any reason other than the issuance of this law;

(b)   Property described in Article I, i (a) shall be used for its normal purposes except as otherwise prohibited by Military Government.

ARTICLE V: VOID TRANSACTIONS

7. Any prohibited transaction effected without a duly issued license or authorisation from Military Government, and any transfer, contract or other arrangement made, whether before or after the effective date of this law, with intent to defeat or evade this law or the powers or objects of Military Government or the restitution of any property to its rightful owner, is null and void.

ARTICLE VI: CONFLICTING LAWS

8. In case of any inconsistency between this law or any order made under it and any German law the former prevail. All German laws, decrees and regulations providing for the seizure, confiscation or forced purchase of property enumerated in Articles I or II hereof, are hereby suspended.

ARTICLE VII: DEFINITIONS

9. For the purposes of this Law:

(a)   "Person" shall mean any natural person, collective person and any juristic person under public or private law, and any government including all political sub-divisions, public corporations, agencies and instrumentalities thereof;

(b)   "Business Enterprise" shall mean any person as above defined engaged in commercial, business or in public welfare, activities;

(c)   "Property" shall mean all movable and immovable property and all rights and interests in or claims to such property whether present or future, and shall include, but shall not be limited to, land and buildings, money, stocks/shares, patent rights or licences thereunder, or other evidences of ownership, and bonds, bank balances claims, obligations and other evidences of indebtedness and works of art and other cultural materials;

(d)   A "National" of a state or government shall mean a subject, citizen or partnership and any corporation or other juristic person existing under the laws of, or having a principal office in the territory of, such state or government;

(e)   "Germany" shall mean the area constituting Das Deutsche Reich as it existed on 31 December 1937.

ARTICLE VIII: PENALTIES

10. Any person violating any of the provisions of this law shall, upon conviction by a Military Government Court, be liable to any lawful punishment, including death, as the Court may determine.

ARTICLE IX: EFFECTIVE DATE

11. This Law shall become effective upon the date of its first promulgation.

BY ORDER OF MILITARY GOVERNMENT

Gesetz No. 52
Abgeändert (3 April 1945)

SPERRE UND KONTROLLE VON VERMÖGEN

ARTIKEL 1: ARTEN VON VERMÖGEN

1. Vermögen innerhalb des besetzten Gebietes, das unmittelbar oder mittelbar, ganz oder teilweise im Eigentum oder unter der Kontrolle der folgenden Personen steht, wird hiermit hinsichtlich Besitz oder Eigentumsrecht der Beschlagnahme, Weisung, Verwaltung, Aufsicht oder sonstigen Kontrolle durch die Militärregierung unterworfen:

(a) das Deutsche Reich oder eines seiner Länder, Gaue oder Provinzen oder eine andere staatliche oder eine kommunale Verwaltung, deren Dienststellen und Organe, einschließlich aller gemeinwirtschaftlicher Nutzungsbetriebe, Unternehmen, öffentlicher Körperschaften und Monopolbetriebe, die durch irgendeine der vorgenannten Verwaltungskörper kontrolliert werden;

(b) Regierungen, Staatsangehörige oder Einwohner von Staaten, — mit Ausnahme des Deutschen Reiches —, die sich mit einem Mitglied der Vereinigten Nationen zu irgendeinem Zeitpunkt seit dem 1. September 1939 im Kriegszustande befanden, und Regierungen, Staatsangehörige und Einwohner von Ländern, die seit diesem Tage von den vorgenannten Staaten oder von Deutschland besetzt waren;

(c) die NSDAP, deren Ämter und Stellen, Formationen und Organisationen, die zur NSDAP gehören, der NSDAP angeschlossen sind oder von ihr betreut werden; deren Beamte und diejenigen ihrer leitenden Mitglieder oder Anhänger, die von der Militärregierung bezeichnet werden;

(d) alle Personen, so lange wie sie von der Militärregierung in Haft oder sonst in Verwahrung gehalten werden;

(e) alle Organisationen, Klubs oder andere Vereinigungen die von der Militärregierung verboten oder aufgelöst werden;

(f) Eigentümer ausserhalb des Kontrollgebietes des Obersten Befehlshabers, sowie Regierungen und Staatsangehörige der Vereinigten Nationen und neutraler Staaten;

(g) alle anderen Personen, die von der Militärregierung durch Veröffentlichung in Listen oder auf andere Weise bezeichnet werden.

2. Der Beschlagnahme hinsichtlich Besitz oder Eigentumsrecht, der Weisung, Verwaltung, Aufsicht oder sonstigen Kontrolle durch die Militärregierung ist gleichfalls Vermögen unterworfen, das Gegenstand von Zwang, rechtswidriger Maßnahmen der Beschlagnahme, Besitzentziehung oder Plünderung in Gebieten außerhalb Deutschlands gewesen ist, gleichgültig, ob dies auf Grund von Gesetzgebung, von Verfahren, die rechtliche Formen zu beachten vorgaben, oder auf andere Weise geschehen ist.

ARTIKEL II: VERBOTENE HANDLUNGEN

3. Sofern nicht nachstehend etwas anderes bestimmt ist oder sofern nicht die Militärregierung ihre Ermächtigung oder Anweisung dazu erteilt hat, darf niemand Vermögen der nachbezeichneten Art einführen, erwerben, in Empfang nehmen, damit handeln, es verkaufen, vermieten, übertragen, ausführen, belasten oder sonstwie darüber verfügen, es zerstören oder den Besitz, die Verwahrung oder die Kontrolle darüber aufgeben:

(a) Vermögen, das in Artikel I aufgezählt ist;

(b) Vermögen im Eigentum oder unter der Kontrolle eines Kreises, einer Gemeinde oder einer sonstigen staatlichen oder kommunalen Verwaltung;

(c) Vermögen im Eigentum oder unter der Kontrolle einer Institution, die dem öffentlichen Gottesdienst, der Wohlfahrt, der Erziehung, der Kunst oder den Wissenschaften gewidmet ist;

(d) Kunstbesitz und Kulturgegenstande von Wert oder Bedeutung, ohne Rücksicht auf Eigentum oder Kontrolle.

ARTIKEL III: VERPFLICHTUNGEN HINSICHTLICH DER VERWALTUNG DES VERMÖGENS

4. Alle Verwahrer, Pfleger, Amtspersonen oder andere Personen, die Vermögen der in Artikel I oder II aufgezählten Art in Besitz, in Verwahrung oder unter Kontrolle haben, unterliegen den folgenden Verpflichtungen:

    (a)   (i) sie müssen das Vermögen nach den Weisungen der Militärregierung verwalten und dürfen bis zum Erlaß einer solchen Weisung dieses Vermögen weder übertragen noch aushändigen noch anderweitig darüber verfügen;

            (ii) sie müssen das Vermögen pfleglich behandeln, unversehrt erhalten und beschützen und dürfen nichts unternehmen, das den Wert oder die Brauchbarkeit derartigen Vermögens beeinträchtigt, noch derartige Handlungen durch Dritte zulassen:

            (iii) sie müssen hinsichtlich des Vermögens und dessen Einnahmen genaue Aufzeichnungen führen und Abrechnungen aufstellen;

    (b) sie müssen nach Maßgabe der Weisungen der Militärregierung:

            (i) Berichte einreichen und darin die hinsichtlich dieses Vermögens verlangten Angaben machen, sowie alle das Vermögen betreffenden Einnahmen und Ausgaben aufführen;

            (ii) die Verwahrung, den Besitz oder die Kontrolle solchen Vermögens und alle darauf bezüglichen Bücher, Aufzeichnungen und Abrechnungen übertragen und aushändigen und

            (iii) über das Vermögen, dessen Einnahmen und dessen Früchte Rechenschaft ablegen.

5. Niemand darf eine Handlung oder Unterlassung begehen, verursachen, noch durch Dritte zulassen, sofern hierdurch Vermögen, das den Bestimmungen dieses Gesetzes unterliegt, beschädigt oder verheimlicht wird.

ARTIKEL IV: BEHANDLUNG VON GESCHÄFSUNTERNEHMEN UND ÖFFENTLICHEN VERMÖGEN

6. Vorbehaltlich anderweitiger Anordnungen und weiterer Beschränkungen, die von der Militärregierung erlassen werden können, wird folgendes bestimmt:

    (a)   jedes geschäftliche Unternehmen, das der Kontrolle auf Grund dieses Gesetzes unterliegt, kann alle Geschäfte eingehen, die normalerweise der gewöhnliche Geschäftsbetrieb innerhalb des besetzten Gebietes Deutschlands mit sich bringt, vorausgesetzt, daß das Unternehmen nicht Geschäfte eingeht, die unmittelbar oder mittelbar die Werte des Unternehmens erheblich vermindern oder gefährden oder sonst seine finanzielle Lage nachteilig beeinflussen. Diese Bestimmung ermächtigt nicht zur Eingehung von Geschäften, die aus anderen als auf diesem Gesetz beruhenden Gründen verboten sind;

    (b)   Sofern nicht die Militärregierung ein Verbot erlässt, darf Vermögen der in Artikel I, i, (a) beschriebenen Art entsprechend seinem normalen Gebrauchszweck benutzt werden.

ARTIKEL V: NICHTIGE GESCHÄFTE

7. Nichtig ist jedes verbotene Geschäft, das ohne ordnungsgemäß erteilte Genehmigung oder Ermächtigung der Militärregierung abgeschlossen wird, sowie jede Übertragung, jeder Vertrag und jede Vereinbarung, gleichgültig ob diese Geschäfte vor oder nach dem Inkrafttreten dieses Gesetzes getätigt wurden, vorausgesetzt, daß die Absicht bestand, die Befugnisse oder Aufgaben der Militärregierung oder die Rückgabe von Vermögen an den berechtigten Eigentümer zu vereiteln oder zu umgehen.

ARTIKEL VI: WIDERSPRUCH ZWISCHEN GESETZEN

8. lm Falle eines Widerspruchs zwischen diesem Gesetz oder einer auf Grund desselben erlassenen Anordnung und deutschem Recht, geht das erstgenannte vor. Alle deutschen Gesetze, Erlasse und Bestimmungen, die Beschlagnahme, Einziehung oder Zwangsankauf von Vermögen der in Artikel I und II aufgezählten Art vorsehen, werden hiermit ausser Kraft gesetzt.

ARTIKEL VII: BEGRIFFSBESTIMMUNGEN

9. Für die Zwecke dieses Gesetzes gelten die folgenden Begriffsbestimmungen:

    (a)   "Personen" bedeutet jede natürliche Person, Gesamthandsgemeinschaft und juristische Person des öffentlichen oder privaten Rechts, ferner eine Regierung einschließlich staatlicher und kommunaler Verwaltungen, Körperschaften des öffentlichen Rechts, deren Dienststellen und Organe;

(b)   "Geschäftliches Unternehmen" bedeutet jede Person der unter *(a)* beschriebenen Art, die sich auf dem Gebiet des Handels und der Industrie oder der öffentlichen Wohlfahrt betätigt;

(c)   "Vermögen" bedeutet jedes bewegliche und unbewegliche Vermögen sowie alle Rechte und Interessen oder Ansprüche auf solches Vermögen, gleichgültig ob diese fällig sind oder nicht. Es schließt ein, ist aber nicht beschränkt auf: Grundstücke und Gebäude, Geld, Beteiligungen, Aktien, Patente, Gebrauchsmuster oder Lizenzen für deren Ausübung und andere Urkunden zum Nachweis von Eigentum, Schuldverschreibungen, Bankguthaben, Ansprüche, Verbindlichkeiten, andere Urkunden zum Nachweis von Verbindlichkeiten, sowie Kunstbesitz und andere Kulturgegenstände;

(d)   ein "Staatsangehöriger" eines Staates oder einer Regierung bedeutet ein Untertan oder Staatsbürger oder eine Personenvereinigung, Körperschaft oder sonstige juristische Person, die auf Grund der Gesetze eines derartigen Staates oder einer derartigen Regierung besteht oder in dem Gebiet eines derartigen Staates oder einer derartigen Regierung eine Niederlassung hat;

(e)   "Deutschland" bedeutet das Gebiet des Deutschen Reiches wie es am 31. Dezember 1937 bestanden hat.

ARTIKEL VIII: STRAFEN

10. Jeder Verstoß gegen die Bestimmungen dieses Gesetzes wird nach Schuldigsprechung des Täters durch ein Gericht der Militärregierung nach dessen Ermessen mit jeder gesetzlich zulässigen Strafe, einschließlich der Todesstrafe, bestraft.

ARTIKEL IX: INKRAFTTRETEN

11. Dieses Gesetz tritt am Tage seiner ersten Verkündung in Kraft.

<u>IM AUFTRAGE DER MILITÄRREGIERUNG</u>

Annex 8

Subject: GENERAL ORDER NO. 6
DECLARATION OF LOOTED PROPERTY IN BRITISH ZONE

Property Control Branch
Main HQ Finance Division

1. On instructions from the Finance Directorate, Allied Control Authority, a General Order calling for the declaration of all looted property in the British Zone and proclaiming it subject to Military control is to be published on 30 April 1946. A copy is attached at Appendix "A".

2. By this Order, the Germans are required to report possession or knowledge of all property removed from United Nations territory while that territory was occupied by Axis armed forces. The only exceptions are articles of trifling value and perishables already consumed. Even if property was received as a gift, or bought and paid for, it must still be reported if it was removed from occupied territory. A list of the United Nations concerned is attached at Appendix "B".

3. Reports will be submitted on Form MGAF(6), copies of which are now being printed. An initial delivery of not less than 10,000 will be made to all Regions on 30 April 1946, and supplementary deliveries as soon as possible thereafter.

4. The Landrat/Oberbürgermeister will be instructed to start a special office to receive and process declarations. Details will be forwarded shortly. Their gist is that the Landrat/Oberbürgermeister is responsible for producing three copies of each declaration, two in English and one in German, and for sending them through Regional HQ to Main HQ R.D.R. Division, MINDEN, B.A.0.R., which will be responsible for the final acts of restitution.

Chief, FINANCE DIVISION

APPENDIX A
MILITARY GOVERNMENT OF GERMANY BRITISH ZONE OF CONTROL
GENERAL ORDER NO. 6
(Pursuant to Military Government Law No. 52 — Blocking and Control of Property)
In pursuance of paragraph 2 of Article I and paragraph 4 (b) of Article III of Military Government Law No. 52, it is hereby ordered as follows:

ARTICLE I: Property Subject to Order
1. Subject to the exceptions contained in paragraph 2 of this Article, this General Order relates to all property in Germany which was situated in the territory of any of the United Nations occupied by the armed forces of Germany or her allies at any time during such occupation, or in such other territory as may be specified by the Military Government.

2. The present Order does not relate to:

(a)   Any article having at the date of this Order a value of less than 10 Reichsmarks, unless the total value of such articles held by one person is greater than 50 Reichsmarks.

(b)   Foodstuffs and perishable household goods which were consumed before the date of this Order.

3. Property shall be reported even although it has already been sequestrated, requisitioned, or declared for any purpose whatever in consequence of any other Order of Military Government.

ARTICLE II: Submission of Reports
 Within two months from the date of this General Order, all persons who have, or at any time have had, possession, custody, control, or knowledge of any property to which this Order relates, will make in respect of such property, and deliver to the Landrat or Oberbürgermeister of the Kreis in which they reside, a report on Military Government Finance Form (No MGAF (6)). Copies of this form can be obtained from the office of the Landrat or Oberbürgermeister. Instructions for completing the form are contained in it. The signature or signatures appended to the declaration must be witnessed by person over the age of 21, who must add his address and occupation.

ARTICLE III: Blocking of Property
 All property to which this General Order relates is hereby declared to be subject to the control of the Military Government under paragraph 2 of Article I Military Government Law No. 52. It must not be destroyed, sold, exchanged, removed without the express authority of the Military Government.

ARTICLE IV: Penalties
 7. Any person who fails to submit a report duly completed in accordance with the provisions of this General Order and the instructions contained in Form MGAF(6), or who omits any required fact or statement from such report, or who makes any misleading, false, or incomplete statement in such report, shall, upon conviction by a Military Government Court, suffer such penalty (including death) as the Court may determine.

ARTICLE V: Definitions
 8. The definitions contained in Article VII of Military Government Law No. 52 apply to this General Order.

ARTICLE VI: Effective Date
 9. The date of this General Order is 30 April 1946.

<u>BY ORDER OF MILITARY GOVERNMENT.</u>

APPENDIX B
UNITED NATIONS

For the purposes of this General Order, the United Nations referred to are as follows:

COUNTRY	DATE OF OCCUPATION
Belgium	10 May 1940
Czechoslovakia	1September 1939
Denmark	9 April 1940
France	17 May 1940
Great Britain (Channel Islands)	1 June 1940
Greece	28 October 1940
Luxembourg	10 May 1940
Netherlands	10 May 1940
Norway	9 April 1940
Poland	1 September 1939
Russia	22 June 1941
Yugoslavia	6 April 1941

Annex 9

LAW No. 59 — RESTITUTION OF IDENTIFIABLE PROPERTY (U.S. Zone)

PART 1: GENERAL PROVISIONS
ARTICLE 1: Basic Principles

1. It shall be the purpose of this Law to effect to the largest extent possible the speedy restitution of identifiable property (tangible and intangible property and aggregates of tangible and intangible property) to persons who were wrongfully deprived of such property within the period from 30 January 1933 to 8 May 1945 for reasons of race, religion, nationality, ideology or political opposition to National Socialism. For the purpose of this Law deprivation of property for reasons of nationality shall not include measures which under recognised rules of international law are usually permissible against property of nationals of enemy countries.

2. Property shall be restored to its former owner or to his successor in interest in accordance with the provisions of this Law even though the interests of other persons who had no knowledge of the wrongful taking must be subordinated. Provisions of law for the protection of purchasers in good faith, which would defeat restitution, shall be disregarded except where this Law provides otherwise.

PART II: CONFISCATED PROPERTY
ARTICLE 2: Acts of Confiscation

1. Property shall be considered confiscated within the provisions of this Law if the person entitled thereto has been deprived of it, or has failed to obtain it despite a well founded legal expectancy of acquisition, as the result of:
   a) A transaction *contra bonos mores*, threats or duress, or an unlawful taking or any other tort;
   b) Seizure due to a governmental act or by abuse of such act;
   c) Seizure as the result of measures taken by the NSDAP, its formations or affiliate organisations, provided the acts described in a) to c) were caused by or constituted measures of persecution for any of the reasons set forth in Article 1.

2. It shall not be permissible to plead that an act was not wrongful or *contra bonos mores* because it conformed with a prevailing ideology concerning discrimination against individuals on account of their race, religion, nationality, ideology or their political opposition to National Socialism.

3. Confiscation by a governmental act within the meaning of paragraph 1 b) shall be deemed to include, among other acts, sequestration, confiscation, forfeiture by order or operation of law, and transfer by order of the State or by a trustee appointed by the State. The forfeiture by virtue of a judgment of a criminal court shall also be considered a confiscation by a governmental act, if such judgment has been vacated by order of an appropriate court or by operation of law.

4. A judgment or order of a court, or of an administrative agency, which, although based on general provisions of law, was handed down solely or primarily with the purpose of injuring the party affected by it for any of the reasons set forth in Article 1 shall be deemed a specific instance of the abuse of a governmental act. The abuse of a governmental act shall also include the procurement of a judgment or of measures of execution by exploiting the circumstance that the opponent was, actually or by law, prevented from protecting his interests by virtue of his race, religion, nationality, ideology or his political opposition to National Socialism. The Restitution Authorities (Restitution Agency, Restitution Chamber and Oberlandeisgericht) shall disregard any such judgment or order of a court or administrative agency whether or not it may otherwise be appealed or reopened under existing law.

ARTICLE 3: Presumption of Confiscation

1. It shall he presumed in favour of any claimant that the following transactions entered into between 30 January 1933 and 8 May 1945 constitute acts of confiscation within the meaning of Article 2:
   a) Any transfer or relinquishment of property made during a period of persecution by any person who was directly exposed to persecutory measures on any of the grounds set forth in Article 1;
   b) Any transfer or relinquishment of property made by a person who belonged to a class of

persons which on any of the grounds set forth in Article 1 was to be eliminated in its entirety from the cultural and economic life of Germany by measures taken by the State or the NSDAP.

2. In the absence of other factors proving an act of confiscation within the meaning of Article 2, the presumptions set forth in paragraph 1 may be rebutted by showing that the transferor was paid a fair purchase price. Such evidence by itself shall not, however, rebut the presumptions if the transferor was denied the free right of disposal of the purchase price on any of the grounds set forth in Article 1.

3. A fair purchase price within the meaning of this Article shall mean the amount of money which a willing buyer would pay and a willing seller would take, taking into consideration, in the case of a commercial enterprise, the normal good will which such enterprise would have in the hands of a person not subject to persecutory measures referred to in Article 1.

ARTICLE 4: Power of Avoidance

1. Any transaction entered into by a person belonging to a class referred to in Paragraph 1 b) of Article 3 within the period from 15 September 1935 (the date of the first Nuremberg laws) to 8 May 1945 may, because of the duress imposed on such class, be avoided by a claimant where such transaction involved the transfer or relinquishment of any property unless:

   a) The transaction as such and with its essential terms would have taken place even in the absence of National Socialism, or

   b) The transferee protected the property interests of the claimant (Article 7) or his predecessor in interest in an unusual manner and with substantial success, for example, by helping him in transferring his assets abroad or through similar assistance.

2. In determining under paragraph 1 a) whether the transaction would have taken place even in the absence of National Socialism, the fact that the transferor himself offered to sell the property to the transferee, or the transferor received a fair purchase price (see Article 3, paragraph 3) the free right of disposal of which was not denied him on any of the grounds set forth in Article 1, shall be considered by the Restitution Authority together with all other facts, but neither fact, either singly or in conjunction with the other shall be sufficient to show that the transaction, would have taken place even in the absence of National Socialism.

3. Similarly neither of these facts, either singly or in conjunction with the other, shall be sufficient to show that the claimant is estopped from exercising the power of avoidance by reason of his own previous conduct or that of his predecessor in interest.

4. The term "claim for restitution" as used in this Law shall be deemed to include all claims based on the right to exercise the power of avoidance. The exercise of the Power of avoidance shall have the effect that the property transferred or relinquished pursuant to the voided transaction shall for the purposes of this Law be deemed to be confiscated property.

5. The filing of a claim for restitution shall, whether or not it is specifically stated, be deemed to be an exercise of the right of avoidance on behalf of the person entitled to exercise such right.

ARTICLE 5: Donations

Where a person persecuted for any of the reasons set forth in Article 1 has transferred property to another gratuitously within the period from 30 January 1933 to 8 May 1945, it shall be presumed that the transfer constituted a bailment or fiduciary relationship rather than a donation. This presumption shall not apply where the personal relations between the transferor and the recipient make it probable that the transfer constituted a donation based on moral considerations (Anstandsschenkung); no claims for restitution may be asserted in such cases.

ARTICLE 6: Bailment and Fiduciary Relationships

1. The provisions of Parts III to VII of this Law shall not apply to bailments and fiduciary agreements entered into in order to prevent damage to property threatened for any of the reasons set forth in Article 1, or to mitigate existing damage to property inflicted for such reasons.

2. The claimant (Article 7) may at any time terminate contracts and any other arrangements described in paragraph 1, such termination to be effective immediately, any contractual or statutory provisions to the contrary notwithstanding.

3. It shall not be an admissible defence for the bailee or fiduciary that the contracts and agreements described in paragraph 1 violated a statutory prohibition existing at the time of the transaction or enacted thereafter, or that a statutory or contractual form requirement had not been complied with, provided that this failure was attributable to the National Socialist regime.

PART III: GENERAL PROVISIONS ON RESTITUTION

ARTICLE 7: Person Entitled to Restitution (Hereinafter called Claimant)

The claim for restitution shall appertain to any person whose property was confiscated (hereinafter called Persecuted Person) or to any successor in interest.

ARTICLE 8: Successorship of Dissolved Associations

1. If a juridical person or unincorporated association was dissolved or forced to dissolve for any of the reasons set forth in Article 1, the claim for restitution which would have appertained to such juridical person and unincorporated association had it not been dissolved, may be enforced by a successor organisation to be appointed by Military Government.

2. The provisions of paragraph 1 shall not be applicable to the organisations referred to in Article 9.

ARTICLE 9: Rights of Individual Partners

If a partnership, company or corporation organised under the Commercial Law, was dissolved or forced to dissolve for any of the reasons set forth in Article 1, the claim for restitution may be asserted by any associate (partner, member or shareholder). The claim for restitution shall be deemed to have been filed on behalf of all associates who have the same cause of action. The claim may be withdrawn or compromised only with the approval of the appropriate Restitution Authority. Notice of the filing of the claim shall be given to all other known associates or their successors in interest and to a successor organisation competent according to Article 10. Within the limits of its authority the successor organisation may represent in the proceedings any associate whose address is unknown, in accordance with the provisions of Article 11.

ARTICLE 10: Successor Organisation as Heir to Persecuted Persons

A successor organisation to be appointed by Military Government, shall, instead of the State, be entitled to the entire estate of any persecuted person in the case provided for in Section 1936 of the Civil Code (Escheat of estate of person dying without heirs). Neither the State nor any of its Subdivisions nor a political self-governing body will be appointed as successor organisation. The same shall apply to other rights in the nature of escheat based on any other provision of law.

ARTICLE 11: Special Rights of Successor Organisations

1. If within six months after the effective date of this Law no petition for restitution has been filed with respect to confiscated property, a successor organisation appointed pursuant to Article 10 may file such a petition on or before 31 December 1948 and apply for all measures necessary to safeguard the property.

2. If the claimant himself has not filed a petition on or before 31 December 1948, the successor organisation by virtue of filing the petition shall acquire the legal position of the claimant. Only after that date, and not prior thereto, shall it be entitled to prosecute the claim.

3. The provisions of paragraphs 1 and 2 hereof shall not apply if, and to the extent to which the claimant, in the period from 8 May 1945 to 31 December 1948, has delivered a waiver of his claim for restitution, in writing and in express terms, to the restitutor, the appropriate Restitution Authority, or the Central Filing Agency.

ARTICLE 12: Obligation of Successors In Interest to Give Information

1. If so ordered by the appropriate Restitution Authority a claimant who acquired the claim for restitution directly or indirectly from the persecuted person shall submit, if known to him, either the address of his predecessors in interest, in particular of the persecuted person, or of his heirs, or execute an affidavit to the effect that he does not know the present address or any data from which it might be ascertained.

2. The successor organisation appointed pursuant to Article 10 shall submit the address of the person entitled to restitution, provided it is known to it, or such data known to it which might serve to locate this person, or an affidavit signed by its legal representative to the effect that it knows neither the address of the person entitled to restitution nor any data which might serve to locate this person.

ARTICLE 13: Designation of Successor Organisations

Regulations to be issued by Military Government will Provide for the manner of appointment of successor organisations, their obligations to their persecutee charges, and any further rights or obligations they may have under Military Government or German law.

ARTICLE 14: Persons Liable to Make Restitution

The person liable to make restitution (hereinafter referred to as restitutor), within the meaning of this Law, is the present possessor of confiscated tangible property or the present holder of a confiscated intangible interest, or of an aggregate of tangible and intangible property.

ARTICLE 15: Effect of an Adjudication of a Restitution Claim

1. Unless otherwise provided in this Law, a judgment directing restitution shall have the effect that the loss of the property shall be deemed not to have occurred and that after-acquired interests by third persons shall be deemed not to have been acquired.

2. Any adjudication of a restitution claim shall be effective for and against any person who participated in the proceeding or who, being entitled to participate, was duly served.

ARTICLE 16: Alternative Claim for Additional Payment

1. If he relinquishes all other claims under this Law the claimant may demand, from the person who first acquired the property, payment of the difference between the price received and the fair purchase price of the property as defined in Article 3, paragraph 3. Proper interest shall be added to this amount in accordance with the provisions on profits contained in this Law.

2. The demand for payment shall not be permissible:

   a) after the property has been restored to the claimant by a judgment no longer subject to appeal;

   b) after the Restitution Agency or Chamber has rendered a decision on the merits; or

   c) after the claimant and the restitutor have reached an amicable agreement with regard to the restitution claim.

ARTICLE 17: Valuation

1. Where the value of property is relevant according to the provisions of this Law, increases in the price caused by the decrease of the purchasing power of money shall not be considered an enhancement in the value.

2. Future implementing regulations may provide for the valuation of property which, because not now determinable, is at present not subject to the property tax. The provision of Article 27, paragraph 2, shall remain unaffected.

PART IV: LIMITATIONS ON THE RIGHT TO RESTITUTION

ARTICLE 18: Expropriation

1. Confiscated property which, after the time of confiscation, was expropriated for a public purpose, or sold or assigned to an enterprise for the benefit of which the right of expropriation could be exercised shall not be subject to restitution if on the effective date of this Law the property is still used for a public purpose, and if such purpose is still recognised as lawful.

2. If property is not subject to restitution for the reasons set forth in paragraph 1, the present owner shall compensate the claimant adequately to the extent to which his claims pursuant to Article 29 *et seq. infra*, do not result in such compensation.

ARTICLE 19: Protection of Ordinary and Usual Business Transactions

Except as provided in Articles 20 and 21, tangible personal property shall not be subject to restitution if the present owner or his predecessor in interest acquired it in the course of an ordinary and usual business transaction in an establishment normally dealing in that type of property. However, the provisions of this Article shall not apply to religious objects or to property which has been acquired from private ownership if such property is an object of unusual artistic, scientific, or sentimental personal value, or was acquired at an auction, or at a private sale in an establishment engaged to a considerable extent in the business of disposing of confiscated property.

ARTICLE 20: Money

Money shall be subject to restitution only if at the time he acquired the money the restitutor knew or should have known under the circumstances that it had been obtained by way of confiscation.

ARTICLE 21: Bearer Instruments

1. Bearer instruments shall not be subject to restitution if the present holder proves that, at the time he acquired the instrument, he neither knew nor should have known under the circumstances that the instrument had been confiscated at any time. Unless special circumstances indicate otherwise, good faith shall be presumed within the scope of this provision, if such property was acquired in the course of ordinary and usual business transactions, especially on the stock exchange, and if the transaction did not involve a dominant participation.

2. The provisions of paragraph 1 shall also apply to interests in bearer instruments deposited in a central account (Sammelverwahrung).

3. Bearer instruments and interests in bearer instruments shall, however, be unconditionally subject to restitution if they represent:

a) a participation in an enterprise with a small number of members, such as a family corporation; or

b) a participation in an enterprise the shares of which had not been negotiated on the open market; or

c) a dominant participation in an enterprise as to which was known, generally or in the trade, that a dominant participation was held by persons who belonged to one of the classes described in Article 3, paragraph 1 b); or

d) a dominant participation in a business establishment which was registered under the Third Ordinance to the Reich Citizen Law (Reichsbürgergesetz) of 14 June 1938 (RGBI. I, p. 627).

4. For the purpose of subsections c) and d) of paragraph 3, a participation shall be deemed to be dominant if it permitted the exercise of a considerable amount of influence upon the management of the business enterprise either by itself or on the basis of a working agreement which existed prior to or at the time of the confiscation.

ARTICLE 22: Restitution in Event of Changes In the Legal or Financial Structure of an Enterprise

If a participation of the type described in Article 21, paragraph 3 had been confiscated and if the enterprise had been dissolved or merged into, or consolidated with, or transformed into another enterprise, or had been changed in any other way in its legal or financial structure, or if its assets had been transferred wholly or in part to another enterprise, the claimant may demand that he be given an appropriate share in the modified or newly formed enterprise or in the enterprise which had acquired wholly or in part the assets of the original enterprise, thereby restoring as far as possible his original participation and the rights incident thereto.

ARTICLE 23: Enforcement of the Principles Set Forth In Article 22

The Restitution Chamber shall take all measures necessary and appropriate to effectuate the rights granted to the claimant under Article 22, provided his claims under Article 29 *et seq.* do not result in sufficient indemnification within the purview of Article 22. To that end the Restitution Chamber shall order, if necessary, the cancellation, new issue or exchange of shares, participation certificates, interim certificates, and other instruments evidencing a participation; or the establishment of a partnership relation between the claimant and the enterprise as described in Article 22, and it shall order the performance of any act required by law in order to effectuate those rights. These measures shall be taken primarily at the expense of those who are liable to make restitution according to the principles of this Law. If such measures would affect any other shareholder they shall be ordered only to the extent to which such other shareholder benefited directly or indirectly from the confiscation in connection with the facts as described in Article 22; or if the enterprise itself would be liable to make restitution or to damages under this Law or under the generally applicable rules of law, especially on the principle of respondent superior.

ARTICLE 24: Other Enterprises

The provisions of Articles 22 and 23 shall be applicable if the object of the confiscation was a business owned by an individual; or a participation in a partnership or a limited partnership; or a personal participation in a limited partnership corporation (Kommanditgesellschaft auf Aktien); or a share in an association with limited liability (Gesellschaft mit beschränkter Haftung) or in a co-operative; or a share of a similar legal nature.

ARTICLE 25: Service

Insofar as it may become necessary pursuant to Articles 22 to 24 to make service on any unknown associate or on any associate whose present address is unknown, service shall be made by publication pursuant to Article 61.

ARTICLE 26: Delivery of a Substitute in Lieu of Restitution

1. Where subsequent to the confiscation the object other-wise subject to restitution has undergone fundamental changes considerably enhancing its value, the Restitution Chamber may order the delivery of an adequate substitute in lieu of restitution; in determining the adequacy of the substitute the Restitution Chamber shall consider the value of the property at the time of the confiscation and the equitable interests of the parties. The claimant may, however, demand the assignment of an appropriate share in the property unless the restitutor offers a substitute of similar nature and of like value. The claimant may avail himself of the provisions of the first and second sentence above even if the fundamental change did not result in a considerable enhancement of the value of the object.

2. The restitutor shall not be entitled to benefits of the provisions of paragraph 1 if he had acquired the object by way of an aggravated confiscation within the meaning of Article 30, or if he knew or should have known under the circumstances at the time the fundamental changes were made that the object at any time had been obtained by way of an aggravated confiscation.

3. Where the restitutor has combined the object subject to restitution with another objects as an essential part thereof, he may separate the latter object and appropriate it. In this case, he shall restore the object to its former condition at his own expense. Where the claimant obtained possession of the combined objects prior to the separation he shall be required to permit the separation; he may, however, withhold his consent unless security is given to save him harmless from any damage resulting from the separation. The restitutor shall not have the privilege of separation if he is not entitled to compensation for expenditures according to the provisions of this Law; or if he is indemnified at least for the value which the separable part of the object would have to him after separation.

4. In determining whether property has been enhanced in value within the meaning of paragraph 1, sentence 1, only such enhancement in value for which the restitutor may claim compensation under the provisions of this Law shall be taken into account.

ARTICLE 27: Restitution of an Aggregate of Properties

1. The claimant may not limit his demand for restitution to separate items out of an aggregate of properties if the aggregate can be returned as a whole and if the limitation of the restitution to separate items would inequitably prejudice the restitutor or the creditors.

2. The claimant may refuse to include in his petition any claim against a public agency falling within the scope of Article 1 of the Laws on Judicial Aid for the Equitable Settlement of Contracts, as uniformly enacted, with the consent of the Laenderrat, in Bavaria, Hesse, and Wuerttemberg-Baden, where such claims are among the assets of a commercial enterprise or of any other aggregate of property subject to restitution.

ARTICLE 28: Protection of Debtors

Until notified of the filing of the petition for restitution, the debtor of a confiscated claim may discharge his obligation by payment to the restitutor. The same rule shall apply in favour of a debtor who prior to the entry in the Land Title Register (Grundbuch) of an objection to its correctness or a notice of restitution makes a payment to a restitutor entered in the Land Title Register.

PART V: COMPENSATION AND ANCILLARY CLAIMS

ARTICLE 29: Subrogation

1. Upon request of the claimant, a former holder of confiscated property who would be liable to restitution if he were still holding it shall turn over any compensation or assign any claim for indemnification which he might have acquired in connection with the event preventing the return of such property. Whatever the claimant receives from one of several restitutors shall be credited against the claims he holds against the remaining ones.

2. The same shall apply with respect to any compensation or any claim compensation which the holder or former holder of confiscated property acquired in connection with deterioration of such property.

3. In case of the confiscation of a business enterprise the claim for restitution shall extend to the assets acquired after the confiscation, unless the restitutor shows that such assets were not paid for with funds of the enterprise. If the purchase was paid for out of the funds of the enterprise, a corresponding increase in the value of the business shall be deemed to constitute profits within the meaning of Articles 30, 32, and 33. This rule shall be applicable also to any other aggregate of property. If the purchase was

not made with funds of the enterprise the restitutor shall have the privilege of separation as set forth in Article 26, paragraph 3, provided, however, that the claimant shall have the privilege of taking over the property pursuant to Article 26, paragraph 3, third sentence, only if otherwise the operation of the enterprise would be hampered considerably.

4. Any claims of the claimant pursuant to Article 30 *et seq.*which are more extensive shall remain unaffected.

ARTICLE 30: Strict Liability

1. Any person who has obtained the confiscated property from the persecuted person through a transaction *contra bonos mores* or as the result of threats made by him or on his behalf, or by an unlawful taking or other tort (hereinafter referred to as aggravated confiscation), shall be liable under the general rules of the Civil Code governing tort liability for damages arising from failure to return such property on the ground of impossibility or from deterioration and also for surrender of profits and for any other indemnification provided therein.

2. The possessor or former possessor of confiscated property shall be subject to the same liability if he knew or should have known under the circumstances (within the meaning of Section 259 of the Penal Code) at the time he acquired the property that had been obtained at any time by way of an aggravated confiscation.

3. If the claimant is entitled to profits he may demand that they be computed on the basis of the usual rate of profits for that particular type of property, such rate to be specified by an implementing regulation, unless it is manifest in an individual case that these standard rules are substantially inappropriate.

ARTICLE 31: Mitigated Liability

1. Any holder or former holder of confiscated property who acquired the property by means of a confiscation not constituting an aggravated confiscation within the meaning of Article 30, paragraph 1, (hereinafter referred to as simple confiscation) shall be liable in damages if he is unable to return the property or if it has deteriorated, unless he can prove that he has exercised due diligence.

2. Any holder or former holder shall be similarly liable from the time when he knew, or should have known under the circumstances, that the property at any time had been obtained by way of a confiscation within the meaning of this Law.

3. Where real property or any interest in the nature of real property has been confiscated, a possessor or former possessor shall be liable according to paragraph 1, unless he shows that because of unusual circumstances he neither knew, nor should have known under the circumstances that the Property at any time had been obtained by way of confiscation within the meaning of this Law.

ARTICLE 32: Return of Profits in Case of Simple Confiscation

1. Any holder, or former holder of confiscated property who at any time obtained such property by way of a simple confiscation shall pay the claimant adequate compensation for the period of time in which such holder enjoyed the profits of the property. Article 31, paragraphs 2 and 3, shall be applicable.

2. The amount of the net profits of the property less the amount of an adequate remuneration for management of the property by the restitutor shall be deemed to be an adequate compensation. The remuneration for management shall not exceed 50 per cent of the net profits drawn from the property, except where relatively small amounts are involved. Profits which the restitutor wilfully diminished or neglected to draw shall be added. Taxes paid on the net income drawn from the property and the interest on the purchase price paid by the restitutor shall adequately be taken into consideration. Paragraph 3 of Article 30 shall be applicable.

ARTICLE 33: Release from Liability

1. A holder or former holder of confiscated property shall not be liable in damages if he is unable to return the property or because the property has deteriorated, nor shall he be liable to account for profits, as long as he neither knew, nor should have known under the circumstances, that the property at any time had been obtained by way of confiscation. The provisions of Article 31, paragraph 3, shall remain unaffected.

2. Profits which under rules of good husbandry are not to be regarded as income from such property shall be returned in any event, pursuant to the rules of the Civil Code on unjust enrichment.

3. Under no circumstances shall remuneration for management be paid for a period for which the claimant cannot claim an accounting for profits.

ARTICLE 34: Compensation for Expenditures

1. Ordinary expenses for the maintenance of property subject to restitution shall not be refunded; they may, however, be taken into consideration in determining the net profits under Articles 30 and 32.

2. For other necessary expenditures compensation may be demanded to the extent that such expenditures should not have been written off in the course of proper management of the confiscated property.

3. For other than necessary expenditures the restitutor may demand compensation only to the extent that such expenditures should not have been written off in the course of proper management of the confiscated property and only to the extent to which the value of the property is still enhanced by such expenditures at the time of the restitution. In this case the liability of the claimant shall be limited to the restituted property and any other compensation to which he is entitled under this Law. The exercise of the claimant's privileges of limiting his liability shall be governed by Sections 1990 and 1991 of the Civil Code.

4. A person who at any time obtained the confiscated property by way of an aggravated confiscation may demand compensation only for necessary expenditures under the conditions set forth in paragraph 2 hereof and under the further condition that such expenditures were in the claimant's interest. The same rule shall apply to any holder or former holder of the confiscated property from the time when he knew, or should have known under the circumstances, that the property at any time has been obtained by way of an aggravated confiscation.

5. Where the provision of Article 26, paragraph 1, are found to be applicable, no compensation can be claimed for any expenditures which resulted in a fundamental change substantially enhancing the value of the property within the meaning of Article 26, paragraph 1.

ARTICLE 35: Duty to Furnish Particulars

The parties shall be liable to furnish particulars, where such information is necessary to effectuate claims under this Law. Sections 259 to 261 of the Civil Code shall be applicable.

ARTICLE 36: Title to Increase

The provisions of the Civil Code shall be applicable to the acquisition of title to the produce and other increase of confiscated property. Where the possessor or former possessor did not obtain the property by way of an aggravated confiscation, he shall be deemed to be the owner of the produce and other increase of the confiscated property, without prejudice, however, to his obligation to return any profits.

PART VI: CONTINUED EXISTENCE OF INTERESTS AND LIABILITY FOR DEBTS

ARTICLE 37: Continued Existence of Interests

1. Any interest in the confiscated property shall continue to be effective to the extent to which it existed prior to the act constituting the confiscation, and insofar as it has not been extinguished or discharged thereafter. The same shall apply to any interest created at a later date to the extent to which the total amount of all claims (principal and accessory claims) does not exceed the total amount of all such claims as they existed prior to the act constituting the confiscation (hereinafter referred to as limit of encumbrances). An interest which does not involve payment of money shall continue to be effective only where an interest of the same kind already existed prior to the confiscation and the interest subsequently created is not more burdensome than that existing at the time of the confiscation, or where such interest would have come into existence even though the property had not been confiscated.

2. The limit of encumbrances shall be raised to the extent to which any interest of a third person results from expenditures for which the restitutor may claim compensation pursuant to Article 34. Any other interest of a third person which exceeds the limit of encumbrances set forth in paragraph 1 of this Article and which results from expenditures for which the restitutor cannot claim compensation pursuant to Article 34 shall be extinguished unless at the time of the restitution the value of the object is still increased correspondingly as the result of the expenditure and the third person shows that he neither knew, nor should have known under the circumstances that the property had been obtained by way of an aggravated confiscation.

3. Interests in the property subject to restitution which, in connection with the confiscation, had been created in favour of the claimant or his predecessor in interest shall continue to be effective irrespective of the limit of encumbrances. This shall be without prejudice to any claim of the claimant for the restitution of such interests in case they had been confiscated.

4. Interests resulting from the conversion of the Home-Rent Tax, with the exception of overdue payments, shall continue to be effective irrespective of the limit of encumbrances.

ARTICLE 38: Devolving of Encumbrances

If real property has been encumbered by any transaction, legal act, or any governmental act constituting a confiscation within the meaning of this Law, such an encumbrance shall devolve on the claimant and shall not be considered in computing the limit of encumbrances as provided in Article 37. This shall apply particularly to encumbrances which were entered in the Land Title Register (Grundbuch) in connection with the Capital Flight Tax, the Property Tax on Jews and similar enactments.

ARTICLE 39: Personal Liability

If, prior to the confiscation of real property, the claimant or his predecessor in interest was personally liable in respect of any debt which was secured by a mortgage, land charge (Grundschuld) or annuity charge (Rentenschuld) on the real property, he shall assume personal liability at the time of recovery of title to the extent to which the mortgage, land charge or annuity charge continues to be effective under the preceding provisions. The same shall apply in case of obligations in regard to which the restitutor may demand to be released pursuant to Article 34 of this Law and Section 257 of the Civil Code. The same shall apply also in the case of liabilities which continue to be effective according to Article 37, paragraph 1, second sentence, and which replace charges for which the claimant or his predecessor in interest had been personally liable.

ARTICLE 40: Demand for Assignment

1. The claimant may demand the assignment to him, without compensation, of any mortgage, land charge or annuity charge against real property subject to restitution which is held by any holder or former holder of such property who at any time obtained the property by way of an aggravated confiscation. This shall not apply to the personal debt on which the mortgage is based. Any interest created prior to the confiscation shall be subject to the provisions of Article 46, paragraph 3.

2. The provisions of this Article shall not apply to encumbrances created pursuant to the provisions of this Law.

ARTICLE 41: Liability for Debts of a Business Enterprise

1. If the claimant recovers a business enterprise or another aggregate of properties, the creditors holding debts incurred in the operation of the enterprise or obligations with which the aggregate of properties has been encumbered may, from the time of the recovery, also assert against the claimant such claims as existed at such time.

2. In this case the liability of the claimant shall be limited to the restituted property and any other compensation to which he is entitled under this Law. The claimant's privilege of limiting his liability shall be governed by Sections 1990 and 1991 of the Civil Code.

3. The claimant shall not be liable under paragraphs 1 and 2 to the extent to which the total amount of liabilities exceeds the limit of encumbrances to be computed in an analogous application of Article 37, and insofar as the excess in the amount of liabilities is not covered by an excess of assets resulting from the application of Article 29, paragraph 3. In such case the Restitution Chamber, in its equitable discretion, shall take the requisite measures in analogous application of Article 37. Debts held by creditors who neither knew nor should have known under the circumstances that the business enterprise or other aggregate of properties at any time had been obtained by way of confiscation within the meaning of this Law shall have preference. Liabilities of equal priority shall be reduced *pro rata*, if necessary.

ARTICLE 42: Leases

1. If a restitutor or any former possessor has leased real property to a third person, the claimant may terminate the lease by giving notice, the termination to become effective on the date prescribed by Law. Such notice cannot be given until the Restitution Authority has determined that the property is subject to restitution, and such determination is no longer subject to appeal, or until the fact that the property is subject to restitution has, been acknowledged in any other way. The notice must be given within three months from such date, or from the date when the claimant in fact takes possession of the real property, if he takes possession at a later date.

2. The provisions of the Law for the Protection of Tenants (Mieterschutzgesetz) in the version of 15 December 1942 (RGBI. I, page 712) shall not apply to any restitutor or his predecessor in interest who obtained the property subject to restitution by way of an aggravated confiscation or who, at the time he acquired the property, knew, or should have known under the circumstances, that the property at any time had been obtained by way of an aggravated confiscation. The provisions of the Law for the Protection of Tenants shall also not apply insofar as the claimant is in need of adequate dwelling space for himself or his close relatives. Similarly, the Law for the Protection of Tenants shall not apply if dwelling space, which at the time of the confiscation or of the filing of the petition for restitution was used in connection with the operation of a business enterprise subject to restitution, is needed for the

continued operation of such enterprise. The provisions of the Law for the Protection of Tenants shall not be applicable to space used for commercial purposes if the claimant has a legitimate interest in the immediate return of such space.

3. Leases entered into with the approval of Military Government may be cancelled only with the consent of Military Government.

ARTICLE 43: Employment Contracts

Irrespective of any contractual provision to the contrary, the claimant may terminate any existing employment contract made since the confiscation by the restitutor or any former holder of a business enterprise subject to restitution by giving notice as provided in a collective labor agreement or in the absence thereof within the statutory period; this shall not prejudice the right of the claimant to terminate an employment contract for just cause without notice. Notice cannot be given until the Restitution Authorities have determined that the enterprise is subject to retribution and such determination is no longer subject to appeal, or until the fact that an enterprise is subject to restitution has been acknowledged in some other way. Such notice must be given within three months from such date, or from the time when the claimant in fact obtains possession of the enterprise, if he obtains possession at a later date.

PART VII: CLAIMS OF THE RESTITUTOR FOR REFUND AND INDEMNIFICATION
ARTICLE 44: Obligation to Refund

1. In exchange for the restitution of the confiscated property the claimant shall refund to the restitutor the consideration received by him, in kind if possible. This amount shall be increased by the amount of any encumbrance against the confiscated property existing at the time of confiscation and discharged thereafter, unless such encumbrance has been replaced by another encumbrance which continues to be effective, and unless the discharged encumbrance was created as the result of a confiscation within the meaning of this Law.

2. Where several items of property were confiscated for a consideration consisting of a lump sum, but restitution takes place in regard to some of these items only, the lump sum shall be reduced *pro rata*, in the ratio which at the time of the confiscation existed between the lump sum and the value of those items to be restituted.

3. If at the time of the confiscation the claimant, for any of the reasons set forth in Article 1, did not obtain, wholly or in part, the power freely to dispose of the consideration received, the refund shall be diminished by a like amount. The claimant shall assign to the restitutor any claim for indemnification to which he may be entitled with respect to this amount.

4. Under no circumstances shall the claimant be required to refund any amount exceeding the value of the confiscated property at the time of restitution, less the value of the encumbrance recognised against the property.

ARTICLE 45: Equitable Lien

The restitutor shall have no equitable lien (Zurueckbehaltungsrecht) for his claims insofar as such lien would substantially delay the speedy restitution of the confiscated property. The same shall apply to any execution or attachment of the confiscated property based on any counterclaim.

ARTICLE 46: Judicial Determination of Terms of Payment

1. The Restitution Authorities shall determine the terms of payments to be made in connection with restitution, taking into consideration the purpose of this Law, the debtor's ability to pay, and existing statutory prohibitions and limitations on payments.

2. In cases involving the restitution of real property and interests in the nature of real property, the claimant may demand that an adequate period not exceeding ten years be allowed for the payment of the refund and expenditures, provided that a refund-mortgage bearing 4 per cent interest be executed on the property in favour of the restitutor. The terms shall be specified by the Restitution Authorities upon application.

3. In cases provided for in Article 34, paragraph 3, and Article 37, paragraph 2, the Restitution Authorities shall determine the maturity dates of debts and the terms of payment in such a way that the restitution of the confiscated property will not be prejudiced under any circumstances nor its enjoyment by the claimant unduly impaired.

ARTICLE 47: Claims for Indemnification

1. Claims for indemnification which the restitutor may have against any of his predecessors in interest shall be governed by the rules of the Civil Law. The liability to make restitution shall be deemed to constitute a defect in title within the meaning of the Civil Code. Section 439, paragraph 1 of the Civil Code shall not be applicable.

2. In case of restitution of real or tangible personal property, any claim provided in paragraph 1

may be asserted not only against the original party to the contract but also against any predecessor in interest who was not in good faith at the time he acquired the property. Such predecessors in interest shall be liable as joint debtors. They shall not be liable, if the restitutor himself was not in good faith.

ARTICLE 48: Lien of Third Persons on Claims of the Restitutor
1. Any interest in confiscated property which ceases to be effective pursuant to Article 37 shall remain a lien on any claim which the restitutor may have for payment of expenditures refund of consideration and for indemnification under Articles 34, 44 and 47; and on the proceeds which the restitutor obtains on the basis of such claims.
2. This provision shall not apply in favour of such persons who by granting loans have aided an aggravated confiscation.

PART VIII: GENERAL RULES OF PROCEDURE
ARTICLE 49: Basic Principles
1. The restitution proceedings shall be conducted in such a manner as to bring about speedy and complete restitution. The Restitution Authorities may deviate in individual cases from procedural rules declared applicable by this Law, if to do so will serve to accelerate restitution, provided that such deviation does not impair complete investigation of the facts or the legal right to a fair hearing.
2. In ascertaining the facts of the case the Restitution Authorities shall bear fully in mind the circumstances in which the claimant finds himself as a result of measures of persecution for the reasons set forth in Article 1. This shall particularly apply where the producing of evidence has been rendered difficult or impossible through the loss of documents, the death or unavailability of witnesses, the residence abroad of the claimant, or similar circumstances. Affidavits of the claimant and his witnesses shall be admitted. This shall apply even though the affiant died after signing the affidavit.

ARTICLE 50: Right of Succession and Foreign Law
1. Any person who bases any claim upon a right of succession on death must establish such right.
2. Foreign law must be proved so far as it is unknown to the Restitution Authorities.

ARTICLE 51: Presumption of Death
Any persecuted person, whose last known residence was in Germany or a country under the jurisdiction of or occupied by Germany or its Allies and as to whose whereabouts or continued life after 8 May 1945 no information is available shall be presumed to have died on 8 May 1945; however, if it appears probable that such a person died on a date other than 8 May, the Restitution Authorities may deem such other date to be the date of death.

ARTICLE 52: Safeguarding
1. The Restitution Authorities shall, if the situation so requires, safeguard confiscated property in a suitable manner. They may to that end issue temporary injunctions (einstweilige Verfügung) or restraining orders (Arrest), either upon their own motion or upon application. Such injunctions or orders shall be modified or vacated if the property can be safeguarded by any other measures than those taken, or if there is no further need for their continuation.
2. The provisions of the Code of Civil Procedure on "Arrest und einstweilige Verfügung", as amended or as hereafter amended, shall be applicable.

ARTICLE 53: Trustee
1. Where supervision of the confiscated property is necessary, a trustee shall be appointed provided no other authority exercises jurisdiction over such property.
2. Unless provided otherwise by implementing regulation, the rules concerning the Administration of Blocked Property shall apply to the appointment and supervision of a trustee.

ARTICLE 54: Jurisdiction of Other Authorities to Take Measures as Set Forth in Articles 52 and 53
Where the safeguarding measures described in Articles 52 and 53 are within the jurisdiction of another agency the Restitution Authorities will request the appropriate agency to take such measures.

PART IX: FILING OF CLAIMS
ARTICLE 55: Central Filing Agency
1. A Central Filing Agency for the filing of petitions for restitution will be established under regulations to be issued by Military Government.

2. The Central Filing Agency shall transmit the petition to the appropriate Restitution Agency or Agencies.

ARTICLE 56: *Form Requirements and Period of Limitation for Filing Claims*

1. A petition for restitution pursuant to this Law shall be submitted to the Central Filing Agency in writing on or before 31 December 1948. Details as to the form of filing will be provided in regulations to be issued by Military Government.

2. The petition shall be substantiated by documents or affidavits.

3. The petition may be effectively filed by any one of several co-claimants.

4. Any petition, filed by a person who is not entitled to restitution of the property, shall be deemed to have been effectively filed in favour of the true claimant, or where Articles 8, 10 and 11 are applicable, in favour of the successor organisations mentioned therein. The same shall apply to the filing of petition by any such successor organisation.

ARTICLE 57: *Relation to Other Remedies*

Unless otherwise provided in this Law, any claim within the scope of this Law may be prosecuted only under the provisions and within the periods of limitation, set forth in this Law. However, any claim based on tort, outside the scope of this Law, may be prosecuted in the ordinary courts.

ARTICLE 58: *Contents of Petition to be Filed*

1. The petition shall contain a description of the confiscated property. Time, place and circumstances of the confiscation shall be stated as exactly as is possible under the circumstances. If a claim is made for the payment of money, the sum demanded shall be specified if feasible; the basis for the claim shall be substantiated.

2. So far as known to the claimant, the petition shall contain the name and address of the restitutor, the names and addresses of all persons having or claiming to have an interest in the property, lessees and tenants, if any, and a statement as to all encumbrances existing at the time of the confiscation of the property.

3. The Central Filing Agency or the Restitution Authorities may request the claimant to supplement his petition by a statement containing the data set forth in paragraphs 1 and 2. They may further require the claimant to swear to his statement.

4. If the claimant does not have his domicile or residence in one of the four Zones of Occupation of Germany or in the City of Berlin, and if he has not appointed there an attorney authorised to accept service of legal papers, he may nominate in his petition a person domiciled there, authorised to receive such papers. If he fails to nominate such a person, the Restitution Agency shall do so and notify the claimant of the appointment

5. After a petition has been filed, a receipt shall be issued by the Central Filing Agency notifying the claimant of the Restitution Agency or Agencies to which the petition has been transmitted pursuant to Article 55, paragraph 2.

6. The period of limitation provided for in Article 56, paragraph 1, shall be deemed to have been complied with by the filing of a written petition with the Central Filing Agency, although it is incomplete or in improper form.

ARTICLE 59: *Venue*

1. Any petition for restitution shall be transmitted by the Central Filing Agency to the Restitution Agency or the district in which the property subject to restitution is located. If it appears that a petition has been transmitted to a Restitution Agency which lacks jurisdiction, such petition shall be referred by such Restitution Agency to the Restitution Agency having jurisdiction. The order of reference shall be binding on the Agency to which the petition has been referred.

2. An implementing regulation may provide for additional rules on venue, especially of claims for compensation and ancillary claims.

ARTICLE 60: *Jurisdiction of Subject Matter*

The Restitution Authorities shall have jurisdiction of the subject matter irrespective of whether under any other law a claim for restitution would come within the jurisdiction of any ordinary, administrative, or other court, or whether no court whatsoever would have jurisdiction.

ARTICLE 61: Notice of Claim

1. The Restitution Agency shall give notice of the petition by formal service on the parties concerned requiring that an answer be filed within two months. Parties concerned shall be deemed the restitutor, persons holding interests *in rem,* lessees or tenants of the confiscated property, as well as any other person the claimant might demand to be joined in the proceedings. If the German Reich, a Land, a former Land, the former NSDAP or one of its formations or affiliated organisations is a party concerned, service shall be made upon the State Minister of Finance. In the cases described in sentence 3 the State shall be authorised to join the proceedings as a party in interest.

2. Where the restitutor or his present address is unknown or where it appears from the petition that any unknown third person may have an interest in the confiscated property, the Restitution Agency shall cause the service by publication of the petition; the restitutor and the unknown third persons shall be requested thereby, within two months, to declare their interests together with proof thereof with the Restitution Agency. Service by publication shall be made pursuant to Section 204, paragraph 2, of the Code of Civil Procedure as amended by Control Council Law No. 38 in the form prescribed for a summons. Service shall be deemed to be effective one month after publication in the periodical specified in Section 204, paragraph 2, of the Code of Civil Procedure.

3. Upon service of the petition the case shall be deemed to be pending (rechtshägig).

4. When the claim for restitution affects real property or an interest in the nature of real property, the Restitution Agency shall request that an entry in the Land Title Register be made to the effect that a claim for restitution has been filed. (Notice of restitution, Rückerstattungsvermerk.) The notice of restitution shall be effective against any third person.

5. The provisions of the Code of Civil Procedure concerning Third Party Practice shall be applicable.

ARTICLE 62: Procedure before the Restitution Agency

1. If no objection has been raised against a petition within the time specified in the notice or in the service by publication, the Restitution Agency shall issue an order granting the petition. Where there is no dispute as to the limit of encumbrances and as to the continued existence of interests, it shall also make the appropriate findings on these matters.

2. If, however, the claim for restitution does not state a cause of action, or the truth of any of the allegations contained therein is controverted by entries in public records or by public documents available to the Restitution Agency, the latter shall order the claimant to submit a statement within an appropriate period of time. The Agency shall dismiss the petition or the merits if the claimant does not submit within this period an explanation justifying his petition or supplementing the facts alleged therein.

3. If an objection is made the Restitution Agency shall attempt to reach an amicable settlement unless the futility of such effort is evident. When an amicable settlement has been reached the Restitution Agency shall, on application, record the settlement in writing, and shall deliver a certified copy of the settlement to the parties concerned.

ARTICLE 63: Reference to the Court

1. If an amicable agreement cannot be reached in whole or in part or if the measures to be taken are not within the power of the Restitution Agency, it shall refer the case to the extent necessary to the Restitution Chamber of the District Court having jurisdiction over the Restitution Agency. This shall apply in particular also to cases where only the limit of encumbrance, or the continued existence of interests or the liability for debts is disputed.

2. Implementing regulations may confer jurisdiction on certain District Courts or on District Courts other than those specified in paragraph 1.

3. The Restitution Agency may stay the proceedings for a period not exceeding six months before referring the case to the Restitution Chamber, if the claimant consents and an amicable agreement may be expected.

ARTICLE 64: Appeal (Einspruch)

1. Any party to the case, by filing an appeal with the Restitution Agency, may appeal to the Restitution Chamber from a decision of the Restitution Agency rendered pursuant to Article 59, paragraph 1, second sentence, or Article 62, paragraphs 1 and 2; the period in which to file the appeal shall be one month; it shall be three months, if the appellant resides in a foreign country. The period to appeal shall begin to run with the service of the decision to be appealed from. Article 61, paragraph 2, shall be applicable.

2. The appeal may be based only on a violation of Article 59, paragraph 1, second sentence, or Article 62, paragraphs 1 or 2.

ARTICLE 65: *Execution*

Agreements recorded by the Restitution Agency and orders of the Restitution Agency which are no longer subject to appeal may be enforced by execution pursuant to the provisions of the Code of Civil Procedure. For this purpose, the Restitution Agency shall have the powers of a court (Vollstreckungsgericht). In effecting execution; the Restitution Agency may avail itself of the services of other agencies, especially of the courts.

PART X: JUDICAL PROCEEDINGS

ARTICLE 66: *Members of the Restitution Chamber*

The Restitution Chamber shall be composed of a Presiding Judge and two Associate Judges, eligible for the office of judge or for the higher Administrative Service. The Presiding Judge shall be a judge normally assigned to a court. The Associate Judges shall be appointed for a term of three years, unless they are professional judges. One of the three judges shall belong to a class of persons persecuted for any of the reasons set forth in Article 1.

ARTICLE 67: *Procedure*

1. The Restitution Chamber shall adjust the legal relations of the parties in interest according to the provisions of this Law.

2.   Unless this Law provides otherwise, the procedure shall be governed by the rules of procedure applicable in matters of non-contentious litigation, subject, however, to the following modifications:

    a)   The Chamber shall order an oral hearing; the hearing shall be public.

    b)   The proceedings may be stayed for a period not to exceed six months, at the request of the claimant. Repeated stays may be granted after the case has been reopened.

    c)   The Chamber shall render partial judgment on one or more of the claims before it, or on part of a claim, where the determination of any counterclaim, offset or equitable lien or any other defence in the nature of an offset or a counterclaim would substantially delay the decision on restitution.

    d)   Without prejudice to the final decision, the Chamber may order the temporary surrender of the confiscated property to the claimant either with or without security. In this case the claimant shall have, with respect to third persons, the rights and obligations of a trustee.

ARTICLE 68: *Form and Contents of the Decision*

1. The decision of the Restitution Chamber shall be pronounced in an order supported by an opinion; the order shall be served on the parties concerned. Immediate execution may be had on this order, a subsequent appeal notwithstanding. The provisions of Sections 713, paragraph 2, and Sections 713a to 720 of the Code of Civil Procedure shall be applicable.

2. An appeal (sofortige Beschwerde) may be taken from this order within one month; the appeal may be filed within three months if the appellant resides in a foreign country. The time to appeal shall begin to run from the date of service of the order; Article 61, paragraph 2, shall be applicable. The Civil Division of the Court of Appeals (Oberlandesgericht) shall hear the appeal. The appeal may be based only on the ground that the decision violated the law. The provisions of Sections 551, 561, and 563 of the Code of Civil Procedure shall be applicable.

3. Implementing regulations may confer jurisdiction to hear such appeals on a certain Court of Appeals.

ARTICLE 69: *Board of Review*

A Board of Review shall have the power to review any decision on any claim for restitution under this Law and to take whatever action is deemed necessary with respect thereto. Regulations to be issued by Military Government will provide for the appointment and composition of the Board, its jurisdiction, procedure, and such other matters as are deemed appropriate.

PART XI: SPECIAL PROCEEDINGS

ARTICLE 70: *Petition by the Public Prosecutor*

Where no petition for the restitution of confiscated property has been filed on or before 31 December 1948, the Public Prosecutor at the seat of the Restitution Chamber may file the petition for restitution on behalf of a successor organisation provided for in Article 10. This provision shall not apply if the claimant has waived his claim for restitution in accordance with Article 11, paragraph 3. The petition of the Public Prosecutor must be filed on or before 30 June 1949.

ARTICLE 71: Conflict of Jurisdiction
1. If claims as described in Articles 1 to 48 are asserted by a person entitled to restitution in a court proceeding including the stage of compulsory execution by way of complaint, defence or counterclaim, the Court shall notify the Restitution Agency. The Court may, and on request by the Restitution Agency must, stay the proceedings or temporarily suspend execution by an order from which no appeal may be taken. The Restitution Agency may direct that the claim be dealt with under this Law to the exclusion of the jurisdiction of the ordinary civil courts, or it may authorise the claimant to prosecute his claim before the ordinary civil courts; such authorisation shall be binding on the latter courts. If an action in the ordinary civil courts is terminated because the claim is being dealt with under this Law, the court fees shall be remitted and neither party shall be entitled to costs incurred out of court.
2. The Court shall report to the Central Filing Agency any action taken under paragraph 1.

PART XII: ASSESSMENT OF COSTS
ARTICLE 72: Costs
1. As a rule no court fees shall be assessed in favour of the State (Gerichtskosten) in proceedings before Restitution Authorities. However, implementing regulations may provide for the assessment of costs, fees and expenses.
2. No advance payment, or bond or security for costs may be demanded from a claimant.

PART XIII: DUTY TO REPORT AND PENALTIES
ARTICLE 73: Duty to Report
1. Anyone who has, or has had in his possession, at any time after it was transferred by or taken from a persecuted person, any property which he knows or should know under the circumstances
   a)   is confiscated property within the meaning of the provisions of Article 2; or
   b)   is presumed to be confiscated property pursuant to the provisions of paragraph 1 of Article 3; or
   c)   has been at any time the subject of a transaction which may be avoided pursuant to the provisions of paragraph 1 of Article 4
shall report this fact in writing to the Central Filing Agency on or before 15 May 1948.
   The report to be filed hereunder shall show the exact circumstances under which the reporting person obtained possession of the property; it shall also contain the name and address of the person from whom the reporting person acquired the property as well as the consideration paid, and in case the property no longer is his possession, the name of the person to whom the property was transferred.
2. The following property need not be reported:
   a)   Tangible personal property which had been acquired in the course of an ordinary and usual business transaction in an establishment normally dealing in that type of property, provided, however, that property acquired at an auction, or at a private sale in an establishment engaged to a considerable extent in the business of auctioning or otherwise disposing of confiscated property, must be reported;
   b)   Tangible personal property, the value of which did not exceed RM 1,000 at the time of the confiscation;
   c)   Donations made to close relatives (as defined in Section 52, paragraph 2 of the Criminal Code) and donations which without doubt were made for moral consideration;
   d)   Property which has already been restituted and property as to which the claimant has relinquished his right of restitution expressly and in writing at any time, between 8 May 1945 and the effective date of this Law.
3. No report filed pursuant to paragraph 1 by any person shall be considered, in proceedings before a Restitution Authority, as an admission of the reporting party that the property so reported is subject to restitution or as a waiver of any defence he might have had if the report had not been filed. It shall be admissible, however, as an admission of the facts stated therein.
4. The Central Filing Agency upon receiving a report under this Article shall forward a copy of the report to the appropriate Restitution Agency or Agencies in each district in which property affected by the report is situated. All reports filed pursuant to the provisions of this Article shall be open to inspection.

ARTICLE 74: Obligation to Inspect the Land Title Register and other Public Registers
1. Anyone holding real property or an interest in the nature of real property, shall ascertain by inspection of the Land Title Register whether or not the property in question must be reported. The

same shall apply with respect to other property interests which are recorded in any other public register.

2. Whenever a public authority or other public agency learns of the whereabouts of property which must be reported, it shall report such fact without delay to the Central Filing Agency. Article 73, paragraph 4, shall be applicable.

ARTICLE 75: Penalties

1. Any person who
   a) intentionally or negligently fails to comply with his duty to report as set forth in Article 73 and 74; or,
   b) knowingly makes any false or misleading statements to the Restitution Authorities
shall be punished with imprisonment not exceeding five years, or a fine, or both, unless heavier penalties under any other law are applicable.

2. No penalty shall be imposed in the case of subparagraph a), where the report required by this Law has been made voluntarily and prior to discovery.

ARTICLE 76: Penalties (continued)

1. Whoever alienates, damages, destroys, or conceals any property coming under the provisions of this Law in order to thwart the rights of a claimant, shall be punished with imprisonment not exceeding five years, or a fine, or both. unless heavier penalties under any other law are applicable.

2. Confinement in a penitentiary up to five years may be imposed in especially serious cases.

3. The attempt shall be punishable.

ARTICLE 77: Penalties (continued)

In the cases within the scope of Articles 75 and 76, nobody may plead ignorance of facts which he could have ascertained by the inspection of public books and registers, if and to the extent to which Article 74 imposed on him the obligation of such inspection.

PART XIV: RE-ESTABLISHMENT OF RIGHTS OF SUCCESSION AND ADOPTION

ARTICLE 78: Exclusion from Inheritance

1. An exclusion from the right of succession or the forfeiture of an estate which occurred during the period from 30 January 1933 to 8 May 1945 by virtue of a law or an ordinance for any of the reasons set forth in Article 1 shall be deemed not to have occurred.

2. The succession shall be deemed to have occurred at the effective date of this Law for the purpose of determining the periods of limitation.

ARTICLE 79: Avoidance of Testamentary Dispositions and of Disclaimers of Inheritance

1. Testamentary dispositions and contracts of inheritance made in the period from 30 January 1933 to 8 May 1945 in which any descendant, parent, grandparent, brother, sister, half-brother, half-sister, or their descendants, as well as a spouse, was excluded from inheritance for the purpose of avoiding a seizure of the estate by the State, expected by the testator for any of the reasons set forth in Article 1, shall be voidable. The power of avoidance shall be governed by Sections 2080 *et seq.* or 2281 *et seq.* of the Civil Code, unless paragraph 3 *infra* provides otherwise.

2. Disclaimers of inheritance by persons described in paragraph 1 shall be voidable, provided that such disclaimers were made within the period from 30 January 1933 to 8 May 1945 in order to prevent an expected seizure of the property by the State for any of the reasons set forth in Article 1. The right of avoidance shall be governed by Sections 1954 *et seq.* of the Civil Code, unless paragraph 3 of this Article provides otherwise.

3. Testamentary dispositions, contracts of inheritance or disclaimers of inheritance must be voided on or before 31 December 1948. The exercise of the power of avoidance within this period shall be deemed timely.

ARTICLE 80: Testamentary Disposition of a Persecuted Person

1. A testamentary disposition, made between 30 January 1933 and 8 May 1945 shall be valid in spite of complete non-compliance with form requirements if the testator made such disposition in view of an actual or imaginary immediate danger to his life based on measures of persecution for any of the reasons set forth in Article 1, and where the circumstances were such that he could not or could not be expected to, comply with the statutory form requirements.

2. Any testamentary disposition coming within the scope of paragraph 1 shall be deemed not to have been made if the testator was still capable of making a testamentary disposition complying with the statutory form requirements after 30 September 1945.

ARTICLE 81: Re-establishment of Adoptions
1. If an adoption relationship was cancelled within the period from 30 January 1933 to 8 May 1945 for reasons set forth in Article 1, such relationship may be reinstated *nunc pro tunc* by a contract between the foster parent or his heirs and the child or his heirs. Section 1741 to 1772 of the Civil Code, with the exception of Sections 1744, 1745, 1747, 1752 and 1753, shall apply to the contract of reinstatement. A contract of reinstatement may be judicially confirmed even after the death of the parties to it. If one of the parties concerned is not available a guardian (Pfleger) may be appointed to represent his interests in the proceedings to reinstate the adoption.
2. Where an adoption was cancelled by decision of a court during the period from 30 January 1933 to 8 May 1945 for any of the reasons set forth in Article 1, and if no facts have appeared which thereafter would have caused contracting parties to revoke the adoption on their own initiative, either party to the contract or his heirs may demand that the decision be vacated.
3. The local court (Amtsgericht) which cancelled the adoption shall have jurisdiction in the cases set forth in paragraph 2. The principles of paragraph 1, fourth sentence, above, shall be applicable. The decision of the court shall be discretionary and shall take into account the equities of the parties. When the cancellation of the adoption is vacated, the adoption shall be reinstated *nunc pro tunc*. The court may exclude the retroactive effect of its decision from certain parts thereof.
4. No costs or fees shall be charged in these proceedings.
5. The application for re-establishment of an adoption must be made on or before 31 December 1948.

ARTICLE 82: Jurisdiction
Any claims arising under Articles 78 to 81 shall be decided by the ordinary civil courts. No filing with the Central Filing Agency is required.

PART XV: REINSTATEMENT OF TRADE NAMES AND OF NAMES OF ASSOCIATIONS
ARTICLE 83: Re-registration of Cancelled Trade Names
1. Where a trade name was cancelled in the Commercial Register within the period from 30 January 1933 to 8 May 1945 after the business establishment had been closed for any of the reasons set forth in Article 1, the cancelled trade name shall be re-registered on application if the business is reopened by its last owner, or owners, or their heirs.
2. If the closed business establishment was conducted at the time of its discontinuation by a single owner, the last owner or his heirs shall be entitled to demand the re-registration of the cancelled trade name. If there are several heirs, and if not all of them participate in the resumption of the enterprise, the re-registration of the cancelled trade name may be demanded, provided the heirs who do not participate in the business assent to the resumption of the trade name.
3. If at the time of its closing the business establishment was conducted by several partners personally liable, re-registration of the cancelled trade name may be demanded if all the partners personally liable establish a business enterprise or if one or several of them do so with the consent of the remaining ones; with respect to heirs of partners the principle of paragraph 2 shall be applicable.

ARTICLE 84: Change of Trade Name
Where a trade name has been changed in the period from 30 January 1933 to 8 May 1945 for any of the reasons set forth in Article 1, the former trade name may be restored upon the application of the person who owned the enterprise at the time change was made or of his heirs, provided they now own the enterprise. The principles of Articles 83, paragraph 2, second sentence, and paragraph 3, shall be applicable.

ARTICLE 85: Names of Corporations
The principles of Articles 83 and 84 shall be applicable to the trade names of corporations.

ARTICLE 86: Reinstatement of Trade Names in Other Cases
Whenever the use of the former trade name is essential for the purpose of full restitution, the Restitution Chamber may permit the reinstatement of a cancelled or changed trade name in cases other than those provided for in Articles 83 to 85.

ARTICLE 87: Names of Associations and Endowments (Stiftungen)
Article 86 shall be applicable to the resumption of the name by an association or an endowment.

ARTICLE 88: Procedure

Applications for the registration in the Commercial Register of former trade names must be filed within the period provided for in this Law for the filing of claims for restitution. The Amtsgericht in its capacity as Court of Registry shall have jurisdiction over these applications except in the cases provided for in Article 86. Otherwise the procedure shall be governed by the rules of procedure applicable in matters of non-contentious litigation. No costs or fees shall be charged in these proceedings.

PART XVI: FINAL PROVISIONS

ARTICLE 89: Claims Reserved to Special Legislation

The reinstatement of lapsed interests arising out of insurance contracts and of lapsed copyrights and industrial rights (patents etc.) may be regulated by special legislation.

ARTICLE 90: Statute of Limitations

To the extent to which the statute of limitations or prescriptive rights of the Civil Code might defeat any claim falling under this Law, the statute of limitations or a prescriptive period shall not be deemed to have expired until six months after such cause of action arises by reason of operation of this Law, but in no event prior to 30 June 1949.

ARTICLE 91: Taxes and Other Levies

1. Taxes and other public levies shall not be imposed in connection with restitution.

2. No taxes, including inheritance taxes, or other public assessments, fees or costs shall be refunded or subsequently levied in connection with the return of confiscated property.

ARTICLE 92: Implementing and Carrying-out Provisions

1. The Restitution Agencies will be designated by implementing regulations.

2. Unless otherwise provided in this Law, or ordered by Military Government, the Minister President of each State or any Ministers designated by him, shall issue the legal and administrative regulations necessary for the implementation of this Law.

ARTICLE 93: Jurisdiction of German Courts

1. German Courts are hereby authorised to exercise jurisdiction in civil cases arising under this Law against any stateless person having the assimilated status of United Nations displaced persons or against any national of the United Nations not falling within categories (3), (4), (5) of Section 10 b) in Article VI of Military Government Law No. 2 as amended or as hereafter amended.

2. German Courts are hereby authorised to exercise jurisdiction in cases involving offences against any of the provisions of Articles 73 to 77 of this Law by persons not exempted from the jurisdiction of the German Courts under Section 10 a) in Article VI of Military Government Law No. 2 as amended or as hereafter amended.

ARTICLE 94: Official Text

The German text of this Law shall be the official text and the provisions of Paragraph 5 of Article II of Military Government Law No. 4, as amended, shall not apply.

ARTICLE 95: Effective Date

This Law shall become effective in Bavaria, Bremen, Hesse and Wuerttemberg-Baden on 10 November 1947.

BY ORDER OF MILITARY GOVERNMENT

Approved: 10 November 1947.

GESETZ Nr. 59 — RÜCKERSTATTUNG FESTSTELLBARER VERMÖGENSGEGSTÄNDE

I. ABSCHNITT: ALLGEMEINE VORSCHRIFTEN
ARTIKEL 1: Grundsatz

1. Zweck des Gesetzes ist es, die Rückerstattung feststellbarer Vermögensgegenstände (Sachen, Rechte, Inbegriff von Sachen und Rechten) an Personen, denen sie in der Zeit vom 30. Januar 1933 bis 8. Mai 1945 aus Gründen der Rasse, Religion, Nationalität, Weltanschauung oder politischer Gegnerschaft gegen den Nationalsozialismus entzogen worden sind, im größtmöglichen Umfange beschleunigt zu bewirken. Eine Entziehung von Vermögensgegenständen aus Gründen der Nationalität im Sinne dieses Gesetzes erstreckt sich nicht auf Maßnahmen, die unter anerkannten Regeln des internationalen Rechts üblicherweise gegen Vermögen von Staatsangehörigen feindlicher Länder zulässig sind.

2. Vermögensgegenstände nach Maßgabe der Bestimmungen dieses Gesetzes sind auch dann an ihren ursprünglichen Inhaber oder dessen Rechtsnachfolger zurückzuerstatten, wenn die Rechte anderer Personen, die von dem begangenen Unrecht keine Kenntnis hatten, zurücktreten müssen. Der Rückerstattung entgegenstehende Vorschriften zum Schutze gutgläubiger Erwerber bleiben außer Betracht, soweit nicht in diesem Gesetz etwas anderes bestimmt ist.

II. ABSCHNITT: ENTZOGENE VERMÖGENSGEGENSTÄNDE
ARTIKEL 2: Entziehungsfälle

1. Vermögegenstände sind im Sinne dieses Gesetzes entzogen, wenn sie der Inhaber eingebüßt oder trotz begründeter Anwartschaft nicht erlangt hat infolge

a)   eines gegen die guten Sitten verstoßenden Rechtsgeschäftes oder einer Drohung, oder einer widerrechtlichen Wegnahme oder sonstigen unerlaubten Handlung;
b)   Wegnahme durch Staatsakt- oder durch Mißbrauch eines Staatsaktes;
c)   Wegnahme durch Maßnahmen der NSDAP, ihrer Gliederungen oder angeschlossenen Verbände

sofern die unter a) bis c) fallenden Tatbestände durch Verfolgungsmaßnahmen aus den Gründen des Artikels 1 verursacht waren oder solche Verfolgungsmaßnahmen darstellten.

2. Niemand wird mit der Einwendung gehört, seine Handlungsweise sei deshalb nicht rechts- oder sittenwidrig gewesen, weil sie allgemeinen Anschauungen entsprochen habe, die eine Schlechterstellung einzelner wegen ihrer Rasse, Religion, Nationalität, Weltanschauung oder ihrer Gegnerschaft gegen den Nationalsozialismus zum Inhalt hatten.

3. Als Wegnahme durch Staatsakt im Sinne des Absatz 1 b) gelten unter anderem Einziehung, Verfallerklärung, Verfall kraft Gesetzes und Verfügung auf Grund staatlicher Auflage oder durch staatlich bestellten Treuhänder. Als Wegnahme durch Staatsakt gilt auch die Einziehung durch strafgerichtliches Urteil, wenn das Urteil durch Gerichtsbeschluß oder kraft Gesetzes aufgehoben worden ist.

4. Als Mißbrauch von Staatsakten gilt insbesondere eine auf allgemeinen Vorschriften beruhende, jedoch ausschließlich oder vorwiegend zum Zwecke der Benachteiligung des Betroffenen aus den Gründen des Artikels 1 ergangene Entscheidung oder Verfügung eines Gerichts oder einer Verwaltungsbehörde, ferner die Erwirkung von Entscheidungen und Vollstreckungsmaßnahmen unter Ausnutzung des Umstandes, daß jemand wegen seiner Rasse, Religion, Nationalität, Weltanschauung oder seiner politischen Gegnerschaft gegen den Nationalsozialismus zur Wahrung seiner Rechte tatsächlich oder rechtlich nicht imstande war. Die Wiedergutmachungsorgane (Wiedergutmachungsbehörde, Wiedergutmachungskammer und Beschwerdegericht) haben eine solche Entscheidung oder Verfügung eines Gerichts oder einer Verwaltungsbehörde als nichtig zu behandeln ohne Rücksicht darauf, ob sie nach geltendem Recht rechtskräftig ist, und ob sie im Wiederaufnahmeverfahren angefochten werden könnte.

ARTIKEL 3: Entziehungsvermutung

1. Zugunsten eines Berechtigten wird vermutet, daß ein in der Zeit vom 30. Januar 1933 bis 8. Mai 1945 abgeschlossenes Rechtsgeschäft eine Vermögensentziehung im Sinne des Artikels 2 darstellt:

a)   Wenn die Veräußerung oder Aufgabe des Vermögensgegenstandes in der Zeit der Verfolgungsmaßnahmen von einer Person vorgenommen worden ist, die Verfolgungsmaßnahmen aus Gründen des Artikels 1 unmittelbar ausgesetzt war;

b)   wenn die Veräußerung oder Aufgabe eines Vermögensgegenstandes seitens einer Person vorgenommen wurde, die zu einer Gruppe von Personen gehörte, welche in ihrer Gesamtheit aus den Gründen des Artikels 1 durch Maßnahmen des Staates oder der NSDAP aus dem kulturellen und wirtschaftlichen Leben Deutschlands ausgeschaltet werden sollte.

2. Vorausgesetzt, daß keine anderen Tatsachen für das Vorliegen einer Entziehung im Sinne des Artikels 2 sprechen, kann die Vermutung des Absatz 1 durch den Beweis widerlegt werden, daß dem Veräußerer ein angemessener Kaufpreis bezahlt worden ist. Dieser Beweis allein widerlegt jedoch die Vermutung nicht, wenn dem Veräußerer aus den Gründen des Artikels 1 das Recht der freien Verfügung über den Kaufpreis verweigert worden ist.

3. Ein angemessener Kaufpreis im Sinne dieses Artikels ist derjenige Geldbetrag, den ein Kauflustiger zu zahlen und ein Verkaufslustiger anzunehmen bereit wäre, wobei bei Geschäftsunternehmen der Firmenwert (good will) berücksichtigt wird, den ein solches Unternehmen in den Händen einer Person hatte, die Verfolgungsmaßnahmen aus den Gründen des Artikels 1 nicht unterworfen war.

ARTIKEL 4: Anfechtung

1. Der Berechtigte kann ein Rechtsgeschäft, das von einer zur Gruppe des Absatzes 1 b) des Artikels 3 gehörigen Person in der Zeit vom 15. September 1935 (Datum der ersten Nürnberger Gesetze) bis zum 8. Mai 1945 vorgenommen worden ist, wegen der Zwangslage, in der sich diese Gruppe befand, anfechten wenn das Rechtsgeschäft die Veräußerung oder Aufgabe eines Vermögensgegenstandes zum Inhalt hatte, es sei denn, daß

a)   das Rechtsgeschäft als solches und mit seinen wesentlichen Bestimmungen auch ohne die Herrschaft des Nationalsozialismus abgeschlossen worden wäre, oder

b)   der Erwerber die Vermögensinteressen des Berechtigten (Artikel 7) oder seines Rechtsvorgängers in besonderer Weise und mit wesentlichem Erfolg, insbesondere durch Mitwirkung bei einer Vermögensübertragung ins Ausland oder durch ähnliche Maßnahmen, wahrgenommen hat.

2. Bei der Feststellung, ob nach Absatz 1 a) das Rechtsgeschäft auch ohne die Herrschaft des Nationalsozialismus abgeschlossen worden wäre, können die Tatsachen, daß der Veräußerer den Vermögensgegenstand selbst dem Erwerber angeboten oder daß er einen angemessenen Kaufpreis (Artikel 3, Absatz 3) erhalten hat, ohne daß ihm dabei aus den Gründen des Artikels 1 die freie Verfügung über den Kaufpreis verweigert wurde, zusammen mit anderen Tatsachen in Betracht gezogen werden. Es sollen aber diese beiden Tatsachen, jede für sich allein oder beide zusammen, noch nicht zum Nachweis dafür ausreichen, daß das Rechtsgeschäft auch ohne die Herrschaft des Nationalsozialismus abgeschlossen worden wäre.

3. Ebensowenig sollen diese beiden Tatsachen, jede für sich allein oder beide zusammen, zum Nachweis dafür ausreichen, daß der Berechtigte sich durch die Anfechtung in unzulässiger Weise zu seinem oder seines Rechtsvorgängers früheren Verhalten in Widerspruch setzt.

4. Der Ausdruck "Rückerstattungsanspruch" im Sinne dieses Gesetzes umfaßt auch das Anfechtungsrecht und die aus diesem folgenden Ansprüche. Die Ausübung des Anfechtungsrechts hat die Wirkung, daß der durch das angefochtene Rechtsgeschäft übertragene oder aufgegebene Vermögensgegenstand als entzogenes Vermögen im Sinne dieses Gesetzes gilt.

5. Die Anmeldung eines Rückerstattungsanspruchs gilt als Ausübung des Anfechtungsrechts seitens des Anfechtungsberechtigten ohne Rücksicht darauf, ob in der Anmeldung eine ausdrückliche Anfechtungserklärung enthalten ist.

ARTIKEL 5: Schenkungen

Hat ein aus den Gründen des Artikels 1 Verfolgter in der Zeit vom 30. Januar 1933 bis 8. Mai 1945 einem anderen Vermögensgegenstände unentgeltlich überlassen, so wird vermutet, daß keine Schenkung, sondern eine Verwahrung oder ein Treuhandverhältnis vorliegt. Die Vermutung gilt nicht, soweit nach den persönlichen Beziehungen zwischen dem Überlassenden und dem Empfänger das Vorliegen einer Anstandsschenkung naheliegt; ein Rückerstattungsanspruch ist in diesem Falle nicht gegeben.

ARTIKEL 6: Verwahrungs- und Treuhandverhältnisse

1. Auf Verwahrungsverträge und treuhänderische Rechtsgeschäfte, die die Abwendung oder

Verminderung eines aus den Gründen des Artikels 1 drohenden oder eingetreten Vermögensschadens bezweckten, finden die Vorschriften des Ill. bis VII. Abschnitts dieses Gesetzes keine Anwendung.
2. Verträge und sonstige Rechtsgeschäfte der in Absatz 1 bezeichneten Art können ohne Rücksicht auf entgegenstehende vertragliche oder gesetzliche Bestimmungen von dem Berechtigten (Artikel 7) jederzeit mit sofortiger Wirkung gekündigt werden.
3. Der Verwahrer oder Treuhänder wird nicht mit dem Einwand gehört, daß Verträge und sonstige Rechtsgeschäfte der in Absatz 1 bezeichneten Art gegen ein zur Zeit ihres Abschlusses bestehendes oder später erlassenes gesetzliches Verbot verstoßen, oder daß ein auf Gesetz oder Rechtsgeschäft beruhendes Formerfordernis nicht erfüllt wurde, sofern die Form wegen der nationalsozialistischen Herrschaft nicht eingehalten wurde.

III. ABSCHNITT: ALLGEMEINE BESTIMMUNGEN ÜBER DIE RÜCKERSTATTUNG
ARTIKEL 7: Berechtigter
Der Rückerstattungsanspruch steht demjenigen zu, dem ein Vermögensgegenstand entzogen wurde (Verfolgter) oder seinem Rechtsnachfolger.

ARTIKEL 8: Rechtsnachfolger aufgelöster Personenvereinigungen
1. Ist eine juristische Person oder eine nicht rechtsfähige Personenvereinigung aus den Gründen des Artikels 1 aufgelöst oder zur Selbstauflösung gezwungen worden, so kann der Rückerstattungsanspruch, der ihr zustehen würde, wenn sie nicht aufgelöst worden wäre, von einer von der Militärregierung zu bestimmenden Nachfolgeorganisation geltend gemacht werden
2. Die Vorschriften des Absatz 1 finden auf die in Artikel 9 aufgeführten Gesellschaften und juristischen Personen keine Anwendung.

ARTIKEL 9: Rechte einzelner Gesellschafter
War eine Gesellschaft oder juristische Person des Handelsrechts aus den Gründen des Artikels 1 aufgelöst oder zur Selbstauflösung gezwungen worden, so kann der Rückerstattungsanspruch, solange keine Nachfolgeorganisation bestimmt ist, von jedem Gesellschafter geltend gemacht werden. Der Rückerstattungsanspruch gilt als zugunsten aller Gesellschafter, denen der gleiche Anspruch zusteht, erhoben. Die Rücknahme des Antrags oder ein Vergleich muß von dem Wiedergutmachungsorgan genehmigt werden, vor dem der Anspruch anhängig ist. Von der Erhebung des Anspruchs müssen die anderen bekannten Gesellschafter oder ihre Rechtsnachfolger einschließlich einer gemäß Artikel 10 zuständigen Nachfolgeorganisation benachrichtigt werden. An die Stelle von Gesellschaftern, deren Anschrift unbekannt ist, tritt für das Verfahren die Nachfolgeorganisation im Rahmen ihrer Befugnisse nach Maßgabe des Artikels 11.

ARTIKEL 10: Nachfolgeorganisation als Erbe von Verfolgten
Im Falle des § 1936 BGB ist Erbe eines Verfolgten hinsichtlich des gesamten Nachlasses an Stelle des Staates eine von der Militärregierung zu bestimmende Nachfolgeorganisation. Als Nachfolgeorganisation darf weder der Staat, noch eine Gliederung desselben, oder ein gemeindlicher Selbstverwaltungskörper bestimmt werden. Das gleiche gilt für Heimfall-, Anfall- und Rückfallrechte auf Grund sonstiger gesetzlicher Bestimmungen.

ARTIKEL 11: Besondere Rechte der Nachfolgeorganisation des Artikels 10
1. Eine nach Artikel 10 bestimmte Nachfolgeorganisation kann, wenn innerhalb von sechs Monaten nach dem Inkrafttreten dieses Gesetzes hinsichtlich eines entzogenen Vermögensgegenstandes kein Rückerstattungsanspruch angemeldet wird, diesen bis zum 31. Dezember 1948 anmelden und alle zur Sicherstellung des Vermögensgegenstandes erforderlichen Maßnahmen beantragen.
2. Sofern nicht der Berechtigte bis zum 31. Dezember 1948 seinerseits den Anspruch anmeldet, erwirbt die Nachfolgeorganisation auf Grund ihrer Anmeldung die Rechtsstellung des Berechtigten. Erst mit diesem Rechtserwerb erlangt sie das Recht, den Anspruch weiter zu verfolgen.
3. Die Absätze 1 und 2 finden keine Anwendung, soweit der Berechtigte in der Zeit vom 8. Mai 1945 bis zum 31. Dezember 1948 schriftliche und ausdrücklich gegenüber dem Rückerstattungspflichtigen, der zuständigen Rückerstattungsbehörde oder dem Zentralmeldeamt auf seinen Rückerstattungsanspruch verzichtet hat.

ARTIKEL 12: Auskunftspflicht von Rechtsnachfolgern
1. Berechtigte, die den Rückerstattungsanspruch mittelbar oder unmittelbar von dem Verfolgten erworben haben, sind auf Anordnung eines Wiedergutmachungsorgans verpflichtet, eine ihnen bekannte Anschrift ihrer Rechtsvorgänger, insbesondere des Verfolgten oder seiner Erben, mitzuteilen oder eine eidesstattliche Vesicherung darüber beizubringen, daß ihnen weder deren gegenwärtige Anschrift noch Anhaltspunkte zu deren Ermittlung bekannt sind.
2. Eine nach Artikel 10 bestimmte Nachfolgeorganisation ist verpflichtet, eine ihr bekannte Anschrift des Berechtigten oder ihr bekannte Anhaltspunkte zur Ermittlung desselben anzugeben oder eine eidesstattliche Versicherung eines gesetzlichen Vertreters darüber beizubringen, daß weder die gegenwärtige Anschrift des Berechtigten noch Anhaltspunkte zur Ermittlung desselben bekannt sind.

ARTIKEL 13: Bestimmung von Nachfolgeorganisationen
Ausführungsbestimmungen der Militärregierung werden des näheren regeln: Das Verfahren betreffend die Bestimmung von Nachfolgeorganisationen, deren Pflichten gegenüber den betreuten Geschädigten und deren sonstige Rechte und Pflichten nach Maßgabe.des Rechts der Militärregierung und des deutschen Rechts.

ARTIKEL 14: Rückerstattungspflichtiger
Unter dem Rückerstattungspflichtigen im Sinne dieses Gesetzes zu verstehen ist der derzeitige Inhaber der Eigentümerstellung an der entzogenen Sache oder derzeitige Inhaber des entzogenen Rechts oder Inbegriffs von Sachen und Rechten.

ARTIKEL 15: Rechtswirkung der Entscheidung über den Rückerstattungsanspruch
1. Eine dem Rückerstattungsanspruch stattgebende Entscheidung hat die Wirkung, daß der Verlust des Vermögensgegenstandes als nicht eingetreten, und später erworbene Rechte Dritter als nicht erworben gelten, soweit nicht dieses Gesetz etwas anderes bestimmt.
2. Eine Entscheidung über den Rückerstattungsanspruch wirkt für und gegen alle Personen, die am Verfahren teilgenommen haben oder zur Teilnahme am Verfahren berechtigt waren und hierzu vorschriftsmäßig aufgefordert wurden.

ARTIKEL 16: Wahlweiser Anspruch auf Nachzahlung
1. Der Berechtigte kann unter Verzicht auf alle sonstigen Ansprüche aus diesem Gesetz verlangen, daß ihm der Ersterwerber den Unterschied zwischen dem erlangten Entgelt und dem angemessenen Preis (Artikel 3, Absatz 3) des Vermögensgegenstandes nachbezahlt. Zu dem Unterschiedsbetrag treten angemessene Zinsen; hierbei finden die Vorschriften dieses Gesetzes über Nutzungen entsprechende Anwendung.
2. Das Verlangen ist nicht mehr zulässig,
a)   wenn der Vermögensgegenstand dem Berechtigten
      rechtskräftig wieder zuerkannt ist,
b)   wenn hierüber eine Sachenentscheidung der Wiedergutmachungsbehörde oder der
      Wiedergutmachungskammer ergangen ist,
c)   wenn sich der Berechtigte mit dem Rückerstattungspflichtigen über den
      Rückerstattungsanspruch geeinigt hat.

ARTIKEL 17: Wertberechnung
1. Soweit es nach den Bestimmungen dieses Gesetzes auf den Wert eines Vermögensgegenstandes ankommt, gelten als Wertsteigerung nicht Preiserhöhungen, die durch Verminderung der Kaufkraft des Geldes hervorgerufen sind.
2. Für die Bewertung von Vermögensgegenständen, die wegen Unbestimmbarkeit zur Zeit nicht zur Vermögenssteuer herangezogen werden, bleiben Ausführungsvorschriften vorbehalten. Die Bestimmung des Artikels 27, Absatz 2, bleibt unberührt.

IV. ABSCHNITT: BEGRENZUNG DER RÜCKERSTATTUNG
ARTIKEL 18: Zwangsenteignung
1. Entzogene Vermögensgegenstände, die nach der Entziehung für einen öffentlichen Zweck

zwangsenteignet oder an ein Unternehmen veräußert oder einem Unternehmen zugewendet wurden, zu dessen Gunsten eine solche Zwangsenteignung stattfinden konnte, unterliegen der Rückerstattung nicht, wenn im Zeitpunkt des Inkrafttretens dieses Gesetzes der Vermögensgegenstand noch für einen öffentlichen Zweck benützt wird und dieser Zweck noch als gesetzmäßig anerkannt ist.

2. Unterliegen Vermögensgegenstände aus den in Absatz 1 bezeichneten Gründen nicht der Rückerstattung, so muß der jetzige Eigentümer den Berechtigten für den Wert des entzogenen Vermögensgegenstandes angemessen entschädigen, soweit die Ansprüche gemäß Artikel 29ff. dieses Gesetzes nicht zu einer solchen Entschädigung führen.

ARTIKEL 19: Schutz des ordnungsmäßigen üblichen Geschäftsverkehrs

Vorbehaltlich der Bestimmungen der Artikel 20, 21 unterliegen nicht der Rückerstattung bewegliche Sachen, die der Eigentümer oder sein Rechtsvorgänger im Wege des ordnungsmäßigen üblichen Geschäftsverkehrs aus einem einschlägigen Unternehmen erworben hat. Dies gilt nicht für Kultgegenstände; es gilt ferner nicht für Gegenstände von besonderem künstlerischen oder wissenschaftlichen Wert oder besonderem persönlichen Erinnerungswert, sofern sie aus Privatbesitz stammten oder im Wege der Versteigerung oder von einem Unternehmen erworben wurden, das sich in erheblichem Umfange mit der Verwertung entzogener Vermögensgegenstände befaßte.

ARTIKEL 20: Geld

Geld unterliegt der Rückerstattung nur, wenn der Rückerstattungspflichtige bei seinem Erwerb wußte oder den Umständen nach annehmen mußte, daß es im Wege der Entziehung erlangt worden war.

ARTIKEL 21: Inhaberpapiere

1. Inhaberpapiere unterliegen der Rückerstattung nicht, wenn der Inhaber nachweist, daß er zur Zeit des Erwerbs weder wußte noch den Umständen nach annehmen mußte, daß das Inhaberpapier zu irgendeiner Zeit Gegenstand einer Entziehung war. Sofern nicht besondere Umstände entgegenstehen, ist guter Glaube im Sinne dieser Bestimmung anzunehmen, wenn der Erwerb im ordnungsmäßigen üblichen Geschäftsverkehr, insbesondere im Börsenverkehr erfolgte, und es sich nicht um eine maßgebliche.Beteiligung handelte.

2. Die Bestimmungen des Absatz 1 finden auch Anwendung auf Anteilsrechte an Inhaberpapieren, die sich in Sammelverwahrung befinden.

3. Inhaberpapiere sowie Anteilsrechte an solchen unterliegen jedoch bedingungslos der Rückerstattung, wenn sie darstellen

a) . eine Beteiligung an Unternehmen mit geringer Gesellschafterzahl, z .B. Familiengesellschaften,

b) eine Beteiligung an Unternehmen, deren Anteile im allgemeinen Geschäftsverkehr nicht gehandelt wurden,

c) eine maßgebliche Beteiligung an Unternehmen, von denen es allgemein oder in Geschäftskreisen bekannt war, daß eine maßgebliche Beteiligung an ihnen in der Hand von Personen war, die zu einer der in Artikel 3, Absatz 1 b) bezeichneten Gruppen gehörten,

d) eine maßgebliche Beteiligung an Gewerbebetrieben, die auf Grund der dritten Verordnung zum Reichsbürgergesetz vom 14. 6. 1938 (RGBl. I S. 627) in ein Verzeichnis eingetragen wurden.

4. Als maßgeblich im Sinne der Bestimmungen in Absatz 3 c) und d) gilt eine Beteiligung dann, wenn sie durch sich allein oder auf Grund einer vor oder bei der Entziehung bestandenen Interessenverbindung einen erheblichen Einfluß auf die Geschäftsführung des Unternehmens ermöglichte.

ARTIKEL 22: Rückerstattung bei Veränderung der rechtlichen oder Kapitalstruktur von Unternehmen

Ist eine Beteiligung der in Artikel 21 Absatz 3 bezeichneten Art entzogen worden und ist das Unternehmen selbst aufgelöst oder mit einem anderen Unternehmen verschmolzen oder in ein anderes Unternehmen umgewandelt oder sonstwie in seiner rechtlichen Struktur oder seiner Kapitalstruktur verändert worden oder ist dessen Vermögen ganz oder teilweise auf ein anderes Unternehmen übertragen worden, so kann der Berechtigte verlangen, daß er an dem veränderten oder neu gestalteten Unternehmen oder dem Unternehmen, das das Vermögen des ursprünglichen Unternehmens ganz oder teilweise übernommen hat, in einer angemessenen Weise beteiligt wird, die, soweit möglich, seine ursprüngliche Beteiligung und die aus ihr fließenden Rechte wiederherstellt.

ARTIKEL 23: *Durchführung des Grundsatzes des Artikels 22*

Die Wiedergutmachungskammer hat, soweit die Ansprüche des Berechtigten auf Grund der Artikel 29 ff. nicht zu einer im Sinne des Artikels 22 ausreichenden Wiedergutmachung führen, alle Maßnahmen zu treffen, die notwendig und geeignet sind, die dem Berechtigten in Artikel 22 eingeräumten Rechte zu verwirklichen. Sie hat zu diesem Zweck insbesondere nötigenfalls die Einziehung und Neuausgabe oder den Austausch von Aktien, Anteilscheinen, Zwischenscheinen und sonstigen Beteiligungspapieren oder die Begründung eines Gesellschaftsverhältnisses zwischen dem Berechtigten und dem in Artikel 22 bezeichneten Unternehmen sowie die Vornahme der zur Verwirklichung der Rechte gesetzlich vorgeschriebenen Handlungen anzuordnen. Diese Maßnahmen haben grundsätzlich zu Lasten derjenigen zu erfolgen, die bei entsprechender Anwendung der Vorschriften dieses Gesetzes rückerstattungspflichtig erscheinen. Zu Lasten sonstiger Anteilsberechtigter an dem Unternehmen sollen solche Maßnahmen nur insoweit angeordnet werden, als diese Anteilsberechtigten aus der Entziehung in Verbindung mit dem in Artikel 22 bezeichneten Sachverhalt mittelbar oder unmittelbar Nutzen gezogen haben oder das Unternehmen selbst auf Grund von Vorschriften dieses Gesetzes oder des bürgerlichen Rechts dem Berechtigten zur Herausgabe oder zum Schadensersatz verpflichtet ist, insbesondere für ein Handeln seiner Organe einzustehen hat.

ARTIKEL 24: *Sonstige Unternehmen*

Die Bestimmungen der Artikel 22, 23 finden entsprechende Anwendung, wenn eine Einzelfirma oder die Beteiligung an einer Offenen Handelsgesellschaft oder Kommanditgesellschaft oder die persönliche Beteiligung an einer Kommanditgesellschaft auf Aktien oder der Anteil an einer Gesellschaft mit beschränkter Haftung oder an einer Genossenschaft oder Anteile ähnlicher rechtlicher Art Gegenstand der Entziehung gewesen sind.

ARTIKEL 25: *Zustellung*

Soweit in den Fällen der Artikel 22 bis 24 eine Zustellung an unbekannte Gesellschafter oder an Gesellschafter, deren gegenwärtige Adresse unbekannt ist, notwendig wird, erfolgt dieselbe durch öffentliche Zustellung gemäß Artikel 61.

ARTIKEL 26: *Ersatzleistung bei Veränderung einer Sache*

1. Wäre eine Sache zurückzuerstatten, die nach der Entziehung wesentlich verändert worden ist und dadurch eine erhebliche Wertsteigerung erfahren hat, so kann die Wiedergutmachungskammer unter Berücksichtigung der berechtigten Interessen der Beteiligten eine nach dem Wert der Sache zur Zeit der Entziehung angemessene Ersatzleistung an Stelle der Rückerstattung anordnen. Der Berechtigte kann jedoch die Einräumung von Miteigentum zu angemessenem Bruchteil verlangen, es sei denn, daß der Rückerstattungspflichtige sich zur Ersatzleistung durch Übertragung ähnlicher gleichwertiger Vermögensgegenstände erbietet. Die Bestimmungen der Sätze 1 und 2 gelten zugunsten des Berechtigten auch dann, wenn durch die wesentliche Veränderung der Sache eine erhebliche Wertsteigerung nicht eingetreten ist.

2. Der Rückerstattungspflichtige kann sich auf die Bestimmungen des Absatz 1 nicht berufen, wenn er die Sache mittels einer schweren Entziehung im Sinne des Artikels 30 erlangt hat oder im Zeitpunkt der Vornahme der wesentlichen Veränderung wußte oder den Umständen nach annehmen mußte, daß die Sache zu irgendeiner Zeit durch eine schwere Entziehung erlangt worden war.

3. Hat der Rückerstattungspflichtige mit der zurückzuerstattenden Sache eine andere Sache als wesentlichen Bestandteil verbunden, so kann er sie abtrennen und sich aneignen. Er hat im Falle der Wegnahme die Sache auf seine Kosten in den vorigen Stand zu setzen. Erlangt der Berechtigte den Besitz der Sache, so ist er verpflichtet, die Abtrennung zu gestatten; er kann die Gestattung verweigern, bis ihm für den mit der Abtrennung verbundenen Schaden Sicherheit geleistet wird. Das Recht zur Abtrennung ist ausgeschlossen, wenn der Rückerstattungspflichtige nach den Bestimmungen dieses Gesetzes für die Verwendung Ersatz nicht verlangen kann oder ihm mindestens der Wert ersetzt wird, den der Bestandteil nach der Abtrennung für ihn haben würde.

4. Bei der Bestimmung, ob ein Vermögensgegenstand eine Wertsteigerung im Sinne des Absatz 1, Satz 1 erfahren hat, dürfen Wertsteigerungen, für die der Rückerstattungspflichtige nach Maßgabe der Bestimmungen dieses Gesetzes keinen Ersatz verlangen kann, zugunsten des Rückerstattungspflichtigen nicht berücksichtigt werden.

ARTIKEL 27: Rückerstattung eines Inbegriffs von Gegenständen

1. Der Berechtigte kann die Rückerstattung einzelner Vermögensgegenstände aus einem entzogenen Inbegriff von Gegenständen nicht verlangen, wenn der Inbegriff zurückerstattet werden kann und die Beschränkung der Rückerstattung auf einzelne Vermögensgegenstände zu einer unbilligen Schädigung des Rückerstattungspflichtigen oder der Gläubiger führen würde.

2. Befinden sich unter den Aktiven eines zurückzuerstattenden geschäftlichen Unternehmens oder sonstigen Vermögensinbegriffs Forderungen gegen die öffentliche Hand im Sinne des Artikels 1 der mit Zustimmung des Länderrats einheitlich in den Ländern Bayern, Hessen und Württemberg-Baden erlassenen Vertragshilfegesetze, so ist der Berechtigte befugt, deren Übernahme abzulehnen.

ARTIKEL 28: Schuldnerschutz

Ist eine Forderung entzogen worden, so kann der Schuldner mit befreiender Wirkung an den Rückerstattungspflichtigen leisten, bis ihm die Anmeldung des Rückerstattungsanspruchs bekanntgegeben wird. Das gleiche gilt für denjenigen, der bis zur Eintragung des Rückerstattungsvermerks oder eines Widerspruchs gegen die Richtigkeit des Grundbuchs an einen im Grundbuch eingetragenen Rückerstattungspflichtigen leistet.

V. ABSCHNITT: ERSATZ-UND NEBENANSPRÜCHE
ARTIKEL 29: Ersatz

1. Ein früherer Inhaber des entzogenen Vermögensgegenstandes. der rückerstattungspflichtig sein würde, wenn er noch Inhaber wäre, hat auf Verlangen des Berechtigten den Ersatz herauszugeben oder den Ersatzanspruch abzutreten, den er infolge des die Rückerstattung unmöglich machenden Umstandes erlangt hat. Der Berechtigte muß sich das, was er von einem oder von mehreren Verpflichteten erlangt hat, auf seine Ansprüche gegen die übrigen Verpflichteten anrechnen lassen.

2. Das gleiche gilt hinsichtlich des Ersatzes oder Ersatzanspruches, den der Inhaber oder ein früherer Inhaber des entzogenen Vermögensgegenstandes für eine Verschlechterung desselben erlangt hat.

3. lm Falle der Entziehung eines geschäftlichen Unternehmens erstreckt sich der Rückerstattungsanspruch auch auf die nach der Entziehung für das Unternehmen neu beschafften Vermögensgegenstände, es sei denn, daß der Rückerstattungspflichtige nachweist, daß die Neubeschaffung nicht mit Mitteln des Unternehmens erfolgt ist. Ist die Neubeschaffung von Vermögensgegenständen mit Mitteln des Unternehmens erfolgt, so gilt eine dadurch eingetretene Steigerung des Wertes des Unternehmens gegenüber dem Zeitpunkt der Entziehung als Nutzung im Sinne der Artikel 30, 32, 33. Die Bestimmungen gelten entsprechend für einen sonstigen Inbegriff von Vermögensgegenständen. Soweit die Beschaffung nicht mit Mitteln des Unternehmens erfolgt ist, steht dem Rückerstattungspflichtigen das Recht zur Abtrennung nach Artikel 26, Absatz 3 zu mit der Maßgabe, daß der Berechtigte das Übernahmerecht des Artikels 26, Absatz 3, Satz 3 nur dann geltend machen kann, wenn ohne dieses Recht der Betrieb des Unternehmens besonders beeinträchtigt würde.

4. Weitergehende Ansprüche des Berechtigten auf Grund der Artikel 30 ff. bleiben unberührt.

ARTIKEL 30: Strenge Haftung

1. Wer den entzogenen Vermögensgegenstand von dem Verfolgten mittels eines gegen die guten Sitten verstoßenden Rechtsgeschäfts oder durch eine von ihm oder zu seinen Gunsten ausgeübte Drohung oder durch widerrechtliche Wegnahme oder sonstige unerlaubte Handlung erlangt hat (schwere Entziehung), haftet auf Schadensersatz wegen Unmöglichkeit der Herausgabe oder Verschlechterung des entzogenen Vermögensgegenenstandes, auf Herausgabe von Nutzungen und auf sonstigen Schadensersatz nach den allgemeinen Vorschriften des bürgerlichen Rechts über den Schadensersatz wegen unerlaubter Handlung.

2. Ebenso haftet ein Inhaber oder früherer Inhaber des entzogenen Vermögensgegenstandes, der bei dem Erwerb desselben wußte oder den Umständen nach annehmen mußte (§ 259 des RSTGB), daß dieser zu irgendeiner Zeit durch eine schwere Entziehung erlangt worden war.

3. Soweit ein Anspruch auf Herausgabe von Nutzung besteht, kann der Berechtigte verlangen, daß für deren Berechnung ein durch Ausführungsvorschriften zu bestimmender, für derartige Vermögensgegenstände üblicher Nutzungsersatz zugrunde gelegt wird, sofern nicht diese Rechtsätze im Einzelfall offenbar in erheblichem Maße unangemessen sind.

ARTIKEL 31: Gemilderte Haftung
1. Auf Schadensersatz wegen Unmöglichkeit der Herausgabe oder Verschlechterung des entzogenen Vermögensgegenstandes haftet auch der Inhaber oder ein früherer Inhaber des entzogenen Vermögensgegenstandes, welcher diesen durch eine nicht den Tatbestand des Artikels 30 Absatz 1, erfüllende Entziehung (einfache Entziehung) erworben hat, es sei denn, daß er nachweist, daß er die im Verkehr erforderliche Sorgfalt angewendet hat.
2. Ebenso haftet der Inhaber oder ein früherer Inhaber von dem Zeitpunkt an, von dem er weiß oder den Umständen nach annehmen mußte, daß der Vermögensgegenstand zu irgendeiner Zeit durch eine Entziehung im Sinne dieses Gesetzes erlangt worden ist.
3. Im Falle der Entziehung eines Grundstücks oder grundstücksgleichen Rechtes haftet der Inhaber oder ein früherer Inhaber nach Absatz 1, sofern er nicht nachweist, daß er infolge besonderer Umstände weder wußte, noch den Umständen nach annehmen mußte, daß der Vermögensgegenstand zu irgendeiner Zeit durch eine Entziehung im Sinne dieses Gesetzes erlangt worden ist.

ARTIKEL 32: Herausgabe von Nutzungen bei einfacher Entziehung
1. Der Inhaber oder ein früherer Inhaber des entzogenen Vermögensgegenstandes, welcher diesen zu irgendeiner Zeit durch eine einfache Entziehung erlangt hat, hat für die Zeit, in der er Nutzungen des Vermögensgegenstandes gezogen hat, dem Berechtigten eine angemessene Vergütung zu entrichten. Die Bestimmungen des Artikels 31, Absatz 2 und 3, gelten entsprechend.
2. Als angemessen gilt der Betrag der gezogenen reinen Nutzungen, abzüglich eines angemessenen Entgeltes für die Geschäftsführung des Verpflichteten. Das Entgelt für die Geschäftsführung soll 50% der gezogenen Reinnutzungen nicht übersteigen, es sei denn, daß es sich um kleinere Beträge handelt. Nutzungen, die der Verpflichtete böswillig nicht gezogen oder vermindert hat, sind hinzuzurechnen. Die aus dem Reinertrag des Vermögensgegenstandes entrichteten Steuern und die Verzinsung des vom Verpflichteten für den Erwerb des Vermögensgegenstandes entrichteten Entgelts sind angemessen zu berücksichtigen. Artikel 30, Absatz 3 gilt entsprechend.

ARTIKEL 33: Haftungsausschluß
1. Der Inhaber oder ein früherer Inhaber eines entzogenen Vermögensgegenstandes ist zum Schadensersatz wegen Unmöglichkeit der Herausgabe oder wegen Verschlechterung des entzogenen Vermögensgegenstandes und zur Vergütung gezogener Nutzungen für die Zeit nicht verpflichtet, während der er weder wußte noch den Umständen nach annehmen mußte, daß der Gegenstand zu irgendeiner Zeit durch eine Entziehung erlangt worden ist. Die Bestimmung des Artikels 31, Absatz 3 bleibt unberührt.
2. Nutzungen, die nach den Regeln einer ordnungsmäßigen Wirtschaft nicht als Ertrag der Sache anzusehen sind, sind in jedem Falle nach den Vorschriften des Bürgerlichen Gesetzbuches über die Herausgabe einer ungerechtfertigten Bereicherung herauszugeben.
3. Für einen Zeitraum, für welchen der Berechtigte keine Nutzungen beanspruchen kann, wird ein Entgelt für Geschäftsführung in keinem Falle gewährt.

ARTIKEL 34: Verwendungsansprüche
1. Gewöhnliche Erhaltungskosten für den zurückzuerstattenden Vermögensgegenstand sind unbeschadet ihrer Berücksichtigung bei Ermittlung der Reinnutzungen nach Artikel 30 und 32 nicht zu ersetzen.
2. Für sonstige notwendige Verwendungen kann Ersatz insoweit verlangt werden, als sie bei ordnungsmäßiger Bewirtschaftung des entzogenen Vermögensgegenstandes noch nicht als abgeschrieben zu gelten haben.
3. Für andere als notwendige Verwendungen kann der Rückerstattungsberechtige Ersatz nur insoweit verlangen, als sie bei ordnungsmäßiger Bewirtschaftung des entzogenen Vermögensgegenstandes noch nicht als abgeschrieben zu gelten haben und durch die Verwendungen der Wert der Sache noch zur Zeit der Rückerstattung erhöht ist. Die Haftung des Berechtigten beschränkt sich in diesem Falle auf den zurückerstatteten Vermögensgegenstand und die sonstigen ihm aus der Rückerstattung zustehenden Ansprüche. Für die Geltendmachung der Haftungsbeschränkung finden die Vorschriften der §§ 1990, 1991 BGB entsprechende Anwendung.
4. Wer den entzogenen Vermögensgegenstand zu irgendeiner Zeit mittels einer schweren Entziehung erlangt hat, kann Ersatz nur für notwendige Verwendungen unter den Voraussetzungen des

Absatzes 2 und unter der weiteren Voraussetzung verlangen, daß die Verwendungen dem Interesse des Berechtigten entsprachen. Dasselbe gilt für den Inhaber oder einen früheren Inhaber des entzogenen Vermögensgegenstandes von dem Zeitpunkt an, von dem er wußte oder den Umständen nach annehmen mußte, daß der Vermögensgegenstand zu irgendeiner Zeit mittels einer schweren Entziehung erlangt worden war. 5. Für Verwendungen, die zu einer wesentlichen Veränderung und dadurch zu einer erheblichen Wertsteigerung einer Sache im Sinne des Artikels 26, Absatz 1 geführt haben, kann kein Ersatz verlangt werden, wenn die Bestimmungen des Artikels 26, Absatz 1 Anwendung finden.

ARTIKEL 35: Auskunftspflicht
Soweit es zur Geltendmachung von Ansprüchen auf Grund dieses Gesetzes notwendig ist, sind die Beteiligten einander zur Auskunfterteilung verpflichtet. Die Bestimmungen der §§ 259-261 BGB finden entsprechende Anwendung.

ARTIKEL 36: Eigentumserwerb an Früchten
Für den Erwerb des Eigentums an Erzeugnissen und sonstigen zu den Früchten der entzogenen Sache gehörenden Bestandteile gelten die Bestimmungen des Bürgerlichen Gesetzbuches. Hat ein Besitzer oder früherer Besitzer die Sache auf andere Weise als mittels einer schweren Entziehung erlangt, so gilt er unbeschadet seiner Verpflichtung zur Herausgabe von gezogenen Nutzungen als Eigentümer der Erzeugnisse und sonstiger zu den Früchten der entzogenen Sache gehörenden Bestandteile.

VI. ABSCHNITT: FORTBESTAND VON RECHTEN UND HAFTUNG FUR VERBINDLICHKEITEN
ARTIKEL 37: Fortbestand von Rechten
1. Rechte an dem entzogenen Vermögensgegenstand bleiben bestehen, soweit sie bestanden haben, bevor die die Entziehung darstellende Handlung vorgenommen worden ist, und sie seither nicht getilgt oder abgelöst worden sind. Das gleiche gilt für später entstandene Rechte, soweit die Gesamtsumme aller Haupt- und Nebenforderungen nicht höher ist als die Gesamtsumme aller Haupt- und Nebenforderungen, die bestanden haben, bevor die Entziehung vorgenommen worden ist (Belastungsgrenze). Rechte, die nicht auf Zahlung von Geld gerichtet sind, bleiben nur dann bestehen, wenn gleichartige Rechte vor der Entziehung bereits bestanden haben und die später entstandenen Rechte nicht lästiger sind als die zur Zeit der Entziehung bestehenden Rechte, oder wenn die Rechte auch ohne die Entziehung entstanden wären.
2. Die Belastungsgrenze erhöht sich, soweit Rechte Dritter aus Verwendungen herrühren, für die der Rückerstattungspflichtige gemäß Artikel 34 Ersatz verlangen kann. Sonstige die Belastungsgrenze des Absatz 1 übersteigende Rechte Dritter, die aus Verwendungen herrühren, für die der Rückerstattungspflichtige gemäß Artikel 34 Ersatz nicht verlangen kann, erlöschen, es sei denn, daß der Wert der Sache zur Zeit der Rückerstattung durch die Verwendung noch entsprechend erhöht ist und der Dritte nachweist, daß er weder wußte noch den Umständen nach annehmen mußte, daß die Sache mittels einer schweren Entziehung erlangt war.
3. Rechte, die für den Berechtigten oder seinen Rechtsvorgänger an dem zurückzuerstattenden Vermögensgegenstand anläßlich der Entziehung begründet waren, bleiben ohne Rücksicht auf die Belastungsgrenze bestehen. Ansprüche des Berechtigten auf Rückerstattung derartiger Rechte, soweit sie ihm entzogen worden sind, bleiben unberührt.
4. Rechte, die aus der Abgeltung der Hauszinssteuer herrühren, mit Ausnahme des Rechtes auf rückständige Leistungen, bleiben ohne Rücksicht auf die Belastungsgrenze unberührt.

ARTIKEL 38: Übergang von Rechten
Wenn ein Grundstück durch ein eine Entziehung im Sinne dieses Gesetzes darstellendes Rechtsgeschäft, Rechtshandlung oder Staatsakt belastet worden ist, so geht das Recht aus einer solchen Belastung auf den Berechtigten über und ist bei Berechnung der in Artikel 37 vorgesehenen Belastungsgrenze nicht zu berücksichtigen. Dies gilt insbesondere für Rechte, die im Zusammenhang mit der Reichsfluchtsteuer, Judenvermögensabgabe und ähnlichen Maßnahmen im Grundbuch eingetragen sind.

ARTIKEL 39: Schuldübernahme
Soweit der Berechtigte oder sein Rechtsvorgänger vor der Entziehung eines Grundstücks persönlicher Schuldner einer Forderung war, für die an dem Grundstück eine Hypothek, Grundschuld oder Rentenschuld bestellt worden war, übernimmt der Berechtigte mit der Wiedererlangung des Eigentums die persönliche Schuld, insoweit als die Hypothek, Grundschuld oder Rentenschuld nach den vorstehenden Bestimmungen bestehen bleibt. Das gleiche gilt, soweit es sich um Verbindlichkeiten handelt, bezüglich deren der Rückerstattungspflichtige Befreiung gemäß Artikel 34 dieses Gesetzes, § 257 BGB. verlangen kann. Das gleiche gilt ferner bei Verbindlichkeiten, die nach Artikel 37, Absatz 1, Satz 2 bestehen bleiben und an Stelle von Verbindlichkeiten getreten sind, für die der Berechtigte oder sein Rechtsvorgänger persönlicher Schuldner gewesen war.

ARTIKEL 40: Übertragungsanspruch
1. Der Berechtigte kann verlangen, daß ihm eine an dem zurückzuerstattenden Grundstück eingetragene Hypothek, Grundschuld oder Rentenschuld, die einem Besitzer oder früheren Besitzer des Grundstücks zusteht, der dieses zu irgendeiner Zeit mittels einer schweren Entziehung erlangt hatte, entschädigungslos übertragen wird. Dies gilt nicht bezüglich der der Hypothek zugrundeliegenden persönlichen Forderung. Bei Rechten, die vor der Entziehung begründet worden waren, findet Artikel 46, Absatz 3 entsprechende Anwendung.
2. Absatz 1 findet keine Anwendung auf Belastungen, die gemäß den Vorschriften dieses Gesetzes einzutragen sind.

ARTIKEL 41: Haftung für Geschäftsverbindlichkeiten
1. Erlangt der Berechtigte ein geschäftliches Unternehmen oder einen sonstigen Vermögensinbegriff zurück, so können die Gläubiger der im Betrieb des Unternehmens begründeten oder auf dem sonstigen Vermögensinbegriff lastenden Verbindlichkeiten von dem Zeitpunkt der Wiedererlangung an ihre zu dieser Zeit bestehenden Ansprüche auch gegen den Berechtigten geltend machen.
2. Die Haftung des Berechtigten beschränkt sich auf den zurückerstatteten Vermögensgegenstand und die sonstigen ihm aus der Rückerstattung zustehenden Ansprüche. Für die Geltendmachung der Haftungsbeschränkung finden die Vorschriften der §§ 1990, 1991 BGB entsprechende Anwendung.
3. Die Haftung des Berechtigten gemäß Absatz 1 und 2 tritt nicht ein, soweit der Gesamtbetrag der Verbindlichkeiten die in entsprechender Anwendung des Artikels 37 zu errechnende Belastungsgrenze übersteigt und der übersteigende Betrag der Verbindlichkeiten auch nicht durch einen nach Artikel 29, Absatz 3 sich ergebenden Mehrbetrag der Aktiven gedeckt erscheint. Die Wiedergutmachungskammer trifft in diesem Falle nach billigem Ermessen die erforderlichen Maßnahmen in sinngemäßer Anwendung des Artikels 37. Hierbei gehen Verbindlichkeiten, deren Gläubiger beim Erwerb der Forderung weder wußten, noch den Umständen nach annehmen mußten, daß das Unternehmen oder der sonstige Vermögensinbegriff zu irgendeiner Zeit durch eine Entziehung im Sinne dieses Gesetzes erlangt worden war, grundsätzlich anderen Verbindlichkeiten vor. Bei gleichrangigen Verbindlichkeiten findet, soweit erforderlich, eine Kürzung nach dem Verhältnis ihrer Beträge statt.

ARTIKEL 42: Miet-und Pachtverhältnisse
1. Hat der Rückerstattungspflichtige oder ein früherer Besitzer ein Grundstück an einen Dritten vermietet oder verpachtet, so kann der Berechtigte das Miet- oder Pachtverhältnis mit der gesetzlichen Kündigungsfrist kündigen. Die Kündigung ist erst zulässig, wenn die Wiedergutmachungsorgane die Rückerstattungspflicht rechtskräftig festgestellt haben oder diese Pflicht anderweitig anerkannt ist. Die Kündigung muß binnen 3 Monaten von diesem Zeitpunkt oder von der tatsächlichen Übernahme des Grundstücks an, wenn diese später erfolgt, vorgenommen werden.
2. Die Bestimmungen des Mieterschutzgesetzes in der Fassung vom 15. Dezember 1942 (RGBI. I, S. 712) findet keine Anwendung auf Rückerstattungspflichtige oder deren Rechtsvorgänger, die den zurückerstattenden Vermögensgegenstand durch schwere Entziehung erlangt haben oder beim Erwerb wußten oder den Umständen nach annehmen mußten, daß der Vermögensgegenstand zu irgendeiner Zeit durch eine schwere Entziehung erlangt worden war. Die Bestimmungen des Mieterschutzgesetzes finden ferner keine Anwendung, soweit der Berechtigte Wohnräume für sich oder seine nahen Angehörigen zum angemessenen Wohnen benötigt. Das gleiche gilt, wenn Wohnraum, der im Zeitpunkt

der Entziehung oder der Erhebung des Rückerstattungsanspruchs im Zusammenhang mit dem Betrieb eines zurückerstattenden geschäftlichen Unternehmens benutzt wurde, zur Weiterführung des Unternehmens benötigt wird. Bei Geschäftsräumen sind die Bestimmungen des Mieterschutzgesetzes insoweit nicht anwendbar, als der Berechtigte an deren alsbaldiger Rückgabe ein begründetes Interesse hat.

3. Miet-und Pachtverträge, die mit Genehmigung der Militärregierung abgeschlossen worden sind, können nur mit deren Zustimmung gekündigt werden.

ARTIKEL 43: Dienstverträge

Der Berechtigte kann laufende Dienstverträge, die der Rückerstattungspflichtige oder ein früherer Inhaber eines zurückerstattenden geschäftlichen Unternehmens in diesem nach der Entziehung abgeschlossen hatte, vorbehaltlich eines etwaigen Rechtes auf fristlose Kündigung, ohne Rücksicht auf abweichende Einzel-Vertragsbestimmungen mit der tariflichen oder gesetzlichen Kündigungsfrist kündigen. Die Kündigung ist erst zulässig, wenn die Wiedergutmachungsorgane die Rückerstattungspflicht rechtskräftig festgestellt haben oder diese Pflicht anderweitig anerkannt ist. Sie muß binnen 3 Monaten von diesem Zeitpunkt an oder von der tatsächlichen Übernahme des Unternehmens an, wenn diese später erfolgt, vorgenommen werden.

VII. ABSCHNITT: ANSPRÜCHE DES RÜCKERSTATTUNGSPFLICHTIGEN AUF RÜCKGEWÄHR UND AUSGLEICH

ARTIKEL 44: Rückgewährpflicht

1. Der Berechtigte hat den Rückerstattungspflichtigen gegen Rückerstattung des entzogenen Vermögensgegenstandes das erhaltene Entgelt, wenn möglich in Natur, herauszugeben. Das Entgelt erhöht sich um den Betrag der vor der Entziehug bestehenden und seither getilgten Belastungen des entzogenen Vermögensgegenstandes, soweit an deren Stelle nicht andere bestehenbleibende Belastungen getreten sind oder die getilgte Belastung nicht selbst auf Grund einer Entziehung im Sinne dieses Gesetzes entstanden ist.

2. Findet im Falle der Entziehung mehrerer Vermögensgegenstände gegen ein Gesamtentgelt die Rückerstattung nur in Ansehung einzelner Vermögensgegenstände statt, so ist das Gesamtentgelt in dem Verhältnis herabzusetzen, in welchem zur Zeit der Entziehung der Vermögensgegenstand, das Gesamtentgelt zu dem Wert der zurückzuerstattenden Vermögensgegenstände stand.

3. Hat der Berechtigte bei der Entziehung ganz oder teilweise aus den Gründen des Artikels 1 nicht die freie Verfügung über die Gegenleistung des Erwerbers erlangt, so vermindert sich das Entgelt um diesen Betrag. Der Berechtigte hat einen ihm etwa zustehenden Wiedergut-machungsanspruch dem Rückerstattungspflichtigen abzuteten.

4. Der Berechtigte hat in keinem Falle mehr zurückzugewähren, als den Wert des entzogenen Vermögensgegenstandes im Zeitpunkt der Rückerstattung abzüglich des Wertes der bestehenbleibenden Belastungen.

ARTIKEL 45: Zurückbehaltungsrecht

Für Ansprüche des Rückerstattungspflichtigen kann ein Zurückbehaltungsrecht insoweit nicht geltend gemacht werden, als dies die schleunige Rückerstattung des entzogenen Vermögensgegenstandes erheblich verzögern würde. Das gleiche gilt für Zwangsvollstreckung und Arrestvollziehung auf Grund von Gegenansprüchen in die entzogenen Vermögensgegenstände.

ARTIKEL 46: Gerichtliche Festsetzung für Zahlungen

1. Die Wiedergutmachungsorgane haben die Zahlungsbedingungen für Geldleistungen, die im Zusammenhang mit der Rückerstattung stehen, unter Berücksichtigung des Zwecks des Gesetzes, der Zahlungsfähigkeit des Verpflichteten und bestehender gesetzlicher Zahlungsverbote und Zahlungsbeschränkungen festzusetzen.

2. Der Berechtigte kann im Falle der Rückerstattung von Grundstücken und grundstücksgleichen Rechten verlangen daß seine Verbindlichkeiten zur Rückgewähr des Entgelts und zum Ersatz von Verwendungen.gegen Eintragung einer mit 4 v. H. verzinslichen Rückerstattungshypothek an dem Grundstück zugunsten des Rückerstattungspflichtigen angemessen, jedoch nicht länger als 10 Jahre, gestundet werden. Die näheren Bedingungen bestimmen auf Antrag die Wiedergutmachungsorgane.

3. In den Fällen der Artikel 34, Absatz 3, und 37, Absatz 2, haben die Wiedergutmach-ungsorgane die Fälligkeit von Verbindlichkeiten und die Zahlungsbedingungen so zu regeln, daß keinesfalls die Rückerstattung des entzogenen Vermögensgegenstandes gefährdet oder die Nutzung des Berechtigten an demselben unbillig beeinträchtigt wird.

ARTIKEL 47: Rückgriffsansprüche
1. Die Rückgriffsansprüche des Rückerstattungspflichtigen gegen jeden mittelbaren Rechtsvorgänger bestimmen sich nach den Vorschriften des Bürgerlichen Rechts. Die Rückerstattungspflicht bildet einen Mangel im Recht im Sinne des Bürgerlichen Gesetzbuches. Die Bestimmung des § 439 Absatz 1 BGB. findet keine Anwendung.
2. Die nach Absatz 1 zulässigen Ansprüche können im Falle der Herausgabe einer Sache auch gegen jeden Rechtsvorgänger geltend gemacht werden, der beim Erwerb der Sache nicht im guten Glauben gewesen ist. Diese Rechtsvorgänger haften als Gesamtschuldner. Ein Anspruch gegen sie ist ausgeschlossen, wenn auch der Rückerstattungspflichtige nicht im guten Glauben war.

ARTIKEL 48: Rechte Dritter an den Ansprüchen des Rückerstattungspflichtigen
1. Rechte an dem entzogenen Vermögensgegenstand, die nach Artikel 37 nicht an ihm bestehen bleiben, setzen sich fort an dem Anspruch des Rückerstattungspflichtigen auf Ersatz von Verwendungen, Rückgewähr des Entgelts und Rückgriff gemäß Artikel 34, 44, 47 und an demjenigen, was der Rückerstattungspflichtige aufgrund dieser Ansprüche erlangt.
2. Diese Bestimmung gilt nicht zugunsten von Personen, die zu einer schweren Entziehung durch Darlehensgewährung Beistand geleistet haben.

VIII. ABSCHNITT: ALLGEMEINE VERFAHRENSBESTIMMUNGEN
ARTIKEL 49: Grundsatz
1. Das Rückerstattungsverfahren soll eine rasche und vollständige Wiedergutmachung herbeiführen. Die Wiedergutmachungsorgane können von Verfahrensvorschriften, die in diesem Gesetz für anwendbar erklärt sind, im Einzelfall abweichen, wenn dies der Beschleunigung und der Rückerstattung dient und dadurch weder die volle Aufklärung des Sachverhalts noch die Gewährung des rechtlichen Gehörs beeinträchtigt wird.
2. Die Wiedergutmachungsorgane haben die Lage, in die der Berechtigte durch die Verfolgungsmaßnahmen aus den Gründen des Artikels 1 geraten ist, bei der Ermittlung des Sachverhalts weitgehend zu berücksichtigen. Dies gilt insbesondere, soweit die Beibringung von Beweismitteln durch Verlust von Urkunden, Tod und Unauffindbarkeit von Zeugen, Auslandsaufenthalt des Berechtigten und ähnliche Umstände erschwert oder unmöglich geworden ist. Eidesstattliche Versicherungen des Berechtigten und von ihm benannter Zeugen sind zuzulassen. Dies gilt auch dann, wenn die die eidesstattliche Versicherung abgebende Person nach Abgabe der Versicherung verstorben ist.

ARTIKEL 50: Erbrecht und ausländisches Recht
1. Wer sich auf eine erbrechtliche Stellung beruft hat diese nachzuweisen.
2. Ausländisches Recht bedarf des Beweises, soweit es den Wiedergutmachungsorganen unbekannt ist.

ARTIKEL 51: Todesvermutung
Wenn ein Verfolgter seinen letzten bekannten Aufenthalt in Deutschland oder in einem von Deutschland oder seinen Alliierten besetzten oder annektierten Gebiet hatte und sein Aufenthalt seit dem 8. Mai 1945 unbekannt ist, ohne daß Nachrichten darüber vorliegen, daß er zu diesem oder einem späteren Zeitpunkt noch gelebt hat, so wird vermutet, daß er am 8. Mai 1945 verstorben ist. Falls nach den Umständen des Einzelfalls ein anderer Zeitpunkt des Todes wahrscheinlich erscheint, so können die Wiedergutmachungsorgane diesen anderen Zeitpunkt als Zeitpunkt des Todes feststellen.

ARTIKEL 52: Sicherungspflicht
1. Die Wiedergutmachungsorgane haben entzogene Vermögensgegenstände, wenn ein Bedürfnis besteht, in geeigneter Weise sicherzustellen. Sie können hierzu auf Antrag oder von Amts wegen einstweilige Verfügungen anordnen oder Arrestbefehle erlassen. Diese sind abzuändern oder aufzuheben,

wenn die Sicherstellung durch andere als die getroffenen Maßnahmen erreicht werden kann, oder das Bedürfnis nach ihrer Aufrechterhaltung entfällt.

2. Die Vorschriften der Zivilprozeßordnung über Arrest und einstweilige Verfügungen sind in der jeweils geltenden Fassung entsprechend anwendbar.

ARTIKEL 53: Treuhänder

1. In Fällen, in denen für entzogene Vermögensgegenstände eine Fürsorge erforderlich ist, ist ein Treuhänder zu bestellen, soweit nicht hierfür die Zuständigkeit einer anderen Behörde begründet ist.

2. Für die Bestellung und Beaufsichtigung des Treuhänders gelten die Vorschriften über die Verwaltung beschlagnahmten Vermögens, soweit nicht durch Ausführungsvorschriften Abweichendes bestimmt wird.

ARTIKEL 54: Zuständigkeit anderer Behörden zu Maßnahmen nach Artikel 52, 53

Soweit zu den in Artikel 52, 53 bezeichneten Sicherungsmaßnahmen andere Behörden zuständig sind, haben die Wiedergutmachungsorgane diese hierum zu ersuchen.

IX. ABSCHNITT: ANMELDEVERFAHREN
ARTIKEL 55: Zentralanmeldeamt

1. Für die Anmeldung von Rückerstattungsansprüchen wird ein Zentralanmeldeamt errichtet. Die näheren Bestimmungen hierüber erläßt die Militärregierung.

2. Das Zentralanmeldeamt hat die Anmeldung den zuständigen Wiedergutmachungsbehörden zu übermitteln.

ARTIKEL 56: Form und Frist der Anmeldung

1. Rückerstattungsansprüche nach diesem Gesetz sind bis spätestens 31. Dezember 1948 schriftlich bei dem Zentralanmeldeamt anzumelden. Die näheren Bestimmungen über die Form der Anmeldung erläßt die Militärregierung.

2. Der angemeldete Anspruch soll durch Urkunden oder eidesstattliche Versicherungen glaubhaft gemacht werden.

3. Die Anmeldung kann rechtswirksam durch einen von mehreren Mitberechtigten erfolgen.

4. Die Anmeldung seitens eines vermeintlichen Berechtigten wirkt zugunsten des wahren Berechtigten und unter den Voraussetzungen der Artikel 8, 10 und 11 zugunsten der dort bezeichneten Nachfolgeorganisationen. Das gleiche gilt für die Anmeldung seitens dieser Nachfolgeorganisationen.

ARTIKEL 57: Verhältnis zum ordentlichen Rechtsweg

Ansprüche, die unter dieses Gesetz fallen, können, soweit in diesem Gesetz nichts anderes bestimmt ist, nur im Verfahren nach diesem Gesetz und unter Einhaltung seiner Fristen geltend gemacht werden. Ansprüche aus unerlaubter Handlung, die nicht unter die Bestimmungen dieses Gesetzes fallen, können jedoch im ordentlichen Rechtsweg gelten gemacht werden.

ARTIKEL 58: Inhalt der Anmeldung

1. Die Anmeldung muß eine Beschreibung des entzogenen Vermögensgegenstandes enthalten. Zeit, Ort und Umstände der Entziehung sollen, so genau als es den Umständen nach möglich ist, beschrieben werden. Soweit tunlich, sollen Geldansprüche beziffert sein; der Grund des Anspruchs soll dargelegt werden.

2. Die Anmeldung soll, soweit dem Berechtigten bekannt, Namen und Anschrift des Rückerstattungspflichtigen, Namen und Anschrift aller Personen, die ein Recht an dem Vermögensgegenstand haben oder geltend machen, etwaige Mieter und Pächter und die Angabe der zur Zeit der Entziehung an dem Vermögensgegenstand bestehenden Belastungen enthalten.

3. Das Zentralanmeldeamt oder die Wiedergutmachungsorgane können die Ergänzung einer Anmeldung durch die in Absatz 1 und 2 vorgesehenen Angaben von dem Berechtigten verlangen; sie können ihm die eidesstattliche Versicherung seiner Angaben auferlegen.

4. Hat der Antragsteller seinen Wohnsitz oder gewöhnlichen Aufenthalt nicht in einer der vier Besatzungszonen Deutschlands oder der Stadt Berlin, und hat er daselbst auch keinen zum Empfang von Zustellungen bevollmächtigten Prozeßvertreter bestellt, so hat er in der Anmeldung einen daselbst wohnhaften Zustellungsbevollmächtigten zu benennen. Benennt er einen Zustellungsbevollmächtigten nicht, so hat die Wiedergutmachungsbehörde einen solchen zu bestellen und den Antragsteller hiervon zu benachrichtigen.

5. Über die erfolgte Anmeldung ist seitens des Zentralanmeldeamtes eine Bescheinigung zu erteilen, in der der Berechtigte davon in Kenntnis gesetzt wird, an welche der Wiedergutmachungsbehörden die Anmeldung gemäß Artikel 55, Absatz 2 übermittelt worden ist.
6. Die in Artikel 56, Absatz 1 vorgesehene Frist für die Anmeldung eines Rückerstattungsanspruchs gilt als gewahrt, wenn diese schriftlich bei dem Zentralanmeldeamt erfolgt ist, selbst wenn sie unvollständig und nicht in der vorgeschriebenen Form vorgenommen worden ist.

ARTIKEL 59: Örtliche Zuständigkeit
1. Das Zentralanmeldeamt hat die Anmeldung des Rückerstattungsanspruchs an die Wiedergutmachungsbehörde des Bezirks zu übermitteln, in dem sich der zurückzuerstattende Vermögensgegenstand befindet. Ergibt sich die Unzuständigkeit einer Wiedergutmachungsbehörde, so verweist sie den Rückerstattungsanspruch an die zuständige Wiedergutmachungsbehörde. Der Verweisungsbeschluß ist für diese bindend.
2. Durch Ausführungsverordnung können weitere Vorschriften über die örtliche Zuständigkeit, namentlich zur Geltendmachung von Ersatz- und Nebenansprüchen, erlassen werden.

ARTIKEL 60: Sachliche Zuständigkeit
Die Wiedergutmachungsorgane sind sachlich zuständig ohne Rücksicht darauf, ob unter anderen gesetzlichen Bestimmungen ein Rückerstattungsanspruch zur Zuständigkeit der ordentlichen Gerichte oder der Verwaltungs-oder sonstiger Gerichte gehören würde oder der Rechtsweg ausgeschlossen wäre.

ARTIKEL 61: Bekanntgabe der Anmeldung
1. Die Wiedergutmachungsbehörde hat den Rückerstattungsanspruch den Beteiligten zur Erklärung binnen zwei Monaten durch förmliche Zustellung bekanntzugeben. Beteiligte sind der Rückerstattungspflichtige, dinglich Berechtigte, Mieter und Pächter des entzogenen Vermögensgegenstandes, sowie diejenigen sonstigen Betroffenen, deren Einbeziehung in das Verfahren der Berechtigte beantragt. Wenn der Beteiligte das Deutsche Reich, ein Land oder ein früheres Land, die vormalige Nationalsozialistische Deutsche Arbeiterpartei, eine ihrer Gliederungen oder angeschlossenen Organisationen ist, so erfolgt die Zustellung an den Staatsminister der Finanzen. Das Land ist in den Fällen des Satzes 3 berechtigt, als Partei im Verfahren aufzutreten.
2. Ist der Rückerstattungspflichtige oder seine gegenwärtige Anschrift unbekannt oder ist auf Grund der Anmeldung anzunehmen, daß unbekannte Dritte in Ansehung des entzogenen Gegenstandes Rechte besitzen, so hat die Wiedergutmachungsbehörde die Anmeldung des Rückerstattungsanspruchs öffentlich zuzustellen und dabei die Rückerstattungspflichtigen und die unbekannten Dritten aufzufordern, ihre Rechte binnen zwei Monaten bei der Wiedergutmachungsbehörde anzumelden und zu begründen. Die öffentliche Zustellung erfolgt nach Maßgabe des § 204, Absatz 2 der ZPO in der Fassung des Kontrollratsgesetzes Nr. 38 in der für Ladungen vorgeschiebenen Form. Die Zustellung gilt als an dem Tage erfolgt, an welchem seit der Einrückung in das in Absatz 2 des § 204 ZPO bezeichnete Mitteilungsblatt ein Monat verstrichen ist.
3. Die Rechtshängigkeit tritt mit der Zustellung der Anmeldung ein.
4. Richtet sich der Anspruch auf Rückerstattung eines Grundstücks oder grundstiicksgleichen Rechtes, so hat die Wiedergutmachungsbehörde die Eintragung der Anmeldung des Rückerstattungsanspruchs im Grundbuch herbeizuführen (Rückerstattungsvermerk). Der Rückerstattungsvermerk wirkt gegen jeden Dritten.
5. Die Bestimmungen der Zivilprozeßordnung über die Streitverkündung und Nebenintervention finden entsprechende Anwendung.

ARTIKEL 62: Verfahren vor der Wiedergutmachungsbehörde
1. Wird innerhalb der Erklärungsfrist oder der durch die öffentliche Bekanntmachung erfolgten Anmeldefrist kein Widerspruch erhoben, so gibt die Wiedergutmachungsbehörde durch Beschluß dem Antrag statt. Wenn über die Belastungsgrenze und den Fortbestand von Rechten kein Streit besteht, so trifft sie auch hierüber die erforderlichen Feststellungen.
2. Ist jedoch der Rückerstattungsantrag nicht schlüssig begründet oder stehen der Richtigkeit der zu seiner Begründung vorgebrachten Behauptungen Einträge in öffentlichen Registern oder öffentlichen Urkunden, die der Wiedergutmachungsbehörde vorliegen, entgegen, so hat die

Wiedergutmachungsbehörde den Antragsteller zur Erklärung darüber binnen einer von ihr zu setzenden angemessenen Frist aufzufordern. Wird innerhalb der Frist eine den Rückerstattungsanspruch rechtfertigende Aufklärung und Ergänzung des Vorbringens seitens des Antragstellers nicht gegeben, so hat die Wiedergutmachungsbehörde den Antrag als unbegründet zurückzuweisen.

3. Wird Widerspruch erhoben, so hat die Wiedergutmachungsbehörde den Versuch einer gütlichen Einigung zu machen, sofern nicht die Erfolglosigkeit eines solchen Versuchs mit Bestimmtheit vorauszusehen ist. Kommt eine gütliche Einigung zustande, so hat die Wiedergutmachungsbehörde die Vereinbarung auf Antrag schriftlich niederzulegen und den Beteiligten von Amts wegen eine Ausfertigung der Niederschrift zu erteilen.

ARTIKEL 63: Verweisung an das Gericht

1. Kommt eine gütliche Einigung ganz oder teilweise nicht zustande oder übersteigen die erforderlichen Maßnahmen die Zuständigkeit der Wiedergutmachungsbehörde, so verweist diese insoweit die Sache an die Wiedergutmachungskammer des für den Sitz der Wiedergutmachungsbehörde zuständigen Landgerichts. Dies gilt insbesondere auch, wenn lediglich über die Belastungsgrenze, den Fortbestand von Rechten oder die Haftung für Verbindlichkeiten Streit besteht.

2. Durch Ausführungsverordnungen kann die Zuständigkeit allgemein auf bestimmte oder andere als die in Absatz 1 bezeichneten Landgerichte übertragen werden.

3. Die Wiedergutmachungsbehörde kann das Verfahren vor der Verweisung bis zur Höchstdauer von sechs Monaten aussetzen, sofern der Berechtigte zustimmt und eine gütliche Einigung zu erwarten ist.

ARTIKEL 64: Einspruch

1. Gegen eine Entscheidung der Wiedergutmachungsbehörde gemäß Artikel 59, Absatz 1, Satz 2 und gemäß Artikel 62, Absatz 1 und 2 kann jeder Beteiligte binnen einem Monat und wenn er im Ausland seinen Wohnsitz hat, binnen drei Monaten die Entscheidung der Wiedergutmachungskammer durch Einspruch zur Wiedergutmachungsbehörde anrufen. Die Frist beginnt mit der Zustellung der anzufechtenden Entscheidung. Artikel 61, Absatz 2 findet entsprechende Anwendung.

2. Der Einspruch kann nur auf eine Verletzung der Vorschriften des Artikels 59, Absatz 1, Satz 2 oder des Artikels 62, Absatz 1 und 2 gegründet werden.

ARTIKEL 65: Vollstreckbarkeit

Aus den von der Wiedergutmachungsbehörde ausgefertigten Vereinbarungen und aus den rechtskräftigen Beschlüssen der Wiedergutmachungsbehörde findet die Zwangsvollstreckung nach den Vorschriften der Zivilprozeßordnung statt. An Stelle des Vollstreckungsgerichts tritt die Wiedergutmachungsbehörde. Sie kann sich bei der Durchführung der Vollstreckung anderer Behörden, insbesondere des Vollstreckungsgerichts, bedienen.

X. ABSCHNITT: GERICHTLICHES VERFAHREN
ARTIKEL 66: Besetzung der Wiedergutmachungskammer

Die Wiedergutmachungskammer besteht aus einem Vorsitzenden und zwei Beisitzern, welche die Befähigung zum Richteramt oder zum höheren Verwaltungsdienst haben müssen. Der Vorsitzende muß ein Richter der ordentlichen Gerichtsbarkeit sein. Die Beisitzer werden, soweit sie nicht selbst Berufsrichter sind, auf die Dauer von drei Jahren ernannt. Einer der drei Richter soll dem Kreise der aus den Gründen des Artikels 1 Verfolgten angehören.

ARTIKEL 67: Verfahren

1. DieWiedergutmachungskammer hat die Rechtsbeziehungen der Beteiligten gemäß diesem Gesetz zu gestalten.

2. Soweit keine anderweitigen Bestimmungen in diesem Gesetz getroffen sind, sind für das Verfahren die Vorschriften über das Verfahren in Sachen der freiwilligen Gerichtsbarkeit mit den folgenden Maßgaben entsprechend anwendbar:

a) Die Kammer muß eine mündliche Verhandlung anordnen. Die Verhandlung ist öffentlich.

b) Auf Antrag des Berechtigten kann das Verfahren bis zur Höchstdauer von sechs Monaten ausgesetzt werden. Die Aussetzung kann nach Fortsetzung des Verfahrens wiederholt werden.

c) Die Wiedergutmachungskammer hat ein Teilurteil hinsichtlich einzelner von mehreren

Ansprüchen oder eines Teils eines Anspruchs zu erlassen, wenn die Entscheidung über eine Widerklage, einen Aufrechnungsanspruch, ein Zurückbehaltungsrecht oder einen ähnlichen Rechtsbehelf die Entscheidung über die Rückerstattung erheblich verzögern würde.

d) Die Kammer kann vorbehaltlich der endgültigen Entscheidung die vorläufige Herausgabe entzogener Vermögensgegenstände gegen oder ohne Sicherheitsleistung an den Antragsteller anordnen. Der Antragsteller hat in diesem Falle gegenüber Dritten die Rechtsstellung eines Treuhänders.

ARTIKEL 68: *Form und Inhalt der Entscheidung*

1. Die Wiedergutmachungskammer entscheidet durch einen mit Gründen versehenen Beschluß, der den Beteiligten zuzustellen ist. Der Beschluß ist vorläufig vollstreckbar. §§ 713, Absatz 2, 713a bis 720 ZPO finden entsprechende Anwendung.

2. Gegen den Beschluß findet innerhalb einer Frist von einem Monat und wenn der Beschwerdeführer seinen Wohnsitz im Ausland hat, innerhalb einer Frist von drei Monaten die sofortige Beschwerde statt. Die Frist beginnt mit der Zustellung; Artikel 61, Absatz 2 findet entsprechende Anwendung. Über die Beschwerde entscheidet der Zivilsenat des Oberlandesgerichts. Die Beschwerde kann nur darauf gestützt werden, daß die Entscheidung auf einer Verletzung des Gesetzes beruhe. Die Vorschriften der §§ 551, 561, 563 ZPO finden entsprechende Anwendung.

3. Durch Ausführungsverordnungen kann die Zuständigkeit zur Entscheidung über Beschwerden allgemein auf eines von mehreren Oberlandesgerichten übertragen werden.

ARTIKEL 69: *Board of Review*

Ein Board of Review ist ermächtigt, alle Entscheidungen nachzuprüfen, die einen nach Maßgabe dieses Gesetzes erhobenen Rückerstattungsanspruch betreffen, sowie die nach Sachlage erforderlichen Maßnahmen zu ergreifen. Ausführungsvorschriften der Militärregierung werden die Ernennung und Zusammensetzung des Board, seine Zuständigkeit, das Verfahren und alle weiteren Einzelheiten regeln.

XI. ABSCHNITT: BESONDERE VERFAHREN

ARTIKEL 70: *Antragsrecht der Staatsanwaltschaft*

Wird bezüglich entzogener Vermögensgegenstände ein Rückerstattungsanspruch bis zum 31. Dezember 1948 nicht geltend gemacht, so kann die Staatsanwaltschaft am Sitze der Wiedergutmachungskammer den Rückerstattungsanspruch zugunsten einer in Artikel 10 vorgesehenen Nachfolgeorganisation geltend machen. Dies gilt nicht, wenn der Berechtigte auf seinen Rückerstattungsanspruch gemäß Artikel 11, Absatz 3 verzichtet hat. Der Antrag der Staatsanwaltschaft kann nur bis zum 30. Juni 1949 gestellt werden.

ARTIKEL 71: *Zuständigkeitsbereinigung*

1. Werden Ansprüche der in den Artikeln 1 bis 48 bezeichneten Art in einem gerichtlichen Verfahren einschließlich der Zwangsvollstreckung vom Berechtigten klage- oder einredeweise geltend gemacht, so hat das Gericht die Wiedergutmachungsbehörde zu benachrichtigen. Das Gericht kann durch unanfechtbaren Beschluß das Verfahren aussetzen und die Zwangsvollstreckung einstweilen einstellen; auf Ersuchen der Wiedergutmachungsbehörde sind diese Anordnungen zu treffen. Die Wiedergutmachungsbehörde kann die Weiterbehandlung des Anspruchs nach Maßgabe dieses Gesetzes mit der Wirkung des Ausschlusses des Rechtsweges anordnen oder mit Bindung für das Gericht den Berechtigten die Geltendmachung des Anspruchs im ordentlichen Rechtsweg überlassen. Findet ein Rechtsstreit durch Weiterbehandlung des Anspruchs nach Maßgabe dieses Gesetzes seine Erledigung, so werden die Gerichtskosten niedergeschlagen, die außergerichtlichen Kosten gegeneinander aufgehoben.

2. Das Gericht hat dem Zentralanmeldeamt jede gemäß Absatz 1 getroffene Maßnahme mitzuteilen.

XII. ABSCHNITT: KOSTENBESTIMMUNGEN

ARTIKEL 72: *Kosten*

1. Das Verfahren vor den Wiedergutmachungsorganen ist grundsätzlich gerichtskostenfrei. Im übrigen werden Ausführungsverordnungen die Tragung und Festsetzung von Kosten, Gebühren und Auslagen regeln.

2. Der Berechtigte ist nicht verpflichtet, Vorschüsse oder Sicherheit für Kosten zu leisten.

XIII. ABSCHNITT: ANZEIGEPFLICHT UND STRAFBESTIMMUNGEN
ARTIKEL 73: Anzeigepflicht

1. Wer Vermögensgegenstände, von denen er weiß oder den Umständen nach annehmen muß,

   a)   daß sie im Sinne des Artikels 2 dieses Gesetzes entzogen sind; oder

   b)   daß eine solche Entziehung nach den Vorschriften des Artikels 3, Absatz 1 vermutet wird; oder

   c)   daß sie zu irgendeiner Zeit Gegenstand eines Rechtsgeschäfts waren, das nach den Bestimmungen des Artikels 4, Absatz 1 angefochten werden kann,

im Besitz hat oder zu irgendeinem Zeitpunkt, nachdem der Verfolgte über sie verfügt hat oder sie ihm entzogen worden sind, im Besitz hatte, muß dies schriftlich dem Zentralanmeldeamt bis zum 15. Mai 1948 anzeigen. Die Anzeige muß genaue Angaben darüber enthalten, wie der Anzeigeerstatter in den Besitz des Vermögensgegenstandes gelangt ist, sie muß Namen und Wohnort desjenigen angeben, von dem der Anzeigeerstatter den Vermögensgegenstand erhalten hat, das entrichtete Entgelt und, falls der Vermögensgegenstand nicht mehr im Besitz des Anzeigeerstatters ist, den Namen desjenigen, an den der Vermögensgegenstand übertragen worden ist.

2. Die Anzeigepflicht entfällt:

   a)   Bei beweglichen Sachen, die im Wege des ordnungsmäßigen üblichen Geschäftsverkehrs aus einem einschlägigen Unternehmen erworben worden sind; anzeigepflichtig sind jedoch Sachen, die im Wege der Versteigerung erworben worden sind, oder in Unternehmen, die sich mit der Versteigerung oder sonstigen Verwertung entzogener Vermögensgegenstände in erheblichem Maße befaßten;

   b)   bei beweglichen Sachen, deren Wert im Zeitpunkt der Entziehung den Betrag von RM 1000.- nicht überstiegen hat;

   c)   bei Schenkungen zwischen nahen Verwandten (§ 52, Absatz 2 STGB) und bei unzweifelhaften Anstandsschenkungen;

   d)   bei bereits zurückerstatteten Vermögensgegenständen und bei solchen Vermögensgegenständen, auf deren Rückerstattung der Berechtigte in der Zeit vom 8. Mai 1945 bis zum Inkrafttreten dieses Gesetzes ausdrücklich schriftlich verzichtet hat.

3. Eine gemäß Absatz 1 erstattete Anzeige darf im Verfahren vor den Wiedergutmachungsorganen nicht als Geständnis des Anzeigenden gewertet werden, daß die angemeldeten Vermögensgegenstände der Rückerstattung unterliegen; ebensowenig darf eine solche Anzeige als Verzicht auf einen Einwand ausgelegt werden, den der Anzeigende hätte geltend machen können, wenn er die Anzeige nicht erstattet hätte. Die Anzeige kann jedoch als ein Geständnis in bezug auf die darin mitgeteilten Tatsachen gewertet werden.

4. Das Zentralanmeldeamt hat nach Erhalt einer auf Grund der Bestimmungen dieses Artikels erstatteten Anzeige eine Abschrift der Anzeige an die zuständige Wiedergutmachungsbehörde oder die zuständigen Wiedergutmachungsbehörden in dem Bezirk weiterzuleiten, in dem sich irgendwelche in der Anzeige in Bezug genommene Vermögensgegenstände befinden. Die Einsicht in alle gemäß den Vorschriften dieses Artikels erstatteten Anzeigen ist gestattet.

ARTIKEL 74: Pflicht zur Einsicht des Grundbuchs und anderer öffentlicher Register

1. Wer ein Grundstück oder ein grundstückgleiches Recht besitzt, ist verpflichtet, sich durch Einsicht des Grundbuchs zu vergewissern, daß es sich nicht um einen anzeigepflichtigen Vermögensgegenstand handelt. Das gleiche gilt von Vermögensgegenständen, die in anderen öffentlichen Registern eingetragen sind.

2. Erlangt eine Behörde oder öffentliche Dienststelle Kenntnis von dem Verbleib eines anzeigepflichtigen Vermögensgegenstandes, so hat sie unverzüglich dem Zentralanmeldeamt Mitteilung zu machen. Artikel 73, Absatz 4 gilt entsprechend.

ARTIKEL 75: Strafbestimmungen

1. Mit Gefängnis bis zu fünf Jahren und mit Geldstrafe oder mit einer dieser Strafen wird, soweit nicht auf Grund anderer Bestimmungen eine höhere Strafe verwirkt ist, bestraft,

   a) wer seiner Anzeigepflicht auf Grund der Artikel 73 und 74 vorsätzlich oder fahrlässig nicht nachkommt,

   b) wer gegenüber den Wiedergutmachungsorganen wissentlich falsche oder irreführende Angaben macht.

2. Der Täter bleibt im Falle des Absatzes 1 a) straflos, wenn er vor Entdeckung die nach diesem Gesetz vorgeschriebene Anzeige freiwillig nachholt.

ARTIKEL 76: Strafbestimmungen (Fortsetzung)
1. Mit Gefängnis bis zu fünf Jahren und mit Geldstrafe oder mit einer dieser Strafen wird, soweit nicht auf Grund anderer Bestimmunqen eine höhere Strafe verwirkt ist, bestraft, wer Vermögensgegenstände, die unter die Bestimmungen dieses Gesetzes fallen, veräußert, beschädigt, vernichtet oder beiseite schafft, um sie dem Zugriff des Berechtigten zu entziehen.
2. In besonders schweren Fällen tritt Zuchthausstrafe bis zu fünf Jahren ein.
3. Der Versuch ist strafbar.

ARTIKEL 77: Strafbestimmungen (Fortsetzung)
Niemand kann sich in den Fällen der Artikel 75, 76 auf die Unkenntnis von solchen Tatsachen berufen, die er auf Grund einer Einsicht in öffentliche Bücher oder Register erfahren hätte, wenn und soweit er nach Artikel 74 zu einer solchen Einsicht verpflichtet war.

XIV. ABSCHNITT: WIEDERHERSTELLUNG VON ERBRECHTEN UND KINDESANNAHME-VERHÄLTNISSEN
ARTIKEL 78: Erbverdrängung
1. Ein in der Zeit vom 30. Januar 1933 bis 8. Mai 1945 aus den Gründen des Artikels 1 durch Gesetz oder Verordnung erfolgter Ausschluß von Erwerb von Todes wegen oder Verfall des Nachlasses gilt als nicht eingetreten.
2. Für die Fristenberechnung gilt der Erbfall mit dem lnkrafttreten dieses Gesetzes als eingetreten.

ARTIKEL 79: Anfechtbarkeit von Verfügungen von Todes wegen und Erbschaftsausschlagungen
1. Letztwillige Verfügungen und Erbverträge aus der Zeit vom 30. Januar 1933 bis 8. Mai 1945, in welchen Abkömmlinge, Eltern, Großeltern, voll- und halbblütige Geschwister und deren Abkömmlinge, sowie Ehegatten von der Erbfolge ausgeschlossen wurden, um ihren Erbteil einem vom Erblasser aus den Gründen des Artikels 1 erwarteten Zugriffs des Staates zu entziehen, sind anfechtbar. Vorbehaltlich der Bestimmungen des Absatz 3 finden auf die Anfechtung die Vorschriften der §§ 2080 ff bzw. 2281 ff. BGB Anwendung.
2. Erbschaftsausschlagungen durch die im Absatz 1 genannten Personen sind anfechtbar, wenn sie in der Zeit vom 30. Januar 1933 bis 8. Mai 1945 erfolgten, um dadurch einen aus den Gründen des Artikels 1 erwarteten Zugriff des Staates auf den Erbteil zu verhindern. Vorbehaltlich der Bestimmungen in Absatz 3 finden auf die Anfechtung die Vorschriften der §§ 1954 ff. BGB Anwendung.
3. Die Anfechtung von letztwilligen Verfügungen und Erbverträgen sowie von Erbschaftsausschlagungen muß bis 31. Dezember 1948 erfolgen. Eine innerhalb dieser Frist er- folgte Anfechtung gilt als rechtzeitig.

ARTIKEL 80: Verfolgten-Testament
1. Der Gültigkeit einer in der Zeit vom 30. Januar 1933 bis 8. Mai 1945 erklärten letztwilligen Verfügung steht das Fehlen jeglicher Form nicht entgegen, wenn der Erblasser zu der Verfügung durch eine aus den Gründen des Artikels 1 erwachsene unmittelbare Todesgefahr, in der er sich befand oder zu befinden glaubte, veranlaßt wurde und ihm die Festlegung in gesetzlicher Form nach den Umständen unmöglich oder nicht zuzumuten war.
2. Eine nach Absatz 1 zu beurteilende letztwillige Verfügung gilt als nicht getroffen, wenn der Erblasser nach dem 30. September 1945 zu einer formgerechten letztwilligen Verfügung noch in der Lage war.

ARTIKEL 81: Wiederherstellung von Kindesannahmeverhältnissen
1. Ein in der Zeit vom 30. Januar 1933 bis 8. Mai 1945 aus den Gründen des Artikels 1 aufgehobenes Kindesannahmeverhältnis kann durch Vertrag des Annehmenden oder seiner Erben mit dem Kinde oder seinen Erben rückwirkend zum Zeitpunkt der Aufhebung wiederhergestellt werden. Auf den Wiederherstellungsvertrag finden die Vorschriften der §§ 1741 bis 1772 BGB mit Ausnahme der Bestimmungen der §§ 1744, 1745, 1747, 1752 und 1753 Anwendung. Die Bestätigung des Wiederherstellungsvertrags kann auch nach dem Tode der am Wiederherstellungsvertrag beteiligten Personen erfolgen. Ist ein Beteiligter nicht erreichbar, so kann für ihn zum Zwecke der Vertretung bei der Wiederherstellung des Kindesannahmeverhältnisses ein Pfleger bestellt werden.
2. Ist das Kindesannahmeverhältnis in der Zeit vom 30. Januar 1933 bis 8. Mai 1945 durch gerichtliche Entscheidung aus den Gründen des Artikels 1 aufgehoben worden und sind keine Umstände

ersichtlich, die die Vertragsschließenden seitdem zur Aufhebung des Kindesannahmeverhältnisses veranlaßt hätten, so können sowohl der Annehmende oder einer seiner Erben, wie das Kind oder einer seiner Erben die Aufhebung dieser Entscheidung beantragen.

3. Zuständig zur Entscheidung gemäß Absatz 2 ist das Amtsgericht, welches das Kindesannahmeverhältnis aufgehoben hat. Absatz 1, Satz 4 gilt entsprechend. Das Gericht entscheidet nach seinem durch Billigkeit bestimmten freien Ermessen. Durch die Aufhebung der gerichtlichen Entscheidung tritt das Kindesannahmeverhältnis rückwirkend wieder in Kraft. Das Gericht kann in seiner Entscheidung die Rückwirkung in einzelnen Beziehungen ausschliessen.

4. Das Verfahren ist gebühren- und auslagenfrei.

5. Die Wiederherstellung von Kindesannahmeverhältnissen kann nur bis spätestens 31. Dezember 1948 beantragt werden.

ARTIKEL 82: Zuständigkeit

Über Ansprüche auf Grund der Artikel 78 bis 81 entscheiden die ordentlichen Gerichte. Eine Anmeldung bei dem Zentralanmeldeamt findet nicht statt.

XV. ABSCHNITT: WIEDERHERSTELLUNG VON FIRMEN UND NAMEN

ARTIKEL 83: Wiedereintragung einer gelöschten Firma

1. Ist in der Zeit vom 30. Januar 1933 bis 8. Mai 1945 eine Firma im Handelsregister gelöscht worden, nachdem der Betrieb des Handelsgeschäftes aus Gründen des Artikels 1 eingestellt war, so ist, wenn der Betrieb eines Handelsgeschäftes von dem oder den letzten Inhabern oder ihren Erben wieder aufgenommen wird, auf Antrag die gelöschte Firma wieder einzutragen.

2. Wurde das eingestellte Handelsgeschäft zur Zeit der Einstellung von einem Einzelkaufmann betrieben, so steht das Recht auf Wiedereintragung der gelöschten Firma dem letzten Inhaber oder seinem Erben zu. Sind mehrere Erben vorhanden und nehmen sie nicht alle den Betrieb wieder auf, so kann die Wiedereintragung der gelöschten Firma verlangt werden, wenn die den Betrieb nicht wieder aufnehmenden Erben der Annahme der gelöschten Firma zustimmen. Wurde das eingestellte Handelsgeschäft zur Zeit der Einstellung von mehreren persönlich haftenden Gesellschaftern betrieben, so besteht das Recht auf Wiedereintragung der gelöschten Firma, wenn die persönlich haftenden Gesellschafter entweder alle, oder einer oder mehrere von ihnen mit Einverständnis der übrigen, den Betrieb eines Handelsgeschäftes aufnehmen. Im Falle des Erbgangs gilt Absatz 2 entsprechend.

ARTIKEL 84: Änderung der Firma

Ist eine Firma in der Zeit vom 30. Januar 1933 bis 8. Mai 1945 aus den Gründen des Artikels 1 geändert worden, so kann die frühere Firmenbezeichnung wiederhergestellt werden, wenn derjenige, der zur Zeit der Änderung Firmeninhaber war, oder seine Erben, es als jetzige Inhaber der Firma beantragen. Artikel 83, Absatz 2, Satz 2 und Absatz 3 gelten sinngemäß.

ARTIKEL 85: Firmen juristischer Personen

Die Vorschriften der Artikel 83 und 84 finden auf Firmen juristischer Personen entsprechende Anwendung.

ARTIKEL 86: Wiederherstellung von Firmennamen in sonstigen Fällen

Die Wiedergutmachungskammer kann die Wiederherstellung einer gelöschten oder einer geänderten Firma auch in anderen als den Fallen der Artikel 83 bis 85 gestatten, sofern die Führung der alten Firmenbezeichnung zum Zwecke der Wiedergutmachung erforderlich ist.

ARTIKEL 87: Vereins- und Stiftungsnamen

Die Bestimmung des Artikels 86 gilt entsprechend für die Wiederannahme des früheren Namens eines Vereins oder einer Stiftung.

ARTIKEL 88: Verfahren

Anträge auf Eintragung von früheren Firmenbezeichnungen im Handelsregister können nur binnen der in diesem Gesetz für Rückerstattungsansprüche vorgesehenen Anmeldefrist gestellt werden. Über diese Anträge entscheidet unbeschadet Artikel 86 das Amtsgericht als Registergericht. Im übrigen sind für das Verfahren die Vorschriften über das Verfahren in Sachen der freiwilligen Gerichtsbarkeit anwendbar. Das Verfahren ist gebühren-und kostenfrei.

XVI. ABSCHNITT: SCHLUSSBESTIMMUNGEN

ARTIKEL 89: Vorbehaltene Ansprüche

Besondere gesetzliche Regelung bleibt vorbehalten für die Wiederherstellung erloschener Rechte aus Versicherungsverhältnissen und erloschener Urheberrechte und gewerblicher Schutzrechte.

ARTIKEL 90: Fristenlauf

Soweit Ansprüchen, die unter dieses Gesetz fallen, Verjährung, Ersitzung oder Ablauf von Ausschlußfristen nach den Vorschriften des bürgerlichen Rechts entgegenstehen würden, gilt die Verjährungs-, Ersitzungs- oder Ausschlußfrist als nicht vor dem Ende von sechs Monaten abgelaufen, gerechnet von dem Zeitpunkt, in welchem ein Klageanspruch auf Grund dieses Gesetzes zur Entstehung gelangt ist, keinesfalls jedoch vor dem 30. Juni 1949.

ARTIKEL 91: Steuern und Abgaben

1. Steuern und sonstige öffentliche Abgaben werden aus Anlaß der Rückerstattung nicht erhoben.
2. Eine Erstattung oder nachträgliche Erhebung von Steuern, sonstigen öffentlichen Abgaben, Gebühren und Kosten aus Anlaß des Rückfalls entzogener Vermögensgegenstände ein schließlich der Erbschaftssteuer findet nicht statt.

ARTIKEL 92: Ausführungs-und Durchführungsvorschriften

1. Die Wiedergutmachungsbehörden werden durch Ausführungsverordnung bestimmt.
2. Soweit nichts anderes in diesem Gesetz bestimmt ist oder von der Militärregierung angeordnet wird, werden die zur Durchführung des Gesetzes erforderlichen Rechts- und Verwaltungsvorschriften vom Ministerpräsidenten eines Landes oder den von ihm bestimmten Staatsministern erlassen.

ARTIKEL 93: Zuständigkeit der deutschen Gerichte

1. Die deutschen Gerichte werden hiermit ermächtigt, die Gerichtsbarkeit in Zivilsachen, die diesem Gesetz unterliegen, gegen Staatenlose, die als verschleppte Personen einer der Vereinten Nationen gelten, oder gegen Staatsangehörige der Vereinten Nationen auszuüben, sofern diese nicht unter eine der in Nr. 3), 4) oder 5) der Ziffer 10 b) in Artikel VI des Gesetzes Nr. 2 der Militärregierung (in seiner jeweils geltenden Fassung) genannten Personengruppen fallen.
2. Die deutschen Gerichte werden hiermit ermächtigt, die Gerichtsbarkeit in Fällen von Zuwiderhandlungen gegen die Bestimmungen der Artikel 73 bis 77 dieses Gesetzes auszuüben, vorausgesetzt, daß der Täter von der Gerichtsbarkeit der deutschen Gerichte nicht gemäß Ziffer 10 a) in Artikel VI des Gesetzes Nr. 2 der Militärregierung (in seiner jeweils geltenden Fassung) ausgenommen ist.

ARTIKEL 94: Maßgeblicher Text

Der deutsche Text dieses Gesetzes ist der amtliche Text; die Bestimmungen des Absatzes 5 des Artikels 11 des Gesetzes Nr. 4 der Militärregierung (in seiner geänderten Fassung) finden keine Anwendung.

ARTIKEL 95: Inkrafttreten

Dieses Gesetz tritt in den Ländern Bayern, Bremen, Hessen und Württemberg-Baden am 10. November 1947 in Kraft.

IM AUFTRAGE DER MILITÄRREGIERUNG

Bestätigt: 10 November 1947

Annex 10

Office of Military Government for Germany (U.S. Zone)
Military Government Regulations

TITLE 18: MONUMENTS, FINE ARTS AND ARCHIVES

18-1 Scope of Title
This title 18 covers the policies and instructions concerning cultural structures and materials found in the U.S. Zone of Occupation of Germany.

Part 1: POLICY AND ORGANIZATION
SECTION A: DEFINITIONS AND ORGANISATION
18-100 Cultural Structures
The term 'cultural structures' includes monuments and other buildings or sites of religious, artistic, archaeological, historic, or similar cultural importance, such as: statues and other immovable works of art; churches, palaces and similar public or private buildings of architectural or historic importance; museum, library and archival buildings; parks and gardens attached to such buildings; and ruins of historical or archaeological importance.
18-101 Cultural Objects
The term 'cultural objects' includes all movable goods of importance or value either religious, artistic, documentary, scholarly or historic, the disappearance of which constitutes a loss to the cultural heritage of the country concerned. This definition includes recognised works of art, as well as such objects as rare musical instruments, books and manuscripts, scientific documents of a historic or cultural nature, and all objects usually found in museums, collections, libraries and historic archives.
18-102 Archives, Books and Miscellaneous Documents
The term 'cultural and historic archives' includes all accumulations of documents, public, private or ecclesiastical, which relate to the functions of institutions now inactive which are not within the province of other military authorities.
18-102.1 Modern Archives
The term 'modern archives' includes all accumulations of documents, public, private or ecclesiastical, which relate or contribute to the functions of institutions now or recently active which are not within the province of other military authorities.
18-102.2 Books
The term 'books' includes printed or otherwise duplicated volumes and pamphlets, except those primarily considered to be works of art (cultural objects).
18-102.3 Miscellaneous Documents
The term 'miscellaneous documents' includes collections of papers, photographs, ephemera and the like which are not, however, the ordered official records of an institution.
18-103 Cultural Materials
The term 'cultural materials' includes both cultural objects and archives, books and miscellaneous documents as defined in MGR 18-102.1, 18-102.2 and 18-102.3, except current commercial activities.
18-104 Looted Cultural Materials
The term 'looted cultural materials' includes all cultural objects and materials which have been acquired since 1 January 1933, by Nazis within Germany or those acquired in territories occupied by the Germans or their allies, either:
    a. Directly by duress or wrongful acts of confiscation, dispossession or spoliation, whether pursuant
      to legislation, or by procedure purporting to follow forms of law, or otherwise; or
    b. Indirectly by purchase or other transactions regardless of whatever consideration may have
      been employed.
18-105 Monuments, Fine Arts and Archives Officers
The term 'Monuments, Fine Arts and Archives officer' refers to a functional specialist designated

as such by OMGUS, or by OMG's of the Länder. The term as used in this Title is abbreviated as 'MFA&A officer'. The assignment to a particular OMG, or category of such officers is indicated where appropriate (e.g., 'Land MFA&A officer').

18-106 Restitution

Identifiable looted works of art and cultural materials will be restituted to the governments of the countries from which they were taken. 'Loot' refers to objects which have been the subject of an act of dispossession by the enemy and which were in existence and located in an occupied territory and removed by the Germans subsequent to the date of commencement of the German occupation of that territory (see MGR Title 19).

18-107 MFA&A Organisation and Channels.

18-107.1 MFA&A Elements of OMGUS

The MFA&A Section of the Restitution Branch, Economics Division OMGUS is responsible, subject to the Deputy Military Governor and the Division Director, for the supervision in the field of Monuments, Fine Arts and Archives.

18-107.2 MFA&A Officers at OMG's of the Länder

Under direction of the Director of OMG for each Land, under supervision of MFA&A, OMGUS, MFA&A officers will take such direct action and will exercise such supervision and make such inspections of the operations of German agencies as are appropriate to ensure that the objectives stated in MGR 18-110 to 18-118 are carried out and to carry out the instructions set forth in this Title 18.

18-108 Intelligence

In locating cultural material MFA&A officers will request assistance from the intelligence personnel of all units in the areas and arrange with them to forward to the MFA&A officers any information or 'lead', which might assist in the discovery of cultural materials. Specially trained MFA&A personnel attached to OMGUS will be made available, on request, to subordinate OMG's to render specialists' advice and to conduct investigations for missing collections or objects.

SECTION B: OBJECTIVES

18-110 Restitution

To restitute identifiable looted works of Art and cultural materials to the governments of the countries from which they were taken.

18-111 Preservation

To protect and preserve Government owned cultural materials and works of art and the contents of museums, libraries and archives pending transfer of custody and responsibility for administration thereof to responsible German agencies.

18-112 Protection of Cultural Structures

Appropriate German authorities are responsible for protection and preservation of certain structures of architectural, artistic or historic importance in accordance with EUCOM directives.

18-113 Transfer of Administrative Responsibility

To complete the transfer of administration of German-owned museums, collections, libraries and archives to responsible German agencies.

18-114 Implementation of Control Council order No. 4 and Directive No. 30

To advise upon the destruction or liquidation of monuments, museums and collections of Nazi inception or which are devoted to the perception of militarism, and to supervise the public use of cultural structures and objects, including exhibitions, to insure the exclusion of material prejudicial to Military Government in accordance with Control Council Order No. 4 and Directive No. 30.

18-115 Interzonal Exchange

To effectuate interzonal exchange of German-owned works of art and cultural materials in accordance with U.S.— British interzonal agreement and such other similar agreements as may be entered into) so as to return such objects or materials to the zone of ownership.

18-116 Replacement in Kind

To make such cultural materials available for replacement in kind as may be ordered by OMGUS.

18-117 Release of Cultural Materials and Structures

To release to other agencies of the U. S. Government such cultural materials and cultural structures as may be directed by competent authority.

18-118 Unidentifiable Cultural Materials

Ultimately to dispose of residue of unclaimed and unidentified materials in collecting points and archival depots.

Part 2: PR0TECTION AND PRESERVATION OF CULTURAL STRUCTURES

18-200 Structures to be Protected

MFA&A officers will ensure that appropriate action is taken for the protection of all structures listed in the Supreme Headquarters Allied Expeditionary Forces 'Official List of Protected Monuments in Germany,' the 'Official List (SHAEF List Revised) of Protected Structures or Installations of Architectural, Artistic, Historical or Cultural Importance in the United States Zone of Germany' (see letter EUCO.M AG 007 (ED), 16 March l947, subject: Protection of Cultural Structures in Germany), or any subsequent official list as well as any additional structures which in their judgment are cultural structures. They will consult the more comprehensive list of cultural monuments in Germany contained in Army Service Forces Manual M 336-17, 'Atlas on Churches, Museums, Libraries and other Cultural Institutions in Germany.' Structures which should be added to the Official List of Protected Structures because of their historic, cultural or architectural value, should be reported to MFA&A Section, Restitution Branch, Economics Division, OMGUS.

18-201 General Responsibility of Military Government

The Ministerpräsidenten of the Länder are responsible for the protection and preservation of all cultural structures in the Land and for the activation or establishment of appropriate German civilian agencies for this purpose. Upon request of the German administration, the OMG for each Land, in co-ordination with unit commanders, may make available to the Ministerpräsident such assistance in the protection of cultural structures as appears appropriate, including:

    a.   Posting of notices placing cultural structures or areas off limits to all personnel;

    b.   Posting of guards; and

    c.   Aiding in the procurement of critical supplies for emergency restoration and protection of cultural structures and materials.

18-202 Inspections by MFA&A Officers

MFA&A officers assigned to OMG's of the Länder will be responsible for the inspections of cultural structures in their areas for the following purposes:

    a.   To record the physical condition;

    b.   To observe the progress of any repairs undertaken and to check on security measures;

    c.   To obtain photographic records showing all damage, structural faults or facts, methods of repair, and the condition before and after repairs.

18-203 Inspection Reports

MFA&A officers will render reports of inspections made pursuant to MGR 18-202 as provided in Part 5 of this Title

18-204 Use of Cultural Structures

18-204.1 General Prohibition

Cultural structures in the U.S. Zone will not be used for any purposes other than those for which they are normally intended. Exceptions for military, American Red Cross, Allied, or UNDP's use, may be made only on the explicit permission in each case of the Director of the OMG for the Land concerned, who will normally act upon the advice of his MFA&A officers. For German requests, exceptions will be made by the competent German official responsible for cultural monuments, with Military Government retaining the right of review.

18-204.2 Duties of MFA&A Officers

Where cultural structures are utilised for military purposes, the MFA&A officer of the Land OMG concerned will ensure, by regular inspections, that the commanding officer of the unit using the building is informed of the necessity of protecting it and its contents from pilfering and defacement; that portions of the building particularly liable to pilferage or defacement are placed off limits; and that valuable movable contents of the building are placed off limits or collected in locked rooms.

18-205 Prohibition of Demolition

The further demolition by military personnel of damaged cultural structures is prohibited except as a measure of public safety, and then only under supervision of an MFA&A officer.

18-206 Preservation of Historic Castles

Instructions on policies of Military Government concerning the preservation and protection of Historic castles and palaces as required by USFET directive will be issued by OMG's of the Länder and Berlin Sector, especially with regard to the following:

    a.   Certain castles and palaces preserved and designated as museums may have been administered as part of Land or Reich trusts. Their operation by German agencies will be subject to present or future policy concerning the continuation or modification of such trusts (MGR 17-312).

    b.   When furnishings or collections which were housed in such buildings before 1939 are not now in situ, the location and return to their point of origin will be effected under the provisions of MGR 18-433. In reassembling such collections, supervision will be exercised by the Land OMG to insure that the exhibits do not extol German militarism or NSDAP doctrines.

    c.   If any building designated and preserved as a museum is presently in use by military units, civilian agencies (other than the normal occupant before 1939), or displaced persons, these units, agencies or persons will be moved unless the Director of OMG of the Land decides that no satisfactory accommodations are available elsewhere, that such a move would be prejudicial to the execution of their assigned mission, and that continued use will not destroy the character of such building for future use as a museum.

18-207 Nazi and Militaristic Structures and Memorials

The Land MFA&A officer will be prepared to render such advice as the Demilitarization Branch of Armed Forces Division may request in the event of an appeal for the retention of structures, memorials and monuments on the basis of great aesthetic value which might otherwise be destroyed through the implementation of Control Council Directive No. 30.

Part 3: RECONSTITUTION AND CONTROL OF CIVIL ADMINISTITATION

18-300 Reconstitution of German Agencies

The Ministerpräsident is responsible for the establishment of MFA&A agencies in the Land governments. Former organisations, records and specialist personnel may be utilised, to the extent available, in accordance, however with the provisions of the Law for Liberation from National Socialism and Militarism (MGR 24-500), and implementation (see Title 24, MGR, Title 2, MGR, and Part 8, Title 9, MGR).

18-301 Return of administration to German agencies

OMG's of the Länder will return to German custody as rapidly as possible all clearly German owned materials (see MGR 18-530). They will, however, satisfy themselves:

    a.   That investigation and search for loot in the collection of cultural materials involved has been made and that the looted cultural materials so discovered have been made secure; and

    b.   all pertinent German public and private records pertaining to the collection involved have been screened for information relating to Nazi looting activities and the dissemination of militaristic and NSDAP doctrines.

18-302 Supervision of German Agencies

Land OMG's after authorising the return of MFA&A administrative responsibility to German agencies will advise and assist the latter in their operations to ensure that they comply with instructions from the Land OMG and with policies set forth herein. To this end the MFA&A officers will:

    a.   Make necessary inspections to ensure that cultural structures and materials in the Land are preserved and protected from deterioration and spoliation;

    b.   Direct German administration to make available information necessary for official MG reports; and

    c.   Supervise important operations such as the evacuation of repositories containing valuable looted cultural materials.

18-303 German Religious Structures and Objects

Land OMG's may require ecclesiastical organisations to submit inventories and/or reports necessary to the fulfilment of the restitution mission of MFA&A.

Part 4: PROTECTION AND CONTROL OF CULTURAL MATERIALS

SECTION A: GENERAL PROVISIONS

18-400 General

The Land OMG's will take the necessary measures to identify and take under control and into custody all Nazi and looted cultural materials and may 'freeze' all cultural materials within their areas, regardless of ownership; pending decision regarding their disposition (see Title 17, Property Control, MGR).

18-401 'Freeze' of Cultural Materials.

18-401.1 Transfer of Works of Art or Cultural Materials of Value or Importance

The OMG for each Land will ensure the observance of Paragraph 3(d) of Article II, MG Law No. 52, as implemented) by AG Letter 007 (ED); 6 December 1946; Transfer of Works of Art or Cultural Materials of Value or Importance, and will Instruct the Ministerpräsident of the Land, or appropriate German authority in Berlin Sector, in the administration of the regulations for the licensing of art dealers and the establishing of conditions under sales and transfers of works of art are permissible as set forth in said letter, which regulations are essential to the fulfilment of the restitution mission of MFA&A.

18-401.2 Location and Report of all Cultural Materials.

Land OMG's will require surveys and inventories, necessary to the fulfilment of the restitution mission, of all cultural materials at repositories and of all collections of cultural materials which have remained in situ.

18-401.3 Regulation of Sale or Exports or Cultural Materials of Value or Importance in Germany.

All transactions will conform with the provisions of MG Law No. 52, as implemented by AG Letter; Transfer of Works of Art or Cultural Materials of Value or Importance, OMGUS, 6 December 1946; USFET Circular 140, 26 September 1946; and such other regulations and directives as may be issued from time to time.

18-401.4 Collections in Situ

All collections of cultural objects found in situ will be closed to the public until the survey required by MGR 18-401.2 is completed, after which they may then be reopened to the public when authorised by the OMG of the Land involved, on recommendation of the MFA&A officer.

18-401.5 Numismatics

Collections of coins and medals in which the numismatic value exceeds the face or intrinsic value will be considered as cultural objects and a responsibility of the MFA&A officer. Such collections will be deposited in the Land Central Bank to be held intact under the provision of MG Law No. 53 and current directives. Publicly owned collections of museums and private collections on loan to museums will be held intact in the museums under the custody of the museum director and in conformity with Law No. 53 and prevailing directives. It is further provided that collections now deposited in the Land Central Bank may be withdrawn and deposited in a museum with the responsible museum official as custodian.

18-401.6 Nazi and Militaristic Collections

All collections of works of art or other cultural objects the intent and purpose of which are the perpetuation of militarism or Nazism will be closed and their contents taken into custody for later examination individually with a view to the possible inclusion of objects of purely cultural or historic value in general museum collections according to their class.

18-401.7 Licensing of Art Dealers

Art dealers will be licensed by such agency as the Ministerpräsident of each Land may direct with the right of review and revocation retained by the Land OMG.

18-401.8 Art Dealers' Reports.

Such reports as may be required will be furnished on Inventory and Sale Card for Art Dealers (MG/MFAA/&/F November 1946) (See MGR 18-540).

SECTION B: REPOSITORIES OF CULTURAL MATERIALS

18-430 Current Lists of Repositories

OMGUS will maintain consolidated records of the location and contents of reported and inspected repositories of cultural materials in the U. S. Zone and will supply information relating thereto, on request, to Land OMG's.

18-431 Discovery and Report of Repositories

MFA&A officers of the Land OMG's will investigate repositories of cultural materials discovered or reported and render reports of such investigations on Monthly Consolidated Field Report Form (MG/MFAA/1/F) (See MGR 18-510) to OMGUS.

18-432 Security

18-432.1 Guards

Where deemed necessary by the Land MFA&A officer repositories containing suspected or identified loot or works of art of great value or importance will be placed under adequate security guard, until evacuated (see MGR 18-440); and repositories not containing such materials will be placed under the care of qualified Germans against custody receipt or, if of minor importance, locked and sealed, until released against custody receipt to responsible German officials or civilians.

18-432.2 Visitor Control

Visitors will not be admitted to any repository without the express written permission of the responsible Land MFA&A officer or of such civilians as may be designated by proper authority.

18-433 Evacuation from Repositories

Cultural materials in repositories may be evacuated to Central Collecting Points (see MGR 18-440) or to other locations only after approval of the appropriate Land OMG. Where movement is so authorised, cultural materials liable to damage or deterioration in their present locations will be evacuated first; thereafter, looted materials; and finally, other cultural materials.

18-434 Spot Surveys

MFA&A officers will ensure that spot surveys of closed crates and of objects not crated will be made of each repository before evacuation. Such surveys will be checked against the custodian's records, and reports thereof will be included in the Monthly Consolidated Field Report (MGR 18-510) to OMGUS.

SECTION C: COLLECTING POINTS AND DEPOTS

18-440 Purpose of Central Collecting Points and Depots

OMGUS will establish Central Collecting Points for the purpose of receiving, surveying and preparing for directed disposition:

    a.   Looted cultural materials;

    b.   Cultural materials evacuated from temporary repositories; and

    c.   Any other materials which the MFA&A officer of the Land OMG may designate.

18-441 Establishment and Operation of Central Collecting Points

The Land OMG will establish additional Central Collecting Points if required and will supervise and control, through their MFA&A officers, the operation of all Central Collecting Points giving due regard in the selection of buildings, to adequacy of space, condition of weather proofing, temperature and humidity, and providing for their custody, maintenance, security and operational functions.

18-442 Personnel

The MFA&A officers in charge of Central Collecting Points may employ and utilise properly vetted or other foreign civilian personnel, in addition to U. S. military and civilian personnel.

18-443 Inventorying

Land OMG's will ensure that cultural materials in collecting points within their areas are inventoried as provided in MGR 18-443.1 and 18-443.2.

18-443.1 Looted Cultural Materials

Unopened cases containing cultural materials clearly identifiable by their markings as loot from one of the United Nations need not be inventoried, but records will be kept to identify the cases and the nature of their contents. Cases containing cultural materials, the contents of which cannot be identified otherwise, will be opened and their contents spot checked or inventoried as and when directed by OMGUS.

18-443.2 German-owned Cultural Materials

Cultural materials in collecting points which are owned by German organisations or nationals will be inventoried and recorded as and when directed by OMGUS.

18-444 Photographic Records

    a.   Photographic reproductions in appropriate size will be made of all cultural materials inventoried whether looted or German-owned. The photographs will be attached to the inventory card (see MGR 18-560). At the discretion of the MFA&A officers, larger size photographs in black and white and colour suitable for study and research may be made of all important objects of which no such record is available to be to be forwarded to the War Department when so instructed by OMGUS.

    b.   All photographs made will be used exclusively by Military Government or the War Department or such agencies as may be authorised by OMGUS.

18-445 Preparation for Restitution of Looted Cultural Materials

18-445.1 Custody

All suspected or identified looted cultural materials will be taken into custody (see MGR 18-400) and may be evacuated to a Central Collecting Point, upon the advice of the MFA&A officer.

18-445.2 Records

Land OMG's will continue to require custodians of all German-owned collections of cultural materials to submit to them lists of accessions since 1 January 1993 and will require such lists to be checked by their MFA&A officers, for the purpose of identifying and locating looted cultural materials.

18-445.3 Restitution of Identified Loot

Clearly identified looted, cultural materials will be released on the authority of OMGUS to the authorised representative of a claimant nation against receipt (see MGR 18-550).

18 -446 Preservation of Cultural Materials

Only such restorative measures to cultural materials will be effected as is necessary to prevent further deterioration or damage.

18-447 Archives

Archives as defined in MGR 18-102 are subsumed under cultural materials as defined in MGR 18-103 and are thus to be considered as cultural materials throughout this Title 18.

18-448 Libraries

The delineation of responsibility between the Education and Religious Affairs Branch, IA&C Division, and the MFA&A Section Economics Division at all levels, for public, church, factory, technical, school, university and all other libraries (except commercial lending libraries) is as follows:

a.   MFA&A is responsible for library materials stored inactively in MFA&A custody, or discovered at some future time to be subject to Restitution.

b.   Education and Religious Affairs Branch is responsible for control of library materials which have been placed on public deposit in a library, whether the library is independent or part of a larger organisation, and for control of operation of such libraries.

c.   A library from which the general public is excluded by official order, and which is for the exclusive use of a restricted group of persons associated with an organisation of which the library is a part, will be subject to the supervision of the authorities which normally control the organisation as a whole. If such a restricted organisation is in any way educational, and one to which any successful applicant is admitted as a member or student, the responsibility for the library materials and for operations will be exercised by the Education and Religious Affairs Branch (see MGR 8-443).

18-449 Exploitation

Preliminary exploitation in situ of libraries, collections, records, archives, miscellaneous books and papers by U. S. intelligence services and technical personnel, or by those accredited through the U.S. intelligence services may be authorised by the OMG for each Land. No removal of libraries, collections, records, archives, miscellaneous books and papers, or parts thereof by U. S. intelligence services or technical personnel, or by those accredited through U.S. intelligence services may ordinarily be effected without prior approval in writing of the OMG for the Land concerned.

SECTION D: INTERZONAL EXCHANGE OF CULTURAL MATERIALS

18-450 Claimants

Upon request of Military Governor of another Zone, cultural materials which have been moved into the U.S. Zone for war time security and are not 'looted materials' as described may be removed from the U.S. Zone in return for the withdrawal of similar material from the requesting Zone, with the following exceptions:

a.   Scientific equipment not easily identifiable as part of a museum collection.

b.   Property of private individuals unless such property has been on loan to a public institution for educational purposes, for exhibition, or for war protection.

c.   Cultural materials, the safety of which would be endangered by the conditions of moving.

d.   Cultural materials, the normal location of which is Berlin.

18-451 Procedure as to materials subject to Interzonal Exchange

18-451.1 Transfer of Custody

When such materials are located, accredited representatives of the requesting zone, invited through OMGUS, assume custody and responsibility against receipt and such representatives effect immediate removal.

18-451.2 Transportation

The removal of materials from the U. S. Zone will be effected entirely by personnel and transportation designated and provided by the Military Governor of the requesting Zone.

18-451.3 Limitation of Disposition

The materials will be held in custody in Germany by the Military Governor of the receiving Zone under adequate conditions of protection and preservation subject to any determination of their ultimate disposition by the Allied Control Council.

18-451.4 Material removed in Error

The Military Governor of the Zone will undertake to restore to the Zone from which delivery has been made any object delivered in error.

18-452 Receipts

Properly accomplished Receipt for Interzonal Exchange of Works of Art and other Cultural Materials will be accomplished and distributed as indicated on the form set forth in MGR 18-520.

18-453 Screening

OMGUS may direct the screening by U.S. personnel of materials subject to interzonal exchange prior to the transfer or may conclude an agreement with the requesting Zone whereby such screening will be the responsibility of the latter. The OMG of the Land concerned will be given notice in either event. Should looted material be found after transfer it will be restituted under agreed Allied procedures. Unless the material has been screened, material shipped into the U.S. Zone will be screened and looted material restituted under agreed Allied procedures.

SECTION E: TRANSFER OF GERMAN OWNED CULTURAL MATERIALS TO GERMAN CUSTODY

18-460 Church Property

OMG's of the Länder may release against receipt clearly identifiable cultural property of religious organisations found in repositories to the authorised representatives of such religious organisation (see MGR 18-530 for receipt form).

18-461 Other Identified Cultural Materials

Cultural materials clearly of German ownership will, on the authority of the OMG of each Land, be released against receipt to the custody of the owner or a responsible German official of the Land in which it is now located (see MGR 18-530).

18-462 Report of Releases

All releases effected pursuant to MGR 18-460 and 18-461 will be reported in the Monthly Consolidated Field Report (see MGR 18-510).

BIBLIOGRAPHY

Akinscha K., Koslow G. with S. Hochfield, Stolen Treasure. The Hunt for the World's Lost Masterpieces. London 1995.

Akinscha K., Koslow G., Toussaint C., Operation Beutekunst. Die Verlagerung deutscher Kulturgüter in die Sowjetunion nach 1945. Nürnberg 1995.

American Commission for Protection and Salvage of Artistic and Historic Monuments in War Areas, *The Department of State Bulletin 1944*, Vol. 11, No. 282.

American policy in occupied areas, Washington 1947.

Anzilotti D., Cours de droit international. Vol. 1, Paris 1929.

Armistice terms for Bulgaria. *The Department of State Bulletin* 1945, Vol. 11, No. 279.

Armistice with Finland. *The Department of State Bulletin* 1945, Vol. 12, No. 295.

d'Arnoux H., Objets et monuments d'art devant le droit des gens. Paris 1934.

Art storage in Germany reported as inadequate. *The Museum News 1945*, Vol. 23, No. 11.

Aubert Z., Controle d'Allemagne. Paris 1949.

Balfour M., Mair J., Four power control in Germany and Austria 1945-1946. London 1956.

Balawyder A., The Odyssey of the Polish treasures. Antigonish 1978.

Bentwich N., International Aspects of Restitution and Compensation for Victims of the Nazis. *British Yearbook of International Law 1955-1956*, Vol. 32.

Berezowski C., Ochrona prawnomiedzynarodowa zabytkow i dziel sztuki w czasie wojny [International legal protection of historic monuments and works of art in time of war]. Warsaw 1948.

Bienkowska B., Losses of Polish libraries during World War II, Warsaw 1994.

Bienkowska B., Kowalski W., Laskarzewska H., Paszkiewicz U., Waligorski S., Straty bibliotek w czasie II wojny swiatowej. Wstepny raport o stanie wiedzy. [Library Losses during World War II within Poland's boundaries of 1945. Preliminary report on the state of information. Parts 1-3. Warsaw 1994.

Bierzanek R., Wojna a prawo miedzynarodowe [War and International Law]. Warsaw 1982.

Bizardel Y., Sous l'occupation. Souvenirs d'un conservateur de musée 1940-1944. Paris 1064.

Bluntschli J., Le droit international codifié. Paris 1870.

Bodkin T., The Reconstruction of Dismembered Masterpieces by International Action. In: XIV Internationaler Kunsttgeschichtlicher Kongress 1936. Kongressakten. Bd. 2. Bern 1938.

Boff L. du, The Deskbook of Art Law. Washington 1977.

Boguslawskyj M.M., Pakt Roericha i okhrana dobr kulturalnikh.[Roerich Pact and the Protection of Cultural Goods] *Sovetskye Gosudarstvo i Pravo* 1974, No. 10.

Boguslawskyj M. M., Probleme der Rückführung von Kulturgütern (Bücher und Archivalien. In: F. Görner (Hrsg), Staatsbibliothek zu Berlin - Preusischer Kulturbesitz. Veröffentlichungen der Osteuropa-Abteilung. 25 ABDOS-Tagung in Kiel. Vol. 20. Berlin 1996.

Borowy W., General Theses on Restitution and Reparations in the Field of Culture and Art. Warsaw 1945.

Boylan P.J., Review of the Convention for the Protection of Cultural Property in the Event of Armed Conflict. [The Hague Convention of 1954] UNESCO 1993.

Brownlie I., International Law and the Use of Force by States. Oxford 1963.

Brownlie I., Principles of Public International Law. Oxford 1979.

Brownlie I., System of the Law of Nations. State Responsibility. Part I. Oxford 1983.

Buckland W. W., McNair A. D., Roman Law & Common Law. A Comparison in Outline. Cambridge 1936.

Buhse K., Der Schutz von Kulturgut im Krieg. Hamburg 1959.

Burnett P., Reparation at the Paris Peace Conference from the Standpoint of the American Delegation. Vol. 1, 2. New York 1940.

Burks S., *Kunstsammlungen zu Weimar v. Elicofon*: Theft of Priceless Art Treasures Gives Rise to Protracted International Legal Battle. *Texas International Law Journal* 1984, Vol. 19, No. 1.

Burr N., Safeguarding our Cultural Heritage. A bibliography on the protection of museums, works of art, monuments, archives and libraries in time of war. Washington 1952.

Calmette G., Recueil de documents sur l'histoire de la question de réparations 1919-1921. Paris 1924.

Calvo M.Ch., Le droit international théorique et pratique. Vol. 4. Paris-Berlin 1888.

Castel J.G., Polish Art Treasures in Canada 1940-1960. A Case History. *American Society of International Law. Proceedings of the 68th annual meeting.* Washington 1974.

Castillon R., Les réparations allemandes. Deux expériences 1919-1932, 1945-1952. Paris 1953.

Chrzaszczewska J., Un example de restitution. Le Traité de Riga de 1921 et le patrimonie artistique de la Pologne. *Mouseion* No. 17-18, 1932, p. 205.

Clute R., The International Legal Status of Austria 1938-1945. The Hague 1962.

Cohn E., A novel chapter in the relations between common law and civil law. *International and Comparative Law Quarterly* 1955, Vol. 4.

Counterparts. Old Master Drawings from the Koenigs Collection in the Museum Boymans-van Beuningen in Rotterdam. A Selection of Drawings Closely Related to the Recovery Drawings Exhibited in the Pushkin Museum Moscow. The Hague 1996.

Cox T., Some signs of recovery in German museums. *The Museum Journal* 1951, Vol. 51, No. 2.

Cultural Losses of Poland. Index of Polish Cultural Losses during the German occupation 1939-1943. Ed. by Ch. Estreicher. London 1944.

Debecker R., La réparation de dommages de guerre en France et en Belgique. Chartres 1950.

Decker A., A Legacy of Shame. *Art News* 1984, No. 12.

Deutsche Malarei. Freundschaftsgeschenk. Des Polnischen Volkes an das Deutsche Volk. Ausstellung. Berlin 1954.

Dlugosz J., Jana Dlugosza Roczniki, czyli Kroniki slawnego Krolestwa Polskiego. Ksiega trzecia [The Annals of Jan Dlugosz,or the Chronicles of the famous Kingdom of Poland. Book Three]. Warsaw 1969.

Dokumentation der durch Auslagerung im 2 Weltkrieg vermisten Kunstwerke der Kunsthalle Bremen. Bremen 1991.

Downey W., Captured Enemy Property. Booty of War and Seized Enemy Property. *American Journal of International Law* 1950, Vol. 44.

Drucker A., Restitution in International Law. *International and Comparative Law Quarterly* 1966, Vol. 15. Review of I. Vasarhelyi, *Restitution in International Law.* Budapest 1964.

Eagleton C., The Responsibility of States in International Law. Washington 1928.

Eggen J., La commission américaine pour la protection et le sauvetage des monuments d'art et d'histoire dans les zones de guerre. *Mouseion* 1946, Vol. 55-56.

Ehrlich L., Pawel Wlodkowic i Stanislaw ze Skarbimierza [Pawel Wlodkowic and Stanislaw of Skarbimierz]. Warsaw 1955.

Ehrlich L, Polski wyklad prawa wojny w XV wieku [The Polish interpretation of the fifteenth century's law of war]. Warsaw 1955.

Elen A.J., Missing Old Master Drawings from the Franz Koenigs Collection. The Hague 1989.

Engstler L., Die territoriale Bindung von Kulturgutem im Rahmen des Volkerrechts. Koln-Berlin-Bonn-Munchen 1964.

Essen van der, Histoire de l'invasion et de l'occupation allemandes en Belgique. Bruxelles-Paris 1917.

Esterow M., A Little Justice in Austria. *Art News.* Vol 94, no. 7.

European Dispersed Heritage. Europaischer Zerstreuter Nachlass. Europejskie Dziedzictwo Rozproszone Gdansk 1993.

Exhibition in Germany of the Returned Collection of Berlin paintings. *The Department of State Bulletin* 1949, Vol. 21, No. 543.

Faterson A., Reparacje. Geneza i rozwoj [Reparations. Origins and development]. Warsaw 1932.

Feliciano H., Le Musée disparu. Enquête sur le pillage des oeuvres d'art en France par les Nazis. Paris 1995.

Feliciano H., The Mauerbach Case. Part. II: An Equivocal Sale. Spoils of War. International Newsletter. No. 3. December 1996.

Fielfer W., Zur Entwicklung des Völkergewohnheitsrechts im Bereich des internationalen Kulturgüterschutzes, in: Staat und Völkerrechtsordnung. Festschrift für Karl Doehring. 1989.

Fiedler W., (Hrsg.) Internationaler Kulturgüterschutz und deutsche Frage. Berlin 1991.

Fielder W., Neue völkerrechtliche Ansätze des Kulturgüterschutzes, in Reichelt G., (ed): Internationaler Kulturgüterschutz. Wien 1992.

Fielder W., Safeguarding of Cultural Property during Occupation — Modifications of the Hague Convention of 1907 by World War II in: Briat M., Freedberg A. (eds): Legal Aspects of International Trade in Art. Paris 1996.

Fiedler W., Internationaler Kulturgüterschutz — völkerrechtlich betrachtet. In: *Spektrum der Wissenschaft.* August 1996.

Fielder W., Notes on the Development of the Protection of Cultural Property Following Armed Conflicts. Law and State. 1997, Vol. 56.

Fielder W., Zwischen Kriegsbeute und internationaler Verantwortung — Kulturgüter im Internationalen Recht der Gegenwart. Zeitschrift für Bibliothekswesen und Bibliographie. 1997, No. 6.

Figlarewicz A., O Komisji Odszkodowan. Ustroj, kompetencje i dzialalnosc na podstawie traktatow pokojowych w Wersalu, w Saint-Germain-en-Laye, w Trianon, w Neuilly-sur-Seine, w Sevres i w Lozannie [On the Commission of Reparations. System, competences and activity on the basis of the peace treaties: in Versailles, in Saint Germain, in Trianon, in Neuilly-Seine, in Sevres and Lausanne]. Warsaw 1927.

Fitzmaurice C., The juridica clauses of the peace treaties. *Recueil des Courses* 1948, Vol. 81, Part 2.

Flanner J., Men and Monuments. New York 1947.

Flemming M., Okupacja wojskowa w swietle prawa miedzynarodowego [Military Occupation in Light of International Law]. Warsaw 1981.

Florisonne M., La Commission Française de Récuperation Artistique. *Mouseion* 1946, Vol. 55-56.

Foundoukidis E., La reconstruction sur le plan culture. Paris 1945.

Freeman A., Responsibility of States for Unlawful Acts of their Armed Forces. *Recueil des Cours* 1955, Vol. 88, Part 2.

Friemuth C., Die geraubte Kunst. Der dramatische Wettlauf um die Rettung der Kulturschatze nach dem Zweiten Weltkrieg [Entfuhrung, Bergung und Restitution europaischen Kulturgütes 1939-1948]. Braunschweig 1989.

Frycz Modrzewski A., De Republica emendanda [O poprawie Rzeczpospolitej, the Polish translation by E. Jedrkiewicz]. Warsaw 1953.

Garner J., International Law and the World War. London 1920, Vol. 1, 2.

Gathings J., International Law and American Treatment of Alien Enemy Property. Washington 1940.

Gentili A., De iure belli libri tres.1598.

Godden G., Murder of a Nation. German Destruction of Polish Culture. London 1943.

Goldschmidt S., Legal Claims against Germany. New York 1945.

Gondek L., Polskie misje wojskowe 1945-1949. Polityczno-prawne, ekonomiczne i wojskowe problemy likwidacji skutkow wojny na obszarze okupowanych Niemiec [Polish Military Missions 1945-1949. Political, Legal, Economic, and Military Problems of the Elimination of the Effects of War in the Territory of Occupied Germany]. Warsaw 1981.

Gondek L., Problemy restytucyjne w pracach Polskiej Misji Wojskowej w Niemczech [Restitutional Problems in the Work of the Polish Military Mission in Germany]. *Przeglad Zachodni* 1979, nr 3.

Götz A., Heim S., Das Zentrale Staatsarchiv in Moskau (*Sonderarchiv*). Rekonstruktion und Bestandsverzeichnis verschollen geglaubten Schriftguts aus der NS-Zeit. Düsseldorf 1993.

Graber D., The Development of the Law of Belligerent Occupation 1863-1914. London 1968.

Grayson C., Austria's International Position 1938-1953. Geneva 1953.

Grieg D. W., International Law. London 1970.

Gross J., Polish Society Under German Occupation. The Generalgouvernement 1939-1944. New York 1979.

Grotius H., *Hugonis Grotii De iure belli et pacis libri tres*, accompanied by an abridged translation by W. Whewell. Cambridge 1853.

Guggenheim P., Les principes de droit international public. *Recueil des Cours* 1952, Vol. 88, Part 2.

Guggenheim P., Schweizerraubgutbeschlusse. *Schweizer Jahrbuch für Internationales Recht* 1949.

Haase G., Kunstraub und Kunstschutz. Eine Dokumentation. Hildesheim 1991.

Hackworth G., Digest of International Law. Washington 1943.

Haggermacher P., Grotius et la doctrine de la guerre juste. Paris 1983.

Hall A., German Libraries in Italy Returned to the Federal Republic of Germany. *College Art Journal* 1953. Vol. 12, No. 4.

Hall A., The Recovery of Cultural Objects Dispersed during World War II. *The Department of State Journal* 1951, Vol. 25, No. 635.

Hall A., The Transfer of Residual Works of Art from Munich to Austria. *College Art Journal* 1952, Vol. 11, No. 3.

Hall W., A Treatise on International Law. Oxford 1909.

Heus A., Der Kunstraub der Nationalsozialisten. Eine Typologie. Kritische Berichte. Zeitschrift für Kunst- und Kulturwissenschaften 1995, Heft 2.

Hollander B., The International Law of Art for Lawyers, Collectors and Artists. London 1959.

Hormats W., Millions of Objects Hidden by the Nazis Were Found in more than 1000 Depots. *Art News* 1975, No. 74.

Howard J., The Paris Agreement on Reparations from Germany. U.S. Government Printing Office 1946.

Howe T., Salt Mines and Castles. The Discovery and Restitution of Looted European Art. Indianapolis-New York 1946.

Hubert S., Zasady restytucji panstwowosci w zastosowaniu do Republiki genewskiej w r. 1814-1815. [The Principle of Restitution of State Authority in the Case of the Republic of Geneva in 1814-1815] Rocznik Prawa I ekonomii 1932.

Hubert S., Odbudowa Panstwa Polskiego jako problemat Prawa Narodow.[The Reconstruction of the Polish State as an Issue of the Law of Nations] Warsaw 1934.

Hubert S., Przywrocenie wladzy panstwowej [The Restoration of the State Authority] Lwow 1936.

Hulin de Loo G., Des compensations à réclamer les dommages artistiques. *Bulletin de la Classe des Beaux-Arts* 1919, No. 4-5.

Humanity in Warfare. The Modern History of the International Law of Armed Conflicts. London 1980.

International Protection of Artistic and Historical Property. A statement released by the Department of State, July 27, 1951. *College Art Journal* 1951, Vol. 11, No. 1.

Iwanejko M., Prawo zdobyczy wojennej w doktrynie XVI-XVIII wieku [War Prize Law in the Doctrine of the sixteenth to eighteenth centuries]. Krakow 1961.

Jackson R., The Case against the Nazi War Criminals. New York 1946.

Jayme E., Kunstwerke als Kriegsbeute: Restitution und Internationales Privatrecht im deutsch-französischen Rechtsverkehr. IPRax 1995, vol. 4.

Jayme E., Neue Anknüpfungsmaximen für den Kulturgüterschutz im Internationalen Privatrecht. In: Dolzer F., Jayme E., Musgnug R.,(Hrsg.), Rechtsfragen des internationalen Kulturgüterschutzes. Heidelberg 1994.

Jolowicz J., Nicholas B., Historical Introduction to the Study of Roman Law. Cambridge 1972.

Kaufman R., Die völkerrechtlichen Grundlagen un grenzen der Restitutionen. *Archiv des öffentlichen Rechts.* Bd. 75. Tubingen 1949.

Kennedy Grimsted P., Displaced Archives on the Eastern Front: Restitution Problems from World War II and its Aftermath. International Institute for Social Studies. Research Paper No 18. Amsterdam 1995.

Kennedy Grimsted P., The Odyssey of the Smolensk Archive. Plundered Communist Records for the Service of Anti-communism. In: The Carl Beck papers in Russian and East European Studies. No. 1201. Pittsburgh 1995.

Khnopff F., Les compensentions pour dommages artistiques. *Bulletin de la Classe des Beaux-Arts* 1919, No. 1-3.

Klafkowski A., Podstawowe problemy prawne likwidacji skutkow wojny 1939-1945 a dwa panstwa niemieckie [Basic legal problems of the liquidation of the effects of the 1939-1945 war and the two German States]. Poznan 1966.

Klafkowski A., Umowa poczdamska z dnia 2 VIII 1945 r. [The Potsdam Agreement of August 2, 1945]. Warsaw 1985.

Kluber J.L., Droit des gens modernes de l'Europe. Paris 1874.

Kobierska-Motas E., Dzialalnosc specjalnego pelnomocnika dospraw zabezpieczania dzielsztuki i zabytkow kultury w GG [Activities of the Special Plenipotentiary for Protection of the Works of Art and Cultural Monuments in Generalgouvernement]. In: Zbrodnie i sprawcy [Crimes and perpetrators]. Ed. by C. Pilichowski. Warsaw 1980.

Kocot K., Problem pojec: reparacje wojenne, restytucja, odszkodowania itp., w aspekcie umowy poczdamskiej ,traktatow pokojowych, umow zawartych przez NRF, wyrokow sadowych i doktryny prawa miedzynarodowego [The Question of the Notions: War Reparations, Restitution, Compensation, etc.,in light of the Potsdam Agreement, Peace Treaties, Agreements signed by FRG, Court Verdicts, and the International Law Doctrine]. Warsaw 1974.

Kovacs E., Loveg Z., The Hungarian Crown and Other Regalia. Budapest 1980.

Kowalski W., Dzialalnosc restytucyjna Karola Estreichera po zakonczeniu II Wojny Swiatowej [Restitutional Activities of Charles Estreicher after the End of World War II]. *Muzealnictwo* 1988, Vol. 31.

Kowalski W., Internationaler Kulturgüterschutz in Europa: deutsch-polnische Fragen. Kritische Berichte. Zeitschrift für Kunst- und Kulturwissenschaften 1995,Heft 2.

Kowalski W., Niec H, Przyborowska-Klimczak A., La protection des biens culturels. Droit international public. Rapport polonais. In: La protection des biens culturels. Paris 1991.

Kowalski W., Liquidation of the Effects of World War II in the Area of Culture. Warsaw 1994.

Kowalski W., Miedzynarodowo-prawne implikacje ochrony dziedzictwa kulturowego na Zachodnich i Polnocnych Ziemiach Polski [International Law Implications of the Protection of the Cultural Heritage in Western and Northern Territories of Poland] W: Ochrona dziedzictwa kulturowego Zachodnich i Polnocnych Ziem Polski [Protection of the Cultural Heritage in Western and Northern Territories of Poland]. Warsaw 1995.

Kowalski W., Praktyczna realizacja Konwencji haskiej z 1954 r.,w okresie 25 lat jej obowiazywania [Practice of the Implementation of the Hague Convention of 1954 within 25 years of its Enforncement]. *Ochrona Zabytkow* 1984, Vol. 3.

Kowalski W., Restytucja dwoch obrazow Duerera do zbiorow Weimaru [The Restitution of Two Paintings by Dürer to the Weimar collection]. *Muzealnictwo* 1985, Vol. 28-29.

Kowalski W., Udzial Karola Estreichera w alianckich przygotowaniach do restytucji dzielsztuki zagrabionych w czasie II Wojny Swiatowej [Contribution of Charles Estreicher to Allied Preparations for the Restitution of Works of Art Looted during World War II]. *Muzealnictwo* 1986,Vol. 30.

Kowalski W., Wladyslaw Tomkiewicz jako teoretyk i praktyk likwidacji skutkow wojny w dziedzinie kultury [Wladyslaw Tomkiewicz as a Theorist and Practitioner of Liquidation of the Effects of World War II in the Field of Culture]. *Biuletyn Historii Sztuki*,1992, Vol. 2.

Kozakiewicz J., Bibliografia komentowana, ocena istniejacej literatury i wnioski badawcze odnoszace sie do stanu badan nad hitlerowska polityka grabiezy dziel sztuki i niszczenia zabytkow [An Annotated Bibliographical Evaluation of the Existing Literature and Scholarly and Editorial Conclusions Drawn from the State of Research on the Nazi Policy of Looting Works of Art and Damaging Monuments]. Warsaw 1970.

Kuhn Ch., German Paintings in the National Gallery: A Protest. *College Art Journal* 1946, Vol. 6, No. 1.

Kumaniecki J., Pokoj polsko-radziecki 1921. Geneza. Rokowania. Traktat. Komisja Mieszana [The Polish-Soviet peace of 1921. The Origins. The Negotiations. The Mixed Commission]. Warsaw 1985.

Kumaniecki J., Tajny raport Wojkowa [Wojkow's Secret Report]. Warszaw 1991.

Kurz M.J., Nazi Contraband. American Policy on the Return of European Cultural Treasures, 1945-1955. New York-London 1985.

Lachs M., Le problème de la propriété dans la liquidation des suites de la Seconde Guerre Mondiale. *Annuaire Français de Droit International* Paris 1961.

Lachs M., Problem prawny podzialu zlota zagrabionego w czasie wojny [Legal Problem of the Division of Gold Looted During the War]. Panstwo i Prawo 1960, No. 6.

Langen E., Die Restitution geraubter Kunstwerke. *Die Weltkunst* 1951, No. 15.

Langen E., Sauer E., Die Restitution im internationalen Recht. Dusseldorf 1949.

Les travaux des Delegations Polonaises aux Commissions Mixtes de Reevacuation et Speciale a Moscou. Varsovie 1922.

Lehmann K-D., Bücher als Kriegsgeiseln. *Bibliotheksdienst* 1996. No. 8/9.

Leistra J., The Mauerbach Case. Part. I. Spoils of War. International newsletter. No. 3. December 1996.

Lemkin R., Axis Rule in Occupied Europe. Washington 1944.

Locke J., Two Treatises of Government. London 1698.

Martin A., Private Property, Rights, and Interests in the Paris Peace Treaties. *British Yearbook of International Law* 1947, Vol. 24.

Matwijow M., Ossolineum. The Case of the Dispersed Library. Spoils of War. International Newsletter. No. 3. December 1996.

McNair A., Watts A., Legal Effects of War. Cambridge 1966.

Merlin O., La récupération du patrimoine artistique français. *Revue de la Défense Nationale* 1945, Vol. 1.

Merryman J. H.; International Art Law: from Cultural Nationalism to a Common Cultural Heritage. *New York University Journal of International Law and Politics* 1983, Vol. 15.

Merryman J. H., Trading in Art: Cultural Nationalism v. Internationalism. *Stanford Lawyer* 1984, Vol. 18.

Merryman J. H., Two Ways of Thinking about Cultural Property. *American Journal of International Law* 1986, Vol. 80.

Merryman J. H., The Retention of Cultural Property. *University of California Davis Law Review* 1988, Vol. 21.

Merryman J. H., Protection of the Cultural Heritage? *The American Journal of Comparative Law* 1990, Vol. 38, Supplement.

Mihan G., Looted Treasure. London 1944.

Missing Art Works of Belgium. Part I: Public Domain. Bruxelles 1994.

Monte Cassino Altarpiece Returned to Italy. *The Department of State Bulletin* 1951, Vol. 25, No. 652.

Moore J.B., A Digest of International Law. Vol. 7. Washington 1906.

Mosley L., The Reich Marshal. London 1977.

Nahlik S.E., Des crimes contra les biens culturels. *Annuaire de l'AAA* 1959, Vol. 29.

Nahlik S.E., Grabiez dziel sztuki. Rodowod zbrodni miedzynarodowej [Plunder of Works of Art. Descent of an International Crime]. Wroclaw-Krakow 1958.

Nahlik S.E., La protection internationale des biens culturels en cas de conflit armé. *Recueil des Cours* 1967, Vol. 120.

Nahlik S.E., L'intérêt de l'humanité à préserver son patrimoine culturel. *Annuaire de l'AAA* 1967-1968, Vol. 27-28.

Nahlik S.E., On Some Deficiencies of the Hague Convention of 1954 on the Protection of Cultural Property in the Event of Armed Conflict. *Yearbook of the AAA* 1974, Vol. 44.

Nahlik S.E., The Case of Displaced Art Treasures - History and Appreciation of a Polish-Canadian Strife. *German Yearbook of International Law* 1980, Vol. 23.

Netl J., Eastern Zone and Soviet policy in Germany. Oxford 1951.

Nicholas B., An Introduction to Roman Law. Oxford 1962.

Nicholas L.H., The Rape of Europa. The Fate of Europes Treasures in the Third Reich and the Second World War. New York 1994.

Niec H., Sovereign Rights to Cultural Property. *Polish Yearbook of International Law* 1971, Vol. 4.

Niec H., Legislative Models of Protection of Cultural Property. *Hastings Law Journal* 1976, Vol. 27.

Niec H., Ojczyzna dziela sztuki. Miedzynarodowa ochrona integralnosci narodowej spuscizny kulturalnej [Fatherland of a Work of Art. International Protection of the Integrity of the National Cultural Heritage]. Warsaw-Krakow 1980.

O'Keefe P.J., Prott L., Law and the Cultural Heritage. Vol.3. Movement. London and Edinburgh 1989.

Oppenheim L., International Law. Ed. by H. Lauterpacht. London 1940.

Pamiatniki isskustva razrushenye nemetskimi zakhvatchikami v SSSR. Sbornik stratel. [Monuments of Art Looted by Germans in USSR. Catalogue of Losses]. Ed. by I. Grabary. Moskva 1948.

Participation of the United States in Emergency Educational and Cultural Rebuilding of the War-torn United Nations. *The Department of State Bulletin* 1944, Vol. 10, No. 249.

Pastusiak L., Polityka Stanow Zjednoczonych w Niemczech 1945-1949 [The United States Policy in Germany 1945-1949]. Wroclaw-Warsaw-Krakow 1967.

Personnaz J., La reparation du préjudice en droit international public. Paris 1939.

Petropoulos J., Art as Politics in the Third Reich. Chapel Hill/London 1995.

Philimore F., Three Centuries of Treaties of Peace and their Teaching. London 1919, p. 8 ff.

Preserving Mankind's Heritage. U.S. Efforts to Prevent Illicit Trade in Cultural Property. Washington 1991.

Prott L. V., O' Keefe P. J., Law and the Cultural Heritage. Vol. 3. Movement. London-Edinburgh 1989.
Proposed Educational and Cultural Organization. *The Department of State Bulletin* 1945, Vol. 13, No. 325.
Przyluski J. (Priluscius), Leges seu Statuta ac privilegia Regni Poloniae omnia /.../. Cracoviae 1553.

Raykher B., Pravovye voprosy reparatsyy [Legal Questions Referring to War Reparations] Leningrad 1948.
Rare Mainz Psalter of 1457, Looted, Returned to U.S. Zone in Germany. *The Department of State Bulletin* 1950, Vol. 22, No. 560.
Ratchford B., Ross W., Berlin reparation assignment. Richmond 1947.
Removal of German Art Objects to the United States. *The Department of State Bulletin* 1945, Vol. 15, No. 327.
Repertoire des biens spoliés en France durant la Guerre 1939-1945. Vol. 1-7, Berlin 1947.
Repertorio delle opere d'arte trafugate in Italia. Roma 1964.
Report of the American Commission for the Protection and Salvage of Artistic and Historic Monuments in War Areas. Washington 1946.
Return of German Art Objects to the United States. *The Department of State Bulletin* 1945, Vol. 13, No. 327.
Return of Looted Objects of Art to Countries of Origin. Memorandum by the State Department Member of SWNCC. *The Department of State Bulletin* 1947, Vol. 16, No. 399.
Rigby D., Cultural Reparations and a New Western Tradition. *The American Scholar* 1944, Vol. 13.
Robinson N., Reparations and Restitution in International Law as affecting Jews. *The Jewish Yearbook of International Law* 1949.
Rorimer J.J., Rabin G., Survival. The Salvage and Protection of Art in War. New York 1950.
Rousseau Ch., Droit international public. Paris 1976, p. 130.
Rousseau J.J., Du contrat social ou principes du droit politique. Strasbourg 1796.
Rundstein S., Szkody wojenne a wspolczesne prawo narodow [War Damages and Current Law of Nations]. Warsaw 1917.

Schivelbusch W., Die Bibliothek von Löwen. Eine Episode aus der Zeit der Weltkriege. München-Wien 1988.
Schmoller G. von, Maier H., Tobler A., Handbuch des Besatzungsrechts. Tubingen 1957.
Schulze D., The Restitution of Works of Art. On the International Legal Dimensions of Restitution, Resolutions passed by the General Assembly of the United Nations. Brement 1983.
Schuster E., The Peace Treaty and its Effects on Private Property. *The British Yearbook of International Law* 1920-1921.
Seeliger K., Das auslandische Privateigentum in der Schweiz. Munchen 1949.
Seferiades S., La question du repatriement des "Marbres d'Elgin" considerée plus specialement au point de vue du droit des gens. *La Revue de Droit International* 1932, Vol. 3.
Seidl-Honenveldern I., Austria. Restitution legislation. *The American Journal of Comparative Law* 1953, Vol. 2.
Semkowicz W., Sprawa rewindykacji archiwow i zabytkow [The case of Revindication of Archives and Monuments]. Krakow 1921.
Seydewitz M., Seidewitz R., Die Dresdner Kunstschatze. Zur Geschichte des "Grunen Gewolbes" und der anderen Dresdner Kunstsammlungen. Dreden 1960.
Siehr K., Kunstraub und das internationale Recht. Schweizerische Juristen Zeitung 1981.
Siehr K., The Return of Cultural Property Expropriated Abroad, in Comparative and Private International Law. Essays in Honor of John Henry Merryman. Berlin 1990.
Siehr K., Nationaler und internationaler Kulturgüterschutz, in Festschrift für Werner Lorenz zum 70. Geburstag. Tübingen 1991.
Siehr K., Manuscript of the Quedlinburg Cathedral back in Germany. *International Journal of Cultural Property*. 1992, Vol. 1.
Siehr K., International Art Trade and the Law. *Recueil des Cours* 1993, Tome 243.
Skilton K., Defense de l'art Europeen. Souvenirs d'un officer americain. Paris 1948.
Smith H., Booty of war. *British Yearbook of International Law* 1946.
Sohm R., Institutionen des romischen Recht. Leipzig 1908. English translation: The Institutes. A Textbook of the History and System of Roman Private Law. Oxford 1907.
Starke J. G., Introduction to International Law. London 1988.
Suchodolski W., Rebuilding Culture. The Meaning of the Reparation for Poland. Warsaw 1945.

Suchodolski W., Zagadnienie prymatu strat kulturalnyh w ogolnym programie odszkodowan [Question of the Primacy of Cultural Losses in the General Program of Reparations]. Warsaw 1945.

Sulc B., Restitution and Succession of Cultural property from Croatian Museums and Galleries. Informatica Museologica 1992, No. 23 (1-4).

Tatarkiewicz W., Ethical Bases for Revindication and Reparations. Warsaw 1945.

Temperley H., A History of the Peace Conference in Paris. Vol. 2: The Settlement with Germany. London 1920.

Tentative List of Jewish Cultural Treasures in Axis-Occupied Countries. By the Research Staff of the Commission on European Jewish Cultural Reconstruction. *Jewish Social Studies* 1946. Vol.8 nr 1, Supplement. The Postwar Settlements of Property Rights. New York, 1945.

Thilo E., La revindication de biens se trouvant en Suisse, dérobés en pays occupés pendant la guerre. Journal des Tribunaux, 1946.

Thilo E., La restitution des rapines de guerre. *Journal des Tribunaux*, 1948.

Thilo E., La restitution des rapines de guerre. *Journal des Tribunaux*, 1952.

Thomas J. A. C., The Institutes of Justinian. Text, Translations and Commentary. Amsterdam-Oxford 1975.

Toman J., La protection des biens culturels en cas de conflit armé. Commentaire de la Convention de La Haye du 14 mai 1954. Paris 1994.

Tomkiewicz W., Catalogue of Paintings Removed from Poland by the German Occupation Authorities during the years 1939-1945. Vol. 1. Foreign paintings. Warsaw 1950, Vol. 2. Polish paintings. Warsaw 1953.

Trevor-Roper H., The Plunder of the Arts in the Seventeenth Century. London 1970.

Treasures Untraced. An Inventory of the Italian Art Treasures Lost during the Second World war. Rome 1995.

Treue W., Art Plunder. The Fate of Works of Art in War, Revolution and Peace. London 1960.

Tyszkowski K., Z dziejow rewindykacji [From the History of Revindication]. Lwow 1924.

Ullrich A., Das Schicksal der Bau- und Kunstdenkmaler in den Ostgebieten des Deutschen Reiches. Bonn 1956.

United States Seeks to Replace Cultural Property Displaced during World War II. *The Department of State Bulletin* 1951, Vol. 25, No. 635.

Valland R., Le front de l'art. Paris 1961.

Vasarhelyi I., Restitution in International Law. Budapest 1964.

Vattel E. de, Le Droit des Gens ou Principes de la Loi Naturelle Appliques à la conduite des affaires des Nations et des Souverines. Tome I & II. A Londres 1758.

Vattel E. de, The Law of Nations or the Principles of Natural Law Applied to the Conduct and to the Affairs of Nations and Sovereigns. Translation of the Edition of 1758 by Ch. G. Fenwick. Washington 1916. Special Edition 1993.

Verlorene Werke der Malerei in Deutschland in der Zeit von 1939 bei 1945 zerstorte und verschollene Gemalde aus Museen und Galerie. Ed. by M. Bernhard. Berlin 1965.

Virally M., L'administration internationale de l'Allemagne. Paris 1948.

Visscher Ch. de, International Protection of Works of Art and Historic Monuments. The Department of State Publication 3590, 1949.

Visscher Ch. de, La protection internationale des objets d'art et des monuments historiques. *Revue de Droit International et de Legislation Comparée* 1935, No. 1 and 2.

Visscher Ch. de, Les monuments historiques et oeuvres d'art en temps de guerre et les traites de paix. In: La protection des monuments et oeuvres d'art en temps de guerre. Manuel technique et juridique. Paris 1939.

Walter B., Ruckfuhrung von Kulturgut im Internationalen Recht. Bremen 1988.

Waxman S., Austria: Ending the Legacy of Shame. *Art News*, vol. 94 no. 7.

Weiss G., Beuteguter aus besetzen Landern und die privatrechtliche Stellung des schweizerischen Erwerbers. *Schweizerische Juristenzeitung* 15 September 1946.

Wengler W., Conflicts of Laws. Problems Relating to Restitution of Property in Germany. *The International and Comparative Law Quarterly* 1962, Vol. 11.

Wermusch G., Tatumstande [un]bekannt. Kunstraub unter den Augen der Alliierten. Braunschweig 1991.

Wheaton H., Elements of International Law. London 1864.

Williams S., The International and National Protection of Movable Cultural Property. A Comparative Study. New York 1978.

Willis F., French in Germany 1945-1949. Stanford 1962.
Woolley L., A record of the work done by the military authorities for the protection of the treasures of art and history in war areas. London 1947.
Wormser R., Collection of international damage claims. New York 1944.

Yevgenev V., Mezhdunarodno-pravovye regulirovane reparatsyy posle Vtoroy Mirovoy Voyny.[International Law Regulations on the Question Reparations after World War II] Moskva 1950.

Zaryn S., Dlaczego chronimy zabytki? [Why do we Protect Historical Monuments?] Warsaw 1966.

ARCHIVES CONSULTED

The Archives of New Records in Warsaw (ANR):
- records of the Bureau of War Reparations (BWR)
- records of the Ministry of Culture and Art, Bureau of Restitution and Reparations (MCA BRR)
- records of the Bureau of War Restitution and Reparations (BWRR)
- records of the Ministry of Congress Affairs of the Republic of Poland (MCA RP)
- records of the Polish Military Mission in Berlin (PMM)
- records of the Delegation of the Government of the Republic of Poland for Home Affairs (DGRP HA)

Department of Archives and Historic Documentation of the Ministry of Foreign Affairs (DAHD MFA):
- records: 10

The Archives of UNESCO in Paris:
- records of Conference of Allied Ministers of Education

National Museum in Krakow: Chief Inventory Division:
- records of restitution documents

Collected Documents and Diplomatic Papers

Acta Pacis Oliviensis inedita. Vratislaviae 1763.
British and Foreign State Papers, 112.
Calmette G., Recueil de documents sur l'histoire de la question de reparations (1919-1921). Paris 1924.
Cassou J., Le pillage par les Allemands des oeuvres d'art et des bibliotheques appartenant a des Juifs en France. Recueil de documents. Paris 1947.
Conventions internationales en vigeur et autres declarations de gouvernements concernant la protection des monuments et oeuvre d'art ou cours des conflits armes. *Mouseion* 1939, supplement.
Documents relating to the termination of the occupation regime in the Federal Republic of Germany. London 1955.
Dogiel M., Codex Diplomatiques Regni Poloniae et Magni Ducatus Lithuanie /.../. Vol. 1. Vilnea 1758.
Dokumente zur Aussenpolitik der DDR. Bd. 4. Berlin 1954; Bd. 5. Berlin 1955.
Dokumenty dotyczace akcji Delegacji polskich w Komisjach Mieszanych Reewakuacyjnej i Specjalnej w Moskwie [Documents on the activities of the Polish Delegations to the Reevacuation and Special Mixed Commissions in Moscow]. Warsaw 1922-1924, z. 1-9.
Dokumenty i materialy do historii stosunkow polsko-radzieckich [Documents and materials on the history of Polish-Soviet relations]. Vol. 8, Warsaw 1974; Vol. 10, Warsaw 1987.
German destruction of cultural life in Poland. Documents relating to the administration of occupied countries in Eastern Europe. No. 2. New York (no date).

Germany 1947-1949. The story in documents. The Department of State Publication No. 3556.

Grenville J., The Major International Treaties 1914-1973. Washington 1975.

League of Nations Treaty Series, LIV, LXXII, CLX.

Mardsen E., Germany (British Zone). Legislation relating to restitution. Bielefeld 1953.

Major peace treaties of modern history 1648-1967 with an introductory essay by Arnold Toynbee. Vol. 1. Ed. by F. Israel. New York 1967.

Martens G.F., Nouveau Recueil General de Traites. 3e ser., Vol. 13, 1924.

Oppen-Ruhm B. (ed.), Documents of Germany under Occupation 1945-1954. London 1955.

Publications de la Cour Permanente de Justice Internationale. Serie A, No. 17, Leyden 1928.

Recueil de Textes a l'usage des Conferences de la Paix. Paris 1946.

Restitution. European legislation to redress the consequences of Nazi rule. London (no date).

Selected documents on Germany and the question of Berlin 1945-1954. London 1961.

Societé des Nations. Recueil des Traites. Vol. 10. 1920.

Stosunki polsko-radzieckie w latach 1917-1945. Dokumenty i materialy [Polish-Soviet relations in the years 1917-1945. Documents and materials]. Warsaw 1967.

Treaties of Peace with Italy, Romania, Bulgaria, Hungary and Finland. Texts for signature in Paris on February 10, 1947. London HMSO, Cmnd. 7022.

United Nations Monetary and Financial Conference. Bretton Woods, New Hampshire, July 1 to July 22, 1944. Extracts from Final Act and related documents. 1946.

United Nations Treaty Series 249, 1956.

United States Department of State. Foreign relations of the United States: Diplomatic papers, 1945. The conference of Berlin. Vol. 1, 2. Washington 1960.

United States Department of State. Foreign relations of the United States: Diplomatic papers, 1945. Political and economic matters. Vol. 2. Washington 1967.

United States Department of State. Foreign relations of the United States: Diplomatic papers, 1945. European Advisory Commission: Austria, Germany. Washington 1968.

United States Department of State. Foreign relations of the United States: Diplomatic papers, 1945. Paris Peace Conference: Proceedings. Vol. 3. Washington 1970.

United States Department of State. Foreign relations of the United States: Diplomatic papers, 1945. Council of Foreign Ministers: Germany and Austria. Vol. 2. Washington 1972.

United States Treaties and Other International Agreements. Vol. 4. Washington 1953; Vol. 17. Washington 1968.

Zbior dokumentow [Collection of documents]. Vol. 1-5. Warsaw 1945-1949.

INTERNATIONAL TREATIES AND CONVENTIONS

INDEX